Matt called Jill Hotz one night, asking questions. The conversation quickly grew heated. "Kari didn't think I was having an affair," he told her.

"Yes, she did, Matt," Jill countered.

"Do you believe that?"

"It doesn't matter what I believe, Matt. Kari thought you were."

"Do you think I could have had an affair?" he demanded.

"Yes. I think you could," Jill responded. "I didn't at the time, and I wish I hadn't said that to Kari."

"I was your pastor! How could you think that of me?" Over and over, Matt screamed, "I was your pastor!"

Praise for **KATHRYN CASEY**

"Casey stakes her claim as one of the best in the business."
M. William Phelps, author of *Perfect Poison*

"Among the elite of true crime writers."
Carlton Stowers, Edgar® Award-winning
author of *Careless Whispers*

"Kathryn Casey joins Carlton Stowers as the premier chroniclers of Texas crime."
Gregg Olsen, author of *Abandoned Prayers*

"She explores incredible crimes . . . with a deft and experienced hand."
Ann Rule

By Kathryn Casey

Non-Fiction
DEADLY LITTLE SECRETS
SHATTERED
EVIL BESIDE HER
A DESCENT INTO HELL
DIE, MY LOVE
SHE WANTED IT ALL
A WARRANT TO KILL

Fiction
SINGULARITY
BLOOD LINES
THE KILLING STORM

True Crime Shorts
THE DRAG QUEEN MURDER
TRUE CRIME FILES
BLUES & BAD BLOOD
TEXAS LOVE TRIANGLE MURDER

KATHRYN CASEY

DEADLY LITTLE SECRETS

THE MINISTER, HIS MISTRESS, AND A HEARTLESS TEXAS MURDER

HARPER

An Imprint of HarperCollinsPublishers

HARPER

An Imprint of HarperCollins*Publishers*
195 Broadway,
New York, NY 10007.

Copyright © 2012 by Kathryn Casey
ISBN 978-0-06-201855-7

First Harper mass market printing: August 2012

HarperCollins ® and Harper ® are registered trademarks of Harper-Collins Publishers.

Printed in the United States of America

Visit Harper paperbacks on the World Wide Web at
www.harpercollins.com

10 9 8 7 6 5 4 3

In memory of my grandparents:
Josephine, Joseph,
Margaret, and Michael

Acknowledgments

*D*eadly Little Secrets took more than a year to complete. Before the writing could even begin, I attended Matt Baker's trial, then fanned out to track down and interview sources. That process alone consumed many months, requiring six trips back and forth to Waco from my Houston home, poring over documents, long weeks filled with face-to-face meetings and, once back in my office, long days on the phone consulting sources I couldn't visit in person.

I would, therefore, like to begin by thanking those people who shared their experiences with me, those who knew Kari and Matt Baker, their families and friends, the law enforcement folks who worked on this case, everyone who talked with me. Many of you are mentioned in the book, some are not, but I'm grateful to you all. Matt's and Kari's stories are important, shedding a light on how religion can be manipulated for evil ends. Without all of you, I couldn't have told it.

Thank you to everyone at HarperCollins, especially my editor, Will Hinton, and art director Gail Dubov and designer Nadine Badalaty, who provided the wonderful cover. Thank you as well to my agent, Jane Dystel.

In addition, I'd like to acknowledge my friend Kathy L. Patrick, founder of the Pulpwood Queens, a book club phenomenon that began in the small town of Jefferson, Texas, one that has grown to become a force in the publishing world. I met Kathy in her combination bookstore/ beauty parlor five years ago, and she's enriched my life in more ways than I can describe through her generosity, her dynamic personality, her enthusiasm for books and literacy, and introducing me to the esteemed PQs, passionate women who advocate for literacy and the power of the written word to change lives.

As always, thank you to my friends and family who've supported me so loyally over the years, understanding when I'm on the road for weeks at a time or locked in my office writing day after day. Please know that although I don't say it as often as I should, I love and appreciate each and every one of you.

Finally, I'd like to express my deep gratitude to my readers, those of you who enjoy my books and recommend them to others. You are *the* most important element in the equation. Thank you.

Some names have been changed in the book:
Jake Roberts, Sarah Parker, Jackie, Nellie,
Tracy Owens, and Sherry Perkins.

Even the Devil can cite scripture for his purpose.

—William Shakespeare, *The Merchant of Venice*

DEADLY LITTLE
SECRETS

Chapter 1

None of it made any sense, absolutely none of it. Not when her sister Nancy tried to tell her on the telephone nor now that Linda Dulin was surrounded by two of her three sisters and her oldest niece, Lindsey, in the backyard of Linda's comfortable home on a Sunday evening. Outside, the rolling hills surrounding Waco, Texas, were replete with beauty, bursting with bluebonnets, Indian paintbrush, and delicate white rain lilies. The days were growing longer, promising summer. Yet it felt like winter in Linda's heart, cold and lonely. She couldn't take any more pain. She'd suffered enough. And what her sisters were saying . . . well, it had to stop. It was impossible, and Linda didn't understand why the others couldn't just see that.

"I want you to drop it," she ordered. "Just let it go."

At fifty-two, Linda was the oldest of the sisters, a lineup that ran from Linda, to Nancy, forty-nine, Kay, forty-seven, and Jennifer, thirty-seven. Nancy's oldest daughter, Lindsey, twenty-six, was almost like another daughter to Linda. She knew they had come out of love, and that they were all trying to help, but that didn't alter things. It was too late to change what had happened. Linda's oldest child, her only daughter, Kari, had died, and there wasn't anything any of them could do about it. They had to come to terms with what had happened; they had to move on with their lives. As impossible as that seemed, that was what Linda, her husband, Jim, and their son, Adam, were all trying to do, and they didn't need anyone filling their minds with groundless suspicions.

"Kari is dead," Linda said. A purposeful woman with short, highlighted dark blond hair and expressively arched eyebrows, she pursed her lips as she sometimes did when standing before her students at McLennan Community College. With a doctorate in organizational communication, she was used to being listened to in a classroom. What she needed now was that same courtesy from her siblings. "There was nothing in Kari that made me think she would take her own life. But we have to accept this."

"Linda, you're not listening," Nancy protested. With shoulder-length dark brown hair and a steady gaze, Nancy might have been younger than Linda, but she was her match. All the women were strong individuals, and they'd grown up both protecting and competing with each other. They'd always been close, held together by a bond that transcended blood. Determined that Linda listen to their theory, Nancy refused to back down. "We don't believe Kari killed herself."

"What's the alternative?" Linda asked, her mind resting uncomfortably on the only conclusion. "If my daughter didn't kill herself, what are you saying? That she was murdered?"

The pause was uncomfortably long, as all the women looked at each other, wondering who should speak next.

"Linda, you have to understand," said Kay, her blond hair in a ponytail and her hands fisted on her lap. She knew this was agonizing, but somehow she had to make her oldest sister listen. Linda was the only one seated at the round patio table who believed that Kari had committed suicide, carried out by an overdose of sleeping pills mixed with alcohol. All the others had come to another conclusion, that Kari's husband, Matt Baker, a Baptist minister, had committed the vilest of sins.

The other women had an advantage over Linda. They'd

understood for years that Matt Baker wasn't the man he pretended to be. Far from being a man of God, Matt lived a double life, one in which he preyed on women.

For those who didn't know better, from the outside it appeared that Kari had the perfect marriage. Just thirty-one, she was a bright, funny, dynamic woman, an elementary-school teacher with shining blond hair cut short, a wide smile, and playful blue eyes. She and Matt had two precious little girls, Kensi, nine, and Grace, five. Another daughter, Kassidy, had died seven years earlier, and her death was the sorrow mentioned in the note found near Kari's body. "I want to give Kassidy a hug. I need to feel her again," it read.

Yet this final missive, including the name at the bottom, was typed. Would Kari have done that? Would she have failed to mention Adam, her only sibling? Kay, Nancy, and Lindsey had discussed it all at length and agreed that the suicide note was a lie.

Linda, however, wouldn't budge. "Matt's the father of my granddaughters, all we have left of Kari," she said, her manner stern. "I want you to drop it. Understand?"

The women nodded. "Okay," Kay agreed. "It's dropped."

Not long after, they hugged Linda at her front door and said good night. Yet after Linda retreated inside, the women congregated near their cars. "So what do we do?" Lindsey asked.

Faith was important to the family, going back to their paternal grandfather, a Baptist minister. The youngest of the sisters, Jennifer, who'd returned home to Florida after the funeral, was married to a music minister. The idea that Matt, the pastor of a small, rural church, could commit murder wasn't to be taken lightly. But they knew Kari. They knew that if it were one of them, she'd move heaven and earth to find justice.

"Linda said to drop it," Lindsey acknowledged. "So what do we do?"

For a moment, no one spoke. Then, Kay said, "We're not going to drop it. Not now. Not ever."

Later, many in Waco would call the three women gathered at their cars "the angels," and Linda, who would eventually come to understand what kind of man her daughter had truly married, "Charlie." This small band of women would join together to uncover the truth, solving the mystery of how Kari Dulin Baker died.

Weeks after that backyard conference, Linda and Jim Dulin reluctantly accepted the heartbreaking truth, that their daughter had been murdered. Yet once they did, the fight had just begun. Their journey would be a long one, requiring the aid of many. Caught in the middle and never far from the Dulins' thoughts were their two granddaughters, Kari's beloved girls. In the end, every step would be a fight in a valiant struggle for justice.

Chapter 2

"From the time she was little, Kari was bursting with life, and always something of a diva," Linda says, a slight chuckle in her voice. "She, of course, fit in with the rest of us. We're a family of she-rahs. All of us, a large, close, extended family. We love each other. We'd do anything for each other. And we all loved Kari."

On August 13, 1974, Kari Lynn was born not among the rolling hills of Central Texas but surrounded by mountains in Salt Lake City. At the time Linda was married to Scott, and they were both students at the University of Utah. It was there one horrible afternoon, when Kari was still a baby, that Linda received the tragic news that her husband had died in a motorcycle accident. "It was hard," she says. "Kari was so small, she didn't even remember Scott."

Leaving the mountains behind, Linda relocated to Waco, Texas, to attend Baylor University, where one of her younger sisters, Kay, was a student. As a child, Linda, her father an army colonel, had lived across the globe, everywhere from Okinawa to Berlin. "I was kind of a military brat," she says. "Growing up, I don't remember ever living anywhere more than three years." But by the midseventies, much of the Dodson family had settled in and around the bucolic hills surrounding Waco, a city of 126,000 situated an hour's drive south of Dallas.

Those unfamiliar with the Central Texas landscape, the tent of bright blue sky, the rich green forests, the grazing cattle, the wildflowers in the spring, and the bright reds and golds of fall, can be unprepared for its beauty. Without the pollution and congestion of Houston, Dallas, or even Austin, the air is clear, and days seem longer. Waco is a place where family values and the belief that a handshake can seal a deal are the norm. Manners still matter in this part of the world. People nod at each other on the streets and wave when they drive by. Mothers teach their sons to hold doors open, and their daughters to say, "Thank you."

In the heart of the Bible Belt, Central Texas is God-fearing country, a place where faith runs as deep as love of family and country, seemingly in the very land. As far back as history extends, the hills around Waco have been considered sacred. Early Spanish explorers christened the river that runs through the city *Rio de los Brazos de Dios,* the river of the arms of God.

Baptists call Waco "Jerusalem on the Brazos." Churches dominate the landscape. Drive down one street and pass an imposing stone-and-brick structure with pillars; take a turn and pass a white clapboard cottage-size church. Both are likely to have slender steeples reaching toward the heavens. The majority are Baptist, busy places on Sunday mornings and Wednesday and Sunday evenings, when their congregations gather to sing, praise, study the Bible, and pray. The result is that in Waco, "God bless" is heard often, accompanied by a smile and a nodding of the head. Grace murmured before a meal in a restaurant is common enough to warrant little notice.

Unfortunately, even in Jerusalem on the Brazos, evil is far from a stranger. As in any part of the United States, anywhere in the world, anger, greed, or jealousy sometimes tears back the peaceful façade and men and women do their worst. At times it twists the very values that promise to help man transcend human limitations. In such cases, those who promise redemption instead bring betrayal and tragedy.

The most famous example in this part of Texas is the one with which many identify Waco's very name. No matter that the city is actually named after the Huaco or Hueco, a tribe of Native Americans that once lived on the land that became the city's downtown. Instead, Waco, Texas, is synonymous with fifty days in 1993, when a man who claimed to be a great prophet, David Koresh, and his cultish Branch Davidians held the combined forces of the ATF and the FBI at bay, until the compound erupted into a fireball that claimed the lives of Koresh and seventy-five others, including twenty-one children.

For some, Koresh became a martyr to individual rights, yet to many he was simply another false prophet, one who abused children and indulged in polygamy, claiming at least one spiritual bride when she was just thirteen.

Yet, belief in God promises not violence but peace, a call to a greater good. If some masquerade as true believers for their own purposes, to manipulate and even violate others, it's surely not God's sin but their own.

In Linda's family, faith ran deep through the generations. "My father's dad and brother were Baptist ministers," she says. "I don't remember a time when faith wasn't important to our family. We raised our children going to church as a family. And we live long lives. Kari knew her maternal great-grandmother, who lived until her nineties and played the organ at church. Faith is part of who we are."

Surrounded by this conservative Christian city, Baylor is the largest of all Baptist universities, begun while Texas was still a republic. The imposing university with its parklike campus is Waco's epicenter of education, an institution held in high regard.

After her husband's death, Linda moved into an apartment with the third of the Dodson sisters, Kay, and enrolled at Baylor, intent on completing her undergraduate degree in communications. "It was a good time in many ways. We had fun together," says Nancy, who visited often. "But it was a rough time for Linda. I remember Kari as this little sprite of a kid with thick blond hair. Just a ball of fire. Linda was never much for doing hair, so Kari would run to me with a brush, and I'd sit on the floor and fix her hair. She'd talk and talk. Even then, Kari was full of life."

At times, Kari was so funny that there was little more to do than laugh. She loved the family dog, a stray cocker mix that showed up one morning and never left. "She was this goofy kid," Linda would say rather proudly. One of Linda's favorite memories was Kari's second birthday, when apparently the toddler decided that since it was a celebration on her behalf, she was exempt from the usual rules. Linda, who wore glasses and contacts, remembers Kari proudly running into the room, hands on hips to tell her, "I ate your tontacts (contacts)!"

"I knew they wouldn't hurt her, and I laughed so hard," Linda says. "She was just this little pistol."

Even at four, Kari loved to belt out a tune, especially church hymns. When the family congregated or friends dropped over, Kari entertained with a song, putting her whole tiny body into it. "Kari was always Kari, a force to be reckoned with," says Kay.

After Scott died, Linda went to counseling for a time, seeking advice as she worked through her grief. "I never thought it was good to hold things in," she says. "Our family is like that. We aren't afraid to ask for help when we need it."

While attending Baylor, Linda studied hard and concentrated on raising her daughter. In the mornings, she dropped Kari at the imposing First Baptist Church, with its tall white pillars and arched windows, for day care. Between classes, Kay and Linda crossed paths often on Baylor's pristine campus, with its redbrick Georgian architecture, windows trimmed in cream, pillars and domes.

It was yet another calamity that brought a young man named Jim Dulin into Linda's life. That Christmas break, 1977, a fire erupted in Linda and Kay's apartment, and they lost nearly everything. A tall, avuncular fellow with glasses, Jim, was a friend of their neighbors, and he offered his pickup to transport the little they had left. Before long, Linda was dating the Texas State Technical College grad, a member of the National Guard who worked for the Department of Defense at nearby North Fort Hood.

"I'd never met a finer man," Linda said years later. Jim was particularly good with Kari, loving and kind. Soon after Linda and Jim married on June 9, 1979, he adopted Kari. And before long, they moved to Gatesville, forty-five minutes southwest by car from Waco, near Jim's job. Linda taught high-school journalism, coached drama and debate. In 1980, the family expanded when Linda gave birth to a son whom they named Adam. Big sister Kari adored her baby brother. Where she was petite and blond, Linda describes Adam as "a giant, round baby, with big brown eyes . . . Kari treated him like a doll . . . carrying him around."

A happy baby, Adam loved it when his big sister lavished him with attention, and Linda would always smile remembering those early days before, as might have been expected, Kari grew weary of Adam's hanging around when her friends came for sleepovers, Kari screaming, "Mommmm, make Adam leave us alone."

The years passed, and Linda continued teaching and getting her education, working on a master's degree. Kari did well in school, played T-ball and took dance classes, and wore her blond hair in curls with a thick fringe of bangs.

Jill Valentine, who met Kari in first grade, would remember her friend as "full of joy and laughter. She never seemed to be afraid of anything." That fearlessness came through in fourth grade, when Jill, Kari, and a friend danced for the school, pretending to be robots. "Kari could never get through the dance without laughing," Jill would later remember. "She wasn't embarrassed; she just thought it was hysterical."

Her friend was also forgiving. In fact, Kari seemed incapable of holding a grudge. The one time she and Jill got into an argument that erupted into a fight, it lasted a full ten seconds. "Then," Jill remembers, "we were hugging."

As Linda's and Jim's lives were grounded in their faith, so was their daughter's. Summers meant Latham Springs, a Baptist camp in Aquilla, Texas, where Kari relished the outdoors, swimming, and campfires. At church, she thrived on being involved. One year, Kari and Jill raised funds for missionaries. "We took groceries to homeless shelters," Jill remembers. "Whatever came up, Kari was there, full of ideas and wanting to help."

One of Jill's favorite pastimes was simply hanging out at her best friend's house. "Linda was funny, with a sarcastic sense of humor," Jill says. "And Jim was a quiet, kind, nurturing man. I loved being there. They were always on the go."

A matter-of-fact woman who doesn't mince words, Linda admits that at times her sense of humor can be a bit biting. "I understand that I can come on rather strong," she says with a shrug. "Some people don't like that. And they may not like me, but I'm okay with that. I work hard not to be hurtful to people, but I try to be honest."

In many ways, Kari was like her mother, outspoken and not letting things that distressed her ride. "Sometimes, Kari lost her temper," Jill remembers. "But the thing was, she was always fair. And if it turned out she was wrong, she'd apologize. She was smart and funny, and none of us doubted that she would succeed in life."

Yet as the years passed, Linda watched her children grow and thought that she could envision them as adults. Despite Kari's boldness, Linda knew that their daughter would remain close. Adam, on the other hand, had a bit of the wanderlust in him. "I knew that our son would travel, but Kari would always stay near," Linda says.

It seemed no matter what the activity, Kari invested herself into it. That pattern held at thirteen when she had her first boyfriend, and he left her for another girl. Convinced it was the end of the world, Kari threw herself on the floor and bellowed, "But I love him!"

Composing herself so she wouldn't laugh, Linda comforted her daughter, explaining that she was young, her life just beginning, and there was time ahead for love.

In eighth grade, Kari played basketball on the junior-high team, wearing a black-and-white uniform with number 33, her hair tied in a yellow bow. Then, in ninth grade, she became a cheerleader. As she came of age, Kari grew into a bright, funny girl, with a slightly heart-shaped face and luminous blue eyes. Rarely did she go unnoticed, and in high school, she appeared center court at the fairgrounds, holding long-stemmed roses and wearing a sash that read: HEART O' TEXAS SWEETHEART.

When the Dulins returned to Waco for visits, which they did often, there were big family get-togethers. As her sisters had children, Linda's family grew, and in high school, Kari spent summers babysitting Kay's children, teaching them to swim, shouting at them from the side of the pool: "You can do it! You can do it!"

Of Kari's cousins, it was Lindsey, Nancy's oldest, that Kari was the closest to. A cute girl with light brown hair, Lindsey was five years younger. As kids, they jumped up and down on Lindsey's bed singing, "Hey, Mickey, You're so fine!" When Kari could drive, Lindsey was as excited as her cousin. The two girls rode around Waco with all the windows down, listening to Vanilla Ice blaring on the radio.

In the end, though, it wasn't family but a job that brought Linda and Jim back to Waco. Linda had earned her master's and was working on her doctorate when she began teaching communication studies at Waco's McLennan Community College, a position that came with long hours coaching the speech team. Jim didn't want his wife commuting, and in 1993, after fourteen years in Gatesville, the Dulin family bought a home on a quiet suburban street lined by trees. Adam enrolled at the local junior high school, and Kari, a sophomore, entered Waco Christian High School.

As it often is, changing schools as a teenager can be difficult. Kari's saving grace would be her belief that if she confronted people, if she was honest and told them what she

thought, they'd understand. It worked at least once, when a
girl decided that the new kid in school was an easy target.
Instead of becoming angry, Kari simply said, "You're a very
bad person, and what you're doing hurts me." At that Kari
walked away and, remarkably, the teasing stopped.

Cute and popular, in her senior year at Waco Christian,
Kari had a boyfriend, but it was a surprise when Jim rushed
their daughter to the emergency room on November 5, 1992,
doubled over with pain. He thought Kari was having an ap-
pendicitis attack, but she was pregnant. She was bleeding
and cramping, and on the chart the doctor who estimated the
pregnancy at seven and a half weeks noted: "likely impending miscarriage."

"Remember, your daughter is eighteen," the physician
told Jim.

When Jim entered the room, Kari sobbed, "Please don't
think I'm a slut."

"I don't think that. I would never think that," Jim said,
and he held her as she cried.

In the days that followed, Kari miscarried. Upset by all
that had happened, Kari turned to her mother for strength.
They were so close that Linda could feel her daughter's pain.
She knew how embarrassed, hurt, and upset Kari was. To
put it in perspective, Linda said: "No matter what happens,
your dad and I are here for you. We love you. Grow and
learn from this experience."

In her high-school graduation photo, Kari has a slight
smile and engaging blue eyes. At the ceremony, she wore a
red gown with a white collar, her hair in blond curls. Life lay
ahead, and Linda and Jim had no doubt that Kari was ready
to grab it with both hands.

Yet there was one issue that Kari seemed to need to look
back on before she moved ahead. With college looming,
Kari asked about her biological father, who'd died so young.
Linda sent Kari to a counselor, where she could talk freely.
"I knew that my daughter might not feel comfortable telling
me everything, that she'd worry that she would hurt my feel-

ings," says Linda. "I wanted her to have a safe place where she could say anything."

It was a brief exercise, only two sessions, and in the end the counselor suggested Kari write Scott a letter, to say good-bye to a father she couldn't remember. Kari did and afterward appeared ready to go on with her life.

That fall, in 1993, Kari left Waco for Lubbock, where she enrolled in Texas Tech, intending to major in family studies. It was there that she met Melody Mabry, another freshman, when they both pledged Pi Beta Phi sorority. "Kari was a hugger," Melody remembers. "Not an uptight sorority girl."

When the other girls talked about being homesick, Kari was the one who comforted them. In some ways, she didn't quite fit in. Most of the other girls had long, straight hair, but Kari still wore hers curly and cut short. And she had a style of her own, one that allowed her to stand her ground the night her sorority sisters asked if she was really wearing *those* red jeans to a party? "Yup," she answered, and she did.

"Kari walked with her shoulders back, with confidence," Melody would recount. "It was obvious that she'd been raised to be her own person. But she was hard on herself, always trying to be a better person."

As the year progressed, Kari would come to believe that Tech wasn't the school for her. There were too many parties and temptations, and Kari told friends that she wanted to get her life back on track. That spring, she told Linda she wanted to stay home and attend college in Waco. "I really want to teach," she said. "I'd like to work with kids, get my master's like you did."

It seemed that Kari was thinking a lot about the future and preparing for her life. There was something else she told her parents. Kari had a plan, and a big part of it was finding the right man. As it was in her parents' home, Kari wanted faith to be the center of the family she'd one day build. "I want a good Christian guy for a husband," she said.

Before long, she'd believe she'd found the perfect man to build that life around. In June 1994, Kari began working at

Waco's First Baptist Church, where as a toddler she'd gone to day care. As a lifeguard at the church youth camp, she met a seemingly affable young man from Kerrville, Texas, Matt Baker. On the surface, they had a lot in common, and in no time Kari Lynn Dulin was in love.

"Love is blind, and lovers cannot see," Shakespeare wrote in *The Merchant of Venice*. Many examples, famous and not, prove his words true. How many have looked back after the haze of passion has worn off and found they didn't know those to whom they'd given their hearts?

To the world, Matt Baker appeared the epitome of the "good Christian boy" Kari said she wanted. But was he really?

Chapter 3

"The last person in the world I would have predicted would ever get in any kind of trouble was Matt Baker," says someone who went through school with the future minister. "He just wasn't the kind. The Matt I knew was always trying to help others. That he could do anything to hurt anyone? Not possible."

It wasn't just Matt but the entire Baker family that many in Kerrville saw as above reproach. Considered staunch Baptists, Matt's parents, Oscar and Barbara, were community mainstays, regular churchgoers, and the kind of people who pitched in when needed. To the outside world it appeared that Matt's life, from youth on, revolved around the principles Christianity teaches. "The Bakers I knew were the first ones to raise their hands when there was a job to be done," says Theron Hawkins, M.D., a retired urologist and friend, who met the family through Kerrville's Trinity Baptist Church. "I've never known a finer family, one more involved in the community. Why, I can't say enough about the family, or Matt for that matter. He always struck me as a fine young man."

"The Bakers went to three services a week," says Jeanne Lehrman, an old friend. "They were involved in all the activities. You won't find finer Christians than the Bakers."

In Kerrville, Trinity Baptist is a low-slung, beige brick

complex on Jackson Road. The church itself has a steeply
pitched roof and a tower rising into a spire. There are Texans
who never worry about seeing the world. For them, the Hill
Country, the rugged terrain west of Austin, is as close to
heaven as one can get on God's good earth. In Kerrville the
hills are jagged, the ground thin layers of soil over rock, and
the scenery spectacular.

Named after James Kerr, a major in the Texas Revolution,
Kerrville rests on I-10, a little more than two hundred miles
southwest of Waco and an hour from San Antonio. A city of
some twenty thousand residents, it's a prosperous place, one
where wealthy Texans buy second homes, a destination for
those searching for a picturesque setting to retire. The result
is that in the midnineties, the *Wall Street Journal* described
Kerrville as one of the wealthiest small towns in America.

Yet few places are as serene as they first seem. The
rugged, thickly forested landscape around Kerrville makes
a good place to hide. For years, no one noticed, for instance,
what was going on in the nearby settlement of Mountain
Home. It was there, in 1984, that federal, state, and local
lawmen converged on what became known as the Texas
Slave Ranch, a thirty-five-hundred-acre spread where hitch-
hikers were allegedly forced into slavery. During the day,
they dug ditches and built fences; at night they carved religious trinkets bearing the phrase "Jesus Loves You." After
one man escaped, the rancher, his son, and one of the ranch
hands were convicted of conspiracy to commit aggravated
kidnapping.

It was marriage that brought Matt's mother, Barbara, to
Kerrville.

As she would describe it, she came from hostile roots, the
unwanted illegitimate daughter of a mother who repeatedly
attempted to abort the pregnancy. "She never wanted me,
and she let me know that. I was an oil-field kid," Barbara
would say. "I went to fifteen different grade schools, never
really knew a home."

Her bitterness still evident many decades later, Barbara,

a short, stocky woman with a thick cap of pin-straight, salt-and-pepper hair, would have little flattering to say about her mother. The picture she drew was of a cold woman, one who demanded much but gave little. "I grew up knowing that if I got a ninety-nine, it was why didn't you get one hundred," she'd say. "I worked hard to get my mother's blessing, but she never gave it to me."

It was her brother who'd stopped their constant moving, and the one who brought Barbara to her faith. "After my mother married and had my brother, we settled down. Then my mother decided that my brother needed to go to church," Barbara says, her frown curling ever downward. "When I was twelve, she told me to find us a church. So I visited some, and when I went to the Baptist church, that felt good to me. So I told my mother we were going to be Baptists."

At the time she met her future husband, Barbara lived in Odessa, running an ice-cream/hamburger parlor. "Oscar grew up in Kerrville and was still living there, farming other people's land, baling and harvesting," she said. After they married in 1967, she relocated to Kerrville. Matthew Dee Baker was born on September 7, 1971, their second child. Their daughter, Stacie June, was nineteen months old at the time. "There was never a bond with my mother, and even as a child I realized I was in this world by myself," Barbara says, her face grim. "That's not the way I would raise my children."

When Matt was one year old, the family moved into a large, rambling two-story, wood-frame house with a wide front porch on Earl Garrett Street, where Barbara and Oscar became house parents of a group home, part of a chain of Dallas-based orphanages and foster homes, the Buckner Baptist Benevolences. From July 1974 through June 1981, the Bakers oversaw the care of up to ten foster children at a time plus their two biological children. "In all, over that ten years, we had about fifty foster kids," Barbara would later explain. "I was just a mom, and ten was the perfect number."

The home was coed, and the children all ages. Some chil-

dren lived in the home for the Bakers' entire tenure there
while others came and went. Some returned to their families
while others were adopted. When one left, another arrived.
Some suffered from handicaps, others were troubled, while
still others simply had the misfortune of not having parents
able to care for them. The majority of the foster children
were boys, and they bunked in two upstairs bedrooms, along
with Matt. Downstairs, the girls, including Stacie, slept in a
bedroom that shared a bath with her parents' bedroom.

Looking back, Barbara described fostering as an idyllic
experience for her own children, saying that Matt learned to
live with children of different races and backgrounds. And
from early on, she'd contend that her son was special. "He
had a God-given talent with the children," she'd say, maintaining that at the young age of six, Matt, a diminutive boy
with shaggy brown hair and denim blue eyes, counseled the
other children. "Even then, Matt had leadership qualities."

Describing his own childhood, Matt would say: "I learned
Christian love. We were all brothers and sisters. Sometimes
the foster kids had been abused, and the kids would show
up with black eyes. But when they were in our house, they
were family."

In her portrayal of her son's early years, Barbara describes Matt as a boy who loved school, his home, his paper
route, climbing trees, and playing word games. "He was
an all-around nice kid. Never got in any trouble," concurs
Hawkins. "Or if he did, I never heard about it."

Why did the Bakers stop foster parenting in 1981? "Because we owed our own, natural-born kids some normal
life," says Barbara. "With the foster kids, we had runaways,
attempted suicides, sometimes the police knocking on the
door."

From the foster home, the Bakers moved into a trailer
planted on a lot outside Kerrville, on a meandering street
made up of a patchwork of houses nestled against the hills
and into the brush. Over the years, the trailer would settle
and appear crooked from the street, as if the foundation

needed work. Matt would later describe his sister, Stacie, as more like his father, a quiet person. "I'm like my mom," he'd insist. "More outgoing."

Unlike in some other Christian churches, Baptists often aren't christened as babies but only when they are old enough to individually accept Jesus. Matt apparently reached that milestone early. "I was baptized at Trinity Baptist in Kerrville when I was six," he would say, with pride. "We attended Sunday school, sang in the choir, and went on mission trips."

The journeys took them into Mexico and deep into the Valley, the expanse of Texas along the Rio Grande, where the Bakers joined with others to build schools and churches, staffing clinics and teaching Bible studies. "It depended on what that particular community needed," says Dr. Hawkins. "Oscar couldn't always go because they couldn't afford for him to take off work, but Barbara and the children went."

In Kerrville's Tivy High School, Matt was a scrawny kid with a cap of bushy brown hair combed down over his forehead. He played the tuba and French horn in the band, enjoyed sports, and worked as a student trainer with the basketball team under the supervision of a teacher who had majored in athletic training at Baylor. Although Matt talked of going to the University of Texas in Austin, it was then that he decided he'd head to Waco and follow in his mentor's footsteps.

"Matt was a good kid. He tutored some of the other kids," says a classmate. "He made good grades. I don't remember anyone's not liking Matt."

But there were some who were struck by something else about Barbara and her son, an unusual similarity. "I don't know how to describe it except that you never saw either one of them show any emotion," says one of Matt's friends growing up. "Barbara was always pretty dour. And Matt was like that, too, kind of expressionless."

In high school, Matt had a couple of steady girlfriends, but his friends say he wasn't one of those boys who "went gaga over the girls." After school and on weekends, he worked with his father, who'd become a handyman, hiring out to do painting, carpentry, mowing grass, whatever work he could find. "From the time I was a kid, I was out working with him," Matt would say. "He taught me a lot."

Those who knew Matt wouldn't be surprised that he'd become a pastor, yet it wasn't something they would have predicted, either. "He never struck me as churchy," says an old friend. "He wasn't quoting scripture all the time or anything."

Yet Matt would say that he felt the calling early on. "It happened gradually," he says, recounting how in his sophomore year in high school, he attended a youth retreat where "I put my intentions on record, announcing that I would dedicate my future to preaching the gospel. It was basically, 'God, I'm here. Take me where you want me to go.'"

Looking back, Barbara would describe her son as exceptional in every way, so well behaved that while parents around the globe are forced to sometimes take their children to task, she'd insist that was never the case with her son. "I can honestly say I can't remember ever punishing Matt," she said, her face blank, as if looking for a memory of some transgression and not remembering any, even a slight one calling for any type of reprimand. "That's hard to believe, I know, but it's true."

In the spring of 1990, Matt graduated from Tivy High with a partial scholarship waiting for him at Baylor, where he planned to major in church recreation and athletic training. In Waco, he moved into a dorm and went to class, earning good grades. "His intention was to become a youth minister," Barbara would say,

But was the Baker family as squeaky-clean as Barbara described it? Was it as grounded in church and doing the right thing, as many thought?

In August 1990, Matt left Kerrville and moved to Waco to enter Baylor. One month later, on September 10, Barbara Baker was ticketed in Kerrville on a shoplifting charge, an item less than $20. The woman with the stoic bearing who spoke of God and held her head high was fined $169.50. Was it a onetime mistake? An aberration? It was a minor transgression, after all, and isn't everyone entitled to one slip? Later, she'd peg the cause on empty-nest syndrome.

Three years later, in 1993, however, Kerr County records would show that it happened again, on June 13, another theft charge, this time a more serious class B misdemeanor for which Barbara was fined $287 and given deferred adjudication. If these run-ins with the law revealed a different side of the staunch churchwoman Barbara professed to be, allegations waited in the future that cast shadows on much, much more, especially what went inside that house on Earl Garrett, the foster home during those seven years when the Bakers were houseparents.

What about Matt? Before long, he, too, would reveal another side, not that of the admired young man with his eye on the ministry, someone dedicated to helping others, but that of a sexual predator.

Chapter 4

Kari Dulin hadn't entered Baylor yet in 1990 when Matt Baker arrived on campus. While known for its majors in business, law, music, philosophy, and science, the heart of the institution is its emphasis on theology. It's a rarefied atmosphere, a religiously based, Ivy-League-feeling school. Thick-trunked oaks line the campus, and roses bloom in front of the library. "It's a different atmosphere than a lot of colleges," says one student. "You don't see torn-up jeans and sloppy T-shirts much. Students are judged by not only how wealthy their parents are but how devout the student appears to be."

That fall, Matt entered as a student majoring in church recreation and specializing in athletic training, preparing to one day work for a church as a youth counselor. As such, he took general classes plus theology. Still the sports aficionado he was as a boy, Matt worked as a trainer with the school's football team, the Baylor Bears, at the time a member of the later defunct Southwest Conference. Home games were played in the aging Floyd Casey Stadium, located blocks off the main campus and seating some fifty thousand fans.

In the Bears' locker room, before the games, the players pounded their chests and slapped their helmets, getting into the zone. Then they prayed, as befitting warriors representing a university dedicated to faith. At such moments, Matt's eyes closed, and he clasped his hands, appearing in tune with the God they worshipped. "Matt always struck me as truly pious," says one team member. "He seemed to be a genuine kind of guy, dedicated to the faith."

As that year progressed, however, there were incidents that, perhaps, should have raised flags. "We thought of Matt as a phenomenal Christian, but we did hear rumors, things like that he tried to kiss women at some of the parties," says another player, one who wrote off Matt's indiscretions as merely youthful hubris. "To me, it was just a college thing. Even ministerial students, even those at Baylor, get horny."

Before the games, Matt and the other trainers wrapped ankles and refurbished helmets with gold spray paint, repairing scuff marks. "Matt always did what he was supposed to do," says one of the other trainers. "He helped the players, bringing ice for injuries, doing what Mike Sims, the head athletic trainer, told him to do. Everybody knew Matt was a good Christian. In the devotionals before the games, he was always reverent."

Despite the rumors about his behavior at parties, Matt went through his first year without major incident. It wasn't until mid-December 1991, during finals week, halfway through his sophomore year, that the allegations turned serious. The young woman was Lora Wilson, a pretty young coed with short blond hair, a freshman majoring in premed. Living on campus, Wilson shared a dorm room with one of Billy Graham's granddaughters. A year behind Matt, Lora met him while they were both participating in the athletic-training program. It hadn't been an easy year for Lora, but then it wasn't for many of the freshmen. Like some sororities and fraternities, the athletic-training students had a tradition of hazing.

As Lora would later describe it, the initiation began at the team doctor's home, where the freshmen were ordered to pretend to be water sprinklers while singing popular songs, such as George Strait's "Ocean Front Property." In the

Baylor version, Strait didn't have oceanfront property in Arizona but Waco. Yet that was only fun. The real hazing took place in the stadium during practice and on Thursday nights before home games. It was there that freshmen worked until after midnight, told to clean toilets and baseboards with toothbrushes and sweep the Astroturf with a broom.

Although Wilson felt as if overall Matt Baker barely noticed her, he was the one who ordered her not to wear gloves while cleaning the toilets and urinals. After she suffered bleach burns on her hands, "I told him to clean the urinal himself and walked out." What that defiance won her was heckling. If she balked, the upperclassmen threatened to have her kicked off the squad. For a while, Wilson did as told, but then she'd had enough. "I got smart when they were attempting to scare me with some treatment or other as I was vacuuming the coach's office," she'd say later. "I looked at them, two senior women with a crowd of about ten behind them, and told them that they had absolutely no authority over me. And unless Mike Sims or the assistant head trainer had a problem with me, there was nothing they could say or do to make me do anything else."

With that, Wilson turned off the vacuum and left it standing in the room as she walked off. On the way out the door, she heard one junior man whisper, "You're gonna get it now."

"Whatever," Wilson said, with a shrug.

Was Matt put up to what happened next? Wilson would never know.

One afternoon during finals week, Wilson was again ordered to clean urinals in the visitors' locker room, to prepare the stadium for high-school playoffs scheduled for the coming weekend. Because it was outside the normal practice hours, much of the stadium was locked. Although she was supposed to have someone with her, she'd ended up alone. As she walked outside the stadium to get to the old training room, Matt offered to help, falling into step behind her. Surprised since it was unusual for an upperclassman, or even a sophomore, to help the freshmen, she agreed. But as they walked, Matt began acting oddly, like an adolescent, poking her from behind with a broom.

"Stop it," she told him, but he didn't. He kept jabbing at her, and she continued telling him to cut it out, until he finally stopped when she reached the doors to the old locker room. Lora thought little of it rather than being annoyed.

Once in the locker room, she told Matt she'd clean the bathroom if he'd work on the rest. He agreed, and she left to get to work. Moments later, while bending over cleaning a stall, she realized that Matt stood directly behind her. Later, all she would remember was that he moved in quickly, pinning her arms behind her back and forcing himself against her, attempting to kiss her. Frightened, she struggled.

"What if I was Brian?" he said, referring to her boyfriend at the time.

"You're not!" Mustering all her strength, she pushed away. "Stop!"

Ignoring her cries, Matt lunged at her, again attempting to kiss her. Her heart pounding, she again shouted for him to stop, but he persisted, picking her up in a bear hug and putting her down on the sink. He then forced her legs open and stood between them, pushing against her while trying to kiss her. Lora used her only weapon, biting his shoulder. Startled, he let go long enough for her to jump off the sink and run.

In the main locker room, Matt caught up, coming at her from behind, wrestling her over to a bench, where he pulled her on top of him, again pushing her thighs apart. Although not a large man, he overpowered her, managing to use one hand to hold her arms behind her back, while he fondled her.

Wilson screamed, but he ignored her, minutes passing.

"Then he suddenly released me. He looked at me, and said, 'I'm done,'" she'd say years later.

As if nothing had happened, Matt walked from the room, leaving Wilson shaking and stunned. Her hands trembling, she started cleaning again, as if determined to finish what she'd begun. She'd later explain, "I think I was in shock."

Tears streaming down her cheeks, she ran from the room

only to make a wrong turn and find the doors locked. Unable to return to the north-end-zone complex where the other students were working, a sobbing Lora called her mother from a pay phone under the stands.

"Find Mike Sims and tell him what happened," Lora's mother told her.

Agreeing that she'd find the head trainer, Lora pounded on the locked doors, but no one answered. Her body shivering, she was forced to walk around the outside of the stadium to get to an open gate. As she passed one coach, the man asked why she was crying. "Did you fail one of your exams?" he wanted to know.

Lora shook her head, then, in tearful gasps, told him what had happened.

"Find Mike Sims and tell him. We won't stand for this behavior," the coach said.

Wilson continued on, searching, but finally gave up. She couldn't find Mike Sims. Instead, she left a note on his desk, asking him to call her at her dorm. Tears streaking her face, Lora left the complex and went to her dorm room, where her mother had said she'd meet her.

When her parents arrived, they accompanied Lora back to the stadium to meet with Sims. Once Lora explained what had happened, Matt was called into Sims's office. "Matt admitted what he'd done, but he said he didn't realize he was hurting me," she said. But there was no doubt that Lora had attempted to fight him off, attested to by the bite mark on his shoulder.

"This will be taken care of," Sims assured her, saying she didn't need to involve the police. Lora and her parents agreed to let the university handle the situation. Lora would later say that she vividly remembered Sims then turning to Matt and warning, "You understand you will have to be disciplined for this, right?"

"Yes," Matt said.

Lora's father returned home, but her mother stayed through the night in Lora's dorm room. Lora had a restless night, reliving the attack. She woke her mother off and on, crying. One thing kept going through her mind: That day her sweats had been dirty, and she'd dressed nicer than usual. Was that why Matt Baker had assaulted her? Had she attracted his attention? Her mother assured her that she'd done nothing to provoke the attack. "She told me that it wasn't my fault," Lora would say later.

The next morning, Lora Wilson woke up in her dorm room, terrified. She looked at her watch, the one with a green dot sticker on it, the athletic insignia that represented leadership and identified her as a trainer. She began furiously scratching at it, attempting to wipe it away. Her mother found Lora on the bathroom floor manically working on the watch. "I have to get this off," she told her. "I can't do this anymore!"

Her mother said, "Lora, we're going home."

In the days that followed, Lora's mother attempted to convince her to go for counseling, but she refused. Going over and over in her mind what had happened, Lora couldn't figure out what to call what Matt had done to her.

As the Christmas holidays ended, the Bears' bowl game was coming up on New Year's Eve day—the Copper Bowl in Arizona, where Baylor would play the Indiana Hoosiers. Lora wanted to go. "I'd worked hard, and I'd earned it," she'd say. Mike Sims had told her that she didn't need to attend the practices, but Lora felt the need to go to at least one, to see if she could be around the other trainers, how it would feel. That first day back at the final practice before the bowl game, Lora saw the other students watching her and whispering. Some accused her of making up stories, and others scoffed at her for being upset about something as minor as being poked by a broom, the story that Matt had apparently told the others. After more giggling and taunts, Lora found one of the assistant athletic trainers and told him that she couldn't stay and that she wouldn't be attending the bowl game.

In the end, the Bears lost the Copper Bowl 24 to 0 to Indiana, and when Lora returned to the campus after Christmas break, she quickly came to the decision that she'd lost as well. When she reported for work at the stadium, Matt was there, and it appeared his only punishment was to be confined to the training room to work with the players. "That was something that usually only the seniors were able to do," Lora says. "It wasn't a punishment. It was more of a promotion."

For Lora, the effects of Matt Baker's attack lingered. She dropped out of athletic training and left Baylor before the semester ended. Months later, she was asked to put her recollection of the events in writing for Matt's file. She did so. At the time, she was told there'd been another episode with Matt. "They said that Matt had been banned from extracurricular activities and could only attend classes," she'd say. The Baylor authorities she spoke with told her that if Matt stepped outside the lines again, he'd be forced to leave.

Departing Waco and Baylor, however, didn't end Lora's suffering. For years after, she endured nightmares in which it happened all over again: Matt's pinning her down, she unable to move as he fondled her. And afterward, the other student trainers laughing and taunting, failing to support her. Such nights, Lora woke up terrified, tears filling her eyes.

Were there any ramifications for Matt? He would later say that when he registered for the spring semester, his paperwork was blocked until he presented himself at the dean's office, where the allegations brought by Lora were discussed. In the story he told his mother and others over the coming years, Matt would deny Wilson's version of the events, instead saying she became hysterical for some unknown reason when the lights went out unexpectedly in the locker room. "They told me not to worry about it," he'd say. "They said they knew I hadn't done anything wrong."

Had the Baylor authorities simply dropped the matter? The university and Mike Sims would later refuse comment, so there would be nothing by which to judge their actions but the results. The undeniable consequence of the attack was that no one at Baylor filed a police report with Waco PD, and Matt Baker was allowed to continue at the university.

Perhaps it would have been expected that Matt would have learned from what he'd done, but then, he'd apparently suffered no punishment, so why should he change his ways? If Baylor had taken action, made sure that he was charged with a crime, Matt might have been held accountable. But they didn't, and he wasn't, and the following January, just weeks after Baker's attack on Lora Wilson, he was home in Kerrville. It was there that he struck up an old friendship with Dina Ahrens, a high-school girlfriend.

"Matt had dated Dina off and on," Barbara Baker would later say. "I always thought she was a nice girl, but I didn't know her all that well."

At a get-together, Dina and Matt saw each other again. She was still in high school, a senior at Tivy, where Barbara Baker worked as an aide. That evening, they were at a party with high-school friends. Dina knew nothing about the Baylor incident when he flirted with her. "It was a cat-and-mouse game," she'd say later, "Rekindling the old flame."

After the party, he followed her to her parents' house. "Heavy petting," she'd say. "Things were getting very physical."

While they'd been boyfriend and girlfriend in high school, Dina would later testify about what happened that night as different than in the past. "He was more aggressive with me," she'd say. "He was . . . relentless."

It took all her physical strength to keep her clothes on. Why did Baker finally stop? According to Ahrens, it was only because he heard her mother at the door.

Looking back, Barbara would scoff at both of the young women's accounts of her son's actions, the perfect son she'd never had to discipline. The incident with Ahrens, she said, was simply Matt getting "maybe a little too aggressive, but what teenage boy doesn't?"

As for Lora Wilson, Barbara insisted that the woman

was lying. Even as the list of women charging her son with improper behavior would grow, Barbara remained steadfast in her son's defense, blaming not Matt but the women who made the allegations.

Meanwhile, all continued to go well for Matt Baker. His grades were good, and the month after Wilson accused him of assault, no one from the university apparently protested when Matt was given a highly coveted position, an internship in the recreation department at the First Baptist Church of Waco, the premier church in the city, one tightly tied to Baylor. Perhaps they didn't realize or maybe didn't care that at the church Matt's duties would include working in the recreation center and at the summer youth camp, often around young, vulnerable women.

The man who hired him, Jake Roberts, was one of Matt's teachers at Baylor, an instructor in church recreation who also worked at First Baptist. Roberts would later say he knew nothing of the charges Lora Wilson had made against his young student. "When it came to church recreation, Matt seemed to know what he was doing, and he was a hard worker and a good student," says Roberts. "He didn't seem girl crazy. I had no reason to doubt him. If I'd known about what had happened at Baylor with that girl, I wouldn't have hired him. Absolutely not. But I didn't. No one told me."

Chapter 5

It was at First Baptist that Kari met Matt, when she took the lifeguard slot in late spring 1994. Held on undeveloped land, mowed and covered with trees, surrounding the church, the youth camp offered canoeing on the nearby Brazos River and swimming in an aboveground pool. The children played softball and volleyball, did crafts, learned archery, cooking, and fire building. Nearly three hundred participants in grades one through six attended, and each day started with a prayer and a song.

When Kari applied for the First Baptist job, Matt's boss, Roberts, had a talk with her. During it, she explained that she didn't want to return to Texas Tech, saying that she felt she'd partied too much and hadn't paid enough attention to her grades. "Kari said she wanted to get back to the values she'd been taught," says Roberts. "She felt she'd gotten a little wild."

Later, Linda would say that she believed what drew her daughter to Matt Baker was Kari's belief that she'd found "a good boy. Someone who shared her faith." In truth, although twenty-three, Matt still looked like a boy, his face round, thin-lipped, with those startlingly blue eyes. He was a senior at Baylor to her sophomore, and when Kari wore high heels she stood nearly shoulder to shoulder with her five-foot-seven-inch boyfriend.

Exactly when her relationship with Matt began would later be unclear, but soon after Kari started, Roberts noticed that she seemed interested in Matt. "She pursued him, I think, rather aggressively," Roberts would say. "Kari was a vivacious girl, and he seemed drawn to her. I didn't think much of it at first, but I started noticing that they were arriving together in the morning and leaving together at night."

To friends, Kari said that she knew from the beginning that Matt was the one. "A lot of the girls at Baylor thought he was a catch," says one of his classmates. "We were Baptist girls looking for the right man to settle down with, and Matt talked a lot about faith. He sounded like a good boy, active in church, and that was very appealing."

Looking back, Matt would say there were many things that drew him to Kari, including that she seemed upbeat and happy, and that she was a woman who obviously loved her family. "Family came first for Kari," he'd say. "You could see that in her."

Their first date was to a just-released Meg Ryan movie, *When a Man Loves a Woman,* in which the actress portrayed an alcoholic wife and actor Andy Garcia her dedicated husband. From the beginning, Matt and Kari's relationship built steam at a pace their parents would later describe as too quick.

When Linda first met Matt, she was less impressed than her daughter. As full of life as Kari was, Matt's manner was subdued, and, Linda thought, perhaps not genuine. "I didn't always have the feeling with Matt that he was the man he portrayed. Jim and I talked about that," Linda says. "It wasn't anything either one of us could put our fingers on. He just seemed okay, to me. I could tell Kari was smitten, but I couldn't understand why."

Kari's aunts and her cousin Lindsey, who'd grown up as her unofficial sister, also had misgivings. Nancy, who worked in real estate, thought Matt seemed a little off. At family gatherings, while the other men congregated around the television, Matt shadowed the women, hovering near

Kari. At times, Nancy wondered if Matt stayed close because he worried about what Kari might say. "It just seemed odd," says Nancy. "It looked strange, looking up and seeing him there, listening."

There was something about Matt that made Lindsey uneasy as well. She didn't like the way he made suggestive motions, not touching but acting as if he were going to squeeze her breasts. And when he hugged her, it seemed invasive, as if he enjoyed it too much. "But Kari was in love with him, and I loved Kari, so I didn't say anything," she explains. "I thought I was just imagining things and let it go."

Of them all, it was Kari's younger brother, Adam, still in high school, who was the most upset about his sister's newfound love. "Adam didn't like Matt right away," says Linda. "I had to tell him to be nice."

A month after Kari and Matt met, he brought her to Kerrville to meet his parents. "I liked Kari. I thought they made a cute couple," says Barbara. "But I talked to Matt because I thought they were moving too fast, getting too serious."

Listening to his mother's concerns, Matt agreed to slow down. Then the living quarters he had lined up for the fall semester fell through. "He didn't have a place to live," Barbara says. "Matt called up and told me and his father that two could live as cheaply as one . . . I think Kari was eager to marry Matt because he was a good man. She could see that in him. And Matt was never serious about anyone before Kari."

Behind the scenes, there were things going on that the Dulins, Kari, perhaps even Barbara, didn't yet know about. At First Baptist, a teenage girl, a young gymnast, had complained to Roberts's secretary that Matt was asking her for sex. According to the girl's allegations, one day Matt tried to corner her, saying he wanted to have intercourse behind the bins that held the roller skates. The secretary told Roberts about the girl's charges, and he called Matt in for a talk. When confronted, Matt denied anything improper had happened, but Roberts felt uncertain. "She said he grabbed her fanny and tried to talk her into meeting him upstairs. But it was a he-said-she-said situation," Roberts would say many years later. "I told him he needed to be more careful, to not be alone with the teenage girls who worked at the camp."

As the summer wore on, just months after meeting Matt, Kari told her parents that they wanted to marry in August before he began his fall semester at Baylor. Worried, Linda asked Kari to wait, arguing that they didn't know each other well enough. "But Mom, this guy is a really good Christian," Kari said. "And we don't want to wait. Matt and I want to get married right away."

Yet Linda and Jim persisted, telling Kari that if she carried through with her plans, they would no longer pay for her tuition or the car note on the Mustang they'd just bought her. "I tried to get them to postpone for a year, but Kari told me there was no need to wait, she was certain Matt was the right one," says Linda.

Before long, Kari was wearing a diamond ring, and she and Matt were engaged. Barbara drove to Waco, and she and Linda met for lunch at a Chili's restaurant. While they ate, Barbara said something that Linda didn't know how to respond to. "You know, Matt's a virgin," Barbara said, looking at her knowingly.

"Oh," Linda said, at a loss for words.

"Too much information from your future mother-in-law," Linda told Kari later, filling her in on the conversation.

"That is a little weird," Kari agreed.

Arrangements for the wedding, planned for August 20, were proceeding at warp speed. Linda hired a caterer and shopped for dresses with Kari. The one she picked had lace on the bodice and a wide, off-the-shoulder neckline that folded over to cover the tops of her shoulders. The veil was a cloud of net anchored by a V-shaped, leafy white, crown.

Just days before the wedding, Linda asked Kari something she'd been wondering about. "Did you tell Matt about the miscarriage?"

"I tell Matt everything," Kari assured her. "He's such a

good guy, and he's led such a clean life, I wouldn't keep anything from him."

It was about that time that Kari told her mother that Matt's best man was going to be one of the Baker family's friends. "Why didn't he pick his best friend?" Linda asked.

"Matt doesn't have one," Kari said. "Matt doesn't have many friends."

The night before the wedding, Kari's cousins and friends took her to a grocery store, where they chuckled and teased as they watched her hold a sign that read, "Tomorrow, I'll be on my honeymoon." Kari laughed, too. She was excited, looking toward the future with a young man she loved.

The next day, in her parents' living room, Kari Lynn Dulin held Matthew Dee Baker's hands and looked into his eyes, promising to love and be true to him as long as they both should live. Matt was twenty-three and Kari twenty. With her wedding gown, she wore a single-strand pearl necklace and earrings. Looking very young, Matt wore a double-breasted suit that hung loose on him, his shirt collar gaping around his neck.

That day, as their wedding pictures were taken, Matt and Kari were at the beginning of their lives together, and she grinned eagerly for the camera. She thought she'd found her knight in shining armor, the man who'd father her children and be her partner for life.

At First Baptist, Roberts didn't know that his two employees had married until Matt and Kari told him the following week. It was about that time that more trouble developed, and Roberts once again pulled Matt into his office for another talk. This time, a middle-aged woman, a custodian who worked in the camp, claimed Matt asked her to have sex with him. According to the woman, Matt said, "I know what it's like to be with a young woman. I'd like to know what it's like to be with a mature woman."

Aghast, the woman reported him. It was the last day of the summer camp when Roberts confronted his young assistant with this second allegation. Matt called the woman a liar. Frustrated, Roberts told his young employee, "I don't know what's going on here, but if you're doing this kind of thing, you'll ruin your life. You need to get professional help."

Matt again denied that he'd done anything improper, but Roberts felt less than sure he could believe him. Yet he had no proof, and he'd say later that he was unwilling to ruin a young man's career based on unproven accusations. Matt would work at the church for one more year, until August 1995, and Roberts would hear of no further incidents. Yet the older man didn't forget what had happened.

Chapter 6

In the fall of 1994, Kari was livid about what she described as groundless allegations being leveled against her new husband by women at First Baptist. Perhaps Matt told her, or she'd simply heard. Rumors were, after all, rampant at the church about Matt and two women, both of whom claimed he'd approached them for sex.

Throughout that summer, Lindsey had also worked at First Baptist's camp. "Everyone was talking about Matt," she'd say later. "We all knew that some women were saying he'd come on to them."

When Lindsey reported the rumors to her mom, Nancy wasn't sure what to do. She didn't want to start trouble by bringing them up with Linda, but she and Kay talked about the allegations, wondering if they were true. Despite his sometimes-bizarre behavior, Lindsey wasn't convinced Matt was guilty. How could it be true when he and Kari looked so much in love? "I was on Matt and Kari's side," says Lindsey. "I never thought, at least not at that point, that it could be true."

Meanwhile, Kari was the one who told Linda and Jim, and when she did, she was indignant. "How could they say that?" she asked, furious. "Matt wouldn't do anything like that." Were the two women jealous, angry because Matt and Kari had married? Was there some other reason for them to make such unprovoked charges? Matt insisted that they were retaliating. The women, he said, had flirted with him, and their claims were nothing more than revenge because he rebuffed them. In a huff, Matt argued that he was being unfairly accused.

For their part, Linda and Jim didn't know what to think. So they listened sympathetically to Kari and watched. What they didn't see was anything happen to Matt. He continued to work at First Baptist, without, it appeared, any repercussions. "We thought, if he'd truly done these things, he'd certainly be fired," Linda would say later. "When that didn't happen, we believed him."

Not long after their marriage, Matt and Kari moved into a two-bedroom unit in the Majestic town homes in Royalton Village, a complex of two-story units that backed up to each other with covered parking at the rear. Nancy had begun acquiring rental property, and the unit the newlyweds lived in was one of hers. Before long, Lindsey moved into the second bedroom.

Despite the turmoil in her nascent marriage, Kari had never looked happier. She adored Matt, talking about him constantly, excited about the life they were building. By then, Matt was back at Baylor and Kari had signed up for classes at the community college. They joked with each other, watched television sports together, studied and worked hard. Lindsey didn't think much at first about the way Matt went everywhere with Kari, even to the beauty parlor when she had her hair cut short and dyed a bright blond, but at times, it was irritating. Lindsey and Kari had been so close, and now they lived together, but Matt was always there. The cousins rarely did anything without him.

Proud of Matt, Kari told her mother she was urging him to continue with his education, to enter Baylor's Truett Seminary, to get a master's degree in divinity. "He'll need it to have a real career," Kari said, making plans for their futures.

Not long after, Matt called Barbara, and said, "Mom, what would you think if I went into the seminary?"

"I wasn't surprised," says Barbara. "I always knew that Matt was destined to do God's work. That was the way he'd been raised."

Although supporting Kari and Matt, Linda and Jim had misgivings. "It just seemed strange," Linda would say. "It just didn't feel quite right. Things like, Matt wasn't the one who suggested we say grace before meals."

Despite their reservations, Jim and Linda understood that Kari believed in Matt and wanted him to succeed. And what was the downside? As far as they could see, there wasn't any. "We kept saying, 'Hey, Matt's going to become a Baptist minister. What could the problem be?'" Jim remembers.

Between attending classes at Baylor, Matt continued to work part-time at First Baptist. After a while, no one talked about the charges against him. When nothing more happened, it quickly became old news.

Then the following spring, Linda was alarmed when she reviewed the roster for the classes she taught and noticed the name of the girl who'd made allegations against Matt. The first months in class, Linda eyed the girl suspiciously, watching her carefully. Based on what Kari and Matt had told her, Linda assumed her new student was a troublemaker. Yet to Linda's surprise, the girl seemed respectful, a good student. Despite that, Linda never made the leap to question whether her son-in-law had told them all the truth. "From the day they married, we accepted Matt as part of the family. We grew to love him like one of our own children," says Linda. "That the girl wasn't what I expected did kind of make me wonder, but I shrugged and forgot about it. After all, Kari believed in Matt, she loved him, and he was my son-in-law. I was Kari's mom. My daughter said the girl was lying. Kari believed Matt, and we believed Kari."

Chapter 7

Later, some would wonder why Kari didn't piece it together, why she failed to understand to whom she was truly married. The rips in Matt Baker's disguise frequently became visible over the years. Yet they were brief if painful interludes, and for the most part, Matt seemed like a good guy. His boss at First Baptist would describe him as a hard worker, someone who said the right things, and to others Matt talked about his future in altruistic terms, his calling to carry the message of God and help others find salvation.

On the surface, Matt was an impressive young man, a future Baptist minister in a city known as Jerusalem on the Brazos, and Kari was not only in love with but dedicated to him. Their lives, after all, didn't revolve around the brief upsets but centered on the day-to-day business of living, hurried breakfasts as they rushed out the door, classes and studying, family dinners, holidays, dreaming of their future together, building a family, and climbing into bed together at the end of the day and turning out the light.

With family, Matt didn't seem like the type of person who would ever cross the line. "Around us, he was always timid. He let Kari be the alpha," says Linda, who'd later maintain that from the beginning Matt and Kari acted less like lovers than buddies.

Over the years, there would be characteristics Linda

noticed in Matt that she wondered about. For instance, he enjoyed taunting others yet he took himself seriously, growing angry if teased. There was the day Matt, who always enjoyed buying himself things, especially new shoes, wore a recently purchased pair of fuzzy black slippers. "Those are women's slippers," Linda pointed out.

"I know," Kari agreed, at which point both the women laughed.

"Matt was unhappy," says Linda, remembering how he sulked. "You couldn't do that."

Another thing Matt didn't like was being questioned. When others made accusations, Matt adamantly defended himself, insisting that if Kari didn't believe him, she was disloyal. He was her husband, a future Baptist minister, one day he would be the father of her children, and he acted as if he expected to be taken at his word.

A year had gone by since the allegations against him, when, in September 1995, Matt turned in his resignation at First Baptist and took a job at the Family Y, a large facility not far off the freeway in west Waco.

That December, Matt graduated from Baylor in a ceremony steeped in tradition, wearing a green gown and a mortarboard, with his parents, Kari, and her family proudly in attendance. He'd earned an education degree, specializing in church recreation.

For a while, all went well at the Y, with Matt running the children's after-school program. Then, six months after he signed on, in January 1996, he approached a young student worker named Jackie. The Y had been quiet that day, with few children in the competition swimming pool where she worked. Matt suggested they go to the youth recreation room to work on the receipts. It was Jackie's last day before leaving to return to college, and she replied that she knew how to fill the forms out. Matt, however, persisted, claiming that she'd made errors and that he needed to walk her though the process.

Moments later, in the recreation room, Matt came up

from behind the teenager, slipping his hand onto her breast. "No!" she ordered, pushing him away.

Rather than backing off, Matt lunged at the girl, trying to kiss her. Jackie again pushed away. "I know you want it," he said, groping between her legs. When she fought, he grabbed her hand and forced it onto his pants, on top of his penis.

"No!" she screamed, as Matt pushed her against a wall.

"I just want to fuck you right here, right now!" he seethed.

At that moment, the phone rang. Appearing startled, Matt let go of the girl. "They must be looking for us," he said. "We'd better head back."

The following week, Jackie left for college without reporting what had happened.

Kari was pregnant with their first child the winter her husband attacked Jackie at the Family Y, and on April 22, 1996, Kensi Baker was born, a blond-haired, blue-eyed, little bundle. Barbara would later describe Kari as an uncomfortable mother, one who wouldn't easily take on the responsibilities of a baby. "Everyone doesn't have a natural parenting instinct," she would say.

It was true that Kensi wasn't an easy infant, suffering from colic in her first months. But the Kari others describe was far from uneasy with her child. In fact, they say Kari was a doting mother, dedicated to her firstborn, dressing Kensi in pretty clothes and pinning her hair back in bows.

Still, Matt did take on a share of the parenting role. "Matt wanted to," Linda would say later. "He was the one who jumped up to bathe Kensi, to wash her hair. It became his thing. It wasn't that Kari didn't want to do it but that Matt insisted he would."

The spring became summer. Kari seemed unaware of the gathering storm clouds, when that June, complaints were filed at the Y by three teenage girls who said Matt had made unwanted advances. The reports were similar, describing clumsy sexual confrontations in which Matt pressured them to have sex. As with Lora Wilson and Dina Ahrens, Matt didn't back off even after the girls turned him down. One said that he approached her and asked about her sex life, then wanted to know if she'd have sex with a married man. The girl said, "No."

"I'm happily married and I plan to spend the rest of my life with my wife, and I wouldn't do anything like that either," he said. Despite those assurances, minutes later he confronted her in the fitness area, asking "How about it?" "It" was a sexual liaison.

"Are you trying to get me fired?" the girl asked.

"No. If we get found out, I'll get fired, too." Matt suggested they steal away to the attic together. He then checked his watch, and said, "I have fifteen minutes before the kids get out of the pool."

Although the girl turned Matt down, he kept propositioning her while she was handing out Pop-Tarts to the children in the recreation room. "I want your cherry," he said.

When he didn't stop, she filed a complaint. Afterward, he came up to her, and said, "You knew that I was just joking, didn't you?"

By then, Jackie had returned from college and was again working at the Y. When she heard what had happened, she decided to talk to the facility's administrator. After she described her experiences, Jackie was asked to document her January encounter with Matt. In her report, she wrote: "I remember this the most. When he had me against the wall, he put his body up against me, and said, 'I just want to fuck you right here, right now.'

"I didn't say anything before because it was just one day, and since I left right after, I didn't know that he was doing this to other girls . . . I have tried to block it from my mind."

On June 14, the Y's administrator called Matt in to discuss the allegations. He never denied the women's claims, and that same day, he was fired. In his termination letter, effective immediately, it pinpointed the cause as "a lack of performance of job duties in a professional and effective manner, for display of poor attitude toward responsibilities of your position, lack of positive influence and direction of supervised staff, and for inappropriate behavior toward female staff members."

What did Matt tell Kari? Most likely what she told Linda about the incident: that Matt was trying to counsel the girls against becoming sexually active, and they misinterpreted his intentions. In this version, Matt's only mistake was attempting, as a future minister, to help the young women. "None of us believed him, but Kari did," says Kay. "Every time Matt got fired, we wondered if it had something to do with harassing some woman."

After his termination, Matt applied for unemployment insurance, but the administrators at the Family Y successfully fought his request, filing a letter with the Texas Employment Commission that said: "We are protesting this claim based on the fact that Mr. Baker was discharged on June 14, 1996, for misconduct . . . inappropriate behavior towards a camp counselor he supervised . . . he did not deny."

The letter also cited a lack of performance on Matt's part, and concluded, "Sexual harassment towards employees or other individuals will not be tolerated." As usual, Kari stood by Matt, accepting his explanation that the girls were confused teenagers who'd misinterpreted his interest.

Three months after he was let go from the Y, Matt gave Kari a gift, a green leather-bound Bible, *The Quest Study Bible*. It was to become a record of her life, a haven where Kari read about the foundation of her faith and one where she wrote her innermost thoughts. On the first page, it bore a quote from Proverbs 2:6, "For the Lord gives wisdom and from his mouth come knowledge and understanding."

Inside, Matt inscribed:

With all my heart and soul, I love you. Kari, I want you to use this to grow closer to the Lord, and also learn more about Him. I love you very much, and hope

that we will forever be rooted together through the
words of this God-breathed masterpiece. I love you,
Matt.

On the page designated to record marriages, Kari wrote
the date of hers to Matt, and on the form recording births,
she noted that on that past April 22, Kensi had been born.

It seemed that by then there was much that could have
been easily discovered about Matt Baker if anyone at Baylor
had taken the time to run even a cursory background check.
Without even leaving the campus, they had only to talk to
his instructors in the athletic training department to learn of
his assault on Lora Wilson. An employment check at either
First Baptist or the Family Y could have uncovered the allegations of sexual misconduct at both. One might have
assumed that such an investigation would have been done
before admitting Matt to the seminary, where he'd study to
be a minister.

Apparently, none of those things were done. In the fall of
1996, Matt would become a student at Baylor's George W.
Truett Theological Seminary, named after a popular minister of the late 1800s. The seminary had only recently opened
and had yet to erect its own building, instead meeting in
classrooms on First Baptist's second floor. That year, fifty-
one students enrolled, putting them on the road to earning
either a master of divinity or a doctorate of ministry degree.
The school's charter said it was "centered on the gospel of
Jesus Christ and consistent with his Baptist commitments
to prepare persons to carry his gospel to the churches of the
world."

Meanwhile, Kari enrolled at Baylor the following January, 1997, and continued her own education, working toward
becoming a teacher. That year, she took a class taught by Dr.
Jeter Brasden, director of the ministry guidance program.
While he didn't have Matt as a student, Brasden knew him as
well and was impressed by the young couple. "Matt seemed
outgoing and pleasant, not wrapped up in his ego," Brasden

would remember. "I'd heard nothing bad about him, and I had no reason to question things about him."

In Kari, Brasden saw a young woman intent on preparing herself for the life she'd chosen. "She was a fine student," he says. "They were just recently married, and she seemed concerned about being a good pastor's wife, about what it meant to be the spouse of someone in the ministry."

How did Kari see her role? Years later, she'd advise another young woman about to marry a man studying for the ministry: "People will attack your husband. They'll say false things because they'll have agendas. Sometimes, women will tell lies because they'll see a good man and want him for themselves."

Looking at the woman meaningfully, Kari appeared to be willing the other woman to understand the importance of what she was saying. "You have to love your husband and believe in him, even when no one else does. The ministry is a hard life, and you have to back up your husband and be there for him, so that he can do God's work."

Chapter 8

Unlike with some other religions, Baptist churches are autonomous. In Texas, many belong to the Baptist General Convention of Texas (BGCT) at the state level and the Southern Baptist Convention at the national level. Yet joining is voluntary, and the conventions have no input regarding an individual church's activities or policies. For the most part, the conventions are used to pool resources for larger projects, including sending members on missions and building schools, hospitals, and churches in impoverished communities. When it comes to the nuts and bolts of daily life, the churches function as individual entities.

"We strongly suggest churches do background checks," says a former member of the BGCT's board. "But we can't force them. And we can't tell them whom to hire. Basically, to be called a pastor of a Baptist church, all you have to do is have a church vote to hire you. We don't license or ordain pastors. That's done by individual churches."

When it comes to ministerial misconduct, including sexual abuse, the Baptist General Convention of Texas keeps complaints on file, yet not all of the churches report. "Many just fire the offending pastor or ask him to find something else and move on," says a former BGCT employee. "They want to get rid of their problem. They don't worry about where that pastor goes next and what he might do once he's there."

Sexual misconduct and the abuse of power by religious leaders, of course, is a problem in many faiths. When it comes to the Baptists, a study was conducted in 1991 by the Fuller Institute of Church Growth that came to a startling conclusion: 37 percent of ministers interviewed confessed to inappropriate sexual behavior with someone in their church. A later Baylor study concluded one out of 33 women in Baptist congregations had been victims of clerical sexual misconduct.

It would later be unclear whether anyone at First Baptist reported to the BGCT regarding the allegations against Matt Baker since BGCT would refuse requests for records. But Matt's supervisor at the church, Jake Roberts, did try to alert churches that inquired about the young seminary student. At one point, a church in Longview contacted Roberts asking for a recommendation for Matt. "I told them that he knew church recreation," Roberts explains. "But I told them they needed to look at other aspects of this young man's life."

"You've told me all I need to know. I'm not hiring him," the Longview pastor responded.

Concerned about Baker, Roberts took an additional step, writing a report on all that had transpired and putting it in First Baptist's safe, to have it on hand for others to refer to in case he wasn't available when a church inquired about his former student, a young man he once thought had potential who he now viewed with different eyes. The problem, it would seem, was that few of the churches would bother to make that phone call.

Later it would be difficult to pin down dates when Matt Baker worked at particular churches since few kept records. According to Matt's résumé, his first church position after First Baptist Waco was as a part-time youth and music minister working under the pastor at the small, metal-sided, beige-painted church of First Baptist of Robinson in August 1995. This was during the same period he worked at the family Y. Like so many of his jobs, his position in Robinson was short-lived, less than a year. "We don't know why, but he was fired pretty quickly," Linda would remember later. "Kari was upset about it, and she asked me to write a letter to the pastor for Matt, which I did. But he didn't hire Matt back."

Meanwhile, Kari was busy taking her classes at Baylor and caring for Kensi. She adored the child, pouring so much of her energy into her. "Kari always had Kensi dressed up in the cutest little outfits, her hair fixed," says a friend. "She looked like a little doll. Half the time, Kari was on the floor playing with her, patty cake, laughing, like two little kids. Matt was a good dad. He doted on Kensi, too. He really seemed taken with her."

The young family still lived in the town house Nancy rented them. Even after he and Kari had married and had a child, Matt hovered at family events, never far from Kari, listening in on the women's conversations instead of watching sports with the men. "It was like he didn't have any boundaries," Nancy would say later. "He'd ask really intrusive questions, like how much money people made. It was just odd."

The younger women continued to feel uneasy around Matt. One day at a family gathering, when he was alone with one of them, he flirted and asked if she wanted to go somewhere with him. Another time, at a family holiday get-together, Kay's fourteen-year-old daughter, Hailey, had on a short skirt. "Have you got any panties on under that dress?" Matt asked.

Hailey didn't answer, she just walked away, and Kay stood nearby but unseen as Matt followed Hailey, asking again, "Hailey, do you have on panties?"

Repulsed, Kay wanted to jump in, but Hailey saw her mother staring at them. She gave Kay a look that said, "Forget it. Don't say anything."

Matt never saw Kari's aunt standing there, watching, furious, as Hailey pushed him aside and walked away. While Kay and Nancy talked about Matt, they didn't tell Linda.

The result was that Linda and Jim knew little of the

rumors and suspicion floating around their son-in-law. Yet
Linda did worry about the effect he was having on Kari.
"I'm not criticizing," Linda said to her daughter one day,
choosing her words carefully. "But I think it's strange that
you don't even go to get your hair cut without Matt, that he's
with you all the time."

"Matt says he just loves me and doesn't want to be without me," Kari answered. "And I feel sorry for Matt. He
doesn't have any real friends."

At that, Linda dropped the matter. "I didn't want to influence her," she explained.

In the summer of 1996, after losing the job in Robinson,
Matt worked as recreation director at the prestigious Columbus Avenue Baptist Church in downtown Waco. An impressive facility, the congregation of more than sixty-five hundred
entered the redbrick sanctuary through doors framed by
elegant white pillars. Matt's sojourn as assistant recreation
director, however, lasted only four months. Had someone at
Columbus Avenue talked to Roberts at Waco's other massive
church, First Baptist, and learned of Matt's past?

Yet, that fall, Matt was given another plum job, to pastor
Pecan Grove Baptist, a small country church outside Waco.
Pecan Grove was known as a good assignment for Truett
students, a place where the seminary's stars were groomed
for the future. "It's one of those places where six families
built a church, and they get a pastor to preach," says one
former pastor. "It's a small church, but it's well-known."

The church was founded in 1882, and the Texas historical
marker outside reads: "Pecan Grove, recognized by Baylor
University for its support of ministerial students . . . As
many as six generations of local families have been members of this congregation."

Dr. Paul Stripling, a Baylor professor of church history
and then head of the Waco Baptist Association, would later
say that the reports of Baker's transgressions weren't reaching those in the Baptist hierarchy. "All in all, I couldn't have
been more pleased with Matt and Kari," he says. "I never

once heard any rumors about his being involved in immoral activities. Not one. As far as I was concerned, he was one of our good young pastors, doing very good things."

With Kensi in her arms, Kari began attending the small church, sitting in the front pew, listening with rapt attention to Matt's sermons. She was proud of him, and Linda and Jim could see that she truly loved him. She talked excitedly about the future, how she would teach while Matt moved on to more impressive jobs at larger churches after earning his master's. Yet while they both worked hard to finish their educations and make that future happen, Matt didn't make it easy for Kari.

One after another, the events would line up, the indications that he wasn't what he pretended to be, like the afternoon a teenage girl who lived in the town house behind theirs cried to her mother, saying that Matt had accosted her in the parking lot. The way the girl recounted the event, Matt first asked her, "Have you ever been kissed by a boy?" then grabbed her and kissed her on the lips.

The mother was a friend of Kari's aunt Nancy, and she told her what happened. "I don't know, she's a teenager, and sometimes she exaggerates," the woman said. "I'm not sure what to think."

Meanwhile, Nancy thought back to what she already knew about Matt, how her own daughters, Ami and Lindsey, felt odd around him, and the only formal allegations she knew of, those made at First Baptist. "I believed what the girl had said," says Nancy. "It broke my heart. But I had to protect Kari, so I acted noncommittal."

This time, Nancy did call Linda to tell her, and Linda relayed the conversation to Kari, who became immediately angry with the girl, insisting she was lying. "Matt didn't do that, Mom," Kari said. "He didn't do anything to her."

After she hung up, Kari pounded on her neighbor's door and burst through. While Matt shadowed her, never saying a word, Kari defended him, sobbing and questioning the girl's mother, asking over and over again, "How can she say something like that?" This would become a pattern: Whenever evidence of Matt Baker's dark side appeared, Kari would not only turn a blind eye but defend him. "Kari was strong, and she loved Matt, she was loyal to him," Linda would say later. "He'd hang back and let her argue for him, and because she believed in him completely, she was persuasive. We believed her. I wondered why my sisters weren't more supportive of Matt. Why they weren't defending him."

On November 20, 1997, when Kensi was nineteen months, Kari gave birth to a second daughter, a round blond baby girl she and Matt named Kassidy. An easier baby than Kensi, without colic or any of her sister's early digestive problems, Kassidy was a stocky child, a Gerber baby with a clear, pale complexion.

Unbeknownst to Matt, Kari, or anyone in their families, that same month Lora Wilson called the Waco police and talked to an investigator. It had been six years, but she was still having nightmares of the afternoon in Casey Stadium when Matt Baker had attacked her. In her dreams, she relived the assault. In those terrifying moments, once again she heard his voice and felt him hold her down, helpless. That day, she talked to a detective, who recorded the information. He seemed interested in pursuing charges against Matt. "This was an attempted sexual assault," he told Lora. "We can charge him with this."

"It was the first time I had a name for what Matt Baker had done to me," she said later. "The first time I realized he had, in fact, committed a crime."

Later, however, the officer called with disappointing news: The statute of limitations had expired. "We can't do anything," he said. "I'm sorry, but it's too late."

Chapter 9

As 1997 drew to a close, Matt was doing well with his studies, and Kari was on track to finish her classes. In another year she was scheduled to begin student teaching. That winter, she and Matt took the girls in sweet dresses—Kensi in red and Kassidy in a blue plaid with a white collar trimmed in lace—for family photos. Each of the girls wore a wide white headband with a large bow at the front. They looked healthy and happy, and no one could have predicted the agony that lay ahead.

The following March, Matt took the pastor's job at Williams Creek Baptist, a congregation of about twenty families in Axtell, a short drive outside Waco. "There's a post office, fire department, general store, and school," says a resident. "It's a small place, mainly farmers, ranchers, and folks who drive into Waco to work."

An unassuming facility, Williams Creek was housed in a beige brick building with a steeply pitched roof. A brick cross in relief decorated the front facing the street. Consecrated in 1979, the church was off the highway, on a quiet country road surrounded by cattle fields. On land adjacent to the church stood the parsonage, a quaint house on a good-sized lot, with a garage and a swing set in the backyard.

Quickly, Matt became popular. He expanded the children's Sunday school program and the Wednesday evening

youth group. Before long, many in the small town grew
used to seeing the young Baptist pastor and his wife at local
events. To bring in families, they attended football and base-
ball games and showed up at festivals. With Kari pushing
the girls in a stroller, they approached townsfolk, inviting
them to try the church and give Matt a chance to win them
over. Some did, others listened politely and went on, but
many were impressed with the young couple's dedication
and energy.

For those who did come, Matt had a message. He wasn't
a fire-and-brimstone preacher, the type who warned of eternal damnation. Rarely did he talk about the consequences
of sin. Rather, he talked of God as a forgiving father who
watched over his flock, pardoned them for their sins no
matter how serious. In one sermon he said: "God is looking
for people who say, 'No longer am I going to be like the rest
of the world.'"

At the church, Kari led the youth group, putting on skits.
Her offerings were more often than not comical, and she
never seemed to mind poking fun at herself. She taught the
women's Bible study, introducing authors like Houston's
Beth Moore with her book *Whispers of Hope*, that came
with daily inspirational messages. And whether it was to
a teenager in the youth group or a woman in Bible study,
Kari made it a point to say she was available whenever they
needed her. "If you want to just spend a little time together
and talk, I'd love to do that," she'd say.

One man took her up on it, confiding that he struggled
with his homosexuality. Kari listened, then hugged him, and
said, "God will always love you. Always."

In the parsonage, Kari decorated, putting Kassidy's
crib in one bedroom and painting another in bright colors
for Kensi. The house was small and homey, a place where
they could sit outside in the evenings and enjoy the rural
quiet. Matt only had to walk across the field to church on
Sundays and Wednesdays for services, usually attended by
about sixty or so church members. When not at Baylor, Kari

walked the girls in a stroller along the road. "She was playful with the girls, loving," says a friend. "But that was just
Kari. She was brimming with life."

At Baylor, Kari made a good friend. Janelle Murphy was
recently married and studying to be a teacher, when they
met in a sign language class. The women became close, and
Janelle and her husband began attending Williams Creek.
Before long, Matt hired Janelle as the church's music minister.

It was also at Williams Creek that Matt and Kari connected with Todd and Jenny Monsey, a teenage brother and
sister. Like Janelle, the Monseys felt drawn to Matt and
Kari. As a pastor, Matt was hip, his sermons not the typical
ones they'd grown up on. Instead, Matt researched on the
Internet, finding sermons that talked about current culture,
bringing the examples back around to religion and God.
And Todd and Jenny saw Kari as a welcome relief from the
straightlaced pastors' wives they'd known. "Kari was really
cool," says Jenny, a solidly built young woman with dark
blond hair.

Many who knew her would mention that Kari wasn't a
typical pastor's wife. She dressed modestly but stylishly. She
wore bracelets that jangled when she walked and flip-flops
in the summer. And like her mom, Kari spoke her mind.
Sometimes she stirred up the church members by disagree-
ing, but it usually ended with a smile and all forgiven.

To the church, Kari brought her love of modern Christian
music, replacing the standard hymns with selections that included Christian Rock. And at youth meetings, she made
up games, once concocting a skit out of a Ray Boltz's song,
"Jesus Real Loud." As she sang, Kari jumped up and down,
and shouted, "What if I say Jesus real loud."

"Kari was fun," says Jenny. "And we loved Matt, too. It
was cool to have people closer to our age. Matt and Kari got
the younger people in the church involved."

"We'd grown up Baptist, and Matt wasn't the kind of
pastor we were used to," says Todd. "He had a clear, delib-

erate style to his worship services, bringing in the younger
people. He was charismatic up at the pulpit. He let us be
young, and he brought more excitement to the church. When
he said it, you believed him. It always sounded like it came
from a higher place. And part of Matt's ministry was Kari.
They were partners."

There seemed to be little that Kari couldn't handle.
Janelle would later describe her as a calm presence. When
Kensi toppled off the top stair of the stage at Vacation Bible
School, Kari heard her daughter's cry and ran from the next
room, scooping her oldest up in her arms. Once she was sure
Kensi wasn't hurt, Kari made a joke and started laughing,
until Kensi forgot about her tumble and laughed along. "She
had a relaxed mothering style," Janelle remembers. "Nothing frazzled her."

As taken as she was with Kari and Matt, when Janelle
brought her father to meet the Bakers, he said something
strange afterward: "Be careful, Janelle. Matt Baker isn't
what he seems. He's one of those pastors who is full of the
devil."

Janelle brushed it off, but at times she did have a strange
feeling about Matt. She'd hear him complain about church
members, bitterly mocking them, in a way that didn't seem
consistent with a man of God.

Yet there was that other side to Matt. "Matt was a preacher
not a pastor. He wasn't warm and welcoming, but he was
great up on the stage, giving sermons. He and my husband
became friends. He laughed and joked with us," says Janelle.
"And he really was a good dad. I kept thinking that my dad
had to be wrong. That Matt couldn't be a bad person."

That summer, a strange thing happened: Pornography
popped up on Matt and Kari's home computer. "Why would
that happen?" Kari asked Linda, who had no answer.

Kari had the hard drive cleaned, but the computer was
slow, and she worried that Kensi would see the images.
Rather than take the risk, Kari bought a new computer and
gave the infected laptop to her brother, Adam, who was in

graduate school. But after a few months, Adam complained that the laptop was so slow, it was nearly worthless. On his next trip home, he gave the computer to their father. Deployed at Lackland Air Force Base in San Antonio that summer, Jim took the laptop with him. Once on base, he asked a computer guru friend if he could increase its speed.

"This thing is packed with porn," the friend told him, after inspecting it. "It's so bad, it's embedded in the hard drive. Porn like you wouldn't believe."

When Matt heard, he shrugged, and said, "Well, Adam's a college kid."

Yet, when Linda asked her son, Adam pointed out that he hadn't used it on the Net, only to do word processing. "I'm smarter than that," he said. "I didn't do it."

Not knowing what to think but never considering that their Baptist minister son-in-law could be viewing pornography, Jim simply discarded the laptop.

Chapter 10

A round, soft, bundle with soft wisps of blond hair and big blue eyes, Kassidy continued to be an easy baby, one who wore a perpetual smile and who didn't balk when Kari passed her around to the other women in church. Kensi was so taken with her baby sister, she called her "My Kassidy."

Based on outward appearances, the second of the Baker girls was thriving. So much so that she'd never even required an aspirin during that first year of life. In mid-November 1998, Barbara and Oscar drove in from Kerrville, and Kari's family gathered to celebrate Kassidy's first birthday. It was after presents and birthday candles that Kassidy threw up. That didn't seem too startling. "We wrote it off as too much cake," Barbara would say.

The next morning at the parsonage, Barbara took a photo of Kassidy before she and Oscar drove home. "Afterward, I looked at it and thought that she didn't look right, just kind of sick. In her eyes, it was like things weren't all right."

That Sunday afternoon, Kassidy vomited again, and it continued throughout the day. The following morning, Kari and Matt bundled up their daughters and went to the pediatrician, who diagnosed the infant with a "stomach bug." Telling them to give her lots of fluids, the pediatrician sent Matt and Kari home. But Kassidy didn't improve.

On that Wednesday, Matt called his mother. "There's something not right with Kassidy," he said. "We've been up all night trying to get fluids in her with a dropper and she's still throwing up. She can't sit up."

Later that day, Matt and Kari again brought Kassidy to the doctor, who again diagnosed her malady as a stomach bug. As the week wore on, however, the toddler didn't appear any better. On Friday, Matt called Barbara. "There's something wrong," he said. "We're trying another doctor. We can't go through another night like last night."

That time, Matt and Kari took Kassidy to Hillcrest Baptist Medical Center's emergency room. There she was examined, but the ER physician found no reason for her illness. Explaining that he worried that the baby was dehydrated, he told Matt and Kari that he wanted Kassidy in the hospital on an IV.

With Kassidy in the hospital and Matt and others watching over her that night, Kari met Janelle at a store, to buy groceries for a needy family in the church. As they walked up to the house to deliver them, Janelle asked, "How can you do this with Kassidy sick?"

"This family needs the groceries," Kari answered. After they finished, Kari returned to the hospital and spent the night at Kassidy's bedside.

The following morning, Barbara drove up from Kerrville and sat in Kassidy's room, holding the child. Kari had convinced Linda to keep a commitment and fly to New York a day earlier to attend a conference, and Matt and Kari had gone to church. It was the weekend before Thanksgiving, and he was speaking at a potluck supper that evening. In the hospital room, Jim talked with Barbara, when Kassidy suddenly threw her head back, her body stiffened and shook. The child was in the throes of a violent seizure.

"Get the nurse," Barbara told Jim, rubbing her granddaughter's stomach and leg. He ran from the room, while she held the child and tried to comfort her. "I know it was only a few minutes, but it seemed to go on twenty minutes or more," Barbara would recount years later. "I kept telling her she'd be all right."

That night, Matt took Kensi home, and Kari and Barbara stayed with Kassidy while they waited for the doctors to figure out what was wrong. During the night, Kassidy awoke, calling for her mother in a hoarse voice. Kari went to her and held her, the child falling back to sleep in her arms.

After a spinal tap ruled out meningitis, Kassidy was sent for an MRI. Back from New York, Linda arrived at the hospital just in time to hear the doctor deliver very bad news. Kassidy had a tumor at the base of her brain. It was growing, and left unchecked, it would be life-threatening. To save her, they'd have to operate quickly. The problem was Kassidy's age. Children so young had delicate lungs. The operation would be lengthy, and the anesthetic was dangerous, possibly even deadly.

The news was crushing. Hillcrest didn't have the facilities to handle the surgery, and that same day Kassidy was transferred via ambulance to Cook Children's Hospital, ninety minutes away in Fort Worth. On medication to suppress the seizures, Kassidy needed to be operated on as soon as possible, and just two days after arriving in Fort Worth, tests were completed and surgery was scheduled. The date was Wednesday, November 25, the day before Thanksgiving.

The surgeon had been blunt, telling the family that there was the chance that Kassidy wouldn't make it through the operation. That afternoon, Matt and Kari kissed their infant daughter and saw her rolled down a hallway and into a surgical suite. They then joined the rest of the family in a waiting room. Five generations of Linda's family were in the waiting room, along with Matt, Kari, Barbara and Oscar, and Matt's sister, Stacie, and her husband. The hours passed, and those gathered prayed. The surgery went on into the evening, before the doctor arrived to say that Kassidy was in the pediatric ICU. The tumor had been completely removed. Encapsulated, it popped out easily. But there were other concerns, including, as they'd warned earlier, the effects of the anesthesia. "I don't know if we're going to be able to pull her through," the surgeon said.

When they first saw her, Kassidy looked small and helpless, tied up to a maze of tubes and machines, but she held up her hand to her parents. Thankful that she had survived, at the suggestion of the doctor, the family went to dinner. When they returned, however, it was to bad news: Kassidy's chest was filling with fluid. "Kassidy had pulmonary edema," says Linda. "Her lungs were hardening. They fully expected her to die."

Thanksgiving Day, church members from Williams Creek, ninety minutes away, brought dinner to the family as they held a vigil inside and outside Kassidy's hospital room. In what was described as a "last-ditch effort," the surgeon cut a tracheotomy in Kassidy's throat to insert a tube for a respirator. They also put the child into a medically induced coma. "The idea was to see if her body would heal itself if it had nothing else it had to do," says Linda.

For one week, Kassidy lay nearly motionless, then she was allowed to awaken, but her condition remained fragile. The coming months were agony. Matt came often, and Kari was almost always at her daughter's side. The anesthetic had also weakened the muscles attached to one eye, allowing it to drift, and affected her gag reflexes, so that she had to be fed through a tube. When they weren't there, Barbara, Linda, or Jim sat in the hospital room, talking to Kassidy, rubbing her soft arms, telling her to hold on and stay with them. There were nights where it seemed her tiny little body was ready to give up, but always the doctors were able to bring her back. "Death was in the room with us those nights," says Barbara. "You could feel it."

As difficult as the times were, Kari and Matt both seemed to hold up well under the pressure. "We can handle this," Kari told one of her friends. "We just have to do whatever we have to do, and then Kassidy will get better, and she'll come home."

In more private times, Kari wrote in her journal, as on

December 3, eight days after Kassidy's surgery: "My little
Kassidy is fighting so hard. There are times where I think
how much longer will she fight. It is so hard to understand
why this has happened, but all I do is pray . . . Matt is being
so strong. He is so solid. I have never wanted this to be over
more than I do now. I want my family back. I miss my little
Kassidy's smile. I want to hear her giggle. I wish I could put
myself in her spot. I hope I have the strength to keep going
because Kassidy and Kensi need me."

In January, Kassidy was still gravely ill in the pediatric
ICU when Lindsey asked a friend who worked with her at
the Cracker Barrel in Waco, Erin Vendetti, to drive to Cook
Children's with her. Erin had never met either Matt or Kari,
and in the car, Lindsey talked about Matt, including his bizarre history with women, describing what happened that
summer at First Baptist. "You have to be careful around
him. He's a little flirtatious," Lindsey warned. "Sometimes,
he says and does strange things."

"He's a preacher?" Erin marveled.

"Yes," Lindsey says. "He is."

An attractive twenty-year-old, Erin brushed it off. "He's
not going to hit on me in the hospital with his daughter
maybe dying. No one would do that."

Lindsey didn't appear convinced.

Once they arrived, they found Matt and Kari outside
Kassidy's room. To protect Kassidy, whose immune system
had been wiped out by chemo, only two visitors wearing
sterile gowns and masks were allowed in at one time.

When Kari and Lindsey left to see Kassidy, Erin claimed
a chair in front of a television in the game room and began
playing a Mario video game with a young boy, a cancer
patient who'd lost all of his hair. Before long, Matt sat
beside her.

"I'm so sorry about your daughter being so ill," Erin said.
"I hope she gets better."

"You know," Matt said, leaning in toward her, "you're a
beautiful girl."

Erin concentrated on the computer game, but said, "Thank you."

Matt moved closer, placing his hand on her leg. "They gave us a room to stay in while Kassidy's here. It's close. Would you like to see it?"

"No," she said, lifting his hand and removing it. "Of course not."

Matt, however, wasn't ready to give up. "Lindsey and Kari will be gone at least fifteen minutes. The room is right down the hall." He placed his hand on her upper thigh.

Again, Erin moved his hand away. "No!" she said, even more forcefully.

With that, Matt stood up, and Erin thought maybe it was over, but then, she felt his hands on her shoulders, rubbing.

Revolted, Erin bolted up and walked away, toward the windows. There she stood, looking out at the hallway in the direction of Kassidy's room. She felt relief flood through her when Kari and Lindsey emerged, peeling off their protective clothing.

To Erin's disgust, Matt walked over to Kari and Lindsey as if nothing had happened. Kari was calm and stoic, while Lindsey sobbed. Matt talked to the other two women as Erin fought an overwhelming urge to flee. "Lindsey, we need to go," she said.

"Just a minute," Lindsey said, wiping away tears.

"No, now," Erin insisted. "We need to go now."

Eyeing Erin, Lindsey told Matt and Kari good-bye, and they walked to the elevator. Once the door closed, and they were alone, Erin began to cry. "He hit on you, didn't he?" Lindsey asked.

Erin nodded.

"I knew he would," she said. "I knew it."

"What do we do?" Erin asked. "Do we tell Kari?"

Lindsey thought for a moment, then said, "I'll tell my mom. She'll know what to do."

After she arrived home that afternoon, Lindsey called Nancy and told her what had transpired in the waiting room at Cook Children's. Lindsey was upset, embarrassed, and angry, and Nancy told her that she'd figure out what to do. After she hung up with her daughter, Nancy dialed her mother. "Mom, I need to tell you about something," she said, then filled her in on Matt's behavior. "What should we do? Should I tell Kari? Or should I tell Linda?"

After considering the situation, the family matriarch, Kari's grandmother, asked Nancy to do nothing. "Kari has a sick baby in the hospital, enough on her mind to worry about," she said. "We can't tell her this now. We need to keep this to ourselves."

Considering all that Kari was going through, Nancy agreed.

The days dragged on, and Kari and Matt tried to live as normal a life as possible. On Sundays, Linda or Barbara sat with Kassidy while Kari took Kensi to Williams Creek to hear Matt preach. No one ever mentioned Erin to Kari or to Linda. Neither had an inkling of what Matt had done. Instead, what Kari saw throughout Kassidy's illness was her husband steadfast by her side, praying with her, supporting her while their daughter fought for her life.

One complication after another threatened Kassidy, but the infant seemed determined to live. Those were hard days. Just to hold their child, Matt or Kari had to sit in a chair and wait until a nurse lowered Kassidy onto their laps, positioning the tubes and alarms that kept her alive.

Some of those who visited said they most often found Matt in the waiting area or outside in the hallway, while Kari stayed at Kassidy's bedside. To some it appeared that he was enjoying the attention he was getting from others as they tried to reassure and comfort him. When asked, he'd go into detail about Kassidy's condition in a clinical way, then talk about all he was doing to help. "He loved the spotlight," says Lindsey. "In his eyes, he was the strong one."

Paul Stripling visited Kari and Matt at the hospital. "To

me, they both seemed overwhelmed," said the Baylor professor. "I went and prayed with them."

Members of Williams Creek, including Todd and Jenny and Janelle Murphy drove to Fort Worth to support the young family. In all, Kassidy spent forty-three days in the pediatric ICU. At one point, the infant had hives all over her body, a reaction to chemotherapy. "It was a roller coaster," says Barbara.

As her time in the ICU ended, Kassidy was not only still alive but appeared to have turned the corner. Her condition was stable, and she was transferred into the tracheotomy unit, a step-down unit with less critical patients. It was then that Kari again wrote in her journal: "Kassidy is such a fighter . . . I know God is healing her. I'm ready for her to come home and have our family back. I love my little girl so much. Also my sweet Kensi doesn't understand why her mommy isn't home."

Before long, Kassidy's doctors talked about releasing her. There were, however, concerns. Kassidy still wasn't swallowing well and was still being fed through a gastric, or a G-tube. And her breathing wasn't to the point where the trach tube could be removed. As preparations began, Matt and Kari were given lessons on how to manage Kassidy's feeding tube, clean her trach, and hook up her monitors. Through it all, Kari appeared not afraid but eager to get her baby home. "Kassidy needed a lot of care, but Kari was prepared to do anything she had to do," remembers Jenny. "She said God had given Kassidy back to them, and she was going to do her best to take care of her."

"Kassidy's prognosis was good," Linda remembers. "She was cancer-free. The chemo was a precaution, and the doctors told us that she should make a full recovery."

With her baby improving, Kari seemed at ease. At times, visitors found her in Kassidy's room bouncing the laughing infant on her knee while she sang "Buffalo gals can you come out tonight," from the Christmas classic *It's a Wonderful Life*.

In late February, the day finally came and Matt and Kari drove home from Fort Worth with Kassidy. She still had her trach and the feeding tube. They'd both been taught how to clean and maintain the lifelines that kept their baby alive. There was also an alarm, one that was designed to notify them if Kassidy stopped breathing. The doctors had said, however, that it should be only a couple of months before both tubes would be removed, and Kassidy would be breathing and eating on her own.

Her two grandmothers would later disagree about Kassidy's condition when she returned home. Barbara would say that the child was still fragile and that, when left unattended, she'd fall over. "You had to blow on her face to remind her to breathe," says Barbara.

Linda, however, maintained that Barbara wasn't in Waco but Kerrville and hadn't seen the child. "Kassidy was learning to walk, pulling herself up on furniture," says Linda. "Her cheeks were pink, and she was smiling. She'd pull the oxygen with her on the floor while she crawled. She was still having chemo, but she was thriving."

Others who saw Kassidy would agree with Linda, saying that they saw a baby who'd been through the worst and was fighting her way back. There was one change. Where in the past, she'd been comfortable on others' laps, she now clung to her mother. "She wanted Kari," says Jenny Monsey. "She didn't want other people to hold her."

One afternoon, Nancy and her husband dropped in at the parsonage to pick up an extra crib. Her second daughter, Ami, had just given birth to a severely premature baby named Joe Joe. The infant was still hospitalized, but Nancy was getting the nursery ready. When she arrived at the parsonage, Kari had Kassidy on her lap tickling her, the infant laughing. "Kassidy looked at us with her blue eyes, so serious," says Nancy. "Then she looked at Kari and just smiled."

Slowly, life was returning to normal. A home health-care nurse watched over Kassidy during the day, so that Kari and

Matt could begin to attend their classes. There were concerns, of course, but the child seemed to be healing. "You could feel it in church," says Jenny. "There was a sense of relief. We'd all been so worried about Kassidy, but our prayers had been answered."

There were more operations ahead. Surgeons would remove the trach and G-tube once Kassidy's lungs and muscles grew stronger, and one eye, damaged in surgery, would need to have the muscles tightened. "But it truly was looking like we got our miracle," says Linda.

All went well, then on Friday, March 19, Matt and Kari took Kassidy to Hillcrest's ER. Later there would be a disagreement about the reason. Matt would say Kassidy had a fever but that she no longer had it when they arrived. What Linda recalled was that the infant's feeding port wasn't seated right, allowing food to ooze out.

Whatever the reason, Matt had called ahead, and instead of exposing the infant to possible infection in the hospital waiting area, a doctor from the ER came out to the car to examine Kassidy. Linda and Jim were there, too, listening. "The doctor said it would be all right," says Linda. "He told them to have the doctor look at Kassidy's G-tube when they brought her in for chemo the following week."

Two days later, Jenny walked with Kari from church after Sunday evening services. "It's wonderful to have her home," Kari said. "I know Kassidy will be okay."

In the small parsonage that night, Matt and Kari watched the Academy Awards and saw Roberto Benigni jump on his chair to celebrate when he won best actor for his role in *Life is Beautiful*. Before Matt and Kari went to bed, they checked both girls and found that Kassidy had diarrhea. They cleaned her up, then went to bed.

When in bed, Kassidy was supposed to wear a monitor, a not-uncommon type used for premature babies who are at risk for Sudden Infant Death Syndrome. If she'd stopped breathing, the alarm would have sounded. Why wasn't Kassidy wearing it? Matt would later say that they often left it off at night. What Kari later told others was that Matt said Kassidy didn't need it.

At about twelve, for no apparent reason, Matt got up to check both girls again. "They were both doing fine," he said.

Oddly, he then rose again, just nine minutes later, and checked Kassidy for a third time. Why? "Something wouldn't let me sleep. I knew I needed to check again," he'd say. Since the monitor wasn't attached, no alarm had sounded, but Kassidy wasn't breathing. "I yelled for my wife. I took Kassidy out of the bed and started CPR."

Describing that horrible night, Kari would later say that she heard Matt scream and rushed to dial 911, begging them to hurry. Meanwhile, Matt continued CPR, using a bag to force oxygen through the trach and into the baby's lungs. Kari never entered Kassidy's bedroom that night. Why? Barbara would later say that Kari said she couldn't go in, and that guilt for that would haunt her. But what Kari told others was that Matt ordered her not to go into the nursery. "She said he didn't want her in there," says Linda. "When she called us, she said Matt was with Kassidy, and he'd told her to wait for the ambulance."

Moments later, Linda called Nancy, and said, "I think my baby is losing her baby."

Meanwhile, Kari and Matt followed the ambulance to the hospital, phoning Barbara on the way to tell her of the unfolding horror. Nancy arrived at the ER just after 12:30 A.M. and saw the staff working on Kassidy. Overcome with emotion, Nancy took an elevator upstairs, where she checked on her own grandson, Joe Joe. At only twenty-eight weeks and two pounds, he was high-risk, and doctors had warned that he might not survive, but he was improving. It struck her as ironic when Nancy returned to the ER and saw the doctors still fighting to restore Kassidy's life. "Joe Joe was supposed to die, and the doctors had said Kassidy was cured, that she would live," Nancy says. "It seemed so strange. He was going to be all right, and Kari was losing her baby."

Finally, the doctor turned to all of them, and said, "There's nothing else we can do."

At that, Kari screamed. As Nancy watched, tears running from her own eyes, she looked at the faces of those around her. It seemed everyone in the room was crying, even the doctors and nurses who'd fought so hard but been unable to save the child. Then Nancy noticed Matt standing in the background watching it all as if it were a mildly interesting television show. "Matt showed no emotion. Zilch," says Nancy. "It was so strange. Everyone crying, and Matt acted like it was just another day."

Thinking to herself that people express grief differently, Nancy couldn't help but wonder, "How can you not cry when you see this beautiful, chubby little baby die?"

At that point, the focus turned to saying good-bye. Family members, one at a time, began entering the hospital room, where Matt and Kari sat with Kassidy's body. Motioned in, Nancy found Kari in a chair cradling her dead child in her arms. "I love you both so much," Nancy said, hugging and kissing Kassidy and Kari.

Later, it would all seem so surreal. Tears coated Kari's cheeks, but Matt stood off to the side, silent and unemotional, until he suddenly rushed forward as if intent on something. As Nancy later described it, Matt began grabbing at Kassidy's tracheotomy tube.

"What're you doing?" Kari snapped. "Leave her alone."

"I just want to remove her trach," Matt said.

"No," Kari responded. "Leave her alone. Don't touch her." But Matt persisted, and Kari protectively swung her arms around, holding the dead child's body away from him.

Before she left the room, Nancy looked down at Kassidy's small, still body, covered with scars from her months of shots, surgeries, and treatments, and thought about how hard the baby had fought to survive. At the time, she thought little of the trach incident beyond that Kari was hurting so deeply, and Matt was being selfish. Later, in light of what lay ahead, it would take on a whole new meaning.

* * *

About three that Monday morning, Kari called her friend Janelle Murphy. "Kassidy is gone," Kari said, then between painful sobs, explained what had happened. "I had to leave Kassidy at that hospital, Janelle. I couldn't bring her home."

Four hours later, at seven, Barbara arrived at the parsonage. The door was open, and she walked inside and found Matt, Kari, and Kensi all in bed together, asleep. Barbara had called from the road and talked to Linda, who told her that Kassidy had died. So Barbara didn't wake them, and instead lay down on the couch to rest.

That morning, at the high school, Jenny saw one of the other teens from the Williams Creek youth group crying. When Jenny asked why, the girl told her that Kassidy Baker had died. Tears gathered in Jenny's eyes as she thought back to the evening before, when she'd left church with Kari and talked about how Kassidy had improved and how happy Kari was to have her home.

From the time the doors opened at the visitation, there was a line of well-wishers wanting to talk to Matt and Kari: family, friends, members of Williams Creek and the other churches where he'd worked, friends and professors from Baylor. Even some of the nurses who'd cared for Kassidy came to say a final good-bye. "It wasn't like a family grieving," says Todd. "Because it was Matt and Kari's baby, because they were so involved in the community, it was the whole town."

When Jenny arrived, Kari took her by the hand and led her to the casket. "Look at my baby," Kari said. She then leaned over and gave Kassidy a kiss.

Throughout the visitation, Kari did the same thing with others, taking them to Kassidy's casket for a final good-bye, including her friend Janelle. Perhaps Kari noticed the way Janelle looked at Kassidy, staring at what appeared to be dark bruises on the child's mouth and nose. "I think those are from CPR," Kari explained.

Like the night before, Matt showed no emotion. "You

don't have to cry," Nancy would say later. "But it didn't seem right that he walked around like it was any other day. As people gave their condolences, it looked like Matt enjoyed all the attention."

To many, it appeared that Kari was grieving enough for both of them. At one point, she jumped up from the couch she was seated on and ran to the casket, draping herself over Kassidy's body. "Why did you do this? Why did you leave me?" she cried.

Janelle followed her and took Kari by her arm, walking her away. "She's not supposed to be in there," Kari sobbed. "My baby is supposed to be home."

It was after the visitation and before the funeral began, that Kari turned to Linda, and said, "Mom, I can't do this."

"Yes, you can," Linda said, wrapping her arms around her. "We're going to do this together."

A former pastor from Trinity Baptist, Matt's home church in Kerrville, conducted the funeral service. There were flowers and a picture of Kassidy on the casket, and a video was shown of her brief life, from her birth through the birthday party when she'd first shown signs of her illness.

Looking at her granddaughter's body, Barbara would say she said to God, "This is one of those situations I don't understand." Later, many would remark how alike she and Matt were that day, how neither shed a tear. Meanwhile, Kassidy's death would test Linda's faith. "God and I had some problems for a while after that," she'd say later. "We agreed to kind of leave each other alone for a while."

After the memorial service, the immediate family followed the hearse to historic Oakwood Cemetery. The burial place of three Texas governors, the cemetery was founded in 1878 on 157 wooded acres. In the summers, crape myrtles bloomed a bright pink at the gate.

The spot chosen for Kassidy's final resting place was in Babyland, a section reserved for the burial of the very young. Not far from a massive oak with branches reaching outward, her grave waited, yawning open just past a stone marker with an etching of Jesus surrounded by children. In a crescent across the top, it read: SUFFER THE LITTLE CHILDREN TO COME UNTO ME.

The day had already taken a terrible toll, and Linda and Jim had to help Kari walk up to the grave. Her body seemed ravaged by grief. Just as he had been at the funeral, Matt appeared businesslike, talking to people, not crying, and not reaching out to comfort his wife. Barbara had a friend with her who snapped photos of Kassidy's casket. When Kari saw it, she asked her mother to ask the woman to stop. Linda did, and the woman appeared unhappy, saying Barbara wanted the photos for her memories. "Kari doesn't want the pictures," Linda told the woman. "Please, put the camera away."

In the little more than a year since Matt had given her *The Quest Study Bible,* Kari had written in it often, sometimes while listening to him preach or during Bible study, noting her thoughts in the margins. She'd also tucked two bookmarks inside, Precious Moments cards with sweet drawings of two little girls and the definitions of her daughters' names: Kensi was the "wise leader," and Kassidy, "a helper of mankind."

In her Bible, Kari had also filled out the family history section with the date of her marriage to Matt and the birth dates of both her children. That spring, she penned another entry, a death date for Kassidy Lynn Baker, March 22, 1999. Later, a granite gravestone marked the site where Kassidy was buried. It read: MY SWEET, SWEET BABY.

Chapter II

"Kari grieved for her child. Oh, how she grieved," Linda would say years later. "But did she let it take over her life? No."

Just a week after Kassidy's death, Kari stopped at her cousin Ami's apartment to see Joe Joe, who'd just been released from the hospital. She held the baby and murmured to him. She stayed to help Ami care for the infant. "We were worried about her, but Kari wanted to be there," says Nancy. "She loved Joe Joe, but it was so hard."

On another level, Kari was plagued by sorrow. The woman so many saw during the first weeks, then months, after her daughter's death struggled trying to understand what had happened, how and why. She wondered, as any mother might, what she could have done to change fate. But for Kari, there was more reason to question, since Kassidy had come home with such an optimistic prognosis.

The day of Kassidy's death, Kari left a message for the oncologist who'd treated her daughter. The physician had worked long and hard to give Kassidy a chance to live, and she'd been successful, sending the child home with the prospect of a healthy future. When the doctor called back, Linda stood with Kari in Kassidy's room and heard the phone conversation. Kari tearfully explained that her daughter had died, but the oncologist didn't respond as Kari expected. Instead of commiserating with her, the doctor protested, "Kassidy wasn't supposed to die. How could she be dead?"

Kari appeared stunned, as the doctor warned, "There's something wrong. I'm going to call children's protective services."

When Kari hung up the phone, she turned to her mother, sobbing, and said, "The doctor thinks we did something to Kassidy. She's calling CPS."

On top of the anguish of her granddaughter's death, Linda heard the hurt in her daughter's voice. She couldn't imagine why the doctor would make such a bizarre statement. "Well, that's crazy," Linda assured Kari. "That's just crazy."

The physician followed through with her threat, and just days after Kassidy's funeral, a CPS worker arrived at the parsonage to talk to Matt and Kari. Anxious, not knowing what to expect, Kari asked her aunt Kay and Kay's good friend, Jo Ann Bristol, a Waco counselor, to be there to support them. They agreed, and the three women and Matt greeted the CPS worker when she came into the house.

A heavyset woman with a notepad, she had questions, and the small group sat in the parsonage and answered. The CPS worker asked about Kassidy's battle with the tumor and the aftermath, and about what happened the night of her death. Matt answered as the woman took notes, describing as he would for so many finding Kassidy's lifeless body. Meanwhile, the woman glanced about, sizing up the house and those gathered.

It was when Matt mentioned that Kassidy had a trained health-care aide in the house eight hours a day taking care of her special needs, that the woman appeared most interested. The aide had even gone to the ER with Matt and Kari days earlier. "Oh, I didn't know that when you went to the ER you had a home health nurse with you," the woman said.

That, it would seem, had settled the matter. "I don't think there'll be any problems," the woman assured them as she left.

Matt would later say: "CPS had a claim we didn't take care of Kassidy properly, and the woman was checking to see if Kensi was okay. She interviewed us, me and Kari. But she didn't find anything wrong. She never did anything."

A few days after the CPS worker walked out the door never to return, Kari had her Bible open to a passage that read: "For unto us a child is born, unto us a son is given." The grieving mother, fighting to find some order in all that had happened stenciled her lost daughter's name, KASSIDY, in all caps beside it.

For Matt, grieving appeared vastly easier. The week after he buried his daughter, he was at the pulpit in Williams Creek Baptist. Some wondered if the young pastor was allowing himself time to grieve, speculating that a father needed time off after the death of a child. Yet there Matt was, standing before the congregation, insisting he followed orders from above: "This is where the Lord wants me. He gives me strength."

This strength of Matt's, it would appear, confused Kari. She expected him to share her pain. "I can't understand why he's not hurting like I am," she told Janelle. "Why is it tearing me apart, and Matt's acting like nothing happened?"

"The fact that it was business as usual for Matt was hard on Kari," says Janelle, who looked at Matt and saw the same thing Kari did, someone who'd moved on. "At one point, I heard him say, 'Now I can get back to work.' It was as if Kassidy's illness had interrupted his life and his preaching, and he was glad to have it over with."

Over the weeks, Kari talked often with Janelle, who was working as music minister at Williams Creek. "Kari questioned the events, how they happened, how Matt found Kassidy, how long he'd been in there, was there more they could have done," Janelle says. "She thought it was strange that Matt was the one who found Kassidy, that he'd decided to go in there and check on her after they went to bed."

At the time, Janelle never considered that Kari could be struggling with a suspicion that Matt had somehow caused their daughter's death. Only later would Janelle believe that was exactly what Kari was attempting to sort through.

One time that would stand out in Janelle's memory was a day she and Kari were at the parsonage and ended up in Kassidy's room. "Kari began talking about the night Kassidy died. She wandered around the room, saying things like, 'I just don't understand what happened. Why did Matt come in here a second time? Did he know something was wrong? What if I had been the one to check on Kassidy, would she still be here? How long did it take for her to die? I mean, Matt checked on her, and she was fine, but then when he went back, she had died. What happened? I hate thinking that Matt did something wrong, like with her feeding tube, that could have caused this. But, why doesn't he hurt like I do?'"

That afternoon, the conversation continued, Janelle listening but able to offer little in response. Talking it through, Kari pondered, "Matt's able to go right back to preaching like nothing ever happened. How does he do that? He wants to have sex, but that's the furthest thing from my mind. It's almost like he's relieved that Kassidy is gone."

Although the conversation was highly emotional, Kari didn't cry. Instead, she looked right into Janelle's eyes. "She was rambling all of these questions while I just empathized. I didn't have answers. Her tone was one of confusion. She couldn't piece together what happened, and speaking aloud her fears of Matt made her feel too guilty. She was careful in how she spoke. She would question what he did that night but then immediately have a look of, *why would I think that?*"

At times, Kari closed her eyes and simply shook her head. Perhaps she felt haunted by what the oncologist had said, her accusations that Matt or Kari must have done something wrong.

Despite all the turmoil inside her, Kari did her best to forge ahead. Yet the sadness seemed to follow her. She was at Target buying clothes for Kensi when she ran into Basy

Barrera, her hairdresser. "Did you hear what happened to Kassidy?" Kari asked.

"No."

"She died," Kari said, and the two women stood in Target, hugging and crying.

"People were probably staring," Basy said later. "But I don't think either one of us cared."

As the weeks passed, Kari talked often of Kassidy, wanting to keep her memory alive, much to Matt's annoyance. "He really didn't seem to have time for it," says Janelle.

To help Kari through the grieving process, Linda suggested that her daughter seek professional help. "I wanted her to be able to talk freely," Linda explains. "She needed someone to help her work through her grief." Kari did, turning to the friend of Kay's who'd come to help the day the CPS worker dropped by, Jo Ann Bristol, a licensed clinical social worker who'd gone back to study psychology and specialized in grief counseling. Bristol had first worked with Linda's family in the early nineties, when Linda's grandfather was dying of cancer. At the time, Bristol worked for a hospice. Over the years, she'd opened her own office, and she and Kay had become good friends.

From that point on, once a week, Matt, with Kensi in her car seat, drove Kari to Bristol's downtown Waco office, on a quaint street lined with shops and restaurants. Matt and Kensi would then leave, while Kari talked to Bristol, a motherly woman with a well-lined face. There was little doubt that Kari was grieving. "I saw that as Kari's way," says Linda. "She lived big, with so much joy in her life. The opposite side was that she grieved hard. Kari never had a feeling that she didn't tell someone."

"I don't want to be here," Kari admitted in the confines of Bristol's office.

"Are you suicidal?" Bristol asked.

"No, that's not what I mean," Kari answered. "I just wish I could be with Kassidy."

Bristol would later say she'd heard these same words

before from others who lamented the loss of a loved one. "Kari wasn't talking about taking her life. She was just saying overall, 'I wish I could be with Kassidy.' "

At one session, Kari complained that Matt was pressuring her for sex, at a time when she felt as if her heart had been torn from her body. At times, Kari confided that she looked for Kassidy everywhere, in other blond babies she saw on the streets, when she looked up to the heavens. In those sessions, Kari laid her soul bare, exposing the deep pain of a mother who'd lost a child. Yet as the hour ended, Kari dried her eyes and took a lipstick from her purse. She put it on, smoothed her hair, said good-bye to Bristol, and walked to the waiting room with a smile, where an unemotional Matt waited with Kensi. They left together until the scene replayed the following week.

On other days, Kari wrote in her journals, calling out to God. One journal was flowered and brightly colored with a Bible verse on the cover, John 3:216: "For God so loved the world that he gave his only begotten Son, that whoever believes in Him should not perish but have eternal life."

It was on the one-month anniversary of Kassidy's death that Kari wrote: "My dearest Kassidy, I haven't written in so long because I just didn't have the words to say how I felt. Now it has been a month, and you are no longer on earth with us. We miss you so much. The thing I miss the most is your smell. I felt that you are so special, and I just never knew how much until you were gone. You are my soul, and you will always have a piece of that.

"Kensi misses you so much. Give her in your own little way something on her birthday that will let her know you are with her . . . Thank you for letting me see you on Friday in the clouds. Please keep that up. I want to feel you all the time."

Two days later, the day of Kensi's third birthday party, Kari wrote again, telling Kassidy: "Oh how I wish you could have been here . . . I am going to keep you by my side forever . . . I know you aren't sad, but I am . . ."

She then wrote: "Dear Jesus. Please help me! This sadness is death feeling. Give me your strength. Please help Matt and I [sic] get through this. I love him so much. You are my rock. Please give me the strength."

When Kari talked about the counseling sessions, Jenny saw it as an indication of her friend's strength. At church, after the first few weeks, Kari had stepped right back into her role of pastor's wife, working with the youth group. "Kari wasn't afraid to say, 'I'm getting help because I need to talk about it,' " says Jenny. "She was the strongest person I knew. Anything the group did, anything we needed, Kari volunteered. One day we played tug-of-war. The devil was pulling us in one direction and Jesus in the other."

In May, Kari wrote to Kassidy again, calling her "my everything" and lamenting that she had nothing left but photographs and videos. "There is something missing, and it is you," she noted. A bracelet Kari wore, one with two intertwined hearts, had broken, and she said it was because Kassidy had died. "I will carry you with me always."

The tension must have been building—Kari struggling with such powerful emotions while Matt watched, stone-faced. On the two-month anniversary of Kassidy's death, Kari again turned to her journal: "I went crazy on your daddy today. I just have so much anger. I don't know how to channel it. I know how you loved your daddy so much, and he misses you so much."

As the letter continued, she asked Kassidy to help her control her anger, and to "help me fall in love with your daddy again. You and Kensi are so lucky to have a father like him. I guess I just wish I had more control of the way I felt." Then, in all capital letters, she printed: "I WANT YOU BACK!"

In those quiet moments, alone with a pen and a blank sheet of paper, Kari pleaded with Kassidy, telling her that she shouldn't have died. "I wish I could explain why you aren't here anymore," she wrote. "But I really don't even know."

One day during Bible study, Janelle sat next to Kari.

Other women were gathered with Bibles open, and Janelle saw Kari write: "I want to be with Kassidy."

"I understood what Kari meant," Janelle said. "I didn't take it as Kari saying she wanted to die. Kari needed to cry, and she did that. She wanted Kassidy back, with her."

The summer came, and in July Matt and Kari accompanied the teenagers to the Glorieta Youth Camp in Santa Fe, New Mexico, near the Sangre de Cristo (Blood of Christ) Mountains. While Jenny and Kensi drove with Kari in her Volkswagen Touareg, Kari talked. On the drive, she recounted a day after Kassidy's death when she stood in the empty sanctuary at Williams Creek alone. "I screamed at God. I told God it wasn't fair."

That afternoon, Kari admitted there were days when the only reason she got out of bed was Kensi. Yet at camp, Kari played games with the teenagers, held worship services, even helped mow the grass. She smiled and laughed. "She was so strong," Jenny said.

The summer wore on, and Kari again confided in Janelle, admitting that she didn't like going in the room that had been Kassidy's, the room where her baby had died. Quickly after the child's death, the room was cleaned out, and Matt converted it into an office. Later, Barbara would say that when she drove to the parsonage with Kari in the car, Kari would become upset as they neared the house. "I don't like coming over this hill," Kari said. "I can't breathe, and my heart starts pounding. I want to keep driving. I don't want to go back to that house where my baby died."

In hindsight, it would seem that the only place Matt showed any emotion about his daughter's death was at the pulpit during his sermons. It was then that he sometimes choked up. "I thought Matt was so great, that he was being so strong," says Todd.

It had been months since Kari had written to Kassidy when Kari opened a journal on August 25 of that year, 1999. After addressing the entry to Kassidy, Kari informed her daughter that she had returned to Baylor that day, picking up her classes to finish her education degree. It would be a milestone, turning the corner toward moving on. Yet Kari admitted, "I don't really want to go. I'm doing it for you. I want you to be proud of me . . . I wish the pain would go away. I wish you would come back."

There was more news to share with her dead daughter. Members of Williams Creek were building a memorial for Kassidy, a small prayer garden in front of the church. On that same day, they'd begun digging to make the beds for shrubs and flowers. And in her journal, Kari again pondered why Kassidy had died. "Why can't I just die?" she asked, pouring out her grief on the journal pages. Finally, she wrote an entreaty to God: "Please help me. I need you so much."

Kari Baker had lost a child, and the grief consumed her private moments. It was with her always, the loss, the slice Kassidy's death had cut through her heart. There were days that would always be reminders. One of the first was in November. As the day that would have been Kassidy's second birthday approached, Kari wrote in her Bible, still lamenting her daughter's death. Yet in counseling, Bristol gave Kari ideas, ways to work through her grief.

That Thanksgiving, Linda's family congregated at her parents' home. They were a large family, about twenty-five in all, and they had gathered in the kitchen when Kari stood with a candle in her hand. "My counselor suggested that as part of the grieving process, I mark holidays by remembering Kassidy," she said. "I'm going to light a candle. Then I'd like you all to say what you remember about her."

With that, Kari struck a match and lit the candle. While the others talked, Linda and Kari began to cry, as Matt stood off by himself, his face rock cold. He leaned against a wall without a tear in his eye as the family surrounding him told anecdotes from the brief life of his dead daughter.

When the ceremony finished, Kari ran sobbing from the room. Matt didn't hurry after her. Instead, it was Linda who followed her daughter to the bedroom, where she held and tried to comfort her.

Chapter 12

That month, November 1999, the congregation at Williams Creek gathered in front of the church for the dedication of Kassidy's memorial prayer garden. They'd fashioned it with stone and mortar in the shape of a Christian fish, the head pointing at the cross on the front of the church. Along the outside stood tall bushes. Inside the border was a lush ground cover. From the street, passersby first noticed a concrete bench and a melancholy cherub on a stone platform, its wings hugging its small body.

Off to the side stood a second concrete angel, its wings unfurled, dressed in Colonial garb and carrying a cross. At its feet lay a slab of granite that read: KASSIDY'S PRAYER GARDEN, and the dates of her brief life, November 20, 1997 through March 22, 1999. Another stone marker tucked into the garden read: MIRACLES GROW WHERE YOU PLANT THEM.

From that day forward, many saw Kari sitting on the lone bench with Kensi. "Kassidy was in that church and in that garden," Janelle would say. At other times, Kari stood alone at the edge of the garden, hands over her face, weeping.

Yet for the most part, those melancholy moments didn't fill Kari's days. She and Matt were both back at Baylor, studying and working toward their degrees, picking up where their lives had taken such a sharp turn a year earlier, when Kassidy first became ill.

It was after the dedication that Matt and Kari made an announcement. Kari was pregnant with another girl. At first, Janelle would say her friend was wary of having another child. Having lost one, Kari worried about exposing herself to more pain. But before long, Kari talked excitedly of the pregnancy. "She said that the new baby was a gift from God," says a friend. "And that they would name her Grace, because the baby was by the grace of God."

In her Bible, Kari had underlined a sentence: *My grace is sufficient for you, for my power is perfect in weakness.*

Yet all wasn't going well for Matt at Williams Creek that fall. He was grumbling even more loudly and more often about the church members. Linda said nothing, but she didn't like it when Kari echoed his complaints. She understood that Kari was loyal to Matt, but it wasn't something Kari would have done before their marriage.

It was late that year when Janelle's water stopped working in her apartment, and she called asking Kari if she could take a shower at the parsonage. Kari quickly agreed, but said she wouldn't be home. When Janelle arrived, Matt let her in. She hurried into the bathroom, in a rush to get to classes. Then while Janelle was in the shower, she suddenly heard the bathroom door close, as if someone had been in the room with her and left. Knowing she and Matt were alone in the house, Janelle knew immediately who it must have been.

Not wanting to upset Kari, Janelle said nothing to either her or Matt about what had happened, but less than a week later Matt approached Janelle at church and fired her. "He told me that I didn't have the calling to be the music minister," says Janelle. "I'd thought that I was fulfilling a service, but Matt said I wasn't needed."

Afterward, Janelle heard Matt had told others, including Kari, that Janelle had quit. Fearing that being truthful could ruin her friendship with Kari, knowing that she would back her husband, Janelle remained silent. "I knew things weren't right with Matt," Janelle said later. "But I loved Kari, and I overlooked it. I didn't tell her that Matt fired me, or what happened in the house that day. If I had, I didn't think she would have believed me."

As the pregnancy progressed, many around Kari understood how worried she was about the baby she carried. "She watched everything she ate, everything she did," says a friend.

"Kari was afraid that Grace would have a tumor like Kassidy," says Barbara. "She was scared."

At the same time, the new baby appeared to have eased so much of the sadness. "Kari had that joy again," says Janelle. "Being pregnant with Grace brought her back."

It wasn't that Kari forgot Kassidy. She talked of her often. And there were those times, like the first anniversary of the baby's death, when she, Matt, and Kensi went to Kassidy's grave. Afterward, they held a small ceremony at the prayer garden, releasing pink balloons to fly up to the clouds. That would become a ritual for them, a way to remember their lost daughter. At times, when the sadness was too great, Kari stayed in bed for a day, watching a video of Kassidy crawling across the floor. One day in a Bible study, the instructor talked about "the baggage of death," and Kari left, crying.

But they were brief interludes in an otherwise busy life. "As time went on, she got better," says Jenny. "You could see it."

It was that May that Kari received her diploma. She was eight months pregnant the afternoon she graduated from Baylor with her education degree. She and Janelle had completed student training in a small country school outside Waco.

Meanwhile, Linda was teaching at the community college full-time and working on her doctorate part-time. In all, it would take eight years to get her Ph.D. She'd passed on that desire for an education to both Kari and Adam, and after Kari finished her degree, she immediately talked of graduate school.

With so much going right in her life, a little more than a

year after Kassidy's death, Kari told Jo Ann Bristol that she wanted to discontinue her counseling. "For five minutes yesterday, I didn't think about Kassidy's death," Kari told her counselor. "You know, I think I'm okay." Bristol had noticed that Kari was less emotional during the sessions and smiling more, that she sounded excited about her future with Matt, Kensi, and the new baby.

As chance would have it, that same month, Kari ran into her old friend from Tech, Melody, at their obstetrician's office. They renewed their friendship, and Melody was surprised at how much Kari had changed. In Lubbock, there'd been nights out at clubs and parties, but Kari explained that she'd married a preacher, that they had a little girl, and that they'd lost a daughter. "She'd settled down. She was calmer and more focused. Where Kari was loud at times in college, she was quieter."

Over the coming months, the two women talked on the telephone, Melody confiding that she was having some problems. "I'll pray for you," Kari told her, then admitting, "You know, I do have my own challenges."

At first, Kari said little about Matt, but then one day she said, "Sometimes I feel like I'm the only one hurting from Kassidy's death. We can't connect on that level. But life truly is beautiful, and I'm so blessed for what I have."

On July 18, 2000, a year and four months after Kassidy's death, Kari went to the hospital in Waco to deliver a third child. Round and blond, Grace was born, and Kari appeared anxious until the pediatrician examined her new daughter. When the doctor pronounced Grace healthy, Kari cried with joy.

That fall, Matt resigned from Williams Creek Baptist Church. Barbara would say that it was Kari who wanted Matt to find another position, that she no longer wanted to live in the parsonage, refusing to put Grace's crib in the room where she'd lost one daughter. Jenny would agree: "Kari said she just needed a fresh start. She said people at

Williams Creek looked at her like 'you're the one who lost your child.'"

Yet there were also indications that not everyone at Williams Creek was sorry to see Matt Baker leave. Some were complaining about his sermons. The very thing that made him popular with the young people in the church worked against him with the more senior members. And at Williams Creek, like many of the churches, the majority of the members were middle-aged and older. "They were saying they wanted to hear more from the Bible. They didn't like his lifestyle sermons," says one former member. Matt's response was on the order of, "I preach what God tells me to preach."

That November 2000, a year after the prayer garden was dedicated, Matt became pastor of yet another small church, First Baptist in Riesel. A tiny burg with a population that hovered near a thousand, Riesel was located on Highway 6, half an hour southeast of Waco. The church itself was a rectangular building with metal sides and a brick front, all painted white. Inside, red-upholstered pews lined up toward an aging oak pulpit. Behind it stood the spalike baptistery visible through a window from the main church. A small communion table was carved with the words IN REMEMBRANCE OF ME. And a banner on the right-hand side read: A WOMAN WHO FEARS THE LORD DESERVES TO BE PRAISED.

A sidewalk ran along the side of the church and behind it, to a long, low-slung building shaded by an ancient oak tree with branches that splayed out over the roof, housing meeting areas and classrooms. Behind that building, on the street that ran along the back of the church, was a small, one-story white frame house: the parsonage. It had a broad porch covered by a roof, and the garage had been enclosed, leaving the gravel driveway as the only parking.

The sign in front of the church was white with red lettering, and it included the times of services. A small plaque hung below it, one that read: PASTOR: MATTHEW BAKER.

Chapter 13

"**M**att hired me as the children's minister," says Todd Monsey. "It was a great experience for my first job. Matt and Kari worked together like they did at Williams Creek, building the youth program. Before long, we had close to fifty kids every Wednesday night, and Kari joked that what made it so much fun was that we all got to be kids again with them. She was happy."

Still, Kassidy's loss continued to haunt Kari, perhaps not during the day but when she tried to close her eyes at night. In November, Kari called her doctor asking for a sleep aid. The reason noted in her chart was that she was having difficulty sleeping "due to the loss of a child." The doctor prescribed 10 mg of Ambien, a powerful sleeping pill.

In the end, the Ambien wasn't to Kari's liking. She never called for more of the pills, complaining that Ambien made her sleep too soundly. She worried that she wouldn't be able to hear Kensi and Grace if they woke in the middle of the night. From that point on, Kari began a nightly ritual, routinely taking a Unisom-type pill, an over-the-counter sleep aid, mild drugs that induced drowsiness. She called them her sleepy-time pills, and habitually bought a less expensive generic brand.

* * *

On the second anniversary of Kassidy's death, Grace went with her sister and parents to the grave, releasing four pink balloons into the sky. Todd would remember that for that one day, Kari wanted to be alone with her family, remembering the little girl they'd lost. It was during that time that Kari and Todd had a long conversation. "We talked about Kassidy whenever she needed to," says Todd.

Todd would later recall something Kari said that day, when he tried to put in order all that lay ahead: "I miss Kassidy, and I want to be with her, but I never want to leave my life with Matt, Kensi, and Grace. I love them all."

In May, Kari wrote the Jabez Prayer in her Bible, in which Jabez called on God to bless him, to enlarge his territory, and protect him from evil. "So God granted him what he requested." Chronicles 4:10.

That spring, a minister with whom Matt had worked in the past attended a Sunday service in Riesel, after which Matt gave him a tour of the facility. Matt's friend would leave thinking that the young pastor had changed. "I never did see the warmth, the touch he'd had before his child died," says the man. "I watched him with the church members, and Matt appeared autocratic, telling them what to do instead of involving them in the church. He wasn't inviting them to attend classes and meetings, but ordering them. He wasn't the same pastor . . . I saw the warmth diminish in Matt."

It was also that May that Matt graduated from the seminary with a Master's of Divinity in Christian Education and Administration. Shortly after, he was ordained as a minister at Pecan Grove, the historic church so closely tied to Baylor where he'd once worked.

That day, Barbara, Oscar, Linda, most of both families watched the ceremony, including Linda's uncle Kenneth from Palestine, who gave Matt books on faith. With Kensi beside her, Kari, holding ten-month-old Grace, smiled proudly. Afterward, there was a celebration, and Kari's family gave Matt an expensive set of golf clubs, something he said he'd been wanting. In the months that followed, Linda asked Kari why Matt never went golfing. "He doesn't have any friends to play with," Kari said.

As May 2001 drew to a close, Kari returned to the journals she had written in off and on since Kassidy's death. She still struggled with her loss, yet the emphasis had changed. A little more than two years after her daughter's death, Kari missed Kassidy, yet she voiced the belief that her daughter was happy in heaven. It was her relationship with God that Kari was exploring. One day, she wrote:

> Dear Lord, Please help me learn to let go of some of the anger . . . Lord, please give me some peace. My heart hurts, and I want to try to be as happy as I can. Lord, I want to serve you, but I need your help again. Thank you for loving me. Amen.

Over a series of days, Kari beseeched:

> The reason it is so hard to ask for blessings is because truly I don't know how to ask. I guess I feel that I am not worthy of such a gift. Also, since Kassidy, I feel my life can't be truly blessed. Today Lord, I want to ask you to bless me . . . I feel I can make a difference. I'm just not sure what it is you want me to do . . . Lord, I want people to see you through me . . . Lord, help me be a better Christian.

At one point, she wrote in her Bible: *I love you God, even if you took my Kassidy.*

Money problems were on Kari's mind on June 11, when she asked God to help her and Matt *"be better with our money,"* then the next day, *"Lord bless my life and give me the blessings you have for me. Bless me in all my endeavors. Lord, I love you. Amen."*

Late that spring, Kari talked with her old friend, Melody. She encouraged her to reach out to God, telling her that if they tried, they could both be better people. "I have to have my faith," Kari said.

Why was Kari having such a difficult time that first summer in Riesel? Perhaps part of it involved a drama going on behind the scenes. Kari called Linda one day, upset. "Mom, someone stole our debit card and charged phone sex and porn on the Internet." She'd discovered the charges when she looked at the account, trying to figure out why it was overdrawn. When she told Matt that their bank account had been emptied out by phone sex and porn charges, he claimed someone had stolen his debit card and that the thief must have used it on the Internet. Kari, as always, believed him.

That day, distraught and indignant, Kari stormed into the bank. Once there, she introduced herself to the manager, explaining that the charges were fraudulent. She hadn't bought porn, and her husband, a Baptist minister, certainly hadn't. The bank manager didn't argue and quickly refunded the money. "Kari was persuasive because she believed what she was saying," says Linda. "Matt was smart. He let her argue for him because she was the stronger one of the two of them."

The furor ended quickly with the return of the money.

Matt's stop in Riesel would again be a short one. A little more than a year after he earned his master's, the tension was rising. That August of 2002, during a church meeting, an argument erupted. Angry, Kari stormed out. "There wasn't criticism of me," says Matt. "But that ended my ministry there. A minister who can't control his wife isn't looked well at."

Jenny and Todd would remember it differently.

They heard rumors that the deacons, a council of five

men who oversaw the running of the church, were disappointed in Matt, and that meetings were being held behind closed doors. However it happened, when Matt announced that he had secured a position in Dallas, it seemed that First Baptist in Riesel was ready for him to move on. "The church as a whole didn't seem upset at their leaving," says Todd. "I heard that people were beginning to question the direction Matt was leading the church."

Kari, always Matt's biggest supporter, didn't hide that she was ready to leave. "She said Matt deserved bigger and better and that he wasn't being appreciated," says a friend.

The church in Dallas was Northlake Baptist, northeast of downtown and inside the 635 Loop, not far from White Rock Lake. The largest church Matt had pastored in his still-burgeoning career, it was set into an elongated corner. Beige brick with a soaring front, a cross surging upward over the front doors, the sanctuary had blue and green block windows framed in white. Built for a congregation of four hundred or more, its membership had dwindled over the years, until at the time Matt was hired, attendance at Sunday services hovered around seventy. In its mission statement, Northlake called itself "a small church with a big vision," and said it hoped "to see people transformed by the power of God."

If Kari's sometime brashness, the high emotion that led her to walk out of the meeting in Riesel, had been a negative in that small town, at Northlake, she was one of the reasons Matt was hired. "We liked Kari, that she was young and modern, a career educator," says one who attended the church. "She was one of the reasons we hired Matt. We interviewed both of them, and we were impressed with her spunk, that she spoke her mind. We wanted not only a pastor but a pastor's wife who'd mesh well."

The neighborhood surrounding the church was comprised of streets lined with modest thirty-year-old, one-story houses, where children played in well-manicured yards. The church offered a mothers' day out program, and as they had at the other churches, Matt and Kari expanded the youth programs. Soon after arriving, Kari began working with the music minister, introducing more modern offerings to the programs.

At first, Kari appeared homesick, but she and Matt quickly made friends among the church members, including Jill and Stephen Hotz. A redheaded mom, Jill taught and coached drama in one of Dallas's tougher schools. Not long after arriving, Matt and Kari also bonded with Aubrey Harbor, a petite young woman with long dark blond hair, and her fiancé, Joe Blodgett, who had plans that included becoming a minister.

In Dallas, Kari appeared happy. At Northlake, she organized and ran the volunteers who staffed the Vacation Bible School. That year, she worked with the children's ministry and youth group to raise money for programs in impoverished countries and taught Bible studies. "Her enthusiasm was contagious," says Jill.

Settling in, Matt and Kari purchased a house in Mesquite, a suburb half an hour west of the church. Linda visited and bought them curtains. At home, Matt and Kari had reversed roles. He did the cooking, and Kari was the one who mowed the yard. He talked often about how he was the one who gave the girls their baths, sounding proud of it. "Matt was more domestic than Kari," says a friend. "He liked to cook, and she didn't."

On weekends, Kari and Matt and Jill Hotz and her family combined efforts on dinners. When Kari cooked, she most often made canned chili and hot dogs. And when the Hotzes cooked and Kari offered to bring a dish, she always brought the same one, cheese grits with jalapenos. "It goes with everything," she told Jill during one dinner.

"Not when Stephen is making stir-fry," Jill answered with a laugh.

When a second-grade slot opened at Lake Highlands Elementary, where Kensi attended kindergarten, Kari applied and was hired. The Bakers' two girls flourished as well.

That summer, Kari signed Kensi up for horseback riding and swim team, and Kari and Matt were in the stands, cheering her on. "After what happened to Kassidy, Kari wouldn't trust a lot of people taking care of the girls," says Jill. "She was protective."

As Kari got to know Jill better, she confided in her. At times, Kari made fun of a woman at the church, one who seemed to spend a lot of time following Matt, often at odd hours. "That woman really likes Matt," Kari said, with a laugh. "I wonder how she comes on to him?" Since Kari didn't appear to take the woman seriously, Jill thought little of it.

Over time, Jill got used to picking up the phone and hearing Kari rattle on about one thing or another without ever taking a breath or bothering to say hello. "It was like the conversation had never stopped from the previous call," says Jill. "Kari just kept talking."

Most of all, they had fun together. "It was hard not to around Kari," Jill says. Even in church, things happened that made Kari laugh. One Sunday, for instance, Kari sat in a chair and turned around to grab Jill's hand in the pew behind her. Instead, Kari latched on to the flip-flopped foot of the man seated beside Jill. "Right in church, Kari started laughing," says Jill. "She laughed so hard, she couldn't control herself."

There were things Jill instinctively knew about Kari. Jill saw her as spontaneous and outspoken and loyal. "When Kari loved someone, she really loved them. She was a really good friend, the kind who's there for you," she says. "No matter what happened, she had your back."

For example, there was the day Jill had car trouble, and Kari wanted to pull Matt out of Bible study to help. "Don't do that," Jill said.

"I'm worried about you," Kari said.

As Jill and her husband saw it, Kari and Matt were well matched, and the Hotz family grew to love him as well. Matt taught their son to tie his shoes, and Matt could be a tease, as he was one afternoon when Kari, Matt, and the girls were visiting. Jill cooked, but had to repeatedly stop to answer the phone. When she did, no one spoke. Without caller ID, Jill didn't know who was calling until she saw Matt holding his cell phone and laughing.

At other times, Matt grew serious, talking about his family and growing up. His parents rarely visited in Dallas, which seemed to disappoint Kari more than Matt. Once he talked to the Hotzes about the foster home his parents ran, saying, "The saddest day in my life was the day I realized the Bakers were my real parents."

Yet when Barbara and Oscar did visit, they appeared proud of Matt. At a skating party for one of the girl's birthdays, Oscar repeatedly asked those gathered if they *really* attended "Matt's church where he preaches."

He asked so often that Jill mentioned it to Matt, who shrugged, and said, "Yeah, my dad's a little different."

While the Bakers rarely came, Kari's family visited often. From what Jill saw, it appeared they had a good relationship with their son-in-law, something Matt confirmed one day when he said, "I think of the Dulins as my parents. They're closer to me than my own parents."

That spring, March 2003, when the anniversary of Kassidy's death approached, Jill saw another side of Kari, watching as she spent the day remembering the child she'd lost. As they had in Riesel, Matt and Kari stayed home that day, and Kari watched videos of Kassidy. They released balloons in her memory. "My sweet little girl. I really do miss her," Kari told Jill. But the sadness passed quickly.

"It was a day, and Kari was up and around again," says Jill.

In her Bible that spring, Kari highlighted in pink the passage that read, "Wives submit to the husband as to the Lord." Then there was the day Kari articulated how she saw her role as a minister's wife. Aubrey and Joe, who was studying to be a minister, were getting ready to marry, and Kari described to the bride-to-be the special stresses faced by a pastor's wife. At times, Kari said, people wouldn't like what Joe was doing. No matter how well-intentioned, there were those who would think they knew better how to run the church. "No matter what, you have to defend your husband," Kari told her. "No matter what."

That May, in Northlake's sanctuary, Matt officiated at Aubrey and Joe's wedding. After a rousing rendition of "Here Comes the Bride," Matt stood before those gathered. "One of the most beautiful expressions of love and tenderness comes from the book of Ruth, where it says, 'don't urge me to leave you or turn back from you. Where you go, I will go. Where you stay, I will stay. Your people will be my people, and your God my God. Where you die, I will die, and there I will be buried. May the Lord deal with me ever so severely if anything but death separates you and me.'"

After finishing the Bible passage, Matt stood before the young couple, and said, "You will work on your marriage. And the only thing that can separate you is death."

Perhaps inspired by Linda's thirst for education, Kari enrolled in Dallas Baptist University and began working on a graduate degree in leadership studies with an emphasis on conflict resolution. She was ambitious for herself and for Matt and the girls. "She never wanted the girls to miss anything because they didn't have enough money," says Jill. "Kari was adamant that they were going to have everything she could give them."

Yet as there had been at the other churches, problems began to develop for Matt at Northlake. It started within weeks of signing on at the church, when Matt fired a staff member. "The woman was well liked, a founding member of the church, so it was a horrible political move," says a church member. The man watched Matt, and thought he saw a pattern, one in which the young pastor went behind the backs of those in charge of different aspects of the church and contradicted their orders. "I came to the conclusion that Matt liked to stir up controversy. He didn't like things to run smoothly."

As in the past, Matt used little scripture in his sermons, instead telling stories, which upset the older members of the church. "Matt always seemed kind of arrogant," says one member. "It was kind of like, this is what I'm preaching, and he expected us to accept that and not question."

Over the months, the complaints multiplied. As always, Kari defended him. "She spent most of her time arguing and standing up for Matt," says Jill. "Kari was a go-getter, with energy to spare, and she was determined that people would back Matt. Because we were their friends, we fell in line behind them. There was a lot of stress at the church."

"Matt would tell Kari that some church member did something, and she'd go find them and take up for him," says another congregant. "She was always defending him, even when he was wrong."

At times, Kari gave Jill knowing glances, poking fun at one or another of the church members, as he or she ranted about Matt's latest sermon or the direction the church was taking. "So, do you want to wrestle?" Kari sometimes asked angry church members. At first, they wouldn't know how to respond. Then they'd laugh and walk away.

There were times when Kari, too, talked about Matt, but never truly complaining, just rolling her eyes, and saying, "Well, you know Matt."

One thing she didn't seem to mind talking about was sex. As she had in Waco, Kari complained that Matt seemed overly interested in lovemaking. "Well, you know Matt's not going to get any," she said with a grimace. To Jill, it sounded as if Kari didn't like sex with Matt. So much so that she called it her "wifely duty."

"It never seemed romantic between them," says Jill. "It was more like they were best friends. He'd dunk her in the pool, and they'd both laugh and chase each other, like kids."

As the year wore on, Kari started complaining about the neighborhood in Mesquite, saying Matt was certain they had a Peeping Tom. Before long, they'd sold the house and moved closer to the church. Later, a church member wondered what was really behind the move. "I always felt Matt kept Kari nervous," he says. "I thought maybe Matt told her about that Peeping Tom wanting to upset her, since no one else I knew out there complained of one."

The second spring in Dallas, as the anniversary of Kassidy's death approached, Kari wrote in her Bible: "Don't grow weary doing good. Because your reward is heaven!"

Jill noticed that her friend didn't seem as sad as she had the year before during the anniversary. "There was a real difference," says Jill, who brought Kari ice cream to assuage her sorrow. "It wasn't like the previous year; it was easing."

That year, a job teaching leadership and business classes opened up at Tarleton State University in Waco. Kari applied, and Jill wrote her a recommendation, touting Kari's passion, high energy and self-motivation. When she got the position, Kari began traveling to Waco one evening a week to teach. The result was that her schedule became even more crowded as she juggled caring for the girls, her day job teaching elementary school, teaching at Tarleton, and finishing up her master's. What complicated the situation even more was that Matt was having increasing problems at Northlake.

During Sunday services, church members angry with Matt were so incensed they'd begun holding up their Bibles and shouting at him to preach from it. At the pulpit, Matt didn't respond. At meetings, voices grew louder, and the Hotzes backed Matt based on friendship, not conviction. The situation flared hotter when Matt cut the hours of the church maintenance man. "People argued against it, and Kari stood up for Matt," Jill says. The deacon who oversaw the facilities, the maintenance man's boss, was so angry about Matt's plan, "he almost broke the door slamming it behind him on the way out of the building."

Meanwhile, others were getting a bad opinion of Matt that had little to do with his preaching. "I caught him lying to me more than once," says one man, who'd recount times Matt told him one thing had happened when it was another.

"I came away with the impression that Matt Baker was a pathological liar. That he'd look at you and tell you the grass was blue."

In Waco, Kari complained to Linda about the church members, echoing complaints Linda heard coming from Matt. While she'd kept quiet in the past, this time Linda spoke up. "Do you hear yourself?" Linda asked. "I want you to think. How could this be at every church? What's the one common denominator at every church?"

Kari didn't answer, but Linda knew her daughter understood that what tied the situations together was Matt Baker. At that, Linda stopped pushing, mindful that Matt was her daughter's husband. But in November 2004, a little more than two years after moving to Dallas, Northlake cut Matt's salary by $5,000. Not long after, he resigned.

"On paper, it said Matt quit," says Jill. "The truth was that he left before he was fired."

When Kari told her family, she insisted that Matt had been treated unfairly. "Bless Kari's heart, she just wanted to believe in Matt," says Nancy. "She defended him through thick and thin."

Chapter 14

"If Matt had tried to abuse Kari physically, she wouldn't have had it. She would never have put up with it. She was too strong for that," says Linda. "Instead, he made her feel sorry for him. And Matt was persuasive. Things happened, and he always had an explanation."

As 2005 began, Matt had a new job, this one with the Texas Youth Commission, in Mart, outside Waco, coordinating volunteers and community relations. Linda would later say that even though Kari had family nearby, she wasn't keen on moving. She'd made friends in Dallas and liked the city. She was also locked into a contract to teach through that May, and Kensi was in school. The decision was made, and Matt moved into Linda and Jim's spare bedroom, while Kari and the girls stayed in Dallas to finish the school year.

All the turmoil in her life appeared to be taking a toll on Kari. She'd always gained and lost weight, but that year she'd gained and hadn't lost, her weight hovering near two hundred pounds. She was still a pretty woman, stylish, with bright blond hair, now cut into a short, spiky, fashionable do. She wore trendy clothes and loved to clomp around in girlish flip-flops, the bangle bracelets on her wrist tinkling as she walked.

Moving again had proved expensive, and that spring Kari

asked Linda for a favor. "Would you add Matt and me to your cell phone, on the family plan?" she requested. "We'll have the bill for our phones sent to our house, but it'll save us money."

Linda barely thought about it before agreeing.

The TYC job not to his liking, Matt had continued to look, when in March he heard about a chaplain's job at the Waco Center for Youth, a residential facility for thirteen- to seventeen-year-olds with emotional or behavioral problems.

In aging dark tan brick buildings on a sprawling campus connected by arched brick walkways, WCY was operated by the Texas Department of Mental Health and Mental Retardation. Its stated mission: *To give each youth a chance for change.* The average stay was eighteen months, and the residents either came voluntarily or by court order. In need of counseling, they weren't considered psychotic, suicidal, or violent. On the campus, they lived in cottages named after Texas rivers: Brazos, Trinity, Rio Grande, and the Red River.

The former chaplain, popular with the residents and staff, had taken a leave five months earlier for family matters, then decided not to return. Matt began working at WCY near the end of April. His duties included holding Sunday afternoon chapel services, Bible studies, and counseling. Early on he was introduced to Terri Corbin, a woman with curly high-lighted hair and a brusque manner, one of his two assistants. She and the other assistant had been covering the chaplain's duties and were both excited about having Matt take on the responsibilities. Terri's and Matt's offices were next to each other on a locked hallway, in the main building near the chapel.

On his first day after training, Matt knocked on Terri's door, then sat in a chair and began talking, at first detailing his credentials. They were impressive, especially his master's degree from Baylor. Then he turned to more personal matters. After talking about Kari, Kensi, and Grace, he turned the conversation around to Kassidy. "We had another little girl," he said. "She died."

"I thought it was so odd," says Terri. "He started talking about Kassidy, and he told me step by step everything that happened, starting at her birth through when she got sick, going to the hospital, what the doctors said. The night she died. Everything."

As the minutes passed, Corbin's eyes filled with tears. Kassidy's story was a sad one, and Terri found it difficult to listen to Matt's account of a beautiful baby who suddenly fell ill. The story turned excruciating, as Matt described finding Kassidy in bed, not breathing, giving her CPR while Kari called 911. "I thought it was strange that he'd share all the details when we'd barely met," says Terri. Something else struck her as odd, that Matt could recount such a painful time without emotion. "He talked for maybe fifty minutes or more, but he never looked upset. Then he just stood up and left. I was in tears."

Once he moved into his office, Matt put photos on his desk of Kensi and Grace and one of Kari in her wedding dress. It wasn't long before Terri met them in person, when Kari dropped in to see Matt, the two girls in tow. *What a cute family,* Terri thought, looking at Kari, who talked non-stop. "Kari was bubbly, fun, and she had the girls all dolled up," says Terri. "They were darling. I was looking forward to working with Matt. I thought with such a sweet family, he must be a good guy."

The honeymoon period, however, was short. Not long after, Matt came into the office of one of his supervisors, Sarah Parker, to review complaints residents had filed about the facility. Parker asked his opinion, then realized that Matt changed his to match hers. "It was odd, like he was trying to gain my approval," she says. Then Matt began coming to her complaining about his staff, especially Terri Corbin. "He used really derogatory terms about them, along the lines of idiots. It was really unprofessional."

* * *

"Kari missed her family, and she wanted the girls to spend time with them," says Jill. "She didn't want to leave Dallas, but she was excited about being back in Waco."

At first, Matt and Kari moved into a house not far from the interstate. But before long, they relocated again, this time to a tidy redbrick one-story at 803 Crested Butte, in Hewitt, Texas, a mushrooming subdivision just outside Waco. The house was perfect in many ways, including that it was just a twenty-minute drive from her parents' home. A bustling suburb, the main business district along Hewitt Drive was packed with banks, strip centers, grocers, vet clinics, fast-food restaurants, and churches.

With a fenced-in yard, the house was situated one house off the corner on a quiet street. Inside, it had a split floor plan, the living room and dining room down the center, with the two children's bedrooms and a bathroom on the right, and the master bedroom and bath on the left.

Making the house perfect, Kari had been offered a third-grade teaching position at Spring Valley Elementary, less than half a mile away, where Grace and Kensi would start in the fall. That spring, another opportunity opened up, a full-time teaching position at Tarleton State. Linda talked to Kari about it, pointing out that college teaching slots were scarce. "I know, Mom," she said. "But I want to be at Spring Valley for the girls. It's Gracie's first year in school, and Kensi's first year at this school."

"You're sure?" Linda asked.

"I'm sure," Kari answered."

Quickly, Kari made the Crested Butte house hers. She and Matt painted the inside and hung her cross collection on a wall. Never faint of heart, she chose a rich brown for the dining room and living room and a celery green for the kitchen, all with a crisp white trim. In the dining room, Kari draped flowing curtains dramatically over the bowed window, and in the beige-walled master bedroom, they positioned the bed with its plank headboard trimmed in a metal lattice in front of the windows. The desk with the computer stood at the foot of the bed, with a flat-screen television. All in all, the house, like Kari, had an unusual style for a pastor's wife, a dose of fun and just a little hip.

Everything undoubtedly felt as if it was working out well that summer. Linda told Kari that in an e-mail, suggesting that the move must be blessed because so much was falling in place. She had no way of knowing what Terri Corbin was experiencing with Matt at work.

In fact, it was just months after he began at WCY, that Matt's behavior started to raise questions with Corbin. She'd slowly begun to wonder about the new chaplain's honesty. It seemed harmless at first, but she'd catch him lying to her about small things, especially what he was doing and where he was going. "I'm going to stop out at one of the cottages," he'd say, sticking his head in her door. "After that, I'll head home."

She wasn't checking on him, but noticed simply by glancing out her office window that Matt wasn't walking toward the residents' cottages but the employee parking lot. "I saw him get in his car and drive off the campus," Terri says. "He wasn't visiting the cottages; he was leaving work early."

Over time, Matt started arriving late in the mornings, but instead of walking in the front door, he entered through the auditorium. "That way, others would think he'd been there on time," says Corbin. "I didn't say anything to him about any of it." Meanwhile, in his reports, he suggested that his workload be cut. Few of the residents attended the weekly Bible study sessions, and Matt's proposal was that if they were held less often, more might participate.

Other things, however, Corbin did speak up about. Where the services in the past had always been reserved for residents and their families, Matt invited members of other churches to WCY on Sunday afternoons. What upset Corbin was that this flew in the face of the residents' confidentiality. WCY policy stated that no one should be on campus unless they registered at the front desk and that they had to be on campus for specific reasons. "People aren't welcome to come and just have a look," she says.

One Sunday, when Terri brought it up, Matt didn't take the criticism well. "How dare you question me!" he challenged.

"It's against policy," she explained yet again. Confused by his reaction, Terri assumed Matt would think it over and understand that she was simply asking him to remember the rules. He was new, and it seemed natural that he'd make a few missteps.

Her assumptions, however, proved wrong. The following morning, Terri turned on her work computer and found a two-page e-mail. In that single e-mail, Matt threatened to fire her for insubordination three times. "I'd never been treated in such a demeaning manner before," she'd later say. "Instead of calling me to his office to discuss the situation, he sent me a hurtful e-mail, threatening to let me go."

Still, Matt was her boss. What was she supposed to do?

In the chapel, Matt hung a banner that read: ANGER: Noise of the Soul; Relentless Invader of Silence. Meanwhile, Terri was unimpressed with his preaching. Instead of writing his own sermons, Matt took ideas off the Internet, including one entitled "Wayne's Rotten Day," where he talked about a boy who starts the day off falling out of bed. "How do you cope with a rotten day?" Matt asked those attending.

Another Sunday, Matt tackled an issue that would have added meaning in the not-too-distant future: suicide. In his sermon, he told the story of a fourteen-year-old boy who took his own life. "What if you were this boy?" Matt asked. "Or if you were his friend? Would you have seen this coming? How could you have stopped it?"

As the summer progressed, Terri saw more that raised questions about Matt's professionalism and his motives. A friend of hers, an employee on the campus, confided that she had a run-in with the new chaplain. The woman said that one day in Matt's office, she was confiding in him about a personal problem. Instead of offering a kind ear or the type of sage advice he'd been trained to dispense, Matt looked at the woman, and asked, "Would you like to fuck me?"

Startled, the woman had no idea what to say. Instead, she quickly jumped up and left. "I'm making sure I'm not alone with him," she told Terri. "That man scares me."

Chapter 15

In August, Matt taught a chapel lesson at WCY: Do we help others? His link to the Bible was in Timothy—"People will love only themselves and their money." Matt's message to the young residents was to stay away from dangerous people.

Meanwhile, Matt's attitude toward Terri Corbin had continued to sour. Weeks earlier, he'd complained to his supervisor about Corbin, then, on September 14, he wrote a list of what he called "Terri's indiscretions" on his computer, including that she'd made unspecified complaints to others about him. Along with that, he filed a report about his duties, including the matter of a resident who wanted demons cleaned from her spirit. In his report, Matt wrote that he'd attempted to remedy the situation by quoting scripture, to illustrate that God loved her. He then showed her a clean sheet of white paper with a small dot on it. "What do you focus on, the clean paper or the spot?" he asked the girl.

"The spot," the girl answered.

"This demonstrates her tendency to focus on the negative aspects of being here," Matt wrote. "I prayed that God would help her focus on the positive." Matt finished his report by noting that he'd discussed the situation with the girl's therapist.

It was also in mid-September that Matt issued what he

called a final warning to Terri, saying that if she complained to others about him, they would talk about "your continuation at WCY."

As 2005 progressed, there seemed one thing missing in Matt and Kari's return to Waco—Matt didn't have a church to pastor. That situation changed in the fall when Steve Sadler, a Baylor religion professor, left his position at Crossroads Baptist, the rural church the Dulins attended, where Jim was a deacon. After discussing the situation with Linda, Jim went to a Crossroads meeting in September and asked the other deacons to interview Matt. "How are you going to feel if we have to jerk him out of here, if he's not for us?" one asked.

"I'm all about this church," Jim assured them. "If we don't want Matt, we'll run him off."

In truth, Linda had mixed feelings about the situation. "I never thought Matt was a very good preacher," she says. "But I wanted to do it for Kari."

That October, Crossroads hired Matt Baker as their pastor. The church, a modest beige-sided building in the bucolic hills, was set back from the road. In the spring, the fields surrounding it were replete with bluebonnets and Indian paintbrush. Summers, a dome of blue sky shone over the church and the small fenced-in playground at the back. Behind the church stood a storage center, one with RVs parked around it. And across the street were single-wide trailers, some with children's toys scattered about.

Most Sundays about fifty members attended Crossroads. Although it was a comedown from Northlake, a smaller church and congregation, Kari looked proud sitting with the girls in the third row from the front, rubbing their backs as they rested their heads on her lap. Every once in a while, she bent down and kissed their softly brushed hair. For Linda, it felt good to have her daughter and granddaughters closer. When Kensi and Grace saw her at church, they ran to Linda, shouting, "Grammy!"

Once word spread that Matt and Kari were back and that Matt had a church, Todd and Jenny Monsey, the brother and sister from Williams Creek, began attending services at Crossroads. From the beginning, Jenny thought Matt had changed. "He wasn't the same person we knew. He seemed bossier, telling people what to do. He didn't seem sincere."

Although they'd returned because he was being squeezed out of his slot in Dallas, Matt told Jenny and others that they'd come back to Waco because Kari was homesick and didn't want to be so far from Kassidy's grave. And as she had at the other churches, Kari jumped in to help, teaching Sunday school and leading Bible studies.

Kimberly Berry met Kari for the first time that August at the Spring Valley teacher's luncheon, when Kari was introduced as the school's new third-grade teacher. When Kari started decorating her classroom with lime green, hot pink, and black, Kimberly immediately liked her. "Kari was always cutting it up with the kids," says Berry. "She sat in a rocking chair to read to them. She always had her makeup on, dressed in the latest styles, and she smiled a lot, and not a teacher's smile, a real one. And she got the kids excited about school."

The other teachers at Spring Valley soon learned that Kari wasn't the quietest of additions. They could hear her calling out spelling words, laughing and joking with the eight-year-olds in her class. When she walked through the halls, the other teachers recognized Kari by the slapping of her flip-flops and the tinkling of her bracelets.

That fall, Kari and another teacher, Shae Dickey, quickly became friends. They had children about the same ages and talked daily while at school. Five years older than Kari, Shae listened sympathetically as Kari told her about Kassidy's death. "I can't imagine what it was like to lose a child. If you ever need to talk about it, I'm here," Shae said.

"Thank you," Kari answered, giving her a warm hug.

Over time, Kari would confide in Shae. "It was horrible when Kassidy died," Kari admitted one afternoon. "Kassidy had been so sick. But then, boom, there was Grace. And what could I do but pull it together and take care of my girls?"

As a remembrance of Kassidy, Kari wore a yellow Livestrong bracelet from Lance Armstrong's cancer foundation, with its mission statement: *To live strong is to not give up.* "Kassidy fought until she couldn't, so now I have to fight for her," Kari told Shae, the day she explained why she wore the bracelet.

Each year, the teachers filled out questionnaires called Panther Profiles, named after the school mascot. The purpose was to introduce themselves to the children and their parents. Kari listed her hobbies as swimming and spending time with family, her favorite flower as the Stargazer lily, her favorite cuisines as Japanese and Mexican, and her favorite candy bar as Hershey's. "Mrs. Baker is funny," one of her students told his mom during the first weeks of school. "She laughs all the time."

While Kari settled in, the move seemed to be going well for the girls as well. Grace blended easily into kindergarten, and Kensi became a popular fourth grader. For one class, she wrote a poem about Kassidy entitled, "I learned so much from my baby sister." The teacher sent it to Kari to read. On her daughter's school folder, Kari wrote: "I love you, Baby. This is great work."

After school, Kensi and Grace ran to Kari's room, where they helped to straighten it for the next morning. Then Kari drove her daughters the short distance home. That fall, Kensi was in swim team at the Family Y, the same one that had fired Matt years earlier, so two nights a week, Kari and Matt hurried out the door, taking the girls to practice. Despite his history at the Y, Matt showed no discomfort. Instead, he walked around with Kari, talking to the other parents, cheering on Kensi's team from the bleachers.

From the outside, they looked like the perfect family. Kari never hid the fact that she was proud of Matt. "She talked about him constantly," says a fellow teacher. "She'd say, 'Come join us at church on Sunday. Give Matt a chance.'"

Before long, some of Kari's fellow teachers, including Kimberly Berry, began attending services at Crossroads, drawn by Kari's enthusiasm. Once she got there, Berry found she liked Matt's sermons. "I could connect with them," she says. "Matt talked about life, like about riding in a car with his parents and having his dad say, 'Now don't make me pull this car over!' Matt was really charismatic, and I felt he was talking directly to me."

Yet, from the beginning, Shea Dickey felt uncomfortable around Matt Baker. And one thing bothered her more than any other, that nearly every time the teachers went out and invited Kari, she'd tell them that she couldn't go, that she had to get home to be with Matt. Shae saw the Bakers everywhere together, even at the grocery store. It appeared that Matt never let Kari be alone. "The few times we did talk Kari into going with us, her phone rang constantly," says one of the other teachers. "It was always Matt needing something. He'd call six or seven times. It felt like he was checking up on her."

"I told Kari that she was entitled to have friends," says one of her fellow teachers. "Kari said, 'I know, but I just feel so sorry for Matt.'"

Chapter 16

At Crossroads that winter, a new member began attending. Vanessa Bulls was twenty-three years old, strikingly beautiful, with iridescent blue eyes, a flawless complexion, high cheekbones, full lips, and long, silky blond hair, a woman in the throes of a divorce and the mother of an infant daughter named Lilly. Vanessa's father was Larry Bulls, Crossroad's music minister who also worked for Discount Tires, and his wife, Cheryl, a high-school teacher.

The Bulls were popular members of Crossroads. Larry was tall and thin, with brown hair, a former high-school football player. His wife, Cheryl, was a gregarious woman, a former high-school cheerleader. Their family roots extended far back in Troy, a town of twelve hundred that lay twenty minutes south of Waco on I-35. "Vanessa never seemed like a wild child," says a friend. "Vanessa was an only child and kind of a quiet kid. As pretty as she was, I remember she had a hard time getting a prom date. She ate lunch with her mom, and I thought she was a good kid."

"Troy High School is small, and I thought it would be rough to be a student and have your mom teach there," says a friend of the family. "In small towns, you live in a glass house. Everyone knows your business. The Bulls were considered middle-income, hardworking people. Cheryl was a good teacher, and the kids loved her. Vanessa seemed like an average girl growing up in an average family. She seemed very close to her parents."

Later, Vanessa would describe her upbringing as "strict Southern Baptist."

From Troy, Vanessa went to Mary Hardin Baylor University in nearby Belton, and one woman who went to college with her would remember Vanessa as socially involved in this strict Baptist college, one that split off from Baylor in 1866. At that time, Baylor became all male, and Mary Hardin was founded as its sister college. While the world changed around them, and both became coed, the schools remained highly conservative. "We had room checks, and everything was supposed to be spotless," says Sara Talbert, who went to Mary Hardin at the time Vanessa enrolled. "Boys weren't allowed in the rooms."

Talbert would later say that while she didn't know her well, she remembered Vanessa. "She came across as superficial, but she might have been really nice. It was just that something rubbed me the wrong way, like one of those girls in high school who are Miss Popular but really not what they appear to be. She had a reputation as a goody/Christian girl, but some people talked about her like she wasn't what she seemed."

Vanessa dressed preppy but wore lots of makeup. "She didn't act like she had money, but she acted like a good Christian girl. At Mary Hardin, it wasn't about money, it was about how religious a girl appeared to be."

In December of 2004, Vanessa married a man who was twenty years older. Vanessa's daughter, Lilly, was born eight months later, in August 2005. A month after Lilly's birth, Vanessa and her husband separated, and he filed for divorce, denying paternity, claiming he'd done a home test that excluded him. In his petition for divorce, he requested DNA testing. Vanessa counterfiled, stating that Lilly was "a child of the marriage," asking for support. But on October 25, the following statement was entered into the case files: "The alleged father [Vanessa's husband] is excluded as the biological father of the child . . . The probability of paternity is 0 percent."

From that point on, the divorce became merely the business of dividing property. In December, Vanessa Bulls's divorce became final. The order read: "There was a child born during the marriage of petitioner and respondent that was not a child of the marriage . . . It is therefore ordered that no orders for conservatorship and support are entered in this cause."

At the time Matt and Kari Baker met Vanessa, she and Lilly lived with her parents in the Bulls's Troy home, and Vanessa was attending classes at Tarleton in the evenings, working on a degree in education. At Crossroads, Kari noticed Lilly quickly. The baby was pudgy and blond and reminded her of the daughter she'd lost. "Lilly looks so much like Kassidy," Kari said to more than one person that fall.

The months passed, and that winter Kari was busy, teaching at Spring Valley during the day, on the community college campus on Monday evenings, and conducting an Internet course one evening a week. In her entrepreneurial class, she gave the students a syllabus for the semester that included writing business plans.

While Kari ran from one job to the next, Matt had his duties at Crossroads and his job at the Waco Center for Youth. At times, he e-mailed Kari on his WCY account to her Spring Valley e-mail, often in the role of the concerned husband and father. "Maybe Grace can use these?" he asked, sending along a link to a Web site that sold connect-the-dot alphabet color pages that read: "Y is for Yarn . . . Z is for Zebra . . . N is for Nightgown."

At Spring Valley that December, Kimberly Berry had health issues and asked Kari to pray for her. In her classroom, Kari took Kim's hands and held them in her own, bowing her head and praying. From that point forward, Kari began talking with Kim about Kassidy, recounting the short time they'd had her. One day, Kari brought a scrapbook she'd made in Kassidy's memory, full of photographs, including some of the child hooked up to the web of machines that kept her alive in the hospital. "Matt doesn't like to look at the scrapbook," Kari said, as they paged through.

"I think she was glad to share Kassidy with someone," Kim would say later. "But she didn't sound sad, more proud of Kassidy, of how hard she'd fought to live."

On the last day of school before Christmas break, Kari made cocoa for her class on a cold day. When she e-mailed Matt, he told her it was quiet at WCY. "I love you," he said.

Kari e-mailed back, sounding a little down because her students had all come in with individual gifts for her. The year before, in Dallas, the students' parents had all donated and given her a hundred-dollar certificate for Borders Books, money she'd used to buy Christmas presents. Matt responded that maybe the parents just didn't do that at Spring Valley, then said, "I love you," a second time.

"Hey, I have a gift from one student that we can give your sister. Ha! Ha! I love regifting," Kari replied, describing "yucky candles." In a later e-mail she said her students were sugared up and having a hard time settling down, so she put on a movie, *The Polar Express*. If they didn't calm down, she joked that she'd have to "Kill them!!!"

"Don't leave a mess!!! ☺" Matt replied.

Matt was noncommittal about whether or not he'd be able to make it to the girls' school Christmas parties that afternoon. "I need to hand out a couple of Bibles, then I will escape," he wrote.

Later that evening, at the teachers' party, Kari presented her gift for the white elephant exchange, a pair of gargantuan panties. Everyone was laughing and having a good time when Kari's phone rang. She answered it, and then said, "That was Matt. I have to go."

On Christmas Day during services, Kensi and Todd Monsey sang "The Christmas Shoes," a song made popular by the group Newsong, in which a child needs money to buy shoes for his dying mother. In his sermon, Matt reminded the faithful that the holiday wasn't about presents and parties but the birth of Christ. "Merry Christmas to all," he said. "I wish the blessings of Christ upon you and your house this season."

"Everything seemed fine," says Jenny. "Matt and Kari looked happy."

Yet during Christmas week, something happened that set the stage for the tragedy that was to come. It was at Crossroads's potluck supper. The church members were in the recreation area eating, while Vanessa Bulls talked on the phone with a friend, saying, "Oh, a new guy is calling me. You know, I'm getting a divorce. I don't know if I can really like, I can date again. . . ."

Later, Vanessa would say that was when Matt Baker motioned for her to follow him into a hallway. She did, and when they got away from the others, he said, "Will you really?"

"Will I really what?" she responded.

"Will you really date your pastor?"

Vanessa just looked at him until he spoke again: "Well, I've had a vasectomy, so I can't get you pregnant. And I don't have any sexually transmitted diseases."

"Have you done that before?" she asked.

Matt nodded. "Kari is clueless."

Chapter 17

In January of 2006, Terri Corbin suspected that Matt was using one of the other employees to set her up. She'd noticed him talking to a young woman named Nellie, who worked with the residents on the campus. Nellie and Matt appeared to be together a lot, especially after Sunday chapel services, and Terri wondered if there was something going on between them although she never saw any real evidence.

One day, Matt called Terri to his office and handed her a report Nellie had filed with a unit manager, saying that several boys on the campus claimed Terri had passed love notes between them and the girls, something that was strictly forbidden.

"This is ridiculous," Terri replied. "It's not true."

Instead of backing up his employee, Matt appeared not to believe her, even when she said, "I'd never break the rules like this. If you don't believe me, ask the boys."

As far as Terri knew, Matt, however, did nothing involving investigating the allegations. Instead, they were kept on Terri's record. Making inquiries on her own, Terri spoke to the boys who had allegedly made the claim. "They didn't know anything about it," she'd say later. "They said they'd never said anything to Nellie about my passing notes, and that they'd never asked me and knew I wouldn't have done it."

Terri knew the allegations were serious. "I believed Matt Baker wanted me to leave Waco Center for Youth, and he was using Nellie to set me up," she'd later say. Two months after the incident, on February 27, Terri Corbin resigned. As much as she loved her job, she'd grown weary of fighting Matt Baker.

In January 2006, Larry Bulls stood before the members at Crossroads and announced that he and Cheryl were leaving the church. The reason, he said, was that he'd told God that when Vanessa's divorce became final, he'd go wherever God led him, which they had decided was back to their church in Troy. Yet even after her parents left Crossroads, Vanessa stayed, showing up on Sundays and sitting in the front row, two rows ahead of Kari and her girls in the sanctuary, listening to Matt preach with a beaming smile.

Early in 2006, Kari took her ExCET, the examination for certification in Texas, to teach English and language arts. She passed, and began talking about changing schools the following year. Grace and Kensi had acclimated well into Spring Valley, and from Baylor on, Kari had talked of wanting to teach middle school. Adolescence is a difficult time, and many teachers find it a tricky age group to teach, but Kari felt drawn to the students who were caught between childhood and their teenage years. "I think that's the population I'm supposed to serve," she told a friend. "It's where I can do the most good."

For the most part, everyday events continued to take center stage in Kari's and Matt's lives, caring for the girls, cooking meals, doing homework, going to work, taking the girls to school, Kensi to swimming practice and meets. At times, the details were mundane, as on January 11, when Matt wrote a report at work saying that he had stopped serving snacks during chapel, to "better assist dietary needs of clients," which translated to not filling them up only hours before WCY served supper.

It was also in January that Kari joined a group of Spring

Valley teachers who'd decided to diet. She went to a doctor she'd been to in the past and began taking phentermine, an appetite suppressant. "Matt and I are sharing the pills," she told Linda. Concerned, Linda looked the pills up on the Internet and formed the opinion that if used correctly, they were safe.

Despite what was developing behind the scenes, at least on the surface, and as far as Kari apparently knew, in the burgeoning New Year, 2006, their lives remained unchanged. At Crossroads, too, all seemed to be churning along. During a Wednesday evening church service, Matt discussed an upcoming mission trip to Brazil and stressed that they'd need to raise funds to help pay for school supplies for the children in the village. "Nothing seemed unusual," Kimberly Berry would say.

The first indication that all wasn't well in the tidy red-brick house on Crested Butte appeared in an e-mail Matt sent Kari on Wednesday January 18. That morning, Matt arrived at WCY early to work on a sermon on the benefits of "living a meek life." Afterward, he e-mailed Kari, attempting to smooth over an argument they'd apparently had the day before. "I was in no way trying to tell you that I couldn't talk or that I did not want to talk to you," he said. "I was in someone's office. I love you, and I love talking to you."

Two weeks later, by early February, Matt was calling the Bulls's household often when Vanessa was home alone with Lilly, and the pressure began to build between Kari and Matt. On February 6, she e-mailed him, talking of not feeling well, yearning for spring break. She'd wanted to go on a family vacation, but he refused, saying that someone in Crossroads was expecting a death and that he'd have to conduct the funeral.

Certainly, she was overtaxed that winter, stretched thin between teaching college and third grade and chauffeuring the girls. On top of everything else, Kari worried about her students' performance on an upcoming standardized test. This was the first year she'd taught a grade level that had to take the TAKS test (Texas Assessment of Knowledge and Skills). She was nervous and was tutoring ten of her students to help them pass.

A day later in a series of e-mails, Matt asked Kari why she was feeling so stressed. He was the one who brought up the upcoming anniversary of Kassidy's death, writing: "Are you feeling depressed? Are you feeling lost? Do you want to stop something? If so, what could you stop? I don't know how to help you any more than I already do. The last time you sounded like this was close to an anniversary of Kassidy's death. I am just asking so I can help. What can I do? Love you, Matt."

In past years, friends and family had judged that Kari was improving, better able to handle the painful anniversary as each year passed. But for some reason this particular year, with so much on her mind, would prove a step backward. In response, she wrote: "Well, this might sound crazy, but I think for the first time I have realized that [Kassidy] is not coming back. So I guess I am feeling like I have lost her all over again. I just have a lot on my plate, and I feel like I am just sinking. So am I depressed or lost? Yes, all of the above. I feel like I am getting sick, and I hate myself because I should be happy because I have you and the girls, but I just can't get going."

In his responses, Matt again professed his love and offered to help, but Kari told him there was nothing he could do. "I will get through this on my own . . . You are wonderful. I couldn't ask for a better husband, but right now I am just sinking, and I have to find out how to pull myself up. So I don't even know how I am going to do it."

Days later, Matt e-mailed apologizing for leaving dirty dishes in the sink the night before, while Kari was teaching her class at Tarleton. "I need to work harder," he said, but she disagreed, saying that it was a combined effort and that they were both too busy. Matt agreed. "I am so ready for summer," she said. "This summer, I am really going to work on things to make it better teaching next year."

The afternoon before Valentine's Day, Kari put together packages for her daughters and students, ones with cards and the traditional small mints in the shape of hearts that read BE MINE and LOVE. She e-mailed and asked Matt, who was doing the grocery shopping, to pick up Cokes, Dr Peppers, and strawberry sauce for the sundaes she planned for her class. But by then the strain between them was building.

While not knowing about Matt's relationship with Vanessa Bulls, Kari had apparently picked up on the fact that something had changed in her marriage, and she'd begun feeling estranged from Matt. Later that day, she sent him an e-mail expressing her inner confusion: " . . . I just want my soul mate back with me forever, and HELL YES, I will do whatever it takes to make sure that happens. I just need you to know that I LOVE YOU MORE THAN ANYTHING IN THE WORLD, AND MY HANG UPS [sic] ARE SOMETHING I NEED TO WORK ON.

"Let's just make it a real habit to try and spend a little time together everyday [sic] to just talk about us and life and just holding each other. I love you, Matt, and I can't even think what my life would be like if you weren't in it."

A minute later, he responded: "Thank you—I needed to hear this . . . I LOVE YOU!"

"I guess we are meant to be since we are always thinking alike," Kari answered.

"Hopefully so, ☺," he responded. " . . . I love you 2."

While Kari didn't know about her husband's new interest, on Crested Butte some neighbors noticed a strange car pulling up to the Baker house on Fridays, when Matt had the day off and Kari and the girls were all at school. The garage door opened, the car with the pretty blonde inside drove directly in. The garage door closed behind her.

Meanwhile, the nervous tension in Kari and Matt's marriage mushroomed, evidenced by e-mails in which she complained that he was increasingly distant and not interested in her physically. They bantered about sex, Kari saying that Matt wasn't reaching out to her, and Matt responding that she was pushing him away. "You know me—I will never ever, ever, ever have enough!!!!!!!!" he wrote.

"Please know that I am thinking of you today. Try not to stress out too much. Your kids will do fine. You're a great teacher, and you've taught them well. I love you!" Matt wrote to Kari on the morning of the TAKS test.

Days later, the tests were over but the results weren't in on the afternoon that Jill and Stephen Hotz and their children drove through Waco and dropped in at the Family Y, where Kensi had swim team, to see Matt, Kari, and the girls. They weren't there long when Jill said, "I could feel the tension between Matt and Kari."

From the Y, they drove to a Chili's restaurant and ordered lunch. Kari talked about her classes' TAKS scores. "I have some kids I'm pretty worried about," she said.

While the visit started out stiff, the old friends quickly fell into a familiar rhythm, laughing and joking, more at ease. When they split up that afternoon, Jill hugged them and said good-bye. Jill had no way of knowing that she'd never again see Kari alive.

Chapter 18

On February 24, 2006, days after Kari's students took the TAKS test, Matt called the Bulls's house at 9:07 A.M. and talked for fifteen minutes and eighteen seconds. The call was initiated from his telephone at Crossroads Baptist.

As she had earlier in the month, Kari confessed to feeling sad as the anniversary of Kassidy's death loomed. She e-mailed Kimberly Berry one day admitting that there was a time soon after Kassidy's death when she had briefly considered suicide. "The thought left me when I thought of the girls. I have to live for my girls," Kari wrote. As upsetting as the approaching anniversary was, Kari said she'd accepted her daughter's death. "I felt at peace with it, with Kassidy being gone."

As the days wore on, the phone calls from Matt to the Bulls's residence continued, sometimes from Crossroads and other times from WCY or his cell phone. At the same time, he e-mailed Kari, closing each with "I love you." Always, he acted concerned about his wife's mood and pegged her building anxiety on something other than him. On March 21, the day before the seventh anniversary of Kassidy's death, Matt e-mailed Kari at school, inquiring if on her diet her sugar intake could be low. Kari responded that she didn't know what was wrong, except that her hands shook, and she couldn't stop it: "I haven't felt this bad in a long time."

In an e-mail that followed, Matt offered to do what he could to help, then said something that would seem infinitely more important years later: "Do you want anything special tonight? How about a chocolate shake with even MORE chocolate syrup? Just joking. :-) Love you!"

"No, I will be okay," Kari responded. "I just want to sleep tonight."

At school, Shae noticed that Kari looked sad and asked if she was all right. Kari gave her a big hug, saying, "I'm okay. I do this every year. It's just hard."

The next day, the actual anniversary, Jenny called Kari at the house, knowing that she would take the day off work. "If there's anything I can do, I'm here," Jenny said.

"You know what day it is?" Kari asked, sounding pleased.

"Yes," Jenny said.

The girls were in school, but Kari said that she and Matt were going to Kassidy's grave. Kari sounded melancholy but not overly so, and Jenny judged that her friend was taking the anniversary in stride.

It was around that time that Kari called Linda to discuss her plans for the future. The two talked every day, but this day Kari had something special on her mind. "I think I'm in a place where I need to reach out and help others who've lost a child," Kari said. "I'll always miss Kassidy, but now that I've found peace with her death, I'd like to find a way to help other parents."

"That's a wonderful idea," Linda said. "You're so good with people."

Nancy didn't sense anything wrong either when Kari called in late March and asked about plans for the upcoming Easter celebration at Nancy's father-in-law's ranch. "What can I bring?" Kari asked. Nancy said they didn't need anything. They were planning a Texas barbecue, and the others had already signed up to bring everything needed.

"No, no, no!" Kari insisted. "If not food, let me bring Easter eggs. We always color so many with the girls."

Nancy agreed and hung up the phone. It would be the last time she talked to her niece.

So many judged that Kari was handling the anniversary well, yet what was wrong? If sad memories weren't causing Kari such upset, making her hands shake, perhaps it was the chasm that had developed in her marriage.

What had been building for months escalated a week after the seventh anniversary of Kassidy's death. Since February, Kari had accused Matt of being distant, and he'd responded by saying she was the one pulling away. But as March drew to a close, Kari began confiding in friends that Matt's overactive sex drive wasn't kicking in as it had in the past. It marked a turnaround in their marriage, one Kari might have understood had she known about Matt's interest in Vanessa Bulls.

"I actually want Matt sexually, but he told me that he doesn't need me like that anymore," Kari told Jill Hotz, her Dallas friend to whom she talked nearly every afternoon.

"Kari seemed really upset, really troubled about it," says Jill. "I told her they'd been married a long time, and it was probably just a phase. It would go away."

After Kari could no longer speak for herself, what would be left was a trail of e-mails, hinting at what went on that final spring behind closed doors, as she struggled to repair her marriage. In those e-mails, Kari seemed willing to sacrifice nearly everything to save her family. Meanwhile, Matt continually shifted the blame for the dire turn in their relationship.

On Monday the twenty-seventh, Kari e-mailed Matt. Hoping to reconnect with her husband, she'd asked Linda to take the girls that upcoming Friday night. "So what are we going to do?" Kari asked.

"NOTHING!!! Sleep," Matt replied.

"I am sure that is what you would want to do," Kari responded. "I am not sure what has changed in you but something has. :)"

"I was just joking, Kari," he responded. "I am not different. I promise. We can go to the movies, out to eat, or rent a movie and order in, whichever you want."

"I tried the other night to make things special, and now the ball is in your court," she responded. "I hope you don't miss the basket."

"Very funny," he responded. "You make me laugh. Hahaha. You did make things special—I never miss the basket."

Yet Friday night, when they'd have a leisurely evening together, was still five days away. The week ahead would prove a tumultuous one.

The next day, Tuesday, March 28, Kari sent Matt another e-mail, apparently after what had been a disappointing sexual encounter: "I know you are not at work yet, but there is something on my mind . . . Matt, I love you very much, and I wasn't joking about what I said last night. I do not doubt your love for me. I just think that something has changed in you, and I can't figure out what it is. Until you open up and tell me what is going on, we cannot go any further . . . Never in our marriage have you ever told me no, and I guess I feel like this is just one way you are pulling away.

"I know you think I am seeing things, but what I feel is real. I have decided that until you open up to me and tell me what is going on and really spend the time needed to make things better, I will not do 'anything' with you. Then again, maybe that is what you want. This morning I thought you would have liked what I did, but I felt like you seemed put out, and I am tired of giving and giving and you not giving back.

"So I guess what I am saying: if you want our marriage to be better than it has ever been, then some things have got to change. Please know I am not in any way saying I do not love you or do not want to be with you, but the way I feel has got to stop, and that means that you have got to tell me what is going on in your mind.

"I love you very much and I am sorry if I have made you mad, but like I said last night I AM SICK OF THIS!!! You are breaking my heart :(."

When Matt got to WCY, he e-mailed back: "Kari, I just want you to know that I love you. Just wanted to say that."

From the outside, it would appear that their relationship was at a crossroads, and the only one who had all the facts, who could have come up with the answers, wasn't talking. Matt could have confessed to his interest in another woman or even simply announced that he didn't love Kari and wanted a divorce. Instead, in his e-mails he blamed Kari for the problems in their marriage. From her response, it would seem logical that he insinuated that their disagreement somehow had something to do with their dead daughter. "Wow," she wrote. "I guess Kassidy has never crossed my mind in what is going on now."

It was all Kari's fault, Matt said. She'd been cold, not fulfilling him sexually. Her response was at first measured. In her e-mail, she accepted that sex had been less important to her than it was to him, referring to it as "the way I was."

Then she wrote: "I understand that I will not expect anything from you like that until you are ready. I want to be real honest with you. I am so sick of talking about this. I just want to focus on us. I will try to not second-guess your feelings for me. BUT you have got to really spend time loving on me as well. It has to go both ways . . . I love you."

Minutes later, perhaps after they'd talked on the phone, it would seem that she'd reconsidered. This time, she sent Matt an e-mail that read: "You know what? I am sick of this. And so that is it. I am finished."

At 11:25 A.M., Matt replied, and this time he attacked Kari on every level, as a mother, wife, and lover: "I guess the whole idea about where Kassidy fits in is the way in which I see her death as a defining moment on [sic] both of our lives. We will never be the same again," he wrote. "I know that you have told me a number of times that you prayed the night that she died, that you wanted her to be pain free . . .

I have never told you before what I did in her room at midnight when I went in to check on her. I guess this is part of the 'not sharing' everything with you. I went to her bed and placed my hand on her back to make sure she was breathing. She was. She looked up at me briefly and went back to snoring quickly. I kept my hand on her back, and I prayed for her that night. I prayed that she would be cancer free, and I prayed for her to start and finish school, graduate college, get married and bring her family home for the holidays. I remember praying the words, 'Please, God, make her well, so we can have her here with us. Please! I need her.'

"I don't know why I never told you this before. Maybe I didn't want to make you mad. You and I have discussed the fact that your prayer was the one that WAS answered that night. I don't know why mine wasn't. I know deep down I hold a grudge against God and you for Him answering your prayer and not mine . . .

"All I know is that I chased you for our entire marriage. You often did make me feel like you did not need nor [sic] desire me. I felt as though I was like the sperm donor for your children, and I was now the butler, cook, babysitter etc. (although I know I am not good at keeping the house clean). We have always been friends.

"I just got off the phone with you and I am just as sick with talking about this as you are. I want to work on us just like you do. I don't want to be looked at weird or blamed or look at you weird or blame you anymore. It has to stop!! We cannot do this much longer, before one of us snaps! I don't know what would happen, but we could snap at each other and say something we can't take back.

"I do love you very much. I love my family very much. My girls are my world! There is nothing I wouldn't do for my girls.

"I do love you—and I am planning for Friday something special for the 2 of us. I just needed you to know what has been on my mind and heart. Please forgive me if anything I say here upsets you. I don't want to make you mad."

His standard signature closed this direct assault, "Matt Baker ~ Chaplain"

That e-mail must have been devastating for Kari. Matt was blameless. He was the dedicated husband and father, the one who prayed over their dying daughter and fought to save her life. Kari? She took without giving back. She'd prayed for their daughter's death. She'd rebuffed her husband and made him feel small.

Twenty minutes later, she responded: "Wow so you finally said it. You blame me for Kassidy's death. I had to read it a few times to make sure I understood what you had said. I feel like you just took a knife and put it through my heart. I have never ever told you that it was your fault that she wasn't alive, ever!!! Yes I carry that guilt of my prayer, but I know in my heart that God knew what he was doing before I ever prayed that prayer. Yes we will never be the same after Kassidy's death, but one thing I have learned is you can either let it change you for the good or the bad and that is up to you.

"Sorry you have felt like you have chased me our whole marriage. Sorry you feel that all you do is cook, clean and take care of the girls. You have truly painted an ugly picture of me. At least now I know how you feel about us and about me. At first I wondered why you would stay with me, and then in your last sentence you said you would do anything for your girls, meaning Kensi and Grace and that is why you have stayed.

"Yes I agree I am very tired of talking about this, but at least one thing happened: I now know how you feel about me and about our relationship. I am not sure what we do from here. I have some things that I need to work out because you said some things that really hurt. I am not mad at you but I am hurt.

". . . I know that marriage isn't easy, even harder with the loss of a child. BUT I am not sure how a marriage can last when one person blames the other for the death of that child. I am in disbelief about what you said. Shocked.

"Thank you for being honest with me finally. I wish it

didn't take so long, but I understand why you did because those words must have been very hard to say, to write. I am just not sure what to do now."

Afterward, Kari called her mother and confided in her. As they talked, Kari said that she and Matt were having problems, and that he blamed her for Kassidy's death. "Mom, I'm going to divorce him," she said. "I don't think we can get beyond this."

As a professor of communications, Linda taught her students that one should never give advice but rather ask others why they thought the way they did and what they believed they should do about it. At that moment, however, she wasn't in a classroom but talking on the phone to her daughter, someone she dearly loved, about ending a marriage. She knew Kari loved Matt, and she knew that a divorce would hurt not only Kari but also Kensi and Grace.

Talking to Kari, Linda reacted not as a professional communicator but as a mother and a grandmother. Most of what Linda knew about Matt Baker was good. She knew he'd moved from job to job, but not about his dalliances or his bizarre sexual advances toward young women. What Linda believed about Matt was that he was, overall, a fine husband and father. And, of course, that he was a minister, a man of God.

"Sweetheart, divorce isn't the answer," Linda said. "What you need is counseling. Clearly Matt hasn't dealt with this yet. You need to go to counseling together."

Years later, Linda brushed away tears. "I will forever live with that. I knew better. I gave my child advice, and I should not have done that. I did not follow the rules I teach. You should never tell people what they should do."

Chapter 19

As the week progressed, Kari continued searching for answers. Although Matt scoffed at her suggestion that he had changed, she was certain that something was very wrong. The next morning, Wednesday, she wrote Matt an e-mail that contained the first clue that she was starting to consider the possibility that her husband was unfaithful. "Haven't heard from you, so I thought I would say, HI! Maybe you are busy with your girlfriend. :) I love you."

"YEAH, Babe," he answered. "I was hooking up with my girlfriend. (By the way—what is her name anyway?) :) Love you very much."

Apparently, Matt had finally acquiesced, and they'd made love the night before. Yet Kari had noticed that Matt had even changed sexually. "Well," she said. "I thought that maybe you have been learning all those crazy moves you did last night some place. [sic] :)."

"You know it, :-)," Matt said, brushing off the insinuation. "Tomorrow I am going to go buy an item or two for FRIDAY!!!!!"

"Why, was that not enough?" Kari asked.

"I am going to shock you," he answered.

Sexually, Kari had always been a modest person, one who didn't wear revealing clothes. She talked of sex as her "wifely duty." But she was trying to save her marriage, and Matt understood that. In the past, she'd been the one in charge, but his withdrawal changed that, and he seemed to enjoy his newfound power. The next day he e-mailed: "I got a couple of needed items [for their romantic liaison on Friday], but I will have to get a couple more . . . I will be ready."

"What in the world do you have planned?" she asked.

"NOT GONNA TELL YOU :-)," he e-mailed back.

"You suck!!!!!!!!!" she replied.

When she asked for a hint, he answered, "You will like it."

That week, the TAKS scores came in, and Kari was elated. Every child in her class had passed. Despite the good news and the sexual banter with Matt, however, she continued to act on edge at work. "She said there were problems at home," says a friend. "She seemed upset. It was odd for Kari. She was usually so bubbly. She even said she thought she was having panic attacks."

The tension in the house on Crested Butte must have been palpable, to the point that even Kensi felt it. On Thursday, March 30, Kari called Linda and told her that she found a note of Kensi's, one in which the child said she felt unloved and that her parents treated her like "crap." Sometimes, Kensi said, she felt as if the only ones who loved her were her swimming coach and Grammy and Paw-paw, Linda and Jim.

"I need to find ways to make Kensi feel better," Kari said. "I need to do some special things with her."

"Bring Grace here, and you and Kensi do some things alone," Linda suggested. "I'd love to have Gracie, and it'll give you an opportunity to find out what's bothering Kensi."

Kari agreed.

The spring semester was half-over, and that afternoon, Kari's thoughts were on the coming fall. Eyeing the possibility of a change, she e-mailed the principal at Midway Middle School, where she'd heard about a language arts job opening, asking to be considered. "Middle-school students have always been my favorite," she wrote, telling him about her class's hundred percent pass rate on the TAKS test. "I would love to talk with you about this position . . . I really connect with this age group."

The following morning, Friday, Matt called Vanessa from Crossroads, at 10:22. They talked for approximately fourteen minutes.

Later that day, at Spring Valley Elementary, Kari stopped in to talk to Shae. While her fellow teachers had sometimes asked Kari to pray for them, this time it was different. "Would you pray for me?" Kari asked. "I'm going out on a date with Matt tonight. I want it to go well."

"I will," Shae agreed.

"I hope he doesn't want to tie me up or do something stupid," Kari said.

Startled, Shae wasn't sure how to take it but decided that Kari had to be joking.

That evening, Linda and Jim babysat while Matt and Kari went out. The following day, Shae called Kari. "She didn't mention the date, but she seemed a little down," Shae would say later. "It sounded like it hadn't gone well. We talked for ten minutes or so, and she had to hang up. I thought Matt was probably there, listening."

When Kari picked up the girls, Linda asked how the evening had gone. "It could have been better," Kari said, sounding a little evasive. Linda thought about Kari, how she liked to feel in control in her life. Whatever was going on with Matt was throwing Kari off kilter. But Kari collected the girls and was quickly out the door.

That afternoon, Kari, with Matt and the girls in tow, had her hair done by Basy Barerra. Kari had come for a cut and color, but Basy didn't have Kari's color in, so they made another appointment for later in the week. While Basy cut Kari's hair, Matt sat with the girls. As far as Basy could tell, Kari seemed in relatively good spirits, talking about the diet she was on with her fellow teachers. Kari had dropped fifteen pounds.

The following day, Sunday, Kari stood before the congregation at Crossroads. As the pianist played, Kari did sign language along with the music to MercyMe's "I Can Only Imagine," a song that wonders what it would be like to be with Christ forever. On the surface, she appeared well.

Yet that afternoon, Kari called a fellow teacher saying she was having a difficult day, fighting off the panic attacks that had by then plagued her for more than a week. At times, Kari said her heart raced, and she felt her blood pressure climb. Still suffering, later that day, Kari e-mailed to officially let the school know she wouldn't be in the next day.

What was behind the attacks? That same day, Kari sat down with her Bible open.

Since Kassidy's death, Kari had poured her heart out on the pages of the green leather-bound Bible Matt had given her. At times, she'd prayed to have her dead child returned to her. At other times, she'd dreamed of someday seeing Kassidy in heaven. This day, Kari's prayer didn't involve Kassidy. On this day, Kari was frightened.

The space on which Kari chose to write was below Galatians 6, near a quote that read: *Finally, let no one cause me trouble, for I bear on my body the marks of Jesus.*

"Peace! Lord, grant me peace. Calm my soul," Kari wrote. "I feel like I have so much worry, and I can't get a hold on it. Lord, be the center of our relationship."

Then Kari wrote something truly alarming: "Lord, I am asking you to protect me from harm. I am not sure what is going on with Matt, but Lord help me find peace with him. You are so mighty, Lord. I love you."

There was a time when Kari questioned what had happened when Kassidy died, wondering aloud if her child would have lived if she'd been in the bedroom instead of Matt. Over time, she'd seemed to convince herself that her fears were unfounded. Yet if that thought remained, even in the shadowy recesses of Kari's mind, could it explain why she might wonder what Matt could be capable of doing to her?

* * *

The next day, Monday, Kari and Matt went to her doctor. The account Kari gave to friends and family afterward was that first a physician's assistant examined her. She told him that she wasn't depressed but anxious, and asked for a prescription for Xanax, an antianxiety drug. Linda had an old prescription for it, one she hadn't used, and Kari had tried one of the pills and liked it. Since it worked, Linda had urged Kari to get her own prescription, to help take the edge off the attacks. But when the doctor came in, he asked Kari if her attacks could be hormonal. When she said no, the doctor wrote a prescription for Celexa, an antidepressant.

"Kari told me that she told the doctor she wasn't depressed, she had anxiety," Linda would say later. "But his response was that depression could rear its ugly head as anxiety. She asked him for something short-term, to get her through the stress she was under, but he said, 'Let's just try this,' and gave her the prescription for the antidepressant."

On the way home, Kari called Linda as Matt drove, telling her mother about the physician, complaining that he hadn't listened to her. Furious, Kari said that she'd torn up the prescription on the way out of the office. But then, as the conversation continued, Kari described how when they'd stopped at a stop sign, she'd opened the door to get some air. Matt had grabbed her. "Mom, Matt thought I was going to jump," Kari said, laughing as if it were the funniest thing Matt could have done.

Although Kari sounded amused by what had happened, Linda worried. She knew Matt and Kari were going through a difficult time and that there were things Kari wouldn't feel comfortable discussing. "She wouldn't tell me anything truly bad about Matt," Linda says. "She wouldn't want me angry with him." Linda thought that Kari needed someone she could trust to confide in.

"Why don't you go see Bristol again," Linda said, suggesting the counselor Kari had seen for a year after Kassidy's death.

Later that day, it would appear that Linda was right; Kari wasn't telling her mother everything. That afternoon, Kari called Jill, who was driving home from work. Kari was sobbing as she said, "I think Matt's having an affair."

Shocked, Jill, who knew only the side of Matt he'd shown her as a friend and her pastor, scoffed. "Kari, be real. Matt loves you. He wouldn't do that."

But Kari wouldn't stop crying.

In Dallas, Jill turned the car around and started driving toward Waco. "I'm coming," she said. "I'll drive right over."

"No," Kari said. "Just pull over and wait. I'll call you back."

Jill did as instructed, and minutes later Kari called back. "I'm okay. You don't have to come. I'll be all right. I have to teach at Tarleton tonight. Don't worry."

"Let me come get you," Jill said. "Please."

"No, no, no," Kari answered. "I'm okay. I'll call you tomorrow."

That night, at the house on Crested Butte, something else happened. Two days earlier, Kari had written in her Bible, asking for God's protection. On that Monday night after returning from teaching her class, Kari saw something that frightened her.

In the bedroom looking for a pen to grade papers, she opened Matt's calf-colored leather briefcase, which he kept next to the bed. Inside, she saw a toothpick container filled with crushed pills. Why would he have that? When she confronted him, Kari would later say that Matt told her that the pills were from WCY, saying that residents sometimes didn't take their pills and spit them into his briefcase. But she must have wondered if that made sense. Why would they be in a powder form? Who'd crushed them?

The next day at school, Tuesday, Kari complained about an upset stomach and mentioned that she wondered if it could have been something she'd eaten, perhaps strawberries she'd had with breakfast. At 8:20, Matt e-mailed: "Hey, hope you

have a good day. Try to keep from becoming anxious . . .
Love you."

Nearly an hour later, she e-mailed back. "I'm doing fine.
Sorry that I freaked out this morning. I guess my mind is
just going crazy. I started thinking about what if this, what
if that. Anyway, I am doing better, and I am trying really
hard to relax."

A while later, Kari e-mailed her mother, asking for
advice about the final she was preparing for her evening college class. The test was a month away, but Kari was making
plans. "I've come up with two ideas," Kari wrote. "One: how
to develop a job from the bottom up. Two: above plus they
will have to video a job interview . . . What do you think?"

When Linda responded, she said they both sounded
great. She also suggested that Kari had no reason to worry
about either the final or the interview for the middle-school
slot she'd applied for. On top of everything else, Kari had
an appointment with Midway Middle School's principal and
hiring committee scheduled for that coming Friday. Kari
was prepared, but with so much going on in her life, she
sounded nervous. "You'll do well," Linda said. "Believe in
yourself. You're a great teacher."

The emotional roller coaster Kari was on climbed that
morning out of the abyss that held her fears. Perhaps Matt
had professed his love as he consistently did in his e-mails.
Or perhaps it was just Kari being Kari, fighting off her own
doubts, attempting to convince herself that the man she
loved, a man who claimed a profound connection to God,
couldn't be having an affair and that she had no need to
fear him.

Whatever the reason, at 10:34 Kari e-mailed Matt, suggesting they meet for dinner. She'd promised the girls that
after school she'd take them to rent *The Chronicles of
Narnia,* which had just been released on DVD. In her e-mail,
Kari wrote: "I do want you to know that I feel a lot better
about us. Do you? I know we have had a bumpy few weeks,
but I feel that we are much closer now. How about you? You

probably think I'm crazy, but I promise I am really trying to work on it. I think after yesterday it really scared me, and it knocked me back into focus of what I need to be doing. Am I better? No. I have to work on some things, but don't we both? I just want you to know that I love you very much, and I am sorry for making you feel like I don't trust you."

What was she referring to? What had frightened her? The crushed pills? Had she accused him of planning to hurt her? Was that why she'd apologized for making Matt feel as if she didn't trust him?

Eight minutes later, Matt responded: "Oh, I have nothing to work on—hahaha. I do agree. I love you."

Despite telling Matt that she was better, that she believed their relationship was improving, around noon Kari followed the advice from her mother and called Bristol and left a message. When Bristol called back, Kari asked for an appointment. "How about four o'clock?" Bristol asked. "I have an opening."

"Perfect," Kari said.

When Kari e-mailed Matt to tell him about the appointment, because as usual he'd said he'd go with her, it was evident that the tension in the marriage hadn't truly eased. "Is that going to put you out?" she asked.

His response sounded angry. "STOP!!!!! Stop judging what I say. Just hear what I say. I said I will meet you at Jo Ann's by 4 p.m. It is not a problem. OK?"

"Matt, YOU STOP IT!!! I wasn't judging you. I was just making sure it wasn't a bad time. GOSH, I CAN'T DO ANYTHING RIGHT. I try to put your feelings first and I get my hand slapped. Sorry."

Three minutes passed, and he responded: "BABE—I am so sorry—I guess I was judging your statement. I am sorry! I CAN & WILL meet you and the girls at Jo Ann's office. OK? I am NOT trying to slap your hand. I promise."

That afternoon, the e-mails flew back and forth, Matt saying he felt like he walked on eggshells around Kari but insisting that he didn't want to make her feel bad. "I am sorry. I hope the meeting with Jo Ann will help." He then suggested that Kari see a counselor through his work, but she replied: "Thanks but no thanks. I don't want to come to your work to get help. I can do it on my own."

A little before four, Kari and the girls arrived at Jo Ann Bristol's office in downtown Waco. When Matt walked in, he sat with the girls in the waiting room, while Kari went inside the private office to talk to the therapist she hadn't visited in six years, not since a year after Kassidy's death.

Assessing Kari, Bristol noted her patient's appearance. Kari was well dressed, her hair combed, her makeup on. That was important, an indication of how Kari felt about herself, one that showed she cared about how she looked. As they talked, it became apparent that much was going well in Kari's life. She was proud of her success with her new diet, mentioning that she was down seventeen pounds that morning. All was well at work, and Kari talked excitedly about her job interview that coming Friday. When the conversation turned to Kensi and Grace, Kari sounded proud, saying both girls were doing well in school.

If Bristol was confused about why Kari was there, she ultimately focused on the reason. "Kari said there were problems in her marriage," Bristol would say later. "That morning, Matt left the house without saying he loved her. He wasn't interested in her sexually and had no desire to be with her that way."

"I've talked to Matt about getting our marriage on track," Kari confided. "But he said, 'Now you're ready, but I was ready for a long time. It will take me a while to catch up.'"

As she talked, Kari brought up the e-mail Matt had sent, the one in which he accused her of being responsible for their daughter's death. Away from Matt's prying ears, Kari told her counselor about her anxiety attacks, including the incident in the car, when Kari had opened the door and Matt grabbed her. "We were stopped. I just needed air," Kari said, laughing at the idea that Matt thought she might jump. Bristol asked Kari if she felt at all suicidal, and Kari said, "No."

Then the conversation took a strange turn, as Kari confided in Bristol about the night before, when she'd found crushed pills in Matt's briefcase. Kari said she'd confronted Matt, and he'd told her that the pills had come from WCY, but Kari admitted that she didn't believe him. "I asked him what they were, and he said, 'Why do you want to know?' I told him, 'Jo Ann will want to know.'" Worried about the pills, Kari said that she woke up in the middle of the night and went looking for them. While she was looking Matt walked in and asked what she was doing.

"I told him, 'I'm looking for the pills because Jo Ann will want to know what they are.'" At that point, Kari said Matt told her that he'd gotten rid of them and that he'd reported to WCY what the residents were doing.

There was more. "I think Matt's having an affair," Kari said. "And I think Matt's planning to kill me."

"Would you say that again?" Bristol asked.

"I think Matt's having an affair," Kari said. "And I think Matt is planning to kill me."

Yet as soon as she uttered those words a second time, Kari did what she'd done throughout her marriage when it came to suspicions about her husband—she quickly made an about-face. "No, he's not. That's ridiculous. I know better than that," she said. "Matt would never do anything like that. He wouldn't."

Listening to Kari, Bristol apparently accepted that her patient hadn't really meant what she'd said because she took no action other than to make suggestions for things Kari and Matt could do together, exercises to help them become closer. One was that Matt and Kari put in writing the things they loved about each other. A second was to rekindle the flame by indulging in the things they enjoyed when they had first met.

Despite that brief interlude when she'd confessed her fears, Kari insisted she was well, saying she was in a better place than she had been in the past, "with regard to the sorrow over Kassidy's death." In fact, Kari felt so at peace with the loss of her daughter that she repeated what she'd told Linda: "I'd like to work with other parents who've lost children. I think that may be my calling."

As the last of their minutes together clicked off the clock, Kari talked again about her girls, how she wanted to spend more time with them. Yet when the session came to an end, Bristol was concerned enough about what Kari had said to ask her to call on Friday, so they could talk on the phone if Kari was still having obsessive thoughts about Matt.

When they opened the door, there stood Matt Baker, the subject of Kari's fears, in the waiting area with Kensi and Grace.

Later that afternoon, Kari called Jill. "Kari said she felt more optimistic about her relationship with Matt," says Jill. "She said she was trying to be more adventurous in the bedroom with him, but that he still wasn't interested. But she said that she really wanted to make the marriage work."

When Kari called Linda, she told her she'd talked to Bristol. Kari didn't, however, voice any of the concerns she'd confided in her therapist, and Linda, seeing the session as private, didn't ask any questions. Later, that was something else Linda would regret. "If Kari had told me what was going on, I would have pulled her out of that house by the hair," Linda says, shaking her head slightly. "I knew something was wrong, but she didn't tell me how bad it actually was."

Chapter 20

At 8:04 the following morning, Wednesday, Matt e-mailed Kari: "Hope you have a good day. Love you."

Despite her assurances to Jo Ann Bristol that she couldn't imagine Matt's hurting her, doubts about Matt apparently continued to plague Kari. Midmorning at Spring Valley Elementary, she again confided in her friend Shae while they were on the playground supervising during recess. Grabbing Shae's hand, Kari said, "I almost called you to come get the girls. I was thinking of leaving Matt. I think he's having an affair, and I found some pills. I'm frightened that Matt's planning to kill me."

Then, as she did with Bristol, however, Kari immediately retracted her accusations, saying, "But I know that's ridiculous."

As worried as Shae was, she decided not to push Kari to talk about it then. In three days, on Saturday, they were planning to do a breast cancer walk with other third-grade teachers, and Shae thought that would be a better time to try to get Kari to open up. Shae had no way of knowing that Saturday would be too late.

That Wednesday, when Kari talked to Shae would turn out to be a good day in at least one way; Kari's grandmother was battling cancer, and that morning she received the report they'd all been hoping for, that the doctors found her cancer-free. Kari appeared overjoyed as she told her friends. Although she complained of a headache, when she talked to Jill on the phone, Kari sounded upbeat. Perhaps her grandmother's good news made Kari feel better about life in general, including her marriage, because she then went on to tell Jill again that she was determined to work the problems out with Matt. "I'm going to do whatever I can," she said. Then she thanked her friend. "I really appreciate having you to talk to."

At 12:19, Kari e-mailed Matt, apologizing for not responding to his morning e-mail sooner, saying she'd been busy teaching math. She'd called earlier from out on the playground and said it was because she'd missed him. "I haven't felt like my heart is going to jump out of my chest today. That's good."

"Good—maybe your heart will only jump inside your body ;-)," he responded.

"I wish you would make my heart jump. :)," she answered.

When he replied, "I do," Kari corrected herself. "Sorry, I meant to say I wish *I* made *your* heart jump."

"Very funny," he replied.

At 1:04, Kari again e-mailed Matt. She'd sent him a message earlier, suggesting a sexual liaison for the evening, and he hadn't e-mailed her in return. Now she wondered, "Did you get my e-mail? Or maybe that is your answer, that you don't want me to do anything with you tonight."

"Whatever," Matt wrote back. "I just got both e-mails right now—we'll see what we can do tonight." A week earlier, Matt had talked about picking up some supplies to augment their sex life. Now he typed, "Might have to use what we used before. :-)"

The following morning, Thursday, Kari e-mailed Matt, but he didn't respond. She wanted him to do what Bristol had recommended, to write down the reasons he loved her. "I know you think that is stupid, but if you don't mind, sometimes it is good to just see the reasons why a person loves

you. I am not saying I doubt your love. I hope you understand and can do this for me. You used to write me little
notes all the time telling me you love me . . . I love you."

A little more than half an hour later, Matt replied: "I did
not get that other e-mail. OK—if your [sic] force me to :-) -
here are a few:

"I love that you make me laugh.

"I love the time we spend together.

"I enjoy the family we have created—how beautiful
they are.

"I love you for loving me.

"I love that you are my best friend.

"I know that these are few—but very important. I DO
love you. You are my wife. I love you."

When Kari responded, she sounded happy: "Thanks for
putting those down. I guess sometimes I just need to be reminded why you fell in love with me. I know that I used to
not ask this, but I really think I am a different person today. I
need to hear more from you. I am sure you are thinking what
happened to the woman that I married? :) I guess I want
more from you. NO. I do want more from you.

"When we first met, you used to always do special little
things to tell me you love me. I guess I just miss that.

"Well my heart slowed down a little this morning. I think
I know why I get the way I do. I really just miss being with
you, and I start thinking about being away from you all day,
and I start feeling strange. I wish there was a way we could
work together. I know that can't happen, but it doesn't hurt
to wish. I love you."

In her final e-mail of the afternoon, at 2:29, Kari wrote:
"We will just talk when I get home. I love you."

During Kari's phone call to Jill that afternoon, she
sounded as if her life had turned an important corner and
that the future looked brighter. "She was elated," says Jill.
"Kari said things were better between her and Matt, that
they were patching things up. I was happy for her."

On the way out the door at school, one of the other

teachers approached Kari to remind her about the breast cancer walk coming up in two days, on Saturday morning. "I'd like to, but I need to talk to Matt," she said. "I'll let you know."

Chapter 21

Friday, April 7, 2006, was a hot day in central Texas. The thermostat was projected to climb to ninety-one, just three degrees below the 1972 record for that date. That morning, Jill called Kari but didn't get an answer. At 8:28, Linda e-mailed Kari, hoping to pump her up before her job interview that afternoon.

"Good luck," Linda typed. "Call me when it's over."

"Okay," Kari responded. "I'm so nervous, I didn't sleep at all last night. In fact, I couldn't remember if I took a sleepy pill at 11:40, so I took another one and now I think two, so my head feels strange. I hope they love me."

"Don't freak yourself out!" Linda responded. "You are a terrific teacher and you interview very well. Remember that you don't have to have this. Don't put so much stress on yourself." At that, Linda talked about wanting to spend time shopping with Kensi for her birthday. They discussed plans. "I do love those girls!!!!!!!!!" Linda said. "I've decided both girls need time with Grammy!"

Meanwhile, at 8:30, Matt Baker called Vanessa at her parents' home. From March 30 through that Friday, April 7, Matt had called the Bulls's house seven times, talking for a total of sixty-three minutes.

* * *

That morning at school, Kari looked happy. She stopped at Shae's classroom about 11:15 with a slice of pizza for her. They came in twos and Kari, on her diet, ate one and offered the other to her friend. Afterward, she exchanged e-mails with some of the other teachers about their plans for workshops that summer, Kari saying she planned to skip the one in June and look for another. Then, she told one of her fellow third-grade teachers that she'd decided not to do the Walk for a Cure breast cancer event the following day. "We're having a celebration for my grandmother on Saturday," Kari said. "I really want to be there."

That afternoon, Kari left Spring Valley at 12:30, stopping on Crested Butte to change into a suit to wear for her interview for the language arts slot. Matt would later say he was there, that they had a snack before she left to drive to Midway Middle School.

At 1:30, Todd Monsey waited at the school's front doors when Kari arrived. She was nervous and excited, and she'd asked him to take her in and introduce her since he taught history at the school. They talked, and Kari joked, saying that if she got the job, they could be coteachers, and that they'd be so good at it that they'd end up on *Oprah* as teachers of the year. Todd walked Kari to the principal's office and introduced her to the secretary, then he left Kari in the waiting area. Later, the secretary would say that Kari appeared happy, enthused about the prospect of teaching seventh-grade English and talking about Kensi and Grace.

After the interview, when Kari walked toward the front doors, she saw Todd again. "How'd it go?" he asked.

"Great," she said, raising her hand. He smacked it in a high five. Seconds later, she was out the door and on her way home.

"I rocked," Kari said, when she called Linda. "I was so good. I slam-dunked it!"

"See, I told you that you would." Linda laughed, relieved to hear Kari happy after the past difficult weeks. "Way to go, Kari!"

As soon as Kari could, she e-mailed Todd asking him to check on how she'd done. "Go in there and find out if I got the job," she said.

Later, when Kari called, her friend had good news. "They were blown away," he responded. "You're one of those being considered for the job."

"Yes," Kari said. "Oprah, here we come!"

Minutes later, Kari walked into Walmart. Shannon Gamble was there shopping when she saw her son's favorite teacher. They talked briefly, Shannon saying for not the first time how delighted she was that her son had passed the standardized test and that she appreciated all Kari had done for him. Shannon noticed how cheerful Kari looked, and they parted as Kari hurried to pick up a few things.

A short time later, Kari logged onto her school e-mail account to send a letter to Midway's principal, thanking him for the interview. "I felt the interview went very well," she wrote. "I was so glad to get to meet some of your great teachers . . . Thank you again for this opportunity, and I look forward to hearing from you. Kari Baker."

Yet at some point late that afternoon, something must have happened, something troubling. For by the time Kari was seen again, her mood was decidedly darker.

That afternoon, one of the other moms, Kim Johnson, saw Kari and Matt walk through the door into the Family Y's pool area for Kensi's swim team at 5:15 and sit in the bleachers with Grace. Immediately, Kim knew something was wrong. On any other evening, Kari would have walked over to Kim, to sit with her and talk. On this evening, Matt and Kari kept to themselves. "Her eyes were red," Kim said. She also noticed that things seemed not right between Matt and Kari. "You could have cut the tension with a knife."

As Kim watched, Kari put her head in her hands and sighed. Without explaining, Matt walked over to Kim and took her youngest daughter and Grace to the vending machines. A short while later, he returned and walked over to

Kari. The two girls were running around, and Kim pulled them to the side and told them not to bother Kari.

"Is she all right?" Kim mouthed at Matt, when Kari again put her head in her hands and stared down at her lap.

"No," Matt mouthed. "I'm going to take her out for some air." At that, he bent down, and pulled Kari up by her arm, then walked her outside to the hallway. To Kim, it didn't appear that Kari was ill but rather that she and Matt had been arguing.

In the hallway, Kari sat on a black leather coach. Another mother walked up and began talking. The second mom, too, noticed Kari's red eyes. The woman was upset with the swim coach and wanted Kari's feedback. Matt was off with Grace at the time.

"This is confidential," the woman said.

"Everyone knows you can trust the Bakers," Kari replied, her inflection sarcastic.

Moments later, Matt returned with Grace, and the other woman, too, sensed a "distance" between Matt and Kari.

Practice ended, and the Bakers left the Y that evening. Matt would say later that at 6:45, he and Kari, together with the girls, pulled into a small pizza restaurant, Rosati's, close to the Walmart where just hours earlier Kari had been happy when she saw Shannon Gamble. The plan was to pick up pizza, but the wait was too long, and they left, instead driving through McDonald's, where the girls asked for Happy Meals.

All Kari had to eat that evening, he'd later say, were two french fries, which she threw up after they got home. From that point on, Matt, Kari, and the two girls were alone inside the house on Crested Butte. The next anyone heard from them was when Matt picked up the telephone just after midnight and dialed 911.

Chapter 22

"This is 9-1-1. Do you have an emergency?" a dispatcher asked.

"Yes. I think my wife just committed suicide," Matt answered.

"Okay. You're at 803 Crested Butte? Stay on the line with me. I'm going to connect you to the ambulance. Okay?"

"Okay. Thank you," Matt responded. Moments later, the dispatcher assured Matt that a unit was on its way.

"Tell me exactly what happened," he then asked.

Kari, Matt said, was on the bed. "Her lips are blue, hands are . . . are . . . are cold, and there's a note that says 'I'm sorry,' basically . . . She's not breathing at all. No pulse or anything."

"Did you see what happened to her?"

"Uh, no. I just tried to push down on her chest, and stuff came out of her nose. No, no, no, no, I do not know. She . . ."

"Listen carefully. I need you to get her on her back flat on the ground, and remove any pillows, okay? Do that and tell me when you're done."

Matt's voice sounded as if it were any other day as he agreed to lower Kari onto the floor. "Hold on. Okay hold on," in the background a brief, low groan was heard. After a long pause, Matt said, "I know how to do CPR."

"Oh, you do."

"Yes. I am certified to do that," Matt answered.

Still, the EMS dispatcher wanted to make sure it was done correctly, and he instructed Matt to check inside Kari's mouth, to be sure her throat wasn't obstructed. Matt responded by saying, "There is fluid all in her nose and in her mouth, it just poured out of her . . . on the floor."

"Put one hand on the floor and one under her neck and tilt her head back," the dispatcher instructed. Once Matt said that was done, he asked Matt to put his ear near Kari's mouth, to make sure that she wasn't breathing.

"There's nothing. There's nothing," Matt responded.

"Okay. We're going to start with compressions first, okay?" Matt agreed, and the dispatcher told him to place his hands on the center of Kari's chest, one hand on top of the other, and push. "You're going to do it fast and hard, four hundred times."

"Four hundred?"

"Four hundred times is the latest we've been instructed to do. Okay? Twice per second," the dispatcher repeated. "It's going to take you about three-and-a-half minutes to do it. So start right now. I'll tell you when to stop."

Matt agreed, as the dispatcher added, "Let the chest come up all the way between the pumps. Okay?"

"Yes, they are." After a pause, Matt added, "I think she urinated on herself, too. It smells like it. There's water everywhere. Something everywhere."

"Okay."

Through it all, as he said he pulled his wife's cold, unresponsive body onto the floor, as he pushed down with his hands on her chest, Matt sounded calm, collected. He asked the dispatcher if he should unlock the door for the ambulance, but the man assured Matt that wasn't necessary yet and that he'd let Matt know when the ambulance got closer.

Then, it seemed something came to mind, the girls, Kensi and Grace asleep in their beds. "I have two kids. In their bedrooms," Matt said, suddenly deciding that he needed to call Linda and Jim. "I want them to come over here and be with the kids." Matt spelled out the Dulins' last name and gave the dispatcher their phone number.

"You still doing compressions?" the man asked. When Matt said he was, the dispatcher explained, "You do those. I'll get someone else started on this, okay?"

"Thank you. Thank you. Thank you." After a long pause, Matt said, "I dropped the phone . . . Oh, she's got foam or something coming out of her nose."

Then, unexpectedly, "Okay, someone's at the front door. I've got to go."

Somehow, EMS had arrived four minutes and twenty-eight seconds into the 911 call, before the dispatcher alerted Matt that the ambulance was approaching, before he instructed Matt to stop doing CPR and to leave Kari's side in the bedroom to unlock the front door.

"Okay, go ahead," the dispatcher said.

What was even odder, however, was that when those first responders arrived on the scene, they didn't have a siren blaring, one Matt might have heard. Yet they didn't have to pound on the front door or ring the bell to get his attention. Matt had told the dispatcher that he was in the bedroom administering CPR to his wife. In fact, Matt Baker wasn't in the bedroom at all. He wasn't even in the house.

What the first EMT on the scene saw at 803 Crested Butte just minutes after midnight on Saturday, April 8, 2006, was Matt with a cordless telephone to his ear, standing at his open front door.

Chapter 23

The dispatcher issued the call as a 2A, high priority. EMT Craig Lott was at home in bed just after midnight when his pager went off. The information relayed to him was that there was a possible suicide. Quickly, he threw on clothes and walked out to his truck, then looked at the address. Lott had recently moved, so it didn't strike him at first, but then he realized that the call address was on his block. Another look, and he recognized that it was the house directly next door. It was then that John Gates, Lott's partner, arrived in the ambulance. Still, they weren't allowed to enter the premises until police cleared the scene, so Lott and Gates walked up to the Baker house but waited. There they saw Matt standing on the front porch talking to the dispatcher.

Moments later, a Hewitt PD squad car pulled up with Officer Michael Irving inside. Irving rushed to the front door, where Baker motioned to come inside. Matt pointed to the bedroom, and there Irving saw Kari on the wood floor, her legs and arms splayed out, wearing a Snoopy Santa T-shirt and a pair of off-white nylon panties. Irving called to Gates and Lott, and the two EMTs rushed in carrying a portable defibrillator.

Once in the bedroom, Lott placed a BVM, a bag valve mask, over Kari's nose and mouth. As Gates began compressions, Lott hooked the BVM up to a tank delivering one hundred percent oxygen at fifteen liters a minute. With the oxygen flowing, Lott then attached leads from an AED, an automatic external defibrillator, to Kari's bare chest, and turned it on. What he was looking for were instructions on how to proceed. If the AED's monitor detected the right type of electrical activity, it would instruct the EMTs to administer a shock. But when Lott pressed the button, the machine's display read NO RHYTHM. That meant that the AED hadn't detected any electrical impulses in Kari's heart, nothing to shock. The only treatment option for Lott and Gates was to continue CPR, which they did as they waited for paramedics to arrive. As they worked, Gates noticed something odd about the scene unfolding around him: The woman's husband showed no emotion, even as the EMTs fought to save his wife.

Instead, Matt stood in the living room calmly answering Officer Irving's questions. The way Matt described what had happened, he'd been gone for about forty-five minutes and returned to find Kari in bed and not breathing. Where had he gone? "My wife asked me to put gas in the SUV and pick up a movie at Hollywood Video. *When a Man Loves a Woman,* the movie we saw on our first date. I left the house about eleven fifteen," he said. "When I got back, just before midnight, the bedroom door was locked. I had to use a screwdriver to get in. She was nude in the bed. I called 911, and then I dressed her, pulled her off the bed, and started CPR while I was talking to the dispatcher.

"I found a note on the nightstand," he then said. In the bedroom, Irving looked and found a sheet of white printer paper, the note read:

Matt,

I am so sorry. I am so tired. I just want to sleep for a while. Please forgive me. Tell Kensi and Grace that I love them VERY much. Tell my mom and dad that I love them to (sic). I love you Matt—I am so sorry

*for the past few weeks. I want to give Kassidy a hug.
I need to feel her again. Please continue to be the
great Dad (sic) to our little girls. Love them every day
for me.*

I am sorry. I love you.

Kari

Did it strike the officer as odd that the note, including
Kari's name, was typed?

Beside the note was a Unisom container with only two
pills remaining. Irving asked about Kari's medications, and
Matt told him that Kari was on weight-loss pills and that she
took a Unisom every night to sleep, something she'd done
ever since their daughter's death.

"Do you know how many were in there?" Irving asked,
referring to the pill bottle.

"No, I don't," Matt said. He also mentioned that Kari
had been drinking that night; they both had. He estimated
that she'd consumed two Bartles & James Fuzzy Navel wine
coolers. Two of the empty bottles sat near the Unisom bottle
and suicide note on the nightstand.

"Has she ever tried to commit suicide before?"

"No, but she talked about it," Matt said. "She's been upset
ever since our second daughter died seven years ago. She's
been depressed, and she's talked about suicide, especially in
the past couple of weeks."

The phone rang at Jim and Linda's home at 12:08 that night.
Linda felt an involuntary shudder. She didn't like late-night
phone calls, especially not around midnight. The last time
Linda had answered the phone at midnight was seven years
earlier, the night Kassidy died.

"There's been an accident at your daughter's house on
Crested Butte," a dispatcher said, following through on
Matt's request to have someone call his in-laws. "You need
to go there."

"Oh, my gosh, something's happened to one of my grand-daughters?" Linda said.

"No, it's your daughter," the man said.

"My daughter? I'll be right there." Minutes later, Linda and Jim had thrown on clothes and were in the car, barreling down deserted suburban streets shrouded in darkness. From the car, Linda called Matt. When he answered, Linda asked, "What's going on? What's wrong with Kari?"

"They're working on her," he said. "She's not breathing."

"We're on our way," Linda said.

Once Matt hung up, Linda called Nancy. "We're on our way to Kari's. There's been an accident," she said.

On Crested Butte, other Hewitt PD officers arrived including Sgt. Chad Kasting, who heard the call as he patrolled. The emergency was described as "an unresponsive female, not breathing." When Kasting called for more information, the dispatcher told him the husband said his wife had committed suicide. Once in the house, Kasting heard the man he'd later identify as Matt tell one of the EMTs that his wife had left a note.

On the bedroom floor, the two EMTs continued to administer CPR, but at least one wondered how long ago the woman on the floor had stopped breathing. When Gates felt Kari's body, it was cool, and he noticed something else, a pale purplish coloring to the woman's hands and back, lividity. Occurring after the heart stops beating, lividity is caused by gravity pooling blood in the lowest parts of the body.

"Looks like she's been unresponsive for some time," Gates mentioned to Kasting.

The sergeant looked at Kari as the CPR continued and noticed that her fingertips, lips, and feet were all blue. About then, a second ambulance arrived, this one manned by two paramedics. They quickly went to work, and Kasting asked one of the other officers on the scene to stand at the hallway to the children's bedrooms. The sergeant didn't want Kari's daughters to wander into the master bedroom. "Keep them from seeing what's going on," he instructed.

On the ambulance that night was Shelton Chapman, a paramedic employed by East Texas Medical Center. He and his partner assessed the situation, and one of the first things he noticed was the same thing that caught Gates's attention, that lividity had already discolored Kari's arms, back, and the back of her neck. That was a bad sign. Quickly, Chapman put a cardiac monitor on Kari's chest, attaching the sensors with tape. The printout verified that there was no electrical activity. Chapman examined the woman's body, touched her skin, and found it cool. Her pupils were dilated and fixed.

As the others assessed Kari, Irving and Kasting stood not far away in the living room, talking to Matt. Listening in to their conversation, Chapman thought that Baker seemed to be continually changing his answers to the officers' questions, as if rethinking what he wanted to say. It was frustrating because the paramedic couldn't get a read on what the man was contending about how long his wife had been unresponsive. But based on the condition of the body, what Chapman knew for sure was that any further attempts to restart Kari's heart were futile.

As the others talked, Chapman picked up his radio and called the doctor overseeing the ambulance service that shift, reporting to him on the condition of the body. The doctor pronounced Kari dead at 12:17.

Minutes later, Matt's phone rang. "What's going on?" Linda asked.

"Kari's dead," Matt replied. "She committed suicide."

"But how could that be?" Linda asked. "I talked to her this afternoon. She was in such a good mood."

Chapter 24

"Kari's dead," Linda told her sister Kay while she and Jim were still driving to the house. "My daughter's gone. Matt said she committed suicide."

Kay insisted that she'd jump in the car and be at Matt and Kari's house quickly, but Linda wouldn't hear of it. "I don't want you to come. Kensi and Grace are there. They're sleeping, and we want to keep things quiet," she said. "I'll talk to you tomorrow."

News always spread quickly in the family. As soon as she hung up, Kay called Nancy, crying. "Kari killed herself."

"Oh, my God, there's no way," Nancy said.

Shaking hard, Nancy dropped the phone and fell back into the arms of her husband. She lay there for moments, wondering what to do, then decided that she had to talk to Linda. She called, and Linda answered, and like Kay, Nancy insisted on coming to help, but Linda again said no.

When Nancy hung up the phone, she decided to go to Kay's house, but first she needed to talk to Lindsey. The two girls were closer than cousins, more like sisters, and although it was the middle of the night, Lindsey needed to know.

Once she got her daughter on the telephone, Nancy delivered the terrible news.

"Kari didn't kill herself. Matt killed her," Lindsey said.

Nancy had been pondering the same possibility. Yet how could they know? They couldn't say anything to Linda. It would be horrible if they were wrong.

"You could be right," Nancy told Lindsey. "But we'll have to wait and see. We need to leave this up to the police. There'll be an autopsy. That will give us answers."

"I'm going over there," Lindsey said.

"Linda doesn't want us to," Nancy replied.

"Mom, I'm going," Lindsey said. "Linda may not want us, but she needs us."

At the house on Crested Butte, as soon as Kari was pronounced dead, Officer Irving called Hewitt PD headquarters and talked with Sgt. Stuart Cooper, the investigator on duty that night, and Captain Tuck Saunders, just under the chief of police in the department's hierarchy. Irving informed them of the unfolding situation.

Meanwhile, Sergeant Kasting called a local justice of the peace, William "Billy" Martin. A gruff-faced man with thick dark hair and a bushy mustache, Martin was a former DEA, Drug Enforcement Agency, investigator, who'd spent time overseas, including working in Peru and La Paz, Bolivia. He talked about his experiences often, and one of his fellow agents would remark how Martin's eyes lit up recounting the days when he lived in foreign lands investigating drug cartels. After retiring, Martin moved to Waco and ran for and won a seat as one of eight justices of the peace in McLennan County.

On the phone, Kasting described the scene, telling Martin about the suicide note and the Unisom and wine-cooler bottles, and what the woman's husband, a Baptist minister, said: that his wife had been depressed and talked of suicide.

The reason Kasting called Martin was that McLennan County, in which Waco and Hewitt were located, had no medical examiner. Not populated enough to support an M.E., decisions involving deaths fell under the purview of the local justices of the peace, elected officials who handled small-claims court and performed marriages. Although not a pathologist or medical expert, it was up to Martin to rule on Kari's cause and manner of death. It was also at his discretion whether or not her body would be autopsied.

After listening to Kasting, Martin asked a few questions, including if there were any stab or gunshot wounds in Kari's body. Kasting answered that there weren't. During their conversation, Kasting read the suicide note to Martin, explaining that the child mentioned in the note, Kassidy, was the couple's dead daughter.

Based on Kasting's answers, Martin apparently decided that he didn't need to leave the comfort of his bed and travel out in the wee hours of a Saturday morning to personally investigate. While just a modicum of care might have convinced Martin that seeing the scene firsthand was a good idea, the law didn't require it, simply stating that a death determination could be made "any place determined to be reasonable by the JP."

Without even looking at her body, still on the telephone, Martin ruled Kari's death a suicide. When asked if he wanted the body autopsied, he answered, "No."

Minutes after she'd heard those awful words, that Kari was dead, Linda and Jim arrived on Crested Butte. The street was lined with ambulances and squad cars. Jim parked, and he and Linda ran toward the house. Before they could enter, an EMT, Chapman's partner, a woman, stopped Linda.

"What happened to our daughter?" Linda asked.

"She overdosed on Unisom," the woman said.

Inside the house, Linda walked toward the master bedroom, but Matt came up to her and hugged her. "I'm so sorry," he said.

"How is this possible?" Linda asked, repeating what she'd said on the phone. "I talked to Kari this afternoon. She was happy. Excited about her interview, about the new job."

Linda began to walk toward the bedroom, but Matt took her arm. "No, don't go in there," he said. "You don't want to see her like this."

Linda thought for a moment, then agreed. When the EMTs emerged from the bedroom, Linda overheard Matt talking to a police officer. "My wife didn't want to be buried. She wanted to donate her body to science."

"No," Linda said. "Kari wouldn't have wanted that."

As soon as she objected, Matt backed down.

In the living room, Linda and Jim, in a state of shock, asked questions. What Officer Irving told them was that Kari's death was a cut-and-dried case of suicide. In fact, the justice of the peace felt so certain of it, he saw no need for an autopsy.

While Irving talked to the Dulins in the living room, Kasting was in the kitchen with Matt. "Is there anyone else in the house?"

"My two daughters," he said.

"Are they okay?"

"You don't think she would hurt them?" Matt said.

Moments later, Kasting had looked in on Kensi and Grace, who were sleeping soundly through all the noise and chaos unfolding in the rest of the house. That done, Kasting asked about Kari's state of mind. Matt repeated what he'd told the other officer, that in the past couple of weeks, Kari had been depressed and talked about suicide. This time he described the incident Kari had told her mother and Bristol about, the one when Kari and Matt were in the car on the way home from the doctor, when she opened the door. Only instead of the way Kari had described it, while the car was stopped, Matt portrayed it as akin to a suicide attempt, saying the car was moving on the freeway and that he'd had to hold Kari in so she wouldn't jump.

When she hung up the phone with Nancy, Kay called the associate pastor from her church and asked her to come over, then she put in another call, this one to her friend Bristol.

Kay didn't know that Kari had just been in to see the therapist days earlier, but as soon as she said Kari was dead, Bristol said, "I'm coming over."

"No, you don't have to do that," Kay objected.

"No. I have to. You don't understand," Bristol said. "I'll be right there."

The moment the grief therapist arrived, she pulled Kay into a bathroom, and said, "I saw Kari this week, and I want to know how she died."

When Kay told her friend that it was from an overdose, that Matt said Kari had taken pills, Bristol said, "Kari told me she was afraid Matt was trying to kill her. She said she'd found crushed pills in his briefcase."

"But Linda said that Kari left a note," Kay said.

"Well, that is odd," Bristol agreed.

"What Bristol said made sense, but I didn't want her to call the police right then," Kay would say later. "I thought the police would investigate. I thought there'd be an autopsy."

Not long after Bristol arrived, Nancy called Kay and said Lindsey was on her way to Kari's house. "Jo Ann is here," Kay said. "Kari talked to her this week, just a few days ago. Kari told Bristol that she was afraid Matt was trying to kill her."

As terrible as those words were, Nancy felt a sense of relief. "I'd known it all along," she'd say later. "I knew Lindsey was right. Kari loved her family. She adored her little girls. She wouldn't have left them."

At eleven minutes before one, Sergeant Cooper arrived on the scene to take over as the lead investigator. While the others waited in the living room, including Jim and Linda, Kasting brought Cooper into the master bedroom to see Kari's body. Kasting showed Cooper the suicide note and the Unisom bottle and told him what Matt had said about Kari's depression over Kassidy's death. The heart-monitor wires were still connected to Kari's chest, hanging out from under her T-shirt as she lay spread across the wood floor, beside the bed. Her short blond hair was disheveled, and there was something dark on her nose and around her mouth.

When Cooper looked at the suicide note, he saw that it was typed and not signed.

"Did you call a JP?" Cooper asked Kasting.

"Judge Martin. He said no autopsy."

A bulky man, Cooper, had been a licensed law-enforcement officer since 1994 and with Hewitt PD for nearly a decade. Although Kasting had told him what Martin had said, Cooper placed a second call to the judge, again presumably rousing him in the middle of the night. Cooper would later say that he described the scene to Martin and asked again about an autopsy. Martin again said no "since the person left the note."

At that, Cooper called Captain Saunders, who told him, "If the judge didn't order an autopsy, one won't be performed."

Later it would seem unfathomable that with a young mother dead, more care wouldn't be taken. With the matter of the autopsy settled, Cooper interviewed Matt in the kitchen. "Did she give you any indication she might do something like this?"

"No, but she's been in therapy ever since our child died," he said. "And she's been erratic. She tried to jump out of the car while it was moving."

When the talk turned to what Kari might have taken, Linda overheard the two men. "So she just took Unisom?" Cooper asked.

"And Xanax," Matt added.

Linda's head whipped around, and she stared at her son-in-law. "Matt, Kari didn't have any Xanax."

"Oh," Matt said. "I didn't mean that. Just Unisom."

Throughout that night, Matt added more detail to his account of what happened earlier that evening. Kari, he said, had thrown up in the bathroom at swim practice and again after they returned home. In the bedroom, she got into bed and drank another Fuzzy Navel. Along with the Unisom bottle and note, the police had the two Fuzzy Navel bottles on the nightstand. It all made a convincing package.

It was at one o'clock that Lindsey arrived on Crested Butte, screaming as she walked up to the house, "What happened to my cousin? What happened to Kari?"

Matt rushed out to quiet her. "Keep it down so you don't wake up the girls," he ordered, putting his arm around her. "Come inside."

Inside the house, Lindsey approached one of the officers and asked to see the note. He refused, saying it was evidence. At that, Kari's cousin sat beside Linda, putting her arm around her. Jim sat quietly in a chair. They both looked as if they were in shock. Meanwhile, Lindsey watched Matt. Just like he had at Kassidy's funeral, he showed no emotion, but he did look nervous, pacing the living room in front of the fireplace, playing with his keys. Repeatedly, he dropped the key ring, having to stoop to pick it up.

By then, Hewitt Police Officer Brad Bond had arrived with a camera. Kasting asked Bond to photograph the scene. While it wasn't unusual in a crime scene to take dozens of photos or more, that night in the Bakers' bedroom, with the body of a young mother dead on the floor, Bond took only eight.

The first one was of the nightstand, a close-in shot showing the suicide note, the two empty Bartles & James Fuzzy Navel bottles, and the Unisom container off to the right edge of the photo. The container had been emptied and two remaining pills lay beside it.

Photographs numbers two and three were of the Unisom bottle, including the upper section of the suicide note. In one the photo extended down far enough to show "Kari" printed at the bottom. Number four was of the wall across from the bed, including the armoire that held the television, and beside it a desk with a computer and printer.

The fifth photo gave the first glimpse of death. The unmade bed dominated the photo, the pillows still in place, and beside it the nightstand, with another view of the wine-cooler bottles, the note, the clock, and the Unisom container. Yet as the officer snapped the photo, extending into the frame were Kari's legs, from the knees down, splayed out on the hardwood floor. Her body lay to the left of the bed, and a bed pillow was thrown against the wall, not far from her left foot.

If that fifth photo was eerie, the last three were truly heartbreaking. The young mother was now nothing more than a lifeless corpse sprawled out, arms above her head. The camera caught a dark spot on her T-shirt and her off-white nylon panties, tight and smooth against her skin. Leads from the heart monitor still trailed from below her shirt. Perhaps saddest were the small reminders of who she had been, the Santa Snoopy on her shirt and the silver bracelets on her right wrist, the ones students at Spring Valley heard tinkling as she walked down the hall, one in the Christian sign of a fish. Her eyes closed, her mouth gaped open, red and raw, as was a spot on her nose. In one taken head to feet, with her limbs extended, she looked like a child making a snow angel.

In the end, those photos did little to explain what had truly happened that night. Adding to the missed opportunities, Hewitt PD collected only two pieces of evidence from the Bakers' bedroom: the Unisom bottle and the suicide note. The sheets weren't taken, not even the Bartles & James bottles.

As the police began to close up shop at the house, Lindsey watched as Cooper talked to Matt, telling him that the JP had ruled Kari's death a suicide. She thought she could see Matt physically relax. "I'll give you a call and get together with you in the future," he said. "We may have more questions."

"That's fine," Matt agreed.

What Lindsey didn't hear was that there'd be no autopsy. If she had, she would have protested. But moments later, the police were outside getting ready to leave when Linda pulled herself together enough to realize there was something she had to do. Lindsey followed her aunt from the house to one of the squad cars, where Linda asked to see Kari's suicide note.

Sergeant Cooper refused. "It's evidence, and we're taking it with us."

"Would you please let me see my daughter's last words?" Linda asked. She wouldn't think until later about how none of the police had asked her or Jim a single question. Wouldn't they have wanted to know what Kari's parents had seen in their daughter in the days leading up to her death? It seemed such an obvious thing to do, yet the only one any of the officers talked to at the scene that night was Matt.

If they had, of course, there would have been many reasons to rethink the course they were taking, to call Judge Martin once again, this time perhaps saying that the girls' parents didn't believe she was depressed, that the young woman's cousin questioned that Kari had committed suicide. At that, the JP would have also had reason to reconsider, perhaps coming to the conclusion that the judicious thing was to spend some of the county's money on an autopsy, so they would know for sure how Kari Baker died.

But that wasn't done.

Cooper did, however, allow Linda to read the note inside its plastic evidence bag. Still reeling from the death of her daughter, Linda read it quickly, then handed it back to the officers and said little.

Meanwhile, peeking over her aunt's shoulder, Lindsey felt even more certain that her cousin hadn't committed suicide. "The note didn't even mention her brother, Adam," Lindsey would say later. "It was eight lines long, all about Matt and what a great guy he was, what a great father. If Kari wrote a suicide note, she would have mentioned her brother, and it would have been longer. If Kari had written that note, she'd have so many people to say good-bye to, it would have been the length of a book."

Chapter 25

At 1:34 A.M., just an hour and a half after the 911 call, a hearse pulled up in front of the house on Crested Butte. Kari's body was placed in the back to be transported to a mortuary to be embalmed. By then, Lindsey had left, not knowing it was a funeral home, not the medical examiner, picking up her cousin's body. "I couldn't be there when they did that," she'd say. "I just couldn't."

Afterward, Matt, Linda, and Jim were alone. With the police gone, Matt repeated his account of the night saying that when they returned home from swimming, Kari hadn't felt well. At 11:15, she asked him to go to the video store to rent the movie and fill up the SUV for the next day. When he returned, the bedroom door was locked. Using a screwdriver to open it, he found Kari naked and unresponsive. He called 911, dressed her, and followed the dispatcher's orders, putting her on the floor and administering CPR.

"I knew Kari was dead because she'd urinated on herself," Matt said.

At one point, Linda noticed the DVD Matt rented on the kitchen counter. In the bedroom, Linda and Jim looked around at the place where their daughter had died. How could Kari have taken her own life? "None of it made any sense, but what else could we believe?" Linda would say later.

As he talked, Matt suggested that Kari bought the Unisom at Walmart that afternoon, on her way home from her job interview. Linda thought briefly that it seemed odd. Kari had been taking a Unisom-type sleeping aid since shortly after Kassidy died; that was true. Kari had made no secret of it, calling them her sleepy-time pills. Yet she always bought the generic brands, cheaper forms of the drug.

"What's this?" Linda asked, pointing at a small amount of something glistening on the floor. She leaned down and touched it, and found it to be sticky.

"That came out of Kari's mouth," Matt said.

Looking around the room, they saw nothing else, no puddles of urine or vomit as Matt had described to the 911 dispatcher. Linda saw nothing on the disheveled bed, and the rumpled sheets didn't appear wet. Perhaps Matt saw his mother-in-law looking about the room, wondering. "I cleaned up where she vomited," Matt said.

That struck Linda as odd. When did he have the time? The police had just left, and Matt obviously hadn't done it while they were there. Still. Why would Matt lie?

Later, it would all seem such a blur.

At that, Matt and Kari's parents discussed what was to be done next. Should they wake the girls? They decided to let them sleep. There would be time enough in the morning to tell them the horrible news. For that night, Kensi and Grace had peace.

In the living room, Linda and Jim sat in chairs while Matt lay on the couch. That night, the girls never stirred. They'd slept through two ambulances arriving, the unsuccessful efforts to save their mother, at least three squad cars pulling up, and officers rushing inside the house. Kensi's bedroom was toward the front of the house, but the nine-year-old didn't even awaken when Lindsey arrived screaming. The police and EMTs had talked directly outside Kensi's window, and she never got up and walked into the living room to investigate. Later Linda and Jim would both wonder why.

Before long, Matt fell asleep, while Linda and Jim sat

in the chairs, wide-awake, watching their son-in-law's even, untroubled breathing. How could he sleep after all that had happened? Kari was dead, and Matt hadn't even shed a tear. How was that possible?

But on this night, the night their daughter died, it wasn't yet time for the Dulins to question. Instead, they quietly contemplated the horror unfolding around them. "We don't have a daughter. Our daughter is gone. How am I still breathing?" Linda wondered. "How is it that I can talk and stand?" She saw herself outside her body, watching herself sitting silently in the chair. "Why am I not prostrate on the floor, screaming?"

Chapter 26

Near sunrise the next morning, Lindsey called the local poison-control phone number and asked about dying from an overdose of Unisom. "The woman didn't think it was possible," Lindsey would say later. By then Nancy had called to tell her what she'd heard from Kay and Bristol: Kari was afraid of Matt, wondering if he could be trying to kill her.

"I wasn't at all surprised," says Lindsey. "In my heart, I already knew. What we were all waiting on was the autopsy."

At 6:00 A.M., Matt called Barbara and Oscar to tell them that their daughter-in-law was dead. "He said it looked like she'd taken sleeping pills," says Barbara, who'd later say she wasn't at all taken aback by the news. "I knew she took them every night."

At 7:45, Kensi finally awoke and found her grandparents in the living room, her father sleeping on the couch. When they told the nine-year-old, she threw herself on the floor sobbing. Grace, too, cried, although Linda wondered if at five she truly understood what Matt meant when he told her that her mommy had gone to heaven to be with God and wouldn't be with them anymore.

By then, the news was beginning to spread to Kari's friends.

Todd Monsey, who'd high-fived Kari at the middle school the afternoon before, ran into a friend who was crying. She told him Kari had committed suicide the night before. "There's no way," Todd insisted. Certain it was all a mistake, he called Kari's cell phone, but there was no answer. He left a message, "Kari, you need to call me back. Why aren't you answering your phone?" Off and on all morning, even after he'd heard from more friends that it was true, Todd kept calling, partly not believing and partly simply wanting to hear her voice.

When Todd called Matt, he said, "Kari took her own life. She passed away."

At that, Todd went to his sister's apartment to deliver the bad news to Jenny in person. "She didn't kill herself," Jenny insisted. "She would have said good-bye."

"Check your e-mail," Todd said. Jenny did, but found nothing.

By then, the girls, Matt, Linda, and Jim were all at the Dulins' house. Not long after arriving, Linda was alone for the first time since learning of her daughter's death. Falling to her knees, Linda prayed. Seven years earlier when Kassidy had died, Linda had been angry with God. This time, her reaction was different. "I knew I couldn't take one more step without Him. He would have to lead me," she says. "I cried out for help."

Afterward, Linda joined Jim and Matt. There were plans to make. It was then that Matt announced that he wanted the funeral the next day, on Sunday. At first, Linda couldn't grasp what he was saying. Kari had only died that morning. She thought about family and friends, the time it would take to make sure everyone knew. "Jim and I literally begged Matt to wait until at least Monday," she'd say later. "I had my sister Jennifer in Florida, who wouldn't be able to even get to a funeral by Sunday."

Matt at first resisted, but then reluctantly agreed.

At that, it was decided that Matt and Linda, along with

Linda's mother and father, would go to the funeral home to make arrangements, while Jim stayed with Kensi and Grace. Heartbroken, Linda and Jim offered to pay for the funeral, which Matt accepted. In the car on the way to the funeral home, Matt turned to Linda, his blue eyes earnest, reaching out to hold her hand. "You know, I love my parents, but you and Jim have been my real family."

At the Oakcrest Funeral Home on Bosque Boulevard, Matt parked in the lot and walked with Linda and her parents under the porte cochere, through the glass doors, and into the lobby. The building was across the street from the Heart of Texas Fair Grounds, where Kari had once worn a banner as one of the fair's sweethearts.

Decorated with silk flowers, the conference room was dominated by a Chippendale table and chairs. They all gathered around it as Matt told the saleswoman that they wanted to move quickly and have the funeral on Monday. With what appeared to be little debate, he picked out flowers, a guest book, and thank-you notes; and then they were escorted into the casket room. Matt looked around matter-of-factly, pointed and said, "We'll take that one." The casket was a baby blue twenty-gauge steel, medium-priced model called "The Lord's Supper." On the four corners were angel figurines.

While Matt appeared not emotionally invested in what they had to do, the import was not lost on Linda. *Oh, my gosh,* she thought. *I'm shopping for my daughter's casket.* She began crying, and while Matt continued calmly making plans with the salesperson, Linda's parents put their arms around their daughter to comfort her. Once the order was completed, Linda wrote a check for a down payment, and they left.

That morning, the phone tree at Spring Valley Elementary sprang into action, the staff and teachers spreading the news to faculty and parents. A group of Kari's friends heard while on the breast cancer walk. "We were all talking about it, trying to figure out how it could be true," says one. "We talked every day, and Kari was upset about problems with Matt, but making plans, talking about taking classes in the summer, hoping for the new job in the fall. We didn't understand what could have happened."

When Shae heard from another teacher that Kari was dead and that it was suicide, she covered her face with her hands and sobbed. All she could think of was what Kari had told her just days earlier: that she worried Matt was planning to kill her. "I knew he went through with it," Shae said. "I knew that Matt killed her."

Meanwhile, Linda and the others returned from the funeral home to find the house filling with family and friends. Kay and Nancy were already there when their parents and sister arrived. Jenny Monsey was at the Dulins' house, too, eager to offer her condolences. While she'd waited, she sat with the girls, who colored at the kitchen table. They both seemed quiet, especially Grace. Jenny noticed Matt's eyes when he walked into the room. He didn't appear to have been crying. "I'm so sorry you're having to go through this," Jenny said, giving him a hug.

"Thank you. I'm sorry you're having to deal with it, too," Matt said, without emotion.

A short time later, Lindsey walked in. Nancy was standing off to the side, when she saw Matt smile at her daughter and make the adolescent gesture he often did when Lindsey entered a room, holding out his hands as if he were going to squeeze her breasts, as he had repeatedly done for years. Disgusted but thinking it wasn't the time to object, "We just kind of brushed it off," says Nancy.

Others began arriving, some bringing casseroles and baked goods for the family, to tide them through the difficult days ahead. For the most part, little was said about suicide, but when one couple offered Nancy their sympathies, Linda's sister didn't mince words. "There's no way Kari would have done this," Nancy said. "Absolutely no way."

The couple looked surprised and walked away.

Both the girls were still coloring at their grandparents' kitchen table when Barbara arrived from Kerrville. Matt's mother put her hands on Kensi's shoulders. "You don't have to worry about the girls," Nancy told her. "We'll all be there for them." At that, Barbara sat in the rocking chair. Before long, the girls found her. Kensi was crying. "What do I tell the kids at school?" Kari's oldest asked.

A pragmatic woman, Barbara thought that through. "By the time you return to school, the other children will know. You won't have to tell your friends."

More people arrived, including teachers who worked with Kari, and then in midafternoon, a car pulled up in front of the Dulins' house, and Vanessa and her parents got out. Once inside the house, Vanessa stood calmly next to her father as her parents offered Matt and Kari's family their sympathies. When Vanessa saw Matt, she gave him a hug. Later, Vanessa would say that when they drove away, Matt winked at her.

That afternoon, Barbara and Matt drove to Crested Butte. Once there, Matt asked Barbara to help clean the master bedroom, scrubbing the wood floor, washing the sheets, erasing all indication of what had transpired there the night before. That done, Matt decided to move the furniture, and, again, Barbara pitched in. "Things were out of control, and this was something Matt could control," she explains. "Matt and I are both like that. We try to do something we can do, not worry about what we can't."

The bedroom sparkling, they then packed suitcases to take to the Dulins', where they were staying through the funeral.

That evening, Steve Sadler, a round-faced man with a fringe of light brown hair, arrived at the Dulins' house. A Baylor religion lecturer, Sadler had been the pastor at Crossroads before Matt, and Linda had suggested that he would be a good choice to conduct the funeral. At first, Sadler conferred privately with Matt.

Meanwhile, Linda's family collected around the patio table overlooking the backyard, talking about Kari. At one point, they began laughing at funny stories from her thirty-one years with them. When Sadler finished talking to Matt, they joined the others outside, and Linda's family told the stories they loved to the minister who would conduct Kari's funeral. They wanted him to know about the woman he'd be eulogizing, that she was smart and funny, and that she had a deep faith.

Afterward, Sadler left with Kari's green leather Bible. Later, he would say that he found something odd inside, the note Kari had written near Galatians just six days earlier: *. . . Lord, I am asking you to protect me from harm. I am not sure what is going on with Matt, but Lord help me find peace with him.*

Sadler read that note in which Kari asked for God's protection but apparently failed to see it as something that should be immediately turned over to the police. He did, however, view it as troubling enough to make a copy.

Meanwhile, the doubt within Linda's family kept growing. When Jennifer arrived, she told her sisters, "Kari wouldn't have done this."

"We know," Nancy answered. When the women discussed what they had to do, they concluded that they had no evidence beyond what Kari had told Bristol. The wisest course, they again agreed, was to wait for the autopsy before voicing their suspicions to Linda and the police.

The visitation took place the day after Kari's death, that Sunday evening, from three to five at the funeral home. Kari's cousin and aunts watched Matt, wondering if at any moment the police would show up armed with the autopsy report, handcuffs ready. Once the results came in, they felt certain there would be scientific evidence to back up their fears. Then the unimaginable happened. Not long after Kay arrived, she heard from Linda that there'd been no autopsy; the justice of the peace hadn't ordered one. "We never considered that a young woman could die, and they wouldn't order an autopsy," says Nancy. "We didn't even think that was possible."

Kay wasn't sure what to do. Regretting that she'd kept Bristol from going to the police, Kay talked with Nancy and Lindsey. Kari's body had already been embalmed. Watching Linda and Jim, seeing the pain they were in, Nancy and Kay decided that they couldn't hurt them any more, not without proof. All they had were suspicions.

As the visitation officially began, a line snaked through the funeral home, family and friends, students and their parents, Kari's fellow teachers. Some had heard that Kari had taken her own life, but others were left wondering if she'd been ill. In the receiving line, some asked Linda, "Did Kari have cancer?" "Was she in an accident?"

Adding to the questions was the fact that the casket was closed. At one point, Linda put both hands on it, as if trying to connect with her daughter one last time.

When Jill arrived, she hugged Matt. Like many who attended, she marveled at how emotionless he was. Lindsey watched, too, thinking that Kari's widower looked pleased with the attention, remembering that Matt had acted the same way at Kassidy's funeral.

"How could this have happened?" Jill asked Linda.

"I don't know," Linda said, feeling trapped in a nightmare.

When Kari's friend Kim hugged Matt, she asked how he was and said she was there to help if he needed anything. When she looked again into his face, he was smiling. As they walked away, Kim's mother said to her, "He doesn't seem like a grieving husband."

A DVD played with photos of Kari from her baby years through growing up, and as a college student and a young mother. Jenny laughed when one popped up of the two of them clowning around with balloons under their shirts in the church kitchen. The time passed, and Bristol arrived and stood in line. When she finally reached Matt, she gave him a slight hug. "I didn't see this coming," he said. Then he asked, "Did Kari tell you she thought I was having an affair?"

"Yes," Bristol said, nodding. "She did."

"Did she tell you she found pills in my briefcase?"

"Yes, she told me."

"Did she say she thought I was trying to kill her?"

"Yes, she did."

"That movie Kari asked me to rent, *When a Man Loves a Woman,*" he said. "That was the first movie we saw together."

At that, Bristol left Matt standing with others around him. Kay had watched him through much of the gathering, and she saw his face darken as Bristol made her way to Jim and Linda. Taking a seat next to Linda, the counselor held her hand and talked quietly with her. But the close proximity felt stifling, and Linda felt as if the therapist was sucking up all the air.

"Was there anything in Kari that makes you believe she'd do this?" Bristol asked.

"No," Linda said. "But what are the options?"

"Linda," Bristol said, more insistently. "Was there anything?"

"No," Linda said again. She had the overwhelming feeling that Bristol wanted her to say something, but she didn't understand what.

A letter went out to Spring Valley's parents the following morning, Monday: *The SV Elementary Community has suffered a tragic loss in the death of third grade teacher Kari Baker.*

Meanwhile at the house, Matt showed Linda and Jennifer the Bible Steve Sadler had returned to him, Kari's *Quest Bible,* pointing out places where Kari had written Kassidy's name, the phrases she'd jotted down including, "Kassidy, I want to be with her."

Understanding, Linda nodded, but in the back of her mind she wondered, why now? Many of the writings Matt showed them were dated six or more years ago, many not long after Kassidy died. Yet it seemed a pointless question. After all, Kari was dead, and the only explanation Linda had was that her daughter had committed suicide.

The expected crowd was too big for Crossroads, so Kari's services began at three that afternoon in the funeral home's large chapel, a room with a soaring ceiling. Despite the substantial accommodations, more chairs had to be brought in. Once the seats filled, mourners stood against the wall and spilled out into the entryway.

Matt cut a sympathetic figure as a widower with two young children abandoned by a wife who'd committed suicide over the death of a child. In his dark suit, he milled through the crowd shaking hands. By then, the church members at Crossroads had voted to donate funds to pay for Kari's funeral and burial. They also gave him a check to help with his rent on the house for the coming months.

As the crowd arrived, Matt stood at the funeral home's podium with the girls, greeting those who came through the door. As Crossroads members entered, he assured them he'd be at church the following week, Easter Sunday. Although they insisted he didn't have to, Matt stressed that he would be there. "I worked right after Kassidy died. I'll do the same thing this time," he told one church member. "God has not abandoned me. He will give me the strength to carry on."

Among those attending were Vanessa Bulls and her parents.

As the service began, Matt and the girls joined Linda and Jim, sitting with Barbara and Oscar in the front row. When he hugged her, Linda said, "I love you."

Much later, someone would tell her that as he turned away, Matt murmured, "I don't love you."

"It was a funeral, nothing stands out that much," Barbara would say later in her dour way. That day many noticed that like Matt, she expressed little if any sorrow. Like him, she didn't cry. Later, Barbara would say: "I saw Matt reacting like I'd react. We're not the type to break down and cry.

Crying and screaming and wringing our hands is not who we are. If people judged on how he reacted, I can't do anything about that."

Jennifer's husband, a Florida music minister, had prepared the music. Behind the lectern, photographs of Kari flashed on a screen. As they looked up at the photos of their mother, Grace and Kensi cried softly.

In front of the crowd, Steve Sadler began the service. Later, Kari's family would say that Sadler said little about Kari. From her Bible, Sadler read underlined passages, many of them about God's love. Yet his words focused on the living. He asked those gathered to watch over Kensi and Grace, and then talked at length about Matt, about all the help he would need not in just the days but months and years to come. Sadler asked them all to pray for Matt, who sat with his head bowed in his hands. "You need to call him, not just today but in the future, and ask what you can do to help him," Sadler said. "Clean his house. Clean his toilets. Be there for him and the girls."

Crying, Linda listened, understanding that Matt would need help with the girls, but disappointed that Sadler hadn't used the dear stories her family had told him about Kari. Then Sadler suggested that the mourners give their condolences to the family, but he urged them not to dawdle, to shake hands and move quickly through the line.

The burial was private, immediate family and close friends only, at the same cemetery where seven years earlier Kassidy's body had been laid to rest. As she watched with the crowd, Nancy prayed, but not as Sadler had suggested during the eulogy for Matt, but it wasn't actually against him either. "I never prayed God would get Matt," she'd say later. "I prayed God would get the truth out."

Chapter 27

The evening after his wife's funeral, Matt Baker called the Bulls's household. Vanessa would later say that he talked first with her, then with her parents, confiding in Larry and Cheryl that Kari had been deeply depressed, detailing all he said he'd suffered with his dead wife. After listening, Cheryl invited Matt and the girls for dinner the following Friday, Good Friday. Over the next three days, Matt called the Bulls's house eight times and talked for a total of 105 minutes.

That same week at Spring Valley Elementary, two teachers cleaned Kari's room, pulling together her personal belongings for Matt to pick up. The teachers found photos of Matt and the girls and the e-mail Matt had sent Kari, the one where he accused her of being responsible for Kassidy's death. "This is what she was so upset about," one said.

Meanwhile, Linda's sisters faced a quandary. Suspecting that Matt had murdered Kari, they now realized that they'd been wrong to stay silent and assume that the Hewitt police would investigate. Talking it over, they worried about the consequences, including that the scene had been scrubbed and cleaned, and Kari's body embalmed and buried. Eager to rectify the situation, they talked about the best way to approach the police. Their decision was that Bristol should talk to Sergeant Cooper, the investigator in charge of the case.

Housed on Chama Drive next to the public library in a modest brick building painted white with blue trim, Hewitt PD was a small operation with twenty-two officers, a department without a considerable amount of resources. The man in charge, Chief James Barton, was a thick-necked, jowly man, with a mustache, graying hair, and wire-rimmed aviator glasses. Over his then-twenty-six years in law enforcement, Barton had worked for a variety of small departments, from the Nueces County constable to the Alice, Texas, police department. He'd hired on in Hewitt in 1983 and worked his way up to the top spot.

Barton's second-in-command was Captain Tuck Saunders. A police officer since 1991, Saunders's entire career had been spent in the employ of Hewitt PD. "Tuck did pretty much whatever the chief told him to do," says a former HPD employee.

The good news was that there wasn't a lot of serious crime in Hewitt. "We have a little bit of everything," Chief Barton would say. "But we don't get a lot of violent crime. Very few murders."

In the past, there had been questions about the department's performance. One case that stood out was the death of Joel Gibbs, who had died under mysterious circumstances ten years before Kari. In the Gibbs case, Joel's body was found with multiple stab wounds, including a slashed throat. Perhaps surprisingly, with those types of injuries, Hewitt PD officers initially assumed the death was a suicide and allowed the scene to be cleaned, even tearing out the bloodstained carpeting, destroying evidence, and hampering the investigation. Perhaps because of the lost evidence, no one was ever charged with the murder.

That first week after Kari's death, Bristol made her way over to Hewitt PD's offices and talked to Cooper, identifying herself as Kari's therapist. Tall and heavyset, a former coworker says that Cooper had a reputation for not liking to be questioned.

When she met with Cooper, the therapist recounted what

Kari had said at their final session, including her suspicions about an affair and that Matt was trying to kill her. Relaying how Kari had then quickly laughed off her suspicions about Matt, Bristol concluded with her assessment of her patient, saying, "I saw Kari three days before she died, and I had no indication that she would commit suicide."

When Cooper appeared not to take the situation as seriously as she expected, Bristol prodded, "What're you waiting for? For Matt Baker to marry and kill a second wife?"

After hearing Bristol's account of her meeting with Cooper, Kay called the police department and talked with the sergeant on the phone. Like her friend, Kay got right to the point, telling Cooper: "I think Matt Baker had something to do with my niece's death."

As she would remember the conversation, the sergeant replied, "We don't have any evidence of foul play."

"Why wasn't an autopsy done?" Kay pressed.

"Judge Martin was notified and didn't order one," Cooper said.

"I don't understand why not," Kay said. "Kari wouldn't have killed herself."

"Well, it's an open case. If you have any more information, let me know," Cooper responded.

"That's it?" Kay asked.

"As I said, if you get any more information, call us and let us know."

Kay hung up, certain Cooper had no intention of investigating Kari's death.

That afternoon, Kay filled Nancy and Lindsey in on Bristol's unproductive visit with Cooper and her follow-up phone conversation. Frustrated, they weren't sure what to do. The only step they could take was one they dreaded. "We didn't know how to tell Linda," says Nancy. "We wanted to, but we knew it would hurt her. And we didn't have proof."

Hoping to gather more information before talking to Linda, Kay called the doctor Kari had seen on the Monday before her death, the one who'd written a prescription for an antidepressant. Kay's attempt to glean any insight, however, proved fruitless. The physician's nurse listened to the news of Kari's death sympathetically but refused to ask the doctor to come to the phone. Citing privacy laws, the nurse said, "The doctor won't be able to talk with you."

After she hung up, the nurse noted her conversation on Kari's chart and notified the doctor, who put in a call to Matt. In Kari's chart, the doctor wrote: "I spoke with Matt and expressed my prayers and thoughts. He states that she must have consumed a large amount of Unisom and mixed drinks, then she aspirated."

Days passed, and the women talked often, yet Linda's sisters and niece remained uncertain about how to proceed. "Hewitt police hadn't done their job," Nancy would say later. "We wanted an investigation."

That same week, on April 12, Kari Baker's death certificate was printed, the cause of death listed as an overdose of Unisom sleep aid. The manner of death was a check in a box beside the word "Suicide." Where the form required information on how the death occurred, someone had typed: "overdose of over-the-counter Unisom. Left note." The death certificate was signed by Justice of the Peace Billy Martin.

Chapter 28

E-mails expressing sympathy arrived for Matt from others within Waco's Baptist pastoral community in the weeks following Kari's death. Some of those who contacted him offered to help if he needed anyone to talk to about his grief. Nearly all said they were praying for Matt and the girls.

At Linda and Jim's house, all thoughts were on their granddaughters. When Matt mused that without Kari's salary he wouldn't be able to afford the rent on the Crested Butte house, Jim and Linda said he and the girls could stay with them for a while until he decided what to do. At first, Matt sounded as if he might agree. And when the girls heard, Kensi, smiling and excited, went through the house, picking out which bedroom would be hers and which would be Grace's. Despite Kensi's enthusiasm, Linda knew her granddaughters were hurting. When alone with Matt, she urged him to take them for grief counseling. They were young, they'd lost their mother, and Linda judged that they needed help. Matt, on the other hand, insisted both the girls were coping and saw no need.

Still feeling as if she were in shock, that first week would be a fog for Linda. One thing she would later remember was how many times she called Kari's cell phone to hear her dead daughter's voice. Todd and Jenny did the same. They

were all surprised when within a week, Matt had deleted
Kari's message and put up his own.

It was that Wednesday, the twelfth, just five days after
Kari's death, when Matt returned to the Waco Center for
Youth. When he walked in the door, his coworkers were
shocked to see him, assuming that he'd need more time
off. They were even more surprised when they offered their
condolences. Instead of simply saying thank you, Matt complained bitterly about his ex-wife. "I'm fine. It wasn't a marriage anyway," he said. "Kari was depressed, so we were just
coexisting."

As he talked, he recounted how he'd found both his infant
daughter and his wife not breathing in bed, that he'd put
both on the floor and administered CPR. It seemed such an
eerie similarity when he mentioned that Kassidy and Kari
had even died at the same time of night. "When Kassidy
died, I felt her spirit go through me," he told one woman.
"It was like she put a small hand on my shoulder, and said,
'Hey, Dad, I'm all right.'"

On his other shoulder, Matt said he'd felt a heavier hand.
"It was God, and he was saying, 'It's okay. She's with me
now.'"

From that day on, others would have similar conversations with Matt, during which he'd talk resentfully of Kari,
branding her a bad mother and wife, saying their marriage
had ended years earlier. He even described her as a dark
cloud that had hovered over the house and said that now that
she was gone, the girls were happier. "Kari was never satisfied," Matt told one woman. "She always wanted more."

That wasn't all that was odd; Matt soon even looked different. It seemed as if overnight he'd changed his hair, gelled
it up and spiked it, and replaced his khakis and button-down
shirts with new, hipper clothes.

Although he'd initially agreed with the Dulins' offer to
move into their home, Matt and the girls remained in the
house on Crested Butte. That first Friday evening, they
drove to the Bulls's house in Troy, where Vanessa's parents

served dinner and had an Easter egg hunt. At the table, Matt again talked about Kari's depression.

That same day, Good Friday, a friend of Kari's called Linda. During the conversation, the friend mentioned that she'd been at the grocery store shopping when she saw Matt with a pretty young woman and a baby, a little girl with blond hair. At that point, Linda had no idea who it could have been.

That Sunday, Matt Baker stood before the congregation at Crossroads officiating over Easter services. "People are surprised that I'm here," he acknowledged. "I'm still your pastor, and I still have a job to do. I'm here because God wants me here."

Some would accept him at his word, including Kari's friend Kimberly. Only later would she look back on Matt's quick return to the pulpit as strange. During his talk, he compared Kari to Jesus, predicting that his dead wife had made a "triumphant entry into heaven . . . Death could not control her."

While Matt remained dry-eyed, Linda and Jim wept. Although she didn't question that it was true, Linda couldn't understand how she'd failed to anticipate her daughter's suicide. One thing she never considered was that Matt could be responsible. "In the eleven years he'd been a part of our family, we'd never even had a cross word," Linda would say later. "We really believed that for reasons we would never understand, Kari had decided she could no longer go on."

After services, Matt and the girls joined Linda and Jim at Nancy's father-in-law's ranch for a barbecue. Kensi and Grace were quieter than usual. "They appeared to be trying to make the most of it," Nancy says. "They were sad, but they were little girls, and they were trying to have a good time."

Nancy noticed that Matt ate well, going back for seconds. "It looks like Kari's dying didn't hurt his appetite," she noted.

* * *

During the following week, the phone calls were frequent and long between Nancy, Kay, Jennifer, and Lindsey. The more they talked, the more certain they became that Matt had murdered Kari. They made lists of the reasons they believed he'd done it, a list that kept growing and included all they'd noticed over the years, including Matt's attitude toward women. They noted the way Matt kept talking about Kari's being depressed when none of them saw that in her. Would a sick Kari, as Matt described her, ask him to pick up a movie at 11:15? They didn't believe it. And Kari would not have been in the bed nude; that they all agreed. It wasn't in her nature. At times they talked about the Unisom bottle. All of them knew Kari bought generic brands. Farther down on the list they added the things Kari had told Bristol, the typed, unsigned suicide note, and the note itself, the way it praised Matt and didn't even mention Kari's brother.

There were reasons, they agreed, but still they wondered, were they being fair? "We talked about how none of us liked Matt," says Nancy. "He was boorish, said the wrong things, and we didn't like the way he talked to women. But we didn't want the police to go after him. We just wanted them to investigate what happened to Kari."

Meanwhile, Linda and Jim, even in their grief, continued to try to support Kari's family. Although Adam had never particularly liked Matt, Kari's brother wrote his brother-in-law a note. In it, Adam told Matt that he cared for him and the girls, and that he hoped that he'd be able to continue to be a part of all their lives.

The week after Easter, Matt dropped in on Linda and Jim. The young widower said he'd been thinking and that he could now see that Kari had been suicidal "for a long time." The woman he described was one who returned from work to spend an hour or more in her bedroom unable to cope.

"What're you talking about?" Linda asked, perplexed. "Kari went to her bedroom to watch *Oprah*. She recorded the shows and watched them when she got home. After that, she went to the girls' events, like Kensi's swimming."

"No," Matt said. "Kari had really stopped taking care of the girls a long time ago. I was the one giving them their baths, fixing their hair, cooking the meals."

"Why are you saying these things?" Linda asked. "They're not true."

Despite her protests, Matt insisted, even insinuating that Linda, who talked to her daughter daily, didn't really know Kari. When Linda again brought up the subject of counseling for the girls, she was shocked by her son-in-law's reaction.

"Grace has already moved on," he said. "She's looking for a new mother."

"Are you crazy, Matt?" Linda asked. "This is a child who just lost her mother and doesn't know how to express her grief. What Grace and Kensi need is counseling."

Not bending, Matt insisted that the girls were adjusting well. Linda was horrified when he then said, "Grace told me, 'Now I can jump on the bed and Mommy can't get mad because she's dead.'"

After he left, Linda thought about what Matt had said, and she knew it wasn't true. She considered how different he looked, how eager he was to go on with his life. She thought about the woman who'd seen him in the grocery store with another woman. And Linda thought about Kari, trying to understand how she could have taken her own life.

Since their daughter's death, Jim had hovered protectively over Linda, and now she asked him a favor. She'd seen the suicide note that night, but couldn't even recall what it said. What she did remember was that Adam wasn't mentioned and that it was unusually short for her talkative daughter. "Go to the police department," she said. "Look at it, and tell me if it sounds like Kari wrote it."

Jim did, talking to Sergeant Cooper, who retrieved the note to show him. Jim read it, nodded, and said, "Thanks. We're satisfied."

At home, Linda asked Jim, "Did Kari write the note?"

"Yes," he said. "I think so."

"Okay then," Linda said with a nod. Later, she'd think about that day, and say, "We were trying to make ourselves believe that Kari had done this. We wanted to believe it."

Around April 13, Jenny Monsey called Matt and offered to help with the party Kari had been planning for Kensi's tenth birthday, scheduled for the twenty-first.

"Do you know who Vanessa Bulls is?" Matt asked.

"The music minister's daughter," Jenny answered.

"Yes," Matt said. "She's going to help, too."

"Okay," Jenny said, thinking it wasn't anything unusual.

That Friday, Jenny arrived at the house and found Vanessa and Matt decorating. Matt had already filled Jenny in on the plans. He had a limo to pick up the girls and Kensi's friends at school. Then they would drop Grace off with Linda and Jim and drive to the house for a slumber party. Jenny was supposed to stay overnight to help with the girls and be with them while he and Vanessa ran out to pick up breakfast the next morning.

When they finished decorating, Matt told Jenny, "Vanessa and I are going to pick up the girls in the limo."

Once Vanessa and Matt left, Jenny looked around the living room. All the photos of Kari were gone. She looked through the rest of the house and saw none. She peeked in Kari's closet and saw it had already been emptied. Then, on the refrigerator, she saw a photo of Vanessa with her daughter, Lilly, Kensi, and Grace. Jenny dialed her brother's number. Todd was coming over later to help with the party, but on the phone, Jenny filled him in, and said, "Something isn't right here."

"Well, maybe it's too hard on Matt to see them all the time," Todd said.

Jenny thought about that. "Well, maybe."

At the elementary school, the teachers had heard that a limo was arriving to whisk Kensi and the partygoers away. Many stood outside after school, waiting when it pulled up. The first one out of the limo was Matt; then a woman's leg emerged, followed by a beautiful young blonde wearing a long brown skirt with a tight white T-shirt, capped by a hot pink shrug that tied just under her breasts. Excited, Kensi and Grace ran to their father, followed by three of Kensi's friends invited to the sleepover. With a flourish, Matt pulled out a birthday tiara and placed it on Kensi, then handed out vinyl leis to all the girls. Someone snapped photos as they bunched together in front of the sparkling white limo. In the pictures, Kensi smiled broadly, showing where she was still missing two of her front teeth.

After they left, the teachers at Spring Valley looked at each other, wondering. Kari had been dead for not quite two weeks, and Matt had shown up with a woman to pick up the girls, a young, beautiful woman, one he put his arm around when they took the photos. "What the heck?" one of the teachers said. "This is just inappropriate."

"Oh, my gosh," Linda thought when Vanessa got out of the limo at the house. Matt had mentioned that the music minister's daughter had offered to help with the party, but as soon as she saw the young blonde with Matt, Linda sensed that the relationship wasn't platonic. Grace ran to her grandmother, and Linda turned to Jim, and said, "Matt's going to marry that girl."

That evening, Linda again wondered what it all meant but then chastised herself. Matt, after all, was still alive. He had to go on. Despite the pain it caused her, she was determined to keep that in mind and accept whatever happened. To Jim she said, "As long as that girl loves Kensi and Grace, if she's a good mother, it's okay." Yet she feared, what if Matt cut them out of Kensi's and Grace's lives?

That evening at the Crested Butte house, the girls played, and Matt took more photos, including of Vanessa clowning with Kensi and her friends in their pajamas, batting a balloon, and playing a spirited game of keep-away. Strewn with crepe paper and banners, pillows scattered around the floor, it didn't look like a house in mourning.

Todd arrived, and Matt introduced Vanessa as someone

from church. "I wondered why he didn't ask Linda to help," Todd would say later. Like his sister, Todd then looked around the house and noticed that every trace of Kari had been wiped away and that Vanessa's photo was on the refrigerator. It was as if Matt had excised Kari from their lives and replaced her.

"Where are Kari's things?" Todd asked.

"I thought it was best for the girls if we put them away," Matt answered.

Later, it would turn out that Matt kept a few items of Kari's that he had a purpose for. That night, the girls dressed Matt and Todd in Kari's dresses and made them up with her cosmetics. "I don't remember whose idea it was," Todd said later. The girls decided they wanted to bake cookies, so a trip to the store was planned. "And then they said we had to go to Walmart."

A first-year teacher, Todd worried about being seen in the store wearing women's clothing but decided he had no options. "Kensi had just lost her mom. I figured that it was the least I could do for her." Matt, despite his position as a pastor of a church, didn't seem at all concerned. They were at the store for only minutes when a woman from church saw them. Todd felt embarrassed, but Matt just smiled.

Back at the house, confused by all that was happening, Todd put his own clothes back on. He'd planned to spend the night but instead left about midnight. Jenny stayed, playing with the girls and watching Matt and Vanessa. At one point, she saw them go into the bedroom. Jenny called Todd, asking what to do. "If you don't feel comfortable, leave," he said.

But Jenny wanted the party to be special for Kensi, so she stayed. Then, about 2:00 A.M., Jenny walked out of the kitchen into the living room. The girls were watching a movie, and Matt was seated on the couch. She felt ill when she saw Vanessa's head on his lap.

That was enough. "I'm leaving," she said.

"Who'll take care of the girls when I take Vanessa to pick up breakfast?" Matt asked.

"One of you can stay here while the other one goes," she answered.

At ten the following morning, mothers began arriving at the Baker house to pick up their daughters and found the girls at the house with Matt and Vanessa. Combined with Vanessa's appearance in the limo at the school the day before, rumors spread through Hewitt in concentric circles, like ripples from a stone thrown in the nearby Brazos River.

Chapter 29

After the slumber party, Matt began showing up at Spring Valley Elementary to pick up the girls with Vanessa Bulls and Lilly in the car. Many of the teachers noticed. "It looked suspicious," says one. "At the very least, it was in bad taste."

It was about that time that Heather Sigler, who worked behind the counter at the Kay Jewelers at Waco's Richland Mall, saw Matt walk in with his daughters and a young blonde carrying a baby. Sigler knew Kari and Matt from attending one of his churches, and she'd seen the Bakers off and on in the store. In fact, Matt and Kari had stopped in at Kay Jewelers just weeks before her death.

This time, however, Vanessa was the one shopping, quickly sidling up to the counter that held the glittering diamond engagement rings. "How do you like this one?" Vanessa asked Matt, pointing at the case.

"It doesn't matter," Matt said. "You're the one who'll be wearing it."

Shocked, Sigler hung back and watched. She didn't yet know that Kari was dead or the identity of the woman Matt Baker seemed so taken with.

As April ground on, Linda had the unmistakable impression that Matt was easing her and Jim from their granddaughters' lives. When she asked, he refused to let her pick them up from school, saying the girls were in an after-school program they enjoyed. Yet both the girls told Linda that the program was boring. Later, Grace said they were actually going to a friend's house after school.

Unbeknownst to Linda, her sisters and niece continued to debate how to tell her their suspicions. Then on the Saturday of the week following Easter, they all talked again. While they understood that Linda was grieving, they weren't seeing any cooperation from Hewitt PD, and their conclusion was that there was no other way; Linda had to be told. That afternoon, Nancy called Linda, and once she had her on the phone, she said, "Linda, there are some things I need to tell you. We don't believe that Kari killed herself."

Linda thought for a moment. "What are you saying?"

"We believe Matt murdered her."

Silence, then Linda said, "No."

To explain, Nancy recounted Bristol's session with Kari.

At first, Linda couldn't process what she was hearing, but then she became angry. How could her sister say such a thing? "No!" Linda ordered. "This isn't true, and I want you to stop talking like this. Matt is my granddaughters' father."

The next morning, Matt was at the pulpit at Crossroads, and Kensi and Grace sat with Jim and Linda. She felt Kensi's forehead, and it was hot. Realizing Kensi wasn't well, Linda asked if she and Jim could take both the girls home with them, so Kensi could rest. Appearing reluctant, Matt agreed.

"You're being a real drama queen," Matt told Kensi, as they walked to the car.

"But my throat hurts," the child responded.

To Linda, Matt looked annoyed.

On the way home, Jim drove through a take-out window and picked up fried chicken for Sunday dinner. At the house, Grace played, but Kensi went straight to bed. Then about 1:00 P.M., Matt stopped over on his way to WCY for afternoon chapel with play clothes for the girls. In the kitchen, Linda offered him chicken, and while he filled a glass with ice and water out of the refrigerator dispenser, she asked him about what Nancy had told her the day before. "Matt, would you help me understand something Kari told Jo Ann Bristol?" she said. "Kari said she looked in your briefcase and found pills. She was worried enough about them to think you might be planning to cause her harm. Will you help me understand why they were in your briefcase?"

As Linda listened, Matt repeated the story Kari had relayed to Bristol, that the pills were from Waco Center for Youth residents who'd spit them into his briefcase. "It happens all the time," he said. "They hide them in their mouths, and then find a place to stash them. I reported it at work to security."

"Okay," Linda said. "That makes sense."

While the girls were with Linda and Jim, in the chapel at WCY that day, Matt's sermon was a very personal one. "I'm angry at my wife for dying," he told the residents. Some of those on staff wondered if he should have been breaking the rule that barred discussing personal matters with residents. None said anything about the transgression, but afterward one employee expressed her sympathies. This time, Matt's attitude was markedly different than it had been during his sermon. "Oh, well," he said. "It doesn't matter. We didn't love each other anyway."

That afternoon, at the Dulin household, Linda and Jim nursed Kensi and played with Grace, but at five thirty, when Matt came to pick the girls up to take them to evening services at Crossroads, Kensi still had a fever. "Why don't you let them stay?" Linda asked. "They don't need to go to the service. They usually spend it in the playroom anyway."

Matt looked so reluctant that Linda thought, *He doesn't want them around us.*

"Can't we stay?" Grace pleaded. "I want to stay with Grammy." Finally, he said yes, but then Matt sat on the edge of the bed and whispered to Kensi.

After her son-in-law left, Linda asked, "Can you tell me what your dad said?"

"He said this is the last time we can stay here on a Sunday evening," Kensi answered.

A short time later, the doorbell rang, and Nancy, Kay, and Lindsey walked in. Linda had been expecting them. She'd asked them over to talk about what Nancy had said on the phone. While her granddaughters watched television in the bedroom, Linda invited her sisters and niece to the patio table, where they'd sat on the evening after Kari died.

"We don't believe Kari killed herself," Kay said as soon as they'd all taken their places.

"Kari is dead," Linda replied. "I know that this doesn't make any sense. There was absolutely nothing in Kari that made me think she would take her own life, but we have to accept this."

"Linda, you're not listening to us," Nancy protested.

As Linda sat stunned, Nancy, Lindsey, and Kay opened up about all they'd seen of Matt Baker over the years, for the first time telling Linda about the accusations women had made against him, including Lindsey's friend Erin, the girl Matt propositioned down the hall from Kassidy's hospital room.

Linda appeared stunned, but Nancy refused to back down. "We don't believe Kari killed herself. We don't."

"What's the alternative?" Linda asked, her mind resting uncomfortably on the only conclusion. "If Kari didn't kill herself, what are you saying? That she was murdered?"

"Kari thought Matt was trying to kill her," Kay said. "Think about that, Linda."

"No. That can't be true," Linda protested. "It's not."

"Linda, if we don't find out why Kari said those things to Bristol, this will haunt us forever," Kay said. The pause was uncomfortably long, as all the women looked at each other, wondering who should speak next.

"Linda, you have to understand," said Kay, her long blond hair held in a ponytail, and her hands fisted on her lap. "We all believe Matt may have murdered Kari."

Linda, however, wouldn't budge, either. "Matt's the father

of my two granddaughters, all we have left of Kari," she said, sternly. "I won't hear this. I won't. And I want you to back off. Do you understand?"

The women looked at each other, and nodded. "Okay," Kay agreed. "It's dropped."

Afterward, they all hugged Linda good-bye at her front door, then the women walked out to their cars on the street. Linda shut the door and went back inside the house, and as soon as she was gone, Lindsey asked, "Are we going to drop it?"

"No," Kay said. "Absolutely not."

Chapter 30

As the days passed, it became increasingly apparent to Linda and Jim that Matt was putting up barriers between them and their granddaughters. After listening to Linda's fears, on April 26, Kay sent Matt an e-mail asking him to please remember that the Dulins loved their granddaughters and to try to include them in their lives. Matt replied that the Dulins had to come to terms with their daughter's death. He then unloaded on Kari, repeating much of what he'd said to others since her death, labeling her a bad wife and an uninvolved mother.

That evening, Kay forwarded both the e-mails, hers and Matt's, to Linda. She read them, disbelieving that Matt would say such things. Upset, she wrote Matt an e-mail she called, "A message from my heart." In it, she recounted how Kari loved Matt and the girls, what a wonderful mother Kari had been. She then reminded Matt that she and Jim loved not only Kari but also all of them.

At 11:11 that same evening, Matt responded, saying that he didn't doubt Linda's love. Then, despite having done so just hours earlier in the e-mail to Kay, he said, "But please don't question my love or devotion to Kari. I will never disparage the memory of Kari. In fact, I have in every way tried to protect you and Jim from any comments that could be construed as damaging to Kari's memory."

Acknowledging that the Dulins were in pain, Matt said that he and the girls, too, were suffering. Throughout, he talked of Kari's depression, claiming that the doctor who'd seen her the week before her death had called him to recommend a therapist, and that the physician remarked at having seen "in Kari's eyes what he called a 'tiredness' that worried him."

Throughout the e-mail, Matt focused on his feelings: "I am grieving—I am hurting—I am trying hard to stay strong for the girls—I am crying with them when they cry . . . I lost a wife and my little girls lost a mother—I am trying to keep everyone happy."

Much of it centered on how hard he was working for others, his missive filling two single-spaced pages. In the end, he wrote: "Please know that I love you guys much. You are family." Yet, what followed read like a warning: "I will do anything I feel necessary for the health of my children. I am not as concerned with other's [sic] feelings at this time."

In early May, Linda's confusion multiplied when she heard that Matt was telling others that Kari's interview for the middle-school job hadn't gone well on that final day of her life. Linda wondered why he was saying that when she knew that it wasn't true. Then a Spring Valley elementary-school mom called Linda. Matt was working on Kensi's fourth-grade talent show. "He's acting like a teenager with a new girlfriend," the woman said. "He's on the phone all the time, giggling. It's like he's giddy."

The uncertainty welled within Linda, and she didn't know what to do. Could her sisters be right? "I didn't believe any of it was possible," she'd say later. "But at the same time, I couldn't understand why Matt was acting the way he was."

To work her way through the bewilderment, Linda called Bristol and asked her about Kari's final session. As she had to others, the therapist recounted what had happened that day. When she repeated what Kari had said about finding the pills, something struck Linda as odd: Why would the pills have been crushed if the residents were spitting them in Matt's briefcase? It didn't make sense. Afterward, Linda called Kay, who knew someone who worked at WCY. "Ask if the kids could have been hiding the pills in Matt's brief-case," Linda asked. "And ask her if Matt filed a report with security."

Kay agreed, then called later to relay the conversation: "She says that couldn't happen. They watch the kids to make sure they swallow the pills, and if Matt had notified security, everyone would have been told to be on alert. That didn't happen."

Still, Linda fought the idea that Matt could have done anything to Kari. "I just couldn't let my mind go there," she said. "It was horrible enough to lose Kari without thinking that Matt might have murdered her."

Field day, a day when the children at Spring Valley played outside running relays and having fun, an event parents and grandparents often attended, came and went, and Matt never told Jim or Linda. Mother's Day approached, and Linda e-mailed Matt: "I imagine that you have something special to do in Kari's memory with the girls. I would love it if you and the girls would have lunch/dinner with us as well."

In his response, Matt said Linda's plans sounded good and that he knew the girls would enjoy a short trip Jim and Linda had planned with them over the summer. Filling them in on the date for Grace's upcoming kindergarten gradua-tion, Friday, May 26, he said that Kensi was "all into rab-bits" and Grace was learning how to play cards. It was a congenial e-mail, one with no sign of strife.

The Saturday before Mother's Day, Jill Hotz drove to Waco to help Matt. She spent the day cleaning the house, cooking dinners for Matt and the girls and freezing them for future use. It was hard not to see how much the house had changed. She noticed that all the photos of Kari were gone, and she saw the same photo Todd and Jenny had, the one of Vanessa with the girls. While Jill worked, Matt and the girls circu-lated through. "Matt complained about Linda a lot," says Jill. "So was Kensi, parroting what her dad said."

When Jill began ironing, Matt complained, "Kari never could iron."

Jill's husband, Stephen, was there as well, and he and Matt began talking about seafood, Matt complaining that Kari had never let them eat it, and prodding Kensi to complain as well. Yet what Jill remembered was that Matt ordered hamburgers when they went to seafood restaurants. "It was like, Kari was so domineering she had a no-fish rule," says Jill. "It was weird. Kari was dead, and Matt was blaming her for everything."

For Jill, the day was especially hard. She'd been feeling guilty about the suicide, convinced that as a good friend, she should have seen the signs. "I'd cry in my car. I felt like I must have been the worst friend in the world not to have known that Kari was so depressed," she says. "But Kari never sounded depressed to me."

The following morning, Mother's Day, a little more than one month after Kari's death, Kensi hung back from her grandparents at church. The ten-year-old didn't even appear excited to see her uncle Adam, whom she'd always adored. When he walked up to her, Kensi bristled, ordering: "Leave me alone."

Matt was busy at WCY that afternoon, and he'd agreed to allow the girls to go to the Dulins' family celebration. Yet Linda sensed something was very wrong. "Kensi, I love you," Linda said to her oldest granddaughter.

In response, the child glared at her.

At her house that afternoon, while extended family gathered around, Kay continued the tradition Kari had begun seven years earlier after Kassidy's death. She put out two candles, one in memory of Kassidy and the second in remembrance of Kari. "Would you like to light them?" Kay asked Kensi and Grace.

Shaking her head, Kensi's eyes filled with tears. Knowing her granddaughter was hurting, Linda took the ten-year-old to Kay's bedroom.

"What's wrong?" Linda asked.

"I am mad at you. You were mean to my daddy," Kensi said.

At first, Linda couldn't understand what Kensi meant. It took a while to wade through the confusion, but it soon emerged that Matt had shown his oldest an e-mail from Linda, one in which she asked why he was telling others that Kari was a bad mother and asked what his plans were with Vanessa. "Why do you have to be so mean to Daddy?" Kensi demanded. Holding up three fingers, she said, "You sent him three bad e-mails! He didn't like the questions you asked about Vanessa!"

Explaining that the e-mails were intended for adults, Linda said she'd simply inquired about Matt's plans. "I know you love your daddy, and I would never do anything to intentionally hurt him," Linda said. "I love you all too much."

"My daddy says you won't move on," Kensi said.

Shocked, Linda struggled for the right words. "I am trying to grieve. I won't forget, and I hope you won't forget your mother."

"We like Vanessa," Kensi said. "And Daddy says you don't like Vanessa."

"We just think it's too early," Linda said.

"We don't think so," Kensi said. "We like Vanessa!"

At that, Linda decided that to ease her granddaughter's distress, she had to let it go. "Then I'm fine with it," Linda said. "I just want you and Gracie to be happy."

Linda talked to Kensi for half an hour, and at the end, they both emerged from the bedroom laughing. But early the next morning, Matt sent Linda an e-mail accusing her of interrogating Kensi, even saying that Linda had physically pulled her granddaughter to the bedroom, hurting her. "Kensi mentioned the context and the manner in which you pursued her even after she attempted to walk away. I was shocked to hear what she had to say."

Linda e-mailed Matt back: "I told Kensi that I was not going to e-mail you again because I didn't want to take a chance that my direct communication style could be mis-

construed. However, I did want to take one final time to reassure you how much we love you and the girls. We want
nothing but for all of you to be happy."

Yet, when Matt responded, he sounded even angrier: "I
noticed that you did not mention anything about grabbing
Kensi's arm to make her continue talking to you or asking
probing questions about Vanessa or the Bulls family . . . I
know that you have always been the 'nosey-in-law'—and I
do not say that as a compliment. I will inform you and Jim of
events/dates/happenings that you need to be made aware of,
but other things will stay in my house where they belong."

By mid-May, there was no doubt that the good relationship the Dulins had with Matt was cratering. So many things
simply didn't seem right, including that Matt had never ordered a headstone for Kari's grave. The church had given
him money to pay for one, but Matt hadn't followed through.
Jim talked to him about the situation, but to no avail. When
Matt said he was deciding on the inscription, Linda e-mailed
suggestions. That Kari's grave remained unmarked bothered Jim so much that he wanted to buy a headstone. Linda
wouldn't hear of it. "Matt needs to do something for Kari,"
she said.

In the end, Matt ordered one with Kari's name and dates
and the phrase: "Always in our hearts."

It would turn out that Mother's Day was the final time
Matt voluntarily allowed the girls to spend time with Jim
and Linda. From that point on, he kept them apart, to the
extent that he even left the girls with others while he was
at Crossroads on Sunday mornings, ensuring that the girls
didn't see their grandparents during services. Meanwhile,
more reports came in from friends and family who said they
saw Matt with Vanessa and that they'd heard Matt say un-
flattering things about Kari.

Despite her reluctance even to consider that her sisters
could be right, that her son-in-law could have murdered her
daughter, one afternoon Linda thought about just that as she
walked out to the mailbox and found her AT&T bill. On her

way back to the house, she thought about Matt and Kari, and remembered how she'd agreed to have them on her cell-phone account. "I'm just so mad, I think I'll cancel Matt's account," Linda told Lindsey on the phone.

"No, don't do that," Lindsey said. "Get the records. Look at his phone calls."

Angry and hurt, Linda called AT&T. When she had a service rep on the line, she asked, "May I get copies of all the phone calls made on this account, for all the phones?"

"It's your account, so yes you can," the man said. "I'll have them sent out to you. But you can also access them on the Internet."

After she ordered copies of three months' billing, Linda logged onto her AT&T account on the Web. Once there, she paused, afraid. "Okay, God," she prayed. "Help me. If there's something I should know, give me some kind of sign."

At that, she pulled up Matt's cell records and looked at the numbers he called in the days following Kari's death. Quickly, Linda noticed one particular number in Troy, one Matt called often, including the morning of Kari's death and the evening after the funeral. When she Googled it, Linda discovered that the number belonged to the Bulls family. It was then that Linda pulled up Matt's previous bills and saw that the calls to the Bulls residence had begun months before Kari died.

Finally, Linda scanned Matt's most recent statements, covering the month since Kari's death. What she saw confused her at first: Matt was calling his dead wife's cell phone. From April 17 through 26 alone, Matt had called Kari's number 181 times for a total of 1,610 minutes. During the following ten days, Matt made 384 calls to Kari's phone and talked for a total of 2.19 hours.

Whom is he talking to? Linda wondered. And then she realized what he must have done. Only one thing made sense; Matt had given Kari's cell phone to someone. Could it have been Vanessa?

Based on the evidence she had before her, Linda could

only surmise that Matt's relationship with Vanessa had started months before Kari's death. And since Kari's death, Matt had called nearly nonstop, starting as soon as he dropped the girls off at school in the mornings.

Saving the phone records on her computer, Linda called Lindsey. When Lindsey heard about the calls to the Bulls's household months before Kari died, she was furious. "I'm going to whomp that woman," she said.

Linda calmed her down. "I need your help," she said. "Let's find out what's going on here. Research these phone numbers for me. Find out who else Matt's calling."

Once Lindsey agreed, they hung up, and Linda ran another search, this one on Unisom caplets, scanning the information she could find on the computer on overdoses. She'd done a cursory search right after Kari died, but now Linda pored over medical journals and perused medical Web sites. "What I found was that it would take an awful lot of Unisom to kill someone," she says.

That night, Linda talked to Jim, who was at summer camp for the National Guard. After she told him about the phone bills, she said, "Jim, there's something wrong here."

Chapter 31

"**K**ari loved life. In her deepest sorrow, she loved life," Linda would say years later. "I just kept trying to convince myself that she committed suicide. I didn't want Matt to be a murderer. But once I saw those phone bills, I had to know what had really happened."

When Todd visited Matt that spring, Matt complained about Kari's family. "Maybe I'll move the girls to a different district," Matt said. "I'd like distance from the Dulins."

Perhaps he realized Linda was questioning. That wouldn't have been a reach after AT&T mistakenly sent the records Linda requested to Matt's address. Later, he'd say that he immediately realized that his mother-in-law was looking at his phone bills. Not long after, Linda received a call from a friend who saw Matt and Vanessa at a fast-food restaurant and another who saw them shopping for cell phones.

Meanwhile, still struggling with what to believe, Linda met with Jo Ann Bristol, to hear in person what Kari had told her. As she had to others since that day, Bristol carefully laid out her final session with Kari, talking of how excited Kari was about the prospect of the new job and finding a way to work with parents who'd lost children. When Bristol turned to the conversation about Matt, however, Linda felt her heart sinking. As the therapist relayed Kari's fears, for the first time Linda had a glimpse into why Kari suffered from anxiety in the final weeks of her life. "Kari was trying to make sense of it all, but still not trusting her instincts," Linda would say later. "Listening to Jo Ann, I hurt for my child. I wished I had known. I wanted to hold Kari. But I couldn't. My daughter was dead."

Afterward, Linda talked with Jim, relaying all she'd learned. With little discussion, they agreed Kari's death needed to be investigated. From what her sisters and niece had said, however, they concluded that Hewitt PD wasn't interested in looking into a death they'd already written off as suicide. Yet Linda wasn't without help. Nancy, Kay, and Lindsey were as eager as she was to uncover the truth.

In the days that followed, e-mails and phone calls flew back and forth among the women, Linda divvying up tasks, issuing orders about who should do what. Before long, the women had renamed themselves. Linda was Charlie, the leader, and began even signing her e-mails that way, and Nancy, Kay, and Lindsey were the angels. Their task, the one they'd gladly accepted, was to look into the strange circumstances surrounding Kari Lynn Dulin Baker's death.

One Friday afternoon, Matt's day off, Lindsey drove to Crested Butte hoping to see Vanessa arrive or leave. She sat there for hours, wondering whether or not Vanessa's car was inside the garage. On the street were piles of garbage. She thought about searching through it but worried that Matt would see her. She had to fight the urge to walk up to the door and tell him what she thought of him. She left that afternoon without ever seeing either Matt or Vanessa.

Another day, Lindsey received an early-morning call. "Your assignment is to call more of the numbers on Matt's phone bill," Linda said. "Let's find out what he's up to."

"Yes, Charlie," Lindsey said. "Will do!"

What Lindsey discovered was Matt was calling Realtors in Lorena, near Crossroads. Matt and Vanessa, it appeared, had been out shopping not just for an engagement ring but a house. Not long after, Linda heard from someone at church that her son-in-law was also looking at homes in Troy, near the Bulls's home.

Meanwhile, in the moments stolen between teaching classes, Linda did more investigating on the Net, much of it about Unisom. What she found were cases of children who took three times more of the drug than prescribed and didn't die. When someone did overdose, it appeared that the result was a slow death, which didn't seem to fit Matt's story. After all, he'd told Linda and Jim that Kari had been awake when he left and that he was only gone forty-five minutes. "That meant that she had to ingest the drugs and die all before he returned," says Linda. "I'm not an expert, but that doesn't make sense."

At other times, instructions went out to Linda's sisters, like the morning Linda e-mailed Nancy asking her to go to Hollywood Video to find out if Matt had done what he said he had the night of Kari's death. The e-mail was signed, "Charlie."

The next day, Nancy drove to the Hollywood Video on Hewitt Drive. Inside the store, she spoke with an assistant manager, a woman, explaining she was there to find out what time Matt was in the store and to get the surveillance tape from that night. Standing in the store with racks of DVDs fanning out around them, the manager said she couldn't give Nancy the surveillance video from the store cameras. "If the police need them, they can come in and get them."

"Okay," Nancy said. "But can you pull them for that night and keep them safe, so that nothing happens to them?"

That the assistant manager agreed to, along with reviewing the records and giving Nancy the time Matt checked out the Meg Ryan movie *When a Man Loves a Woman*: 11:48 P.M.

Then, as their efforts continued, there was another tragedy in Hewitt—one of Kay's friends lost a son to suicide. When Kay heard that Billy Martin had ordered an autopsy for the boy, she called Martin. "I just want to understand why there was no autopsy in my niece's death," Kay said.

"My understanding was that there was a handwritten suicide note," Martin responded.

"No, it was typed, and there was no signature," Kay said. She then detailed what they'd uncovered so far, including Kari's haunting words to Bristol. Stressing that they weren't saying they had proof Matt had killed Kari, Kay said, "We want someone to look into this."

"It definitely needs to be looked into," Martin said. "I'll call Hewitt PD today."

After relaying the conversation to Linda and the others, it was agreed that they would wait one day, giving Martin time to follow through.

The next day, Kay called Sergeant Cooper. He wasn't in and didn't return her call. The following morning, after still not hearing from Cooper, Kay asked to speak to the sergeant's boss, Captain Tuck Saunders. On the phone, she explained what had transpired with Martin. After listening, Saunders said Kari's death was Cooper's case and that the sergeant would call her back.

Meanwhile, that same afternoon, Lindsey and her sister, Ami, arrived at the house on Crested Butte. Lindsey had e-mailed voicing support, hoping Matt would talk to her. In one e-mail, he offered to let her look at what remained of Kari's things, to find a remembrance. Yet when she tried to set a time, he didn't respond. So Lindsey and Ami simply showed up.

At the house, all the drapes and blinds were down. Although it was bright sunshine outside, inside it was pitch-dark. Most of what Kari owned was gone, but Matt showed Lindsey a memory box he'd put together for the girls, including wedding photos and his wedding ring. Kari's diamond engagement ring wasn't there. Kensi and Grace were quiet that afternoon, as they had been often since their mother's death. Like Jenny and Todd before her, Lindsey noticed that all the photos of Kari were gone and saw the one with the girls and Vanessa on the refrigerator.

"I'm just looking for something to remember Kari by,"

Lindsey said, flipping through the box. "I still miss her so much. I want the memories of her to help me move on."

"Well, some people aren't able to move on, are they, Kensi?" Matt asked his oldest, who sat nearby. "Who isn't able to move on in this family?"

At first, Kensi didn't answer, but Matt asked again. The girls had always called their grandmother Grammy, but Kensi finally said, "Linda can't move on."

Hearing Kensi call her grandmother by her first name hit Lindsey hard. "It was just so strange," she says. "That wasn't Kensi."

Nothing of Kari's beyond the memory box remained in the house. In the garage, looking through a few things Matt stored there, Lindsey talked about a movie she wanted to see. Saying he'd wanted to see the movie as well, Matt categorized it as a date movie. Not wanting to interject what she knew about Vanessa Bulls, Lindsey said, "Well, maybe someday that will happen."

"According to you know who, I already have a date, right Kensi?" Matt said. When Kensi didn't answer, Matt said again, "Right Kensi? Grammy thinks I've been dating."

The next day, May 18, Cooper finally called Kay. Grateful to have the sergeant's ear, Kay filled him in on her conversation with Judge Martin and again stressed all that Kari had told Bristol. In response, Cooper asked for the therapist's number. Kay gave it to him, but when Kay talked to Bristol the next day, Cooper hadn't contacted her. With Sergeant Cooper continuing to act disinterested in the case, Linda talked the situation over with Jim, who decided it was time for a personal meeting with the sergeant.

The following morning was a Friday, and Kay and Jim walked together through the doors into the small entry of Hewitt PD's modest offices. The receptionist notified Cooper, who escorted them to an office.

On the desk, Jim laid out paperwork he'd brought, including copies of the bills documenting that Matt was talking with Vanessa Bulls months before Kari's death. Going through the records, Jim showed the sergeant that Matt had even called Vanessa the morning of Kari's death and the evening after the funeral. "It appears this relationship has been going on for quite some time," Jim said.

"Why wasn't an autopsy done?" Kay asked yet again. "I've talked to people who know about these things, and they tell me it's standard procedure in a suicide case where the victim is young and healthy and leaves a typed suicide note."

"That was Judge Martin's decision," Cooper said, sounding defensive.

"How do we get the body exhumed then?" Kay demanded. "We need an autopsy!"

"You need to talk to the judge," Cooper said. "I can't issue that kind of an order."

As they talked, Kay's cell phone rang, and she walked from the room.

"Jo Ann Bristol's testimony will be important in this case," Cooper told Jim, while they were alone. "And we are going to need that autopsy."

When Kay returned, she pressed Cooper again about the autopsy, wanting to know why one wasn't ordered the night of Kari's death. "I could tell he was getting irritated with me," she'd say later. "He didn't like that question."

When Kay explained that Bristol was leaving in just days and would be out of the country for weeks, she suggested that the therapist come in that same afternoon to give a statement, but Cooper, to her dismay, said that wasn't necessary. "I'll tell her to come in today," Kay said, leaving no room for argument.

Bristol arrived at Hewitt PD a few hours later, bringing with her seven pages of notes she'd made on Kari's last session. After again recounting Kari's concerns about Matt, Bristol told the sergeant to call if he needed more. Cooper never called.

That same day, Linda received an e-mail from Matt, one

Kari Dulin and Matt Baker fell quickly in love, so much so that their parents feared that it could be a mistake.

Jim and Linda Dulin wanted to believe that Matt Baker was a good man.

Through it all, Barbara Baker stood by her son.

Kari on her wedding day surrounded by her mother and aunts, the women who would become Charlie's Angels. Left to right: Jennifer, Kay, Kari, Linda and Nancy.

They looked like the perfect family: the Reverend Matt Baker, Kensi, Kassidy, and Kari.

Friends say Kari doted on her girls, Kensi and Kassidy. At first both Baker girls looked happy and healthy, but that would change.

In her darkest times, Kari pored her grief into three journals, yearning for the return of all she'd lost.

The church members at Williams Creek erected a prayer garden in front of the church.

Kari named Grace, saying the child was by the grace of God: here, the Baker family in 2003: Grace, Matt, Kari, and Kensi.

Kari playing in the snow, with Kensi and Grace.

Kari with Kensi and Grace at a church function.

The prim, redbrick house on Crested Butte where the Bakers moved in 2005.

Kari and Jenny Monsey joking around in the church kitchen with balloon breasts.

At the girls' sporting events Kari was always in the stands cheering them on

In her Bible, Kari wrote a plea to God, asking him to protect her from harm.

The Unisom bottle and the suicide note.

Not long after his wife's death, Matt Baker, with Kensi and Grace.

In the fall of 2005, the music minister's daughter, Vanessa Bulls, began attending Crossroads.
Trial exhibit

The limo for Kensi's birthday party, with Matt Baker and Vanessa Bulls, far right. Kensi, wearing tiara, and Grace, front row in front of her father.

Texas Ranger Matt Cawthon wanted to pursue the case but found little cooperation from the Hewitt Police Department.

Bill Johnston was a former U.S. prosecutor, one who'd stepped on toes. He knew how to investigate a case and who to get to help him.

Retired deputy U.S. Marshal Mike McNamara and retired undercover DPS agent John Bennett, who delved into Matt Baker's dark past.

Shannon Gamble, whose son thought the world of his teacher, Kari Baker. When Kari died, Shannon rallied others behind the cause.

Summer 2006, Vanessa Bulls in Matt Baker's new truck.
Trial exhibit

The bumper stickers: a campaign waged throughout Central Texas, as many fought for Justice for Kari.

Guy James Gray was a well-known Texas prosecutor who'd become a defense attorney. In the end, many wondered if the switch had sat well with him.

Abdon Rodriguez, an investigator in the McLennan County DA's office, knew how to lean on a source to get information.

Kari's daughters, Kensi and Grace, were all Jim and Linda Dulin had left of their daughter, and they feared for their safety.

The grand old lady, the McLennan County Courthouse, where the drama would unfold.

Assistant DA Crawford Long took on the case with his fellow prosecutor Susan Shafer, after the McLennan County DA had turned his back on the Dulins for nearly four years.

Judge Ralph Strother controlled his courtroom, keeping a close eye on all involved.

in which he told her that the girls wouldn't be staying with them the coming Sunday afternoon, while he conducted chapel at WCY. A friend's mother had offered to take them shopping.

Tension was building, and Linda e-mailed Matt, inquiring about the upcoming fourth-grade talent show, in which Kensi would be performing. Linda had asked repeatedly when it was without a response, and this time she wrote. "I will get the info . . . the choice is yours. You just need to be on notice that you will NOT keep Jim and me from our granddaughters. No matter how much you are trying to poison them against us."

When he responded, Matt acted like the wronged party: "I am asking for the final time—STOP! Stop accusing me. Stop blaming me. Stop cursing my name. Stop trying to make it appear that I don't care for my girls properly. Stop! Please stop before it causes a rift too deep . . . I have been praying for my family and you and Jim every day."

"Enough of this—I will not be bullied by you," Linda responded. "Do not threaten me in e-mails or anywhere else."

Matt e-mailed again, this time telling Linda she wasn't dealing "properly" with Kari's death and saying that hurt the girls. "I can and will have to keep Kensi and Grace at a distance from you. Stop blaming me . . . Love, Kensi & Grace's FATHER, Matt Baker."

Through it all, Linda could feel her oldest granddaughter being pulled away. In some ways the area around Hewitt is a small town, and when Linda happened by chance upon Matt and the girls at Target, Grace ran to her, but Kensi hung back. "I love you!" Linda said, noticing that Kensi looked up warily at her father, who quickly shuffled the girls away.

It would turn out that Jim and Linda weren't in the audience at Kensi's talent show that month. Matt hadn't notified them of the day. Later, Linda heard that Vanessa was there, however, holding her infant, Lilly. Many of the teachers noticed them, whispering afterward about how strange it was with Kari dead not even two months.

* * *

Three days after Jim and Kay met with Cooper, Linda composed a letter for Jim to take to Hewitt PD. She'd thought of some things she believed the sergeant would like to know. "I wanted to write down a couple of events that Matt Baker described to me regarding the death of my daughter, Kari Baker . . . I just want to be sure you have as much information as possible to help you with this case," she said.

At that, she recounted the events as Matt had told them to her and Jim, everything from the trip to the video store to finding Kari. "I wanted you to have this information, so that you can use this time frame of events when you check the video rental time at Hollywood Video in Hewitt." Not wanting to outright tell the sergeant what to do, she then suggested he could inquire at the video store about the possibility of a surveillance video from the night of Kari's death.

Whether or not Cooper was interested in investigating, Linda was intent on making sure that he understood there were ways he could look into Matt's account of that night, including checking bank records. "Matt and Kari always used a debit card for fuel; you could get information regarding the fuel from the debit card. A toxicology report and autopsy will answer other questions about what she ingested," she pointed out.

The second area Linda wanted to clarify involved Bristol and the pills in Matt's suitcase. She recounted for Cooper how she approached Matt, asking him to "help me understand" where the pills had come from. He'd specifically said that he later reported the breach of security, the pills in his briefcase, to WCY security.

Already certain that Matt had never reported the pills, Linda suggested Cooper inquire with the facility's security. "How would a youth in the WCY facility have access to a bottle of pills?" she asked in her letter. "If pills were being stashed in Matt's briefcase, were other employees notified via e-mail or other means to be aware of such activities?"

Suspecting that the detective wouldn't be happy to hear

from her, Linda then tried to assuage his ego, telling Cooper that she appreciated his work on the case and that she knew he'd do everything possible "to ensure that the facts are uncovered so that we can know for certain what happened surrounding our daughter's death on April 8.

"I know you are a very qualified and competent officer. I don't mean to sound like I am telling you how to do your job in this letter. I just don't want to leave any stone unturned. My husband said you have two daughters. I know you can empathize with what we are going through."

When Jim dropped off the letter, Cooper assured him that the case was a priority, but Linda soon doubted the sergeant's sincerity. "He never even contacted me to ask any questions," she'd say later. "It was as if he'd never received it."

Unbeknownst to Linda and Jim, three days earlier Sergeant Cooper did take some action on the case, going to Waco Center for Youth and talking with Eddie Greenfield, the director, asking about the pills in Matt's briefcase.

"Did Matt report this to you?" Cooper asked.

"No. I have no record of any report like that," Greenfield said.

Perhaps that information, backing up what Kari's family had told him, might have spurred on the investigation. Yet, when Nancy checked back with Hollywood Video, the manager told her that the police still hadn't picked up the surveillance tape. "Release it to me then," she asked, but the manager said she couldn't.

Linda and Jim were in the audience at Grace's kindergarten graduation. When Jenny arrived, she sat with them, and a short time later, Matt entered with Vanessa, pushing Lilly in a stroller. Kensi walked in but didn't rush to Linda and Jim as she would have in the past, instead going directly to Matt on the other side of the room. When Jenny averted her eyes from Matt and Vanessa, Linda leaned over, and said, "You know?"

"I don't know what you're talking about," Jenny said.

"We'll talk afterward," Linda said, as they watched Grace queue up with the other kindergarteners in her gown and mortarboard.

Later, in the parking lot, Jenny described what she'd seen at Kensi's birthday party, including Vanessa's head on Matt's lap. "I didn't want to tell you. You had just lost your daughter," Jenny said.

"I don't blame you," Linda said. "I wouldn't have wanted to hear it." At that, she looked up and saw the hurt in Jim's eyes.

"Do you think Kari could have killed herself?" Linda asked.

"No." Jenny answered. After they parted, Jenny wrote out an account of everything she remembered about Kensi's birthday party. When she got it, Linda placed Jenny's notes in a growing stack of paperwork she was collecting in what was becoming her personal investigation into her daughter's death.

For Jim, the anger was building inside of him. He didn't like that. He was a military man, a man who took action. Sitting back and waiting for others to do something was an untenable situation. Linda was still at times unable to believe that Matt had truly murdered Kari, but Jim knew it with his heart, which ached. He felt the guilt of a father who was unable to protect a daughter.

Looking for an outlet, Jim went to a T-shirt shop at the mall, clutching a photo of Kerry with Kensi and Grace. The following Sunday when Matt stood at the Crossroads' pulpit, Linda and Jim sat in the front row, and Jim stared up at him, his eyes burning but a smile on his face, wearing a new T-shirt, one with the photograph of Kari with her beloved daughters front and center.

"Oh, I like your T-shirt," Matt said sarcastically afterward.

Jim just smiled.

The church seemed to be taking up little of Matt's attention that May. He repeatedly canceled Sunday evening services to spend time with Vanessa. He'd sold both his car and Kari's and bought a new four-door pickup, and he took a photo of Vanessa, her blond hair falling about her shoulders, a smile on her pretty face, behind the wheel. When the church flooded in a spring deluge, Matt walked through the sanctuary and said hello to those cleaning it up but didn't offer to help. Instead, he kept walking. He was on his way to Troy to visit Vanessa.

As May drew to a close, the Dulins became increasingly frustrated with Hewitt PD in general and Sergeant Cooper in particular. They continued to funnel him information as they uncovered it. Unaware of the actions he had taken, they saw no evidence that he was conducting any kind of investigation. Kay delivered information from the director of the Family Y regarding Matt's activities while he was there, the sexual harassment of young girls that resulted in his firing. But when she checked, Kay was told that Cooper never called the woman at the Y to follow up. When Kay visited Billy Martin to ask him about exhuming the body for an autopsy, Martin said he hadn't heard from anyone at Hewitt requesting one.

Meanwhile, Linda called experts who told her that every day an autopsy was postponed and Kari's body lay in the grave meant more evidence was lost. Searching for help, Linda consulted with a friend who suggested she contact the Texas Rangers. Linda did and talked with a veteran ranger named Matt Cawthon.

Tall and fit, Cawthon had steel blue eyes and a studied gaze that could cut to the quick. He'd started at DPS as a trooper in 1982, fulfilling a childhood dream. Seven years later, Cawthon was promoted to criminal intelligence and from there to the state's elite law-enforcement group, the Texas Rangers. Over the years, he'd worked on vice, homicide, theft, gambling, and corruption cases. One murder-for-hire case took him to Honduras, where he uncovered a child-pornography ring. For that, he was honored as a policeman of the year, and Janet Reno, then the attorney general, gave him an award.

On the phone, he listened quietly to Linda, not at all surprised. He'd encountered other officers and police departments over the years who'd dug their heels in once they made a decision, unwilling to reconsider when they were presented with evidence that suggested their take on a case was wrong. But the Rangers have a tradition of rarely entering a case except at the invitation of local police.

"You need to go through channels," Cawthon said. "You need to talk to the detective in charge in Hewitt, and then you need to talk to the chief. Once you've done that, if they don't help you, you can write a letter to the district attorney and ask him to request our assistance."

Linda listened, took notes, and thanked him.

It was on May 26 that Jim and Linda arrived at Hewitt PD for yet another conference with Cooper, asking if he had done anything toward getting Kari's body exhumed. "We don't have any probable cause for an autopsy," Cooper replied.

Linda couldn't believe what she heard. Texas law allowed autopsies of any questionable death, and she believed that they'd certainly given Cooper enough evidence to find that to be true. "Isn't the information from Kari's therapist probable cause?" Linda asked.

"No, we need evidence for probable cause. I am not sure that we will ever be able to do an autopsy. The judge wants more," Cooper said.

Frustrated and growing angry, Linda noticed that Cooper wasn't taking notes. When he asked Linda where Matt banked, she'd had enough, telling the detective that she'd given him that information weeks earlier. "Are you doing any work on this case yourself, or are you waiting for me to do it all for you?" she asked. "I'm done talking to you. I want to talk to the person in charge."

After Captain Tuck Saunders walked into the room, the

discussion continued. Linda and Jim continued to prod. As they would later recount it, Cooper eventually said that he had no way of knowing what Martin would say about an autopsy since he'd never talked to the judge about one.

"I want to remain calm with you," Linda said.

"You don't have to. There's nothing you can do to upset me," Cooper responded.

"You told us you were trying to get an autopsy and the judge was resisting," Linda said. "So, Sergeant, which one is it? Billy Martin won't exhume my daughter's body, or you haven't even talked to him? Let's get this story right."

Furious, Cooper stalked out, leaving them alone with Saunders. In his reports, the sergeant had written that he'd talked with the justice of the peace a week earlier about the case and that Martin was the one who'd told him that they'd need evidence to dig up Kari's body. Cooper had perhaps interpreted the conversation as the judge saying that he needed clear-cut proof of a homicide. In his report, the sergeant had discounted everything the Dulins had given them, typing: *I have no definite indication of any criminal activity.*

"We're not going to have this. I want to talk to the chief," Linda said, mindful of the instructions the Texas Ranger had given her. "Today."

The meeting with Chief Barton took place just after four that afternoon, but from the beginning the Dulins sensed that the top officer in Hewitt law enforcement had no interest in what they had to say. "If you're just here to rehash the same old stuff, you're just wasting your time," he said. "My men are not going to discuss this case with you."

"I don't want them to. But I want an autopsy," Linda argued. "Every day that goes by, the evidence is more compromised. We just want the truth. We want to know what happened to our daughter. That's all we're asking."

Growing red-faced, Barton argued vehemently that it didn't matter how long a body was in the grave, it wouldn't affect the accuracy of an autopsy, but Linda had done her homework, contacting forensic experts, and they'd all told her that wasn't true. Neither one backed down. Through it all, Jim kept cool although he had to fight the urge to jump over the table and grab the chief by his collar. In the end, the Dulins' arguments fell on deaf ears, and they walked out, shaking their heads.

Later, someone who was in the police station that day would say that after Jim and Linda left, Chief Barton stalked around the station swearing about the Dulins and their audacity at coming into his department and making demands. "It was like he was backing Cooper, no matter what," the observer said. "He didn't like that anyone questioned one of his men. I heard him say, 'That bitch killed herself, and her parents are fucking crazy.'"

Yet something apparently did make an impression, for just days later, Sergeant Cooper decided to have a sit-down with the man they were all talking about, Matt Baker.

Chapter 32

Fifty-two days after Kari's death, Cooper finally asked Matt to come to Hewitt PD to give an official statement. While Kensi and Grace waited in the squad area, Cooper and Matt met in a small, wood-paneled room with two metal and brown vinyl chairs and a table pushed against a wall. A video camera ran, and Cooper sat just off camera to the right while Matt leaned back in a chair, his legs crossed. He wore a striped polo shirt and jeans, tennis shoes, and his hair was carefully combed, a new addition, a thin goatee, encircled his lips.

"I want to talk about what happened that night," Cooper began. "We can clear all this up, as far as Linda and Jim."

Matt nodded and quickly launched into a soliloquy of the events of April 7 of that year, the last day of Kari's life. Much of it would be unchanged from the report he'd given on the scene. They arrived home from swimming at approximately seven fifteen, and he'd spent the evening taking care of the girls while Kari went to the master bedroom to lie down. As Matt explained it, she'd vomited twice after they arrived home. "Now, I've played some mind games and I wonder if she'd already taken some medicine before that time," he said, his speech quick and unemotional.

Although he said she'd thrown up as recently as eight thirty that evening, Matt said Kari asked him to get two wine coolers out of the garage refrigerator. She was half-asleep, half-awake, in bed watching television, at ten thirty, when she asked him to fill her car up with gas and rent a movie. "She wanted to see *When a Man Loves a Woman*," he said. "That was the movie we watched on our first date. That's cool. We've done that a few times."

In detail, he described to the sergeant how he left the house at approximately ten after eleven. This time, however, the account included details Matt hadn't mentioned earlier, eating up more of the forty-some minutes he claimed to have been gone. First, he said he went to the corner convenience store near the house, only to find it shuttered for the night. "Hewitt closes down at eleven," he said, and Cooper agreed.

From there, Matt said he stopped at a second gas station, one that wouldn't take cards at the pump. When he went inside, "I found out they only sold diesel." In this new account of his activities that night, Matt took three stops to buy gas, eventually filling up at an Exxon. That task completed, he drove north to Hollywood Video, where he bought a Diet Pepsi, Peanut M&Ms, and rented the movie.

"How long do you think you were in Hollywood Video?" Cooper asked.

"Ten minutes," Baker said, estimating that he'd arrived at around eleven forty, and left at eleven fifty. He then drove straight home, and upon arriving found the bedroom door locked.

"I thought maybe she was trying to be romantic," Matt said, with a shrug. But when he opened the door with a screwdriver, Kari was pale, her lips blue, and she wasn't moving. "I thought: *That's not good.*"

Recounting the trauma of finding his wife dead, Matt Baker shed no tears. Describing his talk with the dispatcher, Matt said he'd pulled Kari's lifeless body off the bed and onto the floor. She'd urinated in the bed, and vomited as he moved her, and as he gave her CPR, fluid poured from her mouth and nose. "On the floor, everywhere," he said. "When I did chest compressions, foam was coming out of her nose."

Later, it would seem odd that Cooper didn't ask more

questions at junctures like this. The sergeant had been at the scene, and no one had noted urine or vomit on the bed or floor. When Cooper asked if Matt saw the note, he said, "It's a whirlwind. I know there was a note . . . I know it said I'm sorry, and tell my parents I love them."

Through it all, Matt acted as if he were still trying to piece together what drove Kari to kill herself. Although she'd told others how excited she was about the prospect of a new job, Matt said he wondered if that played into her motives. "She dreaded changing classes again," he said. "She's changed classes every year. I know she was playing that game of, I like junior high, but do I want to move again?"

That afternoon, when he was at the grocery store, Kari called from Walmart to say she was stopping to pick something up. He'd offered to get it for her, but she'd said she wanted to. "I bet she was getting the pills," he told Cooper.

Since his wife's death, Matt claimed that he'd "played a mind game" with those events, and that he'd talked with Kari's friends. "If we'd pieced it all together . . . things she said to me . . . we might have thought she might have been at a point . . . You know what I'm saying?"

"Explain to me what was said," Cooper suggested.

Matt then went into greater detail, this time talking about what he described as Kari's nature. As he often did, he put it in his daughters' mouths instead of his own. "My oldest daughter said this recently, that Kari would blow up over nothing. It could be if there wasn't a cold Diet Pepsi in the refrigerator, and it's a heated battle."

Sounding like the victim, Matt shrugged and said, "I loved Kari, don't get me wrong, but that's just who she was."

As an example, he said that two weeks prior to her death, Kari hadn't wanted to go to Kensi's swimming team practice. Matt said he told her he'd take the girls. "Well, maybe you'd all be better off if I wasn't here," he quoted Kari as saying. "I asked her what she meant, and she said that maybe she'd just move out and move in with her mom and let me have the girls."

That last anniversary of Kassidy's death was a "real down time" for Kari. Yet when her doctor wrote her a prescription for an antidepressant, Kari was furious. "She didn't want to be labeled depressed," Matt told Cooper. "I don't know if she thought sickos are labeled depressed, but she fought not to be labeled depressed."

On the way home, Matt said Kari fell apart, screaming at him in the car, grabbing the door handle and attempting to open it. In this version, unlike what Kari had described to others, Matt contended that she'd tried to jump out of the car on the freeway. Yet if that were true, wasn't it reasonable to pull off the road and park? Instead, he claimed he drove around holding on to Kari while he "circled blocks."

"It was just a weird week, odd behavior," he said. "I knew she was depressed."

As the interview continued, Matt talked of the e-mails Kari had sent, including the one in which she said she'd suddenly realized Kassidy would never come back. "I don't know what she thought," Matt said. "That one day Kassidy was just going to walk in the door?"

As proof of his wife's depression, her desire to die and be with their daughter, Matt told Cooper about the notations in Kari's Bible. Most were years old, yet Matt said he had looked at them, and thought, "Wow. Should I have reached out to her before this?"

When it came to Linda and Jim, Matt sounded magnanimous. "I know they're grieving differently than I am. They lost a daughter. Our girls are grieving differently. They lost a mother," he said. "We're all in this weird grieving state. Some not-so-good things have been said back and forth, and a lot of it is anger that Kari's not here anymore . . . It's just been an interesting time."

Perhaps Matt knew that Linda had questioned whether Kari could die so quickly from an overdose of a sleeping aid. "This is my thing," he said, as if confiding in Cooper. Repeating what he'd told Kari's doctor the week after her death, Matt said, "I don't think the medicine is what killed Kari. I think she threw up into her mouth, and it choked her."

Cooper didn't comment but asked Matt more questions about the time line the night of Kari's death, particularly about Kari having been naked when Matt found her body. Why would she undress? Matt's theory was that perhaps she'd felt trapped, as she had in the car when she attempted to open the door. Suddenly, he added another detail to his account, one that suggested Kari's disrobing was part of a pattern—as she'd tried to jump from the moving car, Matt said that she'd tugged at her shirt, as if trying to pull it off. So how was it that Kari was wearing panties and a T-shirt when the first EMT arrived? "I put her panties on while in the bed and I'm getting her on the floor, then I put her shirt on."

All this, he said, was while he held the phone to his ear and talked to the dispatcher. In those brief four-plus minutes, Matt claimed to have dressed Kari's lifeless body, pulled it off the bed, and administered CPR. Was that possible? Could anyone have done that while continuing to talk to the dispatcher?

Yet Cooper didn't bring up the logical questions about Matt's account. Perhaps he was waiting, wanting to make sure Matt kept talking. When Cooper asked about the pills Kari found in his briefcase, Matt again changed his story. In contrast to what he'd told Linda, he now claimed that he'd never seen the pills in his briefcase, and, in his opinion, the likeliest scenario was that the pills weren't his but Kari's. "I told Kari to go have them tested," he said.

"You told her that?" Cooper repeated. Bristol had said that Kari had wanted to have them tested, but Matt had disposed of them.

"I told her that," he insisted. "But she washed them down the sink."

"Did you tell her that someone else put them in there, one of the kids?"

"One of my things I said, that if it is from my work, that's what it would be," he said, gesturing palms open. "I know there are kids who hide things. If you want me to, I'll talk to security, but she said no, no, no, and that's when she washed them down the sink."

"Did you tell anyone at work about them?" Cooper asked. Since he'd already talked to Greenfield at WCY, the sergeant knew Matt hadn't reported any pills.

"No. I truly didn't believe it was from the kids at work," he said.

At nearly every juncture, there were differences from what Matt had said in the past, from what he'd told Linda, and from what Kari had told Bristol.

"Who is Vanessa Bulls to you?" Cooper asked.

"A good friend of mine now," Matt shrugged. "We knew her before. Her mom and dad were members at Crossroads. Her dad was the music minister." As Matt told it, Vanessa and Kari were friends, and he and Kari were concerned about Vanessa's messy divorce and that she'd been left with a small child. After her parents left the church, Vanessa came to Sunday evening services three or four times. Then, after Kari died, Matt contacted the Bulls. Why? Matt said only to ask what it was like having Vanessa and Lilly live in their home because he was considering moving in with the Dulins.

"I wanted to know how they handled it," he said. "Since then it has grown into a friendship. I know my in-laws don't like that. I guess they think I'm moving on too quickly . . . She makes my girls happy, and that's my number one concern right now."

When Cooper asked about Matt's relationship with Linda and Jim, Matt said, "It's frayed. They've attacked me for everything and nothing."

Then Matt talked about Mother's Day, repeating his charge that Linda grabbed Kensi's arm, this time expanding it to claim that she'd held Kensi's arms so tightly that it had left a mark. "The Dulins think I'm trying to keep the kids away from them," he said. "Even though we've been there more in the last month than we were there the six months preceding it . . . Linda is a very controlling person."

As he had earlier, Matt then relayed what he said his girls had told him about the house on Crested Butte. "Kensi has said to me that she wants out of that house so bad. It's dark. It's dreary. It's such a sad house," he said. "And Grace said recently that there's no happiness in that house."

Did that sound like a five-year-old? Was it possible?

So many questions Cooper didn't ask. Why didn't he bring up the cell-phone records that proved Matt had called Vanessa well before Kari's death? Jim had given Cooper copies, highlighting the calls. Instead, Cooper asked, "Do you think that your mother- and father-in-law think you played a part in Kari's death?"

Matt looked indignant. "I don't know. They've never said that. I'd be very hurt if they thought that. Personally, that would destroy any relationship I have with them."

"I understand," the sergeant agreed.

"I wouldn't want them around if they believed that," Matt said. "I don't think they think I was involved."

Leaning back against the chair, his legs still crossed, Matt had his hands folded over his chest. Kari had told Bristol about the pills. "Do you think at any time Kari might have thought you were trying to hurt her?" Cooper asked.

"I don't know. For a while, she was paranoid," Matt replied.

"It's a question I had to ask," Cooper said, apologetically.

"She never said to me that I was trying to kill her," Matt then said.

"Do you think Kari would have said that to anyone else?"

"The only one would be Jo Ann Bristol that week," Matt admitted. "The only thing is if she accused me of trying to do something with those pills."

When it came to Kari's fears that he was having an affair, Matt said she had a history of accusing him of being unfaithful even if he casually mentioned a woman. How could he be having an affair? he asked dismissively. With two jobs, he said he had no time for anything other than work.

"Okay," Sergeant Cooper said. "I just wanted to sit down and talk to you about that night and everything. One last thing that would really put the icing on the cake, quell everything. If I asked you to, would you take a polygraph test?"

Matt nodded, yes.

"Would you have a problem with that?" Cooper asked.

Matt shook his head and mumbled, "No." Then, after a pause, he asked, "Are you thinking I did have something to do with it?"

"I'm just looking at everything," Cooper said. " . . . I'm not accusing you of anything . . . the Dulins are asking questions. So I just want to clear it all up."

"Are they accusing me of anything?" Matt asked, appearing agitated.

"No, no one is accusing you of anything," Cooper assured him. "They're not doing anything. I'm just clearing things up for myself. So will you take the polygraph?"

Without hesitation, Matt said, "Absolutely."

The meeting ended, Matt agreeing to track down bank records to substantiate the exact times when he'd filled the SUV's tank and rented the video. "I knew people would question, but I think anybody who knew Kari the last month or so knew there was something different with her," he said. "I did see a change. I did see her act differently."

"Hindsight," Cooper said.

"I know," Matt agreed. After shaking hands, they left the room.

Finally, police had interviewed Matt Baker, but had he told the truth? And why hadn't more questions been asked? Why hadn't Cooper pushed harder? Wasn't that the time to ask the tough questions?

Chapter 33

As May drew to a close, Linda gave up on Hewitt PD. "I got the feeling that they weren't going to be wrong, even if a murderer went free," she'd say later. She and Jim talked over the situation, agreeing to pursue it on their own, and she asked him a favor: "Is it okay if I take the lead?"

"Sure," Jim said. "Of course." To Linda, it was as if her husband had given her a gift, the ability to look into their daughter's death and do one last thing for Kari.

The day after Cooper's interview with Matt, Linda went to Hewitt PD and requested anything that was public on the case. She was given the cover sheet from the police report. The only information on it that helped was the exact time of the 911 call: 12:03 A.M. Once she had that, she asked Nancy to once again go to Hollywood Video, this time to verify when the movie had been checked out. It was 11:48.

At her desk at home, Linda plotted the two events on a time line. She then made more phone calls, including to the EMT service, to determine what time the first responders arrived on the scene. Every fact Linda nailed down added another piece to the puzzle of what happened the night Kari died.

Off and on, Charlie and the angels met at one of their favorite Mexican restaurants, holding lunchtime meetings where they debated what they knew and plotted how to learn more. Topics ranged from, if Matt didn't kill Kari, why wasn't the suicide note signed? To: Why did Kari leave two pills in the Unisom bottle instead of taking them all?

Perhaps feeling the pressure, Matt called Jenny in early June and asked her to go to a movie and to a Wendy's for dinner with him and with the girls. Although she wanted to see Kensi and Grace, Jenny worried about being with Matt, thinking that he might push her for details on what Linda was doing. "I already have plans," she said.

Meanwhile at Crossroads, dissent was growing. Rumors circulated, a growing number of the members questioning whether Kari had committed suicide and their pastor's relationship with Vanessa Bulls. A deacons' meeting was scheduled to address the situation. Before it, Matt contacted church members, pleading his case. Talking to one woman, Matt attacked Kari, saying that she wasn't a good mother. The woman would have none of it. "I knew Kari," she said. "She was a wonderful mother."

The evening of the meeting, Jim was out of town and didn't take part. Later, he would hear that the deacons laid out the accusations, including that Matt had been calling the Bulls's household to talk to Vanessa before Kari's death. Matt denied every charge. The problem was that one deacon had already confirmed some of the facts before the meeting, and he judged that their pastor was lying. And there were the practical matters of running the church. Distracted, Matt had become less involved. The members had had enough of his canceling Sunday evening services to be with Vanessa.

Matt put up a fight, but the deacons were determined. They gave him a sixteen-hundred-dollar severance, but his services were no longer required at Crossroads Baptist. Afterward, Matt told a church member that he was disappointed and needed the extra money from his pastor's job to buy a house he and Vanessa were considering. "I'm going to take the girls and move to Kerrville," he said. "Away from all this gossip."

* * *

As the days ticked past, Linda carried out the plan Matt Cawthon, the Texas Ranger, had given her. She'd talked to Hewitt PD's chief and gotten nowhere, and on June 2, she wrote a letter to McLennan County's longtime district attorney, John Segrest. "My daughter, Kari Baker, died on April 8, 2006. Her death was ruled a suicide by Judge Billy Martin and the Hewitt Police Department . . . Martin didn't conduct an autopsy. In fact, Judge Martin didn't come to the scene," Linda wrote. Filling Segrest in on the details, including the typed, unsigned suicide note, she laid out what she knew, including the time line she'd pulled together with her family's help.

In the letter, she mentioned Kari's visit with Bristol, noting that after the therapist talked with Cooper, she'd come away believing that nothing would be done with the information. Linda described her dilemma, trying to work with the justice of the peace and Hewitt PD, who continually referred her to each other but took no action. "I have additional information to share with you. However, I wanted to give you an idea of what my family is dealing with here . . . We want to move forward. We don't want to play any sort of blame game."

At that point, Linda asked Segrest to take the case out of Hewitt PD's hands and call in the Texas Rangers. "While I have no doubt that the Hewitt PD are fine men and women, this case may not be something they are trained to handle. I don't mean to dismiss or disparage the work of the Hewitt Police Department. I want to ensure that this case is investigated properly, however." She concluded by writing, "Thank you very much for your time. All my family wants is the truth."

While Linda waited to hear from Segrest, Matt sent her an e-mail on June 4, a Sunday, informing the Dulins that Barbara would be spending time with them over the summer. "I need to inform you that Kensi, Grace, and I have talked and are not at a point to have any extended time away from each other," he wrote regarding short vacations with the girls that the Dulins had proposed for the summer. "I feel any trip apart from each other this summer is not of the best interest of Kensi, Grace, nor [sic] myself."

"It was evident that he was cutting us off from our granddaughters," Linda would later say. After talking over the situation, she and Jim hired an attorney to sue for visitation. When Matt was notified, he e-mailed claiming they had no reason to do so, that he would never keep his daughters from their maternal grandparents. Linda was blunt in her response, saying she knew Matt was turning their granddaughters against them. "You don't need to respond to this e-mail," she concluded. "I think we have both said what needs to be said. Have a good day."

Three days later, the Dulins' civil attorneys formally filed a petition for visitation with Kensi and Grace. Along with time with their granddaughters, the Dulins wanted court-ordered counseling for both girls.

The distractions must have been piling up for Matt that summer. He had the battle with the Dulins, the worries of knowing that they were questioning Kari's death, the girls to care for, and, of course, the relationship with Vanessa to nurture. The same afternoon that the Dulins filed their petition, Matt was at his computer at WCY working on that latter complication, Vanessa. Using an *mbaker18@hot.rr.com* e-mail address, he sent an e-mail to Turtlefiji.com, a company that booked trips to the island of Fiji. When a reply came, it read: "I am responding . . . regarding your honeymoon in Fiji . . . congratulations on your engagement. What an exciting time for both of you!"

All wasn't going as well at the Dulins'. The following day, Linda received more bad news. In a letter, Segrest, the district attorney, expressed his sympathies but then backed Hewitt and Billy Martin. While admitting that they could make mistakes, Segrest urged the Dulins to trust the JP and the Hewitt officers' judgment. And in the end, he refused to help in any way, writing, "My office is not involved and won't become involved in the inquiry at this stage."

Disappointed, Linda and Jim talked. In the end, they agreed that their best option was to reach out to everyone they knew and ask for help. Linda carried out the plan, calling friends and family. A day later the phone rang. A friend of Kari's from high school had some advice. "Mrs. Dulin," he said. "There's an attorney in Waco, a former federal prosecutor, Bill Johnston. You need to call him."

Chapter 34

"Let's get started," Bill Johnston said on the afternoon of Friday, June 9, 2006, two months after Kari's death. Six feet four inches, lean, with a thick mop of curly dark brown hair, Johnston had a brusque incisiveness. They were seated around a conference table in a mid-rise office decorated with Western art. The appointment calendar said only that Linda Dulin wanted to talk about her daughter's death, a suicide that the family believed was suspicious.

Johnston and Linda weren't alone in the room.

At Camp Swift for his annual training, Jim wasn't able to be there, but Nancy had come to support Linda. And Johnston had invited two old friends to sit in on the meeting: John Bennett, a wiry, gray-haired man in a leather bomber jacket, and Mike McNamara, tall and angular with a fringe of white hair habitually topped by a cowboy hat. Both men had hung out shingles as private investigators after retiring from long careers in law enforcement, Bennett as an undercover agent for the Texas Department of Public Safety and McNamara as a deputy U.S. Marshal.

A former assistant U.S. attorney, Johnston had worked with McNamara and Bennett for more than a decade. The law was a family legacy. Johnston's father, Wilson Johnston, had been an assistant Dallas district attorney for decades, the one who prosecuted Jack Ruby for the murder of President John F. Kennedy's assassin, Lee Harvey Oswald. "My dad was a courageous guy, and I grew up wanting to do what he did," says Johnston. As a prosecutor, he had a reputation for working with law enforcement to help along investigations, giving officers advice and the tools they needed when he believed a crime had been committed.

"If Bill saw a problem like a drug-infested apartment complex, he'd say, 'We've got a nest of rats over here to work on,'" says Bennett. "Bill is fearless."

"I took cases where I thought it was the right thing to do," says Johnston. "I wanted to be the person who picked up the flag, and said, 'Follow me.'"

Over the years, Johnston had forged a close relationship with McNamara and his older brother, Parnell, also a deputy U.S. Marshal. Like Johnston's, the McNamara brothers' family had a long history in law enforcement; their father, T. P. McNamara, grandfather, Emmett Parnell McNamara, and uncle, Guy McNamara, had all worn badges for the U.S. Marshal's office.

Then there was Bennett. Not as tall as McNamara and Johnston were, Bennett measured a hair over five-foot-six, with a wide smile and a glint in his eyes. In the late 1960s, Bennett, nicknamed "Little John," joined the navy out of high school and was sent to Vietnam, where he was stationed outside Da Nang. Once home, like Johnston and the McNamara brothers, Bennett enrolled in Baylor. His intention was to go into law. But by graduation, he'd grown weary of school. Instead, Bennett hired on as a state trooper, working his way up the ladder, promoted to undercover narcotics investigations.

Over twenty-five years, Bennett traveled the U.S. pulling together major drug cases, including air conspiracies, where his targets flew in planeloads of drugs, and vast indoor growing operations, some with fingers stretching out to Oklahoma, Virginia, and Florida. A meticulous investigator, Bennett had a talent for detail. "It's a hard life because of who you're dealing with," he says.

All the men had a conjoined history.

John Bennett had been the first narcotics officer Johnston had ever worked with, and it had been the McNamara brothers who in 1992 brought a brutal murder to Johnston's attention, that of Melissa Northrup, a convenience-store clerk. About that time, the McNamaras noticed that a lot of young women were turning up dead, including three Waco-area prostitutes and an Austin accountant. The lawmen quickly suspected Kenneth McDuff, a serial killer who'd been paroled out of a Texas prison. What Johnston did first was take the information to Segrest, the McLennan County district attorney. When Segrest refused to pursue the case, Johnston took it on himself to go after McDuff on a federal drug charge, based on a single tab of LSD. At the same time, the McNamara brothers and others investigated the killings. Based on the information gathered, Segrest then prosecuted the case. In the end, McDuff was convicted of Northrup's murder and executed in 1998.

"The plague of law enforcement is weak prosecutors," says Johnston. "You can have a great investigator, but if he can't get a prosecutor to take a risk . . . he's stymied."

After thirteen years as a prosecutor, it was the Branch Davidian fiasco that convinced Johnston to become a defense attorney. The one who wrote the initial warrant for David Koresh's arrest on a weapons charge, Johnston got caught up in the finger-pointing that followed the lethal fire. The switch to the other side of the courtroom wasn't an easy one. "I missed prosecuting," he admitted. "It's not the same."

Looking across the table at Linda, Johnston said, "Tell me why you're here."

After taking a deep breath, she told the three men about Kari, Matt, Kari's death, Vanessa, and all that they'd uncovered, from the phone calls to Matt's bizarre behavior.

"What do you want us to do?" Johnston asked. It wasn't unusual for family members to balk at the idea that a loved one had committed suicide. For all Johnston knew, that was the case with the two women seated across from him.

Linda had thought long and hard, and what she didn't want was for Johnston to think this was a hunting party out to get Matt Baker. "I don't want you to assume my son-in-law did anything wrong. I just want the truth," Linda said. "I need to know what happened to my daughter."

Linda had feared Johnston would write off her concerns, the way Cooper and Segrest had. So when Johnston said, "We can do that," she felt an overwhelming sense of relief.

Yet Johnston then explained that Linda really didn't want to hire him, at least not yet. Instead, she needed McNamara and Bennett. "I think the world of these two men," Johnston said. "Let's ask them to do a little digging. Let's see what they find out."

"We'd all worked closely together from the time Bill became the deputy U.S. attorney in Waco," says McNamara. "We were used to working as a team."

Once Johnston turned the floor over to the two investigators, McNamara explained the situation the way he saw it. "If we take this case, we will try to find the facts as best we can," he said. "Those facts will speak for themselves."

"That's all I want," Linda answered. "If Kari committed suicide, I can live with that. It's painful, but I can. I just want to know the truth."

It was Bennett who then detailed how they'd proceed. "First, we'll investigate your daughter," he said. "We're going to go at this with the assumption that she did take her own life and see if that's true. So let's get started. What do we need to know?"

As the investigators took notes, Linda and Nancy laid out all they knew about Kari's death, including their suspicions about Vanessa, and Kari's haunting words to Bristol. In a folder, Linda had copies of the phone bills and all the documents they'd collected, which she gave to the two men. That done, Nancy repeated what she knew of the accusations women had leveled against Matt over the years. "These things happened, and they've made us wonder what's going on," Nancy said. "From my view, Matt was always pretty sketchy."

For the investigators, Linda then compiled a list of places Matt had worked, some of which he'd left under a cloud. She told him about the time Kari went to the bank after their debit card had been maxed out on Internet pornography. Listening and taking notes, Bennett and McNamara took their time coming to any conclusions. "I thought it sounded a little suspect, but you don't know one way or the other," says McNamara. "But it seemed there was enough that it needed to be looked into."

The list of names the women supplied included Matt's and Kari's friends and families. As the meeting wrapped up, little more than an hour after it started, Bennett stressed again that the first thing they'd do was to focus on Kari, on the likelihood that she had taken her own life. "Then we'll talk to Bill and get back to you," he said. "Let us find out the facts, and we'll see where we are."

As they walked out the door of Johnston's office, Linda felt better than she had in a long time. "All of a sudden, all the shock I was feeling, all the numbness, was gone. Someone was looking into Kari's death. That was all I wanted."

Chapter 35

That summer, 2006, Barbara Baker traveled to Waco often. She'd say later that she was concerned about the relationship between her son and Vanessa. "I could see that this woman was attached to my son. Her hands were all over him. Physical touch." Frowning, Barbara added, "I saw a high-school girl crush all over a young man." Yet at the same time, Barbara insisted that nothing happened. Matt was home every night, in his own bed, alone. "I don't remember anything but her coming over for dinner a few times."

If his mother didn't see signs of her son's intentions, others certainly did. Early that summer, Matt went to the Bulls' house and asked Larry if he could officially date his daughter. Crossroads' former music minister replied that was Vanessa's decision. As for Vanessa and Matt never having a date, on the very evening after Linda and Nancy met with Johnston, Bennett, and McNamara, Matt arrived at the Bulls' household. Lilly was left with her parents, and Vanessa climbed into Matt's new truck and left.

Meanwhile, at Crossroads, a storm brewed.

Although he'd been fired, Matt hadn't returned the Dell laptop he'd been supplied for church business. At the time he'd been let go, he argued that it had personal files including the girls' games on the hard drive. A deacon told Matt that the computer was church property and needed to be returned. When that didn't happen, one of the deacons, Monty Toombs, called his son, Ben, who worked as a detective at Hewitt PD. "Matt Baker's refusing to return the church laptop," he said.

After substantiating that the church had a receipt for the computer to prove ownership, Toombs said, "If he's not willing to return it, the church can file a report for theft."

Based on that advice, the deacon called the ex-pastor again, stressing that if the laptop wasn't returned, the church would file a formal police report. Only then did Matt turn the computer over to Toombs.

Once he had it, Monty Toombs took the laptop to Hewitt PD and turned it over to his son. Ben then took it to Waco PD and asked to have it examined for anything that could tie into Kari's death. A week later, Waco called. "They said that they couldn't find anything useful," says Ben. "I returned it to the church."

On June 12, Matt received a report from a home inspector on a house he was considering buying in Lorena, Texas, near Crossroads. On a corner lot with a detached garage, the price was more than $200,000, a considerable step up from the homes he'd lived in with Kari.

That afternoon, John Bennett drove to Troy and tracked down the Bulls's house. For a few hours, he sat outside in his truck with a camera, hoping to see Vanessa and/or Matt, to substantiate that the rumors were right and that they were a couple. Neither one appeared. At the end of the afternoon, Bennett drove back to Waco.

The following day, McNamara and Bennett met with Bristol. In her cozy office, she offered them a cup of coffee and spent the next three hours talking about Kari. The woman the therapist described wasn't one who appeared on the threshold of suicide. "She was well dressed. She was clean and taking care of herself," Bristol said. "She was upset about her marriage, but she had plans, including a new job and finding ways to help other parents who had lost children. I asked more than once if she was suicidal, and she said, 'No.'"

To both the investigators, it was easy to see that Kari's counselor was struggling with what had happened. "It was weighing on her, very much so," says McNamara.

When they believed they'd heard everything the therapist could tell them, McNamara and Bennett left, walking toward the parking lot. Bristol followed, talking as they walked, saying over and again, "I don't believe Kari committed suicide."

As the summer went on, two investigations unfolded, separate and unbeknownst to one another: the one mounted by Linda Dulin with Bennett and McNamara in the lead made progress; at the same time, Hewitt PD's lukewarm investigation stumbled along.

About that time, Sergeant Cooper walked in the door at the Waco Center for Youth, following up on his interview with Matt, hoping to set up the polygraph Matt had agreed to. After Matt and Cooper talked briefly, the officer left. Afterward, Matt appeared nervous and disappeared into his office, then left the campus a short time later. Later that day, it wasn't Matt who called Cooper but a criminal defense attorney the pastor had hired, Gerald Villarrial. If Cooper had held off on asking Baker the tough questions until he was attached to a lie detector, it had been a bad decision. "Matt won't be talking with you anymore," the lawyer said. "And I've advised him not to take a polygraph."

Cooper might have been stymied, but Bennett and McNamara were moving on.

About that time, Bennett called Jill Hotz, hoping to hear what Kari had said the final days of her life. Since the day her friend had died, Hotz had struggled with all that had happened. She was still having days when it weighed heavily on her. Off and on, she'd called and talked to Linda, and they'd discussed the theory that maybe Kari hadn't killed herself.

After seeing the photo of Vanessa on Matt's refrigerator, Jill had begun to feel more confident that it was true. "It made sense," she says. "That Kari killed herself, that didn't make sense."

In the Hotz household, Jill was the only one who believed Matt could be a murderer. Stephen, Jill's husband, considered Matt a friend, and he was loyal. "It was hard," Jill said later. "We had arguments. I kept saying, 'I know Kari didn't kill herself,' and Stephen would say, 'Matt couldn't have done it.'"

The Kari that Jill described to John Bennett wasn't depressed. "Kari thought her husband was having an affair," Jill said. "But the Kari I knew loved her girls too much to ever leave them. She was excited about the future but worried about her marriage."

Writing up what Hotz told him, Bennett shared the information with McNamara. That evening, their investigation continued in the living room of a home not far from Spring Valley Elementary, where a group of teachers congregated. They'd all worked with Kari, seen her day after day. The gathering was a somber one as the women described Kari when she first began at the school and in the months that followed, culminating in the turmoil they saw in her life during the final months. One after another, the women recounted how anxious Kari had become about her marriage. What Bennett and McNamara heard was not that Kari was obsessed with Kassidy. While the loss of her daughter was on her mind that spring, what the teachers agreed on was that Kari seemed infinitely more concerned about Matt.

One of those in attendance was Shae, the teacher Kari had confided in. "Kari told me that she almost dropped the girls at my house and left," she said, detailing how just days before Kari died, she'd said she feared that Matt might be trying to kill her.

As the investigators talked over what they'd discovered, things started to line up. "Not a single person we talked to thought Kari Baker committed suicide," said McNamara.

"Every person we talked to said she would not. We even heard from one woman that Kari had called suicide a copout."

Behind the scenes, the Dulins' lawsuit to get court-ordered visitation with their granddaughters gained steam. It was on June 16, the Friday following the investigators' meeting with the teachers, that an agreement was reached. Under it, Linda and Jim had Kensi and Grace two Sundays and one Saturday a month. There were also weekends scheduled for summer visits, including one from July 24 to 26, while Linda's sister Jennifer visited from Florida. As part of the decision, Matt also agreed to enroll the girls in counseling. It all appeared congenial, at least on paper, with the exception of one admonition: "There would be a mutual injunction prohibiting any party from making disparaging remarks regarding any other party or any other party's family."

The same afternoon that the ruling on visitation came down, Bennett and McNamara had lunch with an old friend, Texas Ranger Matt Cawthon, along with Detective Kristina Woodruff from the Waco PD. While they ate, the investigators talked about their latest endeavor. Cawthon already knew of the Baker case because he'd advised Linda on how to proceed weeks earlier. He didn't know if there was anything beyond a family unwilling to accept suicide, but what he heard piqued his interest. Cawthon had worked with Johnston, Bennett, and McNamara often in the past, and he trusted them. "These guys are men of grit," says Cawthon. "They see an injustice and go after it. They're righteous in what they do. I've never known them to be on the wrong side."

As he considered what the others were saying, Cawthon regretted that more hadn't been done at the scene. If he'd been there that night, he felt certain that Kari's body would have been autopsied and Matt thoroughly questioned. "Mistakes were made when you looked at the case," he said. "There should have been someone there with common sense who said we've got a healthy young woman dead with an unsigned suicide note. We need to investigate."

When he considered what had happened, Cawthon wondered if money had been behind the decision. "Autopsies are expensive," he says. "Maybe there was a move to keep costs down?"

Detective Woodruff knew nothing about the case, but she listened as the others talked. After they parted, she called Bennett with an idea: "You should do a public information request on Baker with Waco PD."

It wasn't an unusual thing to do. In fact, such a request was standard procedure. "But Matt's being a preacher, we hadn't thought we'd find anything," says Bennett. "But oh my gosh. We did."

The paperwork that was turned over to McNamara and Bennett was the first real red flag. It contained a detective's notes on an alleged attempted sexual assault on the Baylor campus. The frustrating thing was that while the report was public information, many of the names had been blacked out. Once they had it, the investigators worked on the documents, deciphering what was below the black marker. The name of the woman who'd called Waco PD years after the attack hoping to file charges was listed as a Laura Mueller. Yet when they accessed other records to find her, nothing came up.

Chapter 36

Six days after Cooper talked to Matt, June 19, the WCY campus was quiet. Most of the employees had the day off in honor of Juneteenth Day, the state holiday that commemorated the post–Civil War day when Texas slaves first heard of the Emancipation Proclamation. Only a skeleton staff was on-site at WCY that morning, and Christina Salazar was covering the switchboard when Matt walked up.

"Oh, I guess you were the one who walked past me earlier?" Salazar asked. She'd heard someone walk in but hadn't been sure who it was.

"Yes," Matt replied.

A conversation commenced, and Matt mentioned insurance he had on Kari through his job. Salazar replied that she doubted that it would pay since the cause of death was suicide. "You need to call HR, but usually there's a waiting period," she explained. "I don't know if you've been here long enough."

Matt looked disappointed, and Salazar offered her sympathies for his loss.

"Our relationship ended a long time ago," he said, his voice flat. "I wasn't Kari's husband, more her counselor and her friend." When Salazar asked about the welfare of the girls, making observations about how they'd miss their mother and all the things Kari did for them, Matt shrugged.

"I've really been the one taking care of the girls, not Kari," he said. "She was so depressed, she never really did anything with them. Kari was like a black cloud around the girls. The girls always felt like they had to tiptoe around her."

Salazar then listened in disbelief as Matt said that he was giving the girls more freedom. He'd even given Kensi permission to use "the F-word," if she wanted to. After they talked for a while, Matt retrieved a photo of Vanessa with all three of their daughters from his wallet. "We're into each other," he said. "The girls want a new mommy." When he pointed at Lilly, he asked, "Doesn't she look like me? She could be mine." Vanessa, he said, looked so much like Kensi and Grace that she could have been their mother. "She has a year left in college, then I think we'll get married."

The conversation continued, and Matt launched into an account of the night Kari died. Yet there were differences from what he'd said in the past. No longer did he say Kari was awake when he left the house; instead, his dead wife had "a hard time holding her eyes open." He also said police found the note. "It wasn't signed," Matt said, saying that he'd been called in to talk to police.

"You could tell when the note was typed," Salazar offered. "If it was written on a computer, there's a time on it. If it was while you were gone, that should answer any questions."

"Oh, I got rid of our home computer," he said. "Maybe Kari wrote it at work."

"Well, they can subpoena her computer from work and your computer from your work," Salazar explained.

Not long after, Matt excused himself and left. Later that afternoon, a security guard noticed the chaplain carrying a box through the parking lot toward his truck.

Chapter 37

It would turn out that Salazar was right; Matt's insurance wouldn't pay anything on Kari's death. Her retirement fund money came in a few weeks later, however, and he pocketed $51,644.80. Matt also filed for social security survivors' benefits, including stipends for each of the girls.

On June 20, Barbara e-mailed Matt about his plans to move to Kerrville, saying she'd heard of a job opening for a hospital chaplain. "In rethinking about you bringing Vanessa and Lilly," she wrote, "I think you might make some people question your quick relationship, marriage etc. I think if you and the girls come for a little while, then they come, it would probably be more acceptable. If you and the girls stay with us, I think it will make it look more innocent . . . Do you understand what I am trying to say?"

Apparently, Vanessa's parents were also against her plans to move to Kerrville with Matt. Barbara wrote: "You don't need two sets of in-laws having problems with you."

That same day, Mike McNamara questioned another of the third-grade teachers at Spring Valley Elementary. What she said was that the week after Kari's death, she happened upon Matt and the girls at Walmart. As they talked, Matt described finding Kari's body, saying that when the police asked if the girls were all right that night, he went into their bedrooms to check them. "If Kari did anything to my girls,

I would go get her out of the ambulance," he said. The problem was that no one saw Matt enter his daughters' bedrooms that night. It was what the teacher said Matt had in his Walmart cart, however, that caught McNamara's attention: a new computer, printer, and monitor.

Baker replaced the home computer, McNamara thought. *Why?*

Computers were the topic of conversation again three days later at WCY, when chaplain's assistant Gene Boesche went into Terri Corbin's deserted office to use the printer and discovered that her computer tower was missing. Immediately, Boesche reported the situation to Matt, his boss. The two men then inspected Corbin's office, Matt looking around the filing cabinet and the desk. "I'll report it," he said.

Five days later, Matt reported the missing computer to security, and Keith Lowery, the facility's tech expert, was notified. He, too, looked through Corbin's office and verified that the computer was, indeed, gone. Then he went back to the system and ran a check, to see when it was last connected to the network. What he discovered was that Corbin's computer was still being used. Investigating further, he determined that the one using Corbin's computer was Matt Baker.

Lowery then went to Matt's office and inspected the computer on the chaplain's desk. A WCY sticker identified it as Matt's, but when Lowery checked the serial number, he determined that the computer was actually the one from Terri Corbin's old office. Apparently someone had switched the computers. The question then became: Where was Matt Baker's computer?

To find out, Lowery searched Matt's office, but to no avail. Matt's computer was gone, apparently stolen. The only conclusion was that someone had taken Matt's computer and covered up the theft by replacing it with the one from Terri Corbin's old office, going so far as to change the WCY tags to hide the thievery. When Lowery asked Matt where his computer was, Matt said he didn't know.

Not long after, Matt wrote a report. In it, he claimed that he'd noticed something that could explain what had happened: "I do not remember the exact date that I found my computer turned out at a different angle, but it would be approximately two weeks ago, around the time the tower might have been exchanged." Although his office was down a locked hallway, he then suggested that volunteers and others who came on the campus had access to the offices and would have been able to make the switch, including a rabbi who'd used Matt's office. "I do not see any other items missing from my office," he concluded, signing it Chaplain Matt Baker.

In the weeks that followed, the campus was searched, but Matt's CPU was never found. In hindsight, two things stood out. First, Lowery would recall how Matt had once asked him if deleted e-mails could be retrieved off a computer. They could. The other was that tracing Matt's IP address back, Lowery discovered that the missing computer was disconnected from the WCY network at 11:37 on the morning of June 19, the holiday when Matt talked with Christina Salazar, who'd told him that his work computer could be subpoenaed. That was the same day Matt was seen walking to his truck carrying a box.

WCY's security notified Waco PD, where a case file was opened on the missing computer.

Rumors had been stirring in Hewitt since Matt had first shown up at the school with Vanessa just two weeks after Kari's death, but once two private investigators were looking into the case, the word spread quickly. At Crossroads, many doubted that Kari had committed suicide. After Matt's firing, the pastor who had preceded him, Steve Sadler, returned. He was the one who'd presided over Kari's funeral, the one who'd seen her plea for God's protection in her Bible. Perhaps hearing the rumors convinced Sadler that the police needed to know what he'd seen.

Whatever the reason, on June 26, Sadler wrote a letter on

his Baylor stationery to Ben Toombs, the Hewitt PD officer
whose parents attended Crossroads: "As of conversations
at Crossroads Baptist Church yesterday, I feel it is time for
me to give you this Xerox copy of a page in Kari Baker's
Bible . . .

"On Sunday night April 9 as I was thumbing through
Kari's Bible, I came across this notation attached. It had a
very sobering and lingering impact. I xeroxed it but filed
it away as 99% unrelated to anything of significance. Matt
and I have never discussed this or any of the other markings
I read in the Bible.

"With the knowledge I now have concerning an investigation into Kari's death, I feel I should give this to you. I am
available for further conversation should you want it."

The Hewitt police now had in their hands Kari's own
words: *Lord, I am asking you to protect me from harm. I am
not sure what is going on with Matt, but Lord help me find
peace with him.*

Chapter 38

Linda's crusade to have an official investigation into her daughter's death appeared to reap benefits on July 6, nearly three months to the day after Kari's death, when Captain Tuck Saunders informed the detective in charge of the investigation, Cooper, that Judge Martin said he was now willing to order an exhumation and an autopsy. The news hadn't come directly from the judge but from Texas Ranger Matt Cawthon, whom McNamara and Bennett had been keeping informed.

Three days later, Cawthon dropped in at Hewitt PD headquarters to talk to the chief, personally putting pressure on him to take a look at the case. Voices rose, especially when the chief questioned why Cawthon was interjecting himself into the case. "Who are you working for, Bill Johnston?" Chief Barton demanded.

"No, that dead woman. And you should be, too," the Texas Ranger replied.

That same afternoon, Cooper was no longer the lead investigator on the case. Saunders called twenty-eight-year-old Toombs into his office and told him the Baker case was now his. The dark-haired young detective with a crooked smile protested. He explained that he had connections to the case: His father was a deacon at Crossroads, and he'd met Matt and the Dulins. Toombs and his family had briefly lived in

Troy and attended the same church as Vanessa. "She seemed like a nice girl from a good family," he says.

From what he knew, Toombs didn't think Matt Baker was guilty. Ben's mother spoke well of the former pastor, and, as the young officer saw it, even if Matt and Vanessa had an affair, it wasn't important. "Because he's having an inappropriate relationship, that doesn't prove he killed his wife," says Toombs.

Toombs protested the assignment, but Saunders insisted. "The case is yours," the captain said. "Get with Matt Cawthon on this."

Assigned to help Toombs was Mike Spear, a baby-faced Hewitt detective, one with a slight dimple in his chin, who'd joined the department five years earlier, at the tender age of twenty-one. "I always thought it would be fun to be a cop," says Spear, who'd heard about the Baker case around the office, always in the context of "some lady committed suicide, and her parents were causing problems."

The first thing Toombs did on his new assignment was to call a Waco detective he knew, one in special crimes, to talk about the procedure for exhuming a body for an autopsy. After he hung up, he called the judge's office and got the plans rolling. The affidavit Ben Toombs wrote on July 10, 2006, was entitled "for disinterment of a dead body," and it said that while Kari's death had been initially determined to be a suicide, the cause had "come into question due to suspicious circumstances." The ones referred to as requesting the exhumation were her parents, Jim and Linda Dulin, and the reason to have it autopsied was so that an official manner of death could be determined.

That same day, Judge Martin signed the order for the disinterment from Oakwood Cemetery, section 1, lot 96, space 2. From the judge's office, Toombs and Spear proceeded to the cemetery, where a backhoe was waiting. As they stood to the side, the operator removed the rich dark earth. A hoist was then used to bring the baby blue coffin up, and when it emerged, the earth had dented the top and one side.

The coffin was then transferred into the back of a hearse to be taken to the Southwest Institute of Forensic Science in Dallas. Toombs and Spear followed in a slow-moving procession, then accompanied the casket into the autopsy suite. Before long, Dr. Reade Quinton, a pathologist, arrived, and the casket was opened.

Dressed in a teal sweater and skirt set, Kari's body was transferred onto an exam table. For the most part, the autopsy wasn't all that unusual. Photos were taken, and Kari's organs were each removed and weighed. Yet, when it came time to take samples for toxicology, there was a problem: The tests were usually done on blood, but it had all been drained and replaced by embalming fluid. Instead, Dr. Quinton harvested muscle tissue, labeling it to be sent to the lab.

While they waited, Toombs called Matt's attorney, informing him of what was transpiring. When he heard, Matt rushed to the cemetery with his mother at his side and stood above the empty grave, his phone to his ear, talking to Vanessa. For some reason, his thoughts weren't only of Kari that day. "I wonder if they dug up Kassidy, too," he said.

Moments later, after he'd traversed the short distance to the child's grave, the one marked "My sweet, sweet baby," Matt sounded relieved. "No, she's still here," he said.

Meanwhile in Dallas, after the autopsy, Spear and Toombs talked to Dr. Quinton. "I don't see anything that would suggest either suicide or homicide," he told them. "And I'm afraid that the toxicology I've ordered won't help much. Without blood, having to use muscle tissue, it's not likely to be conclusive."

When the sad caravan returned Kari's body to Oakwood Cemetery, one lone man waited. Jim Dulin had heard that his daughter's body had been exhumed and would be reburied. In a new casket, one identical to the last, Kari's body was removed from the back of the hearse. The casket was slipped back into the ground as Jim prayed. Then, before the two young detectives left, Jim approached them. "I just want to tell you; you get him, or I will," he said, weeping. "If I get him, y'all will be coming after me."

When the autopsy report came back, as Quinton had suggested, there were no clear answers, but there was more information. In Kari's muscle tissue, the toxicologists found traces of phentermine, the diet drug she was taking, diphenhydramine (Unisom), and something else, something that Kari Baker didn't have a prescription for, a drug she wasn't known to take: zolpidem, better known as the sleeping pill Ambien.

When Dr. Quinton reviewed all the results, he wrote: "After a complete autopsy and scene investigation the cause of death of Kari Baker, a thirty-one-year-old white female, remains undetermined. The combined effects of phentermine, diphenhydramine, and zolpidem, in conjunction with the possible use of alcohol (per history), may have contributed to the cause of death. However, accurate blood concentrations of these drugs cannot be determined due to embalming. If additional information becomes available, the cause and manner of death may be amended."

So much anticipation had gone into that autopsy suite with Kari's body, so much excitement that the question that was her death might finally have an answer, all to end in uncertainty. Yet, now, those investigating had something to work with, toxicology results that added a new piece to the puzzle: Ambien.

Once he had a copy of the autopsy, Bill Johnston contacted Dr. David Stafford, a well-known forensic toxicologist and former professor at the University of Tennessee in Memphis, asking for his opinion. Days later, Stafford called Johnston. "This woman did not die of an overdose," Stafford said. He then went on to explain the chemistry of death by overdose. If Kari had downed a bottle of pills, the individual pills would have broken down and been absorbed at different rates. As they took effect, her system would have slowed. At death, some of the pills would have remained undigested in her stomach. Those would have been easily apparent during autopsy. But there were none, not in Kari's stomach or intestines. "That means she didn't die of an overdose," Stafford maintained. "It's not possible."

"Could she have aspirated and choked?" Johnston asked.

"No," Stafford said. "Her lungs were clear."

Chapter 39

The finding of undetermined on the autopsy had been disappointing, but the investigation forged ahead. The day after the exhumation, Bennett and McNamara went to Baylor to talk to Steve Sadler, Crossroads' current pastor. They'd heard that Sadler had found something potentially interesting in Kari's Bible. In a university conference room, they asked what Kari had written. "He didn't cooperate. He was evasive," says McNamara. "Sadler brought someone with him, apparently afraid to meet us alone."

"There's a privilege, maybe not a legal one, but there's one to me, as a minister," Sadler contended.

Bennett and McNamara asked questions, however, and Sadler finally admitted that the rumors were true; he had found something troubling in the Bible. "Will you show it to us?" Bennett asked.

"No," Sadler said. "But I did give it to the Hewitt police."

Despite all the accumulating evidence, the Dulins had a tie with their son-in-law that they couldn't break, their granddaughters. On July 18, Jim and Linda attended Grace's birthday party at a pizza restaurant. Baker didn't know that one diner at a separate table had a special interest in the case. It was the first time John Bennett had seen Baker, and he wondered about the preacher's body language. Matt had lost weight and looked on edge. He was dressed not as a pastor but in clothes a teenager might wear.

The following afternoon, Toombs's partner on the case, Mike Spear, talked with Cawthon, who urged him to meet with McNamara and Bennett, vouching for the two men. That evening at six, Spear, Toombs, Cawthon, McNamara, and Bennett congregated at Bennett's house. Toombs brought along a copy of Cooper's interview with Matt, and Bennett popped it in his DVD player. Before long, the two seasoned investigators wondered why the detective let the subject control the interview. Bennett noticed that every time a difficult subject was broached, Matt clenched his jaw, and his face flushed.

The DVD ended, and it was McNamara and Bennett's turn to divulge what they knew for the detectives. "It was typical for them to say, 'Did you meet with this person yet? You may want to talk to this person who may have some information for you,'" says Spear.

Two days later, Bennett and McNamara met with Spear again. This time the detective brought the eight crime-scene photos. The first thing the two investigators noticed was the purplish hue of Kari's hands and arms, her back, and the back of her neck. What they recognized was lividity. "That shouldn't be there," Bennett pointed out. "Not if she'd only been dead a short time."

The meeting ended, and the investigation continued. Now that they had more to work with, John Bennett used the information from Baker's interview with Cooper to retrace the former pastor's account of his whereabouts on the night his wife died. Leaving the Crested Butte address at just after eleven one night, Bennett drove out of the subdivision and turned right, taking the road underneath the highway to the first stop, a convenience store. Matt had said the store was closed, and Bennett saw that it was; pulling back out, he drove up onto the freeway and toward downtown Hewitt. From there, he drove into a second gas station, one that sold only diesel, then into the Exxon, estimating the time it took to pump twenty-six gallons, the amount on the receipt Baker supplied to Hewitt PD. Pumping at twelve seconds a gallon, the standard, that stop took a total of seven minutes and twelve seconds.

After going into Hollywood Video, picking up a video and checking out, Bennett drove back to Crested Butte. Bennett's conclusion? The route Matt said he drove, including the stops, shouldn't have taken more than thirty-five minutes and forty-seven seconds. Matt should have been home at least ten minutes before he said he was, well before 12:03, when he called 911.

"We lived the investigation every day. We talked about it every day," says Bennett, with a frown. "We'd say, was it possible this happened, or that. Was there any way we could think of where Matt didn't do it? Any way that it could have been suicide? But that didn't seem to work. We had no evidence she would kill herself."

"We kept trying to point the arrow away from Matt Baker, and it kept turning and pointing right back at him," says McNamara.

To get more information on Matt's past, McNamara investigated the former pastor's work experience. At First Baptist in Waco, he talked to a man he'd known for years, Jake Roberts, who'd been Matt's boss in the youth program. From Roberts, McNamara learned about the young girl who'd charged that Matt pushed her for sex, even the cleaning woman he'd propositioned. From there, McNamara went to the Family Y and heard about the allegations from teenage girls that had led to Matt's firing. All of it fit the police report Bennett and McNamara already had from Waco PD, the one from the woman who said Matt assaulted her at Baylor.

As McNamara and Bennett assessed it, there'd been many opportunities to hold Baker accountable, but no one had taken the step of reporting his actions to police. "What I found disturbing was that he was allowed all these years to engage in criminal acts," says McNamara. "Matt Baker is a coward and a bully. He bullied these women, and no one stood up for them."

There were others to whom Nancy directed Mike and John, including the teenage neighbor Matt kissed in the parking lot and the friend of Lindsey's he'd propositioned in the hospital. As McNamara made his way from church to church asking questions about the former pastor, at times he was rebuffed, as in Riesel, where he was told that those in charge of the church had received a letter from Matt's lawyer warning them to be careful what they said about his client. "I can't talk with you," a man there told McNamara. "I have to protect our church!"

Another meeting was held with Bill Johnston. Linda attended, and the two private investigators reported all they'd learned. "More and more I realized that Matt had a dark side I knew nothing about," says Linda. "Matt was incapable of truly loving a woman. And I felt sadness for Kari, that she'd died never really having been loved by a man."

Meanwhile, Jim continued to fight his own demons, carrying the guilt of not having been able to protect his daughter. At times he daydreamed about finding a way to even the score, hunting Matt down, and throwing him into a pit. Frustrated and angry, one night in his dreams, Jim believed that he heard God's voice. "You're not going to do anything about this. I know what he did was wrong, but what gives you the right to take their daddy away?" the voice asked. "I will take care of this. And you will wait on my will."

In July, Matt wrote a letter of resignation to WCY, explaining that he was moving to Kerrville. To coworkers, he blamed the move on gossip his in-laws were stirring up. "I want to get the girls away from all this," he said to one.

Evidence mounting, decisions were being made. As Johnston saw it, his two investigators were very different. McNamara tended to go with his heart, and he'd believed within weeks of taking the case that Matt had killed his wife. Bennett was the more systematic of the two. He'd been the one who kept questioning, pushing, trying to look at the case from all sides before coming to a conclusion. That day, Bennett told Johnston, "You know, based on Matt's own story, it couldn't have happened that way. She couldn't have killed herself in that period of time. All the experts are saying the same thing. The only other one with opportunity is Matt."

During a meeting with McNamara and Bennett, the lawyer told Linda that with the investigation apparently stalling at Hewitt PD, it was time to move ahead on their own. The course of action Johnston recommended was the filing of a wrongful death suit. A civil suit, Johnston explained, would give them subpoena powers, allowing him to obtain employment, medical, police, and other records. He'd also be able to depose witnesses, including Matt Baker. The objective wasn't the money they'd be asking for in the suit, but to arm them with the powers to keep digging. The ultimate goal was to gather enough evidence to move the criminal investigation forward.

"I told you before you didn't need to hire me yet," Johnston told Linda. "Now, if we're going to take this any further, you do."

After talking the situation over with Jim, Linda called Johnston back and said they agreed, giving the attorney the go-ahead to draw up the paperwork and file suit.

In Dallas, Jill and her husband continued to debate whether or not Matt Baker could have or would have murdered his wife. Jill was still having those moments when she'd forget and pick up the phone, wanting to call Kari to tell her something that happened at work or at home. Off and on, Jill called Linda to reminisce about Kari. "We were laughing at all the funny things Kari did," Jill would say later. "It was fun just to have someone to share them with."

It was during one such call that Linda told Jill they were moving forward with the civil suit. "I need to know if we can count on you," Linda said.

Jill considered her response for only a moment. "Kari was like a sister to me, and I'll do whatever I can. I don't believe she killed herself."

Afterward, when she again talked to her husband, Stephen said, "I don't know how you can be so comfortable with the idea that Matt did this."

"You're just not getting it," Jill responded. "Kari couldn't have committed suicide. What are the other options?"

Not long after, Matt called the Hotzes one night, asking questions, Jill believed to see if she'd tell him what Linda had planned. The conversation quickly grew heated. "Kari didn't think I was having an affair," he told her.

"Yes, she did, Matt," Jill countered.

"Do you believe that?"

"It doesn't matter what I believe, Matt. Kari thought you were."

"Do you think I could have had an affair?" he demanded.

"Yes. I think you could," Jill responded. "I didn't at the time, and I wish I hadn't said that to Kari."

"I was your pastor! How could you think that of me?" Over and over, Matt screamed, "I was your pastor!"

Meanwhile, Bennett and McNamara continued to pull information together. One hole they'd been trying to fill for more than a month was the identity of the Baylor woman who'd accused Matt of attempting to sexually assault her. "We had her date of birth and what we finally did was pull up everyone born in Texas on that date," says Bennett. "Then I went through the list, and what I found wasn't a Laura Mueller but a Lora Wilson." With a little more digging, Bennett discovered that the Waco detective who'd taken the report had misspelled the woman's first name, and she'd married, taking her husband's last name, Mueller.

Once he had the right name to work with, Bennett used the Internet to search and uncovered an old phone number. Calling it, he found someone who knew Lora Wilson Mueller and left a message. He hung up not knowing if the

woman who'd fled Baylor after the attack would call or want
to forget the incident and refuse to talk.

The following morning, on July 22, Mueller called Bennett. "I can't speak to what happened to Kari Baker," she
said. "But I can tell you what Matt Baker did to me. I left
Baylor feeling as if they'd turned their backs on me and supported Matt. They treated me like I was some screwed-up
slut who wanted to ruin the life of a good ministerial student."

Before the call ended, she begged, "Please, get him before he does it again!"

On July 26, the final day of her sister Jennifer's weekend
visit, Linda drove the girls home to the house on Crested
Butte. While Jennifer took the girls inside, Linda noticed a
cooler she and Jim had lent Matt in a pile of boxes on the
curb for the garbage collectors. At the time, Matt was getting ready to move to Kerrville. Linda decided to reclaim
her cooler. When she stood over the garbage, she saw family
photos and some of Kari's things, including cards she'd written Matt for birthdays, Christmases, and Valentine's Days.
Inside, Kari had inscribed messages professing her love.

Linda kept looking until she noticed a stack of computer
disks. Deciding those were the most important, she grabbed
the CDs and ran back to her car. Minutes later, Jennifer
emerged, and they drove away.

The wrongful death suit brought by Linda and Jim on behalf
of their granddaughters, Kensi and Grace, was filed on the
last day of July 2006. It read, "On or about April 7, 2006,
Matthew Baker intentionally caused the death of his wife,
Kari Baker. The defendant then falsely reported the death
to the police as a suicide . . . The Dulins suffered because
of Kari's death the loss of a daughter, and Kensi and Grace
lost a mother."

A day later, Bennett drove the two hundred miles from
Waco to Kerrville, and found Matt unpacking a U-Haul

in front of a small duplex. As Bennett watched, a process server handed Matt an envelope. Inside was a copy of the lawsuit. "Have a good day," he said, before he walked away.

Afterward, Matt called Linda, something he hadn't done in months. On the phone, with Jim sitting next to Linda, Matt tried to talk them into dropping the suit.

"Matt, we know you did it," Linda answered.

"Linda, you know . . ." Matt never finished the sentence.

"He never said he hadn't murdered Kari," says Linda.

In early August, in Kerrville, Matt settled in, enrolling the girls in school. He found a position at a funeral home delivering bodies and counseling families. He also found a part-time job at a local university, working with students.

Meanwhile, in Waco, the investigation continued.

One afternoon, Bennett followed up on his interest in the Bulls family, driving again to Troy, and this time talking to Vanessa's father, Larry. An amiable man, Bulls listened as Bennett explained that he was an investigator hired by the Dulins, looking into their daughter's death. Under questioning, Larry Bulls confirmed that Matt had begun calling Vanessa months before Kari's death, in December.

Based on what they now knew from the autopsy, Bennett had an important question: "I asked if anyone in the household had a prescription for Ambien. Larry said that his wife, Cheryl, did. Then I asked if Vanessa could have given Matt Ambien."

"I don't know," Bulls responded, according to Bennett.

Meanwhile, McNamara continued his investigation into Matt's past employment. At the Waco Center for Youth, he heard from Matt's coworkers about his odd behavior, the strange statements he'd made after Kari's death, including how he'd flaunted his relationship with Vanessa and claimed the marriage to Kari had been loveless. Then someone brought up a matter McNamara was particularly interested in: Matt Baker's missing computer. "Matt's computer had gone missing the same day someone saw him walking through the parking lot with a box," says McNamara. "My thought was, of course, what was on it that it was so important, he was willing to steal state property?"

That afternoon, the retired deputy U.S. Marshal took a tour of the facility, and Matt's assistant, Boesche, explained how the doors to the wing that included the chapel and chaplain's office were kept locked, limiting access. When they reached Matt's old office, the facility's head of security, Dennis Edwards, attempted to use a master key to open the door. To his surprise, the key didn't work. Later, Edwards determined why. Months earlier, Matt had asked the complex's handyman to change the lock.

"Do you dispense Ambien here?" McNamara asked Edwards.

"I don't know," he answered. "But we follow national patient safety regulations, and the nurses dispense the medicines."

Another piece of the puzzle clicked into place when McNamara talked to Salazar, and she recounted the events of June 19, the day Matt's computer disappeared, including that she'd told him that the computer was subject to subpoena.

Before he left WCY, McNamara asked Edwards to secure any data off the main network from Matt's old computer. "We'll be getting a subpoena," he said. "I'll be back."

Later, at a meeting in Johnston's office, McNamara filled in Linda, Johnston, and Bennett. Everyone at the meeting immediately realized the importance of what McNamara had found out. "As more information came in, it was like bombshells exploding," says Bennett.

"It was obvious that this was a deliberate plan to get rid of the computer," says Johnston.

For Linda, it was another piece of evidence proving how little she knew about her son-in-law. "I could see she really didn't want to believe all of it," says McNamara. "But the evidence just kept piling up."

As reluctant as she'd been to embrace the possibility,

by then even Linda was convinced that there was no other feasible explanation. Matt had murdered Kari. "I knew my child. She wasn't perfect, but she was a good woman. She tried her best to be a good wife and mother. She just didn't know whom she'd married. Maybe Matt killed my daughter because he'd fallen in love with his latest conquest. Whatever the reason, it was becoming obvious that Matt Baker wanted my daughter dead."

As they talked, the conversation often wound back to another tragedy, Kassidy's death. There were so many similarities, too many to ignore. When Johnston wondered out loud if Matt might have killed Kassidy, too, the possibility terrified Linda. "I began to worry that Kensi or Grace could become inconvenient for Matt," says Linda. "What if they were in danger as well?"

Chapter 40

Bill Johnston began a war room in his office. Brown butcher paper lined the walls, and each time a new piece of evidence was found in the Baker case, he wrote it on the time line. One afternoon, Matt Cawthon stopped in, and he, Johnston, Bennett, and McNamara looked over the chart and discussed the case, Cawthon making suggestions. As the meeting ended, Linda arrived.

"I don't know what I can do," Cawthon said. "But before this is over, I'm going to arrest Matt Baker."

Tears in her eyes, Linda hugged him, and whispered, "Thank you."

"It's not a favor to you," he replied. "It's the right thing to do."

A similar process was under way at Hewitt PD's headquarters, where Spear and Toombs tracked all the incidents and facts they hoped would reveal how Kari had died. One day, Toombs called Matt's attorney, Villarrial, asking again about the possibility of Matt's taking a polygraph. To his surprise, the defense attorney informed him that Matt had already done just that, a private one set up through the law office. "I'll send you the results." When they arrived, however, it was Toombs's opinion that it was worthless: "There were three questions, all about the pills, none of which were conclusive."

"The questions weren't substantial enough," Toombs told Villarrial on the phone. "I'd like to have him take one given by law enforcement."

"I'll check with Matt," the attorney answered, but Toombs never heard from him.

Leads continued to funnel in, often through those who contacted Linda. One was Heather Sigler, the young woman who worked at Kay Jewelers on the day Vanessa and Matt looked at engagement rings. After Linda talked to her, she passed the information on to Bennett and McNamara, who in turn called Matt Cawthon with the lead.

The Ranger was still trying to collaborate with Hewitt PD, but while Spear and Toombs were working on the case, Chief Barton seemed intransigent about pushing it. Cawthon had a hard time understanding that. "He should have been admitting that they screwed up, asking what can we do to fix it," he says. "But he just wanted it to go away."

When he looked at the case, Cawthon believed Bulls was the key. He began calling Vanessa, but she ignored his messages. The one time Cawthon got her on the phone, she was at work. "You wait, and I'll be right there," he told her. "We're going to talk."

"I'm leaving. I don't want to talk to you," Bulls said.

"I told her exactly what I thought of her," says Cawthon. "I knew I wasn't going to catch a fly with honey with her. I told her, 'I'll be coming after you.'"

Frustrated, Cawthon decided that the best way to get Bulls to talk was to put her in front of a grand jury. Yet, his badge didn't give him that power. The only one who could order Vanessa to appear was the county's district attorney. Determined, Cawthon drove his SUV downtown and parked in front of the grand stone, more-than-a-century-old McLennan County Courthouse. Once there, he ran up the long flight of stairs, through the doors, and into the balconied lobby, under a dome topped with open-winged eagles and a sculpture of Themis, the Greek goddess of law and justice.

Once inside, Cawthon dropped in to talk to Melanie Walker, a slender woman with long dark hair, a prosecutor who'd successfully taken on a spate of murder cases. "I went over all we had with her," says Cawthon. "I told her what I needed, and that I wanted Bulls brought in front of a grand jury, that I believed that could open up the case. She said, 'Let's do it.' But later, when I talked to her, Melanie had a sheepish look on her face. I asked what was wrong, and she said she'd had a meeting with her boss, Segrest."

"We're not going to be able to help you," Walker said, according to Cawthon. When he asked why, she explained, "Because of Bill Johnston. The district attorney says he won't have anything to do with anything involving Bill Johnston."

Later, Walker would deny the above scene, saying she was unsure who gave her the order not to proceed. But Cawthon stood firm on his account, saying he saw the situation as purely political. Over the years, according to Cawthon, when Johnston was a federal prosecutor, he'd taken cases Segrest refused. "Bill Johnston was strong where Segrest was weak," says Cawthon. "It's as simple as that."

What Cawthon said he told Walker was: "You're telling me that there's a state law-enforcement agent standing in front of you, requesting the tools you would afford any investigator, and you're telling me you're not going to provide me with the tools to continue this investigation? And this is a murder case?"

According to Cawthon, Walker answered, "Don't kill the messenger."

As soon as he'd filed the wrongful death suit, Johnston had his office write subpoenas for records from all Matt's former employers, the Hewitt Police Department, the EMT service that sent paramedics to the scene, Baylor University, Kari's medical records, and something else: records pertaining to little Kassidy Lynn Baker.

While they didn't have anything solid, Johnston, McNamara, and Bennett had mounting suspicion that if Matt murdered Kari, it might not have been his first killing. They'd talked often about the similarities between Kassidy's and Kari's deaths, from the time of night, just after midnight, to Matt's being the only one with both of them. Bennett involuntarily shuddered when Jill Hotz repeated what Matt had told her: that both Kassidy and Kari were in fetal positions when he found them.

Now something in particular had McNamara's attention, something he and Bennett found on one of the computer disks Linda had pulled from Matt's trash: a paper entitled "The Eyes of a Child." Matt had written it a month after Kassidy's death for his Human Growth and Faith Development class at Truett Seminary. The paper told Kassidy's story, but what seemed odd to McNamara was the way Matt repeatedly described his daughter's eyes. "Kassidy's blue eyes can pierce the hardest of hearts and melt a heart of stone," Baker had written.

"What do you think about that?" Bennett asked.

"That is so weird," McNamara said, explaining that it brought to mind something he'd noticed over the years, that law-enforcement officers who'd taken a life, even in the line of duty, often later remembered looking into the eyes of the person they'd killed. "That Baker wrote about Kassidy's eyes gave me the chills," says McNamara. "It made me think about that little girl looking up at him from her bed that night, seeing her daddy. And I wondered what Matt might have done to her."

Chapter 41

In Waco, especially at Crossroads, rumors circulated that Vanessa and Matt had broken up. "We heard that Larry Bulls told people that he and Cheryl asked Vanessa not to see Matt until the investigation into Kari's death was over," says a church member.

On August 4, 2006, Cawthon and Ben Toombs again discussed strategy, and it was decided that Toombs and Mike Spear would confront Vanessa and bring her in without prior warning. "We didn't know for sure what her situation was with Baker," says Toombs. "We didn't want her calling him and having him tell her not to talk to us."

That evening, they went to Tarleton, where Vanessa had a class. She'd say later that not enough students had shown up, and the professor sent her on her way about eight forty-five. Spear and Toombs followed her car to a grocery store.

When they walked up, Vanessa at first looked stunned, perhaps a bit frightened, but she agreed to talk. At the station, they escorted her into the same small interview room in which Cooper had talked to Matt months earlier. They suggested she take a chair in the corner, then they stepped out for a few minutes. At that point, the video camera was turned on, aimed at where Bulls sat. Her long blond hair pulled back in a ponytail, she wore a short-sleeved, dark green and gold John Deere T-shirt and black athletic shorts.

She had a tube-shaped pink purse on the table beside her. While the officers talked in an adjacent office, Vanessa fidgeted. She alternated between appearing bored and bothered, yawning one moment and peering peevishly at her watch the next.

"Do you want water?" Toombs asked, sticking his head in the door. When she said yes, he returned with a clear plastic bottle. She unscrewed the top and took a swig. A longer wait, then the interview began, with Toombs reading Bulls the Miranda warning. At first, he asked the essentials, including her birth date. At one point she grabbed a tissue and dabbed at her eyes. "I'm sorry," she said. "This is just scary."

The officers murmured that she had no reason to be upset; they simply had a few questions. At first, they let Bulls talk while planting the occasional prod to keep the conversation flowing. Yet, they needed to say little. From the tone of it, Bulls had been thinking for a long time about what she would say if ever questioned by the police. As if she'd rehearsed, she laid out her version of the events that had transpired since she met Matt and Kari in the fall of 2005, when he became pastor at Crossroads, where Bulls's father was the music minister. "Kari and I became good acquaintances," she said.

As she described it, Kari often talked with Bulls about her divorce and Lilly. Appearing as angry as sad, Bulls cried when she talked about how her ex-husband had signed away his parental rights "because he doesn't want anything to do with Lilly." What Bulls didn't mention was that this came after a paternity test proved her ex-husband wasn't Lilly's biological father.

Rather than Matt, Vanessa said that when the Bakers arrived at Crossroads, it was Kari who reached out to her. "I have a daughter they loved, and their daughters loved mine. Kari and I talked about getting together for dinner and to get the kids and eat out or something."

It was Matt, however, who Bulls said began calling her house in either late January or early February 2006, two months before Kari's death. "He asked for my father, but he wasn't there," she explained. "He said he didn't know I'd be home."

Vanessa was home afternoons with Lilly and going to school at Tarleton in the evenings. From that point on, Matt called often, spiraling from a couple of times a week to two or three calls a day. "He wanted to chat. I thought that he was doing the pastor thing. It didn't get inappropriate or out of context," Bulls assured the officers. "He asked about my divorce and said God would work everything out."

"Did it seem like he was pursuing you a little bit?" Toombs asked.

"He seemed happily married. He never talked bad about his wife or anything," Bulls answered, gesturing with her hands. "I felt sorry for him. He talked a lot about Kassidy, and my heart went out to him . . . It was nice to have someone to talk to."

On the phone, Matt went into detail recounting Kassidy's illness and death. "He said that Kari had never quite gotten over it and was depressed," Bulls said. "Sometimes she made the other girls feel like she loved Kassidy more than she loved them."

Answering questions, Bulls related how she'd gone with her parents to the Dulins' house the afternoon of Kari's death, then to the funeral. That night, Matt called and spoke with Vanessa's parents, talking about what Matt described as Kari's depression. The first time he came to their home was one week to the day after Kari's death, when Vanessa's parents invited Matt and the girls for dinner and an egg hunt on Good Friday. "We wanted to be there for him and the girls," Vanessa stressed. "For the long haul."

That evening, at the Bulls's home, Matt suggested that he and Vanessa could take the girls out together for dinners. It was the girls, she said, who drew her to agree. "He really wasn't my type. He's shorter than I am," she said, smacking on a piece of gum she chewed steadily throughout the interview. "But I really loved Kensi and Grace."

After that, they took the girls to McDonald's and the movies. It was a surprise, she said, when her father told her about a month after Kari's death that Matt had come to him and asked if he could begin dating Vanessa. "I just thought all we were doing was taking the kids out," Vanessa said.

"And what did your parents say?" Toombs asked.

"At that point, they thought he was just a great person who had just suffered so much in his life," she said, gesturing with her hands. "From what he had started to tell us about Jim and Linda and some other people at Crossroads being out to get him, we all felt sorry for him. . . ."

"How did you feel about his asking your father that?" Toombs asked.

"I was upset about it that he didn't talk to me first," she answered. But "it was good to have a friend. I'd be lying if I didn't say that it would be nice . . ." Bulls began crying again, as she mentioned her daughter, "to have someone who had two daughters and who would possibly be the dad to my child . . . I loved his kids more than him."

Their dating, she said, had been more than sanitary, chaperoned at all times by their three children. "It was never a one-on-one thing," she stressed.

Even that, she insisted, had been short-lived. Her parents began telling her that much of what Matt said didn't make sense and that they were hearing conflicting stories from people at Crossroads, including that the police were investigating Kari's death.

At first, Bulls said she hadn't wanted to hear it. With the breakup of her marriage, she said, "I didn't care about the rumors. I was going to stand by him with those two girls. He made me believe he was totally great, and everyone was out to get him. Another part of me just didn't want my parents to be right about another guy."

Her parents, she said, asked her to stop seeing Matt, but she'd initially refused.

From the beginning, much of what she said tracked closely what Matt had told Cooper. And it often appeared that Vanessa wanted to control the interviewing, telling the officers only what she wanted them to know. When one asked a question, she cut him off, then smiled. Despite initially supporting Matt, she said she began to see that he wasn't being honest. She heard from others about his sordid past. "My parents told me some of the stuff, and it made me want to throw up," she said, grabbing a tissue.

When she broke it off, Matt was angry but "didn't rage violent or anything." How had it affected her? Bulls shrugged again. "I've been fine since. I haven't lost any sleep."

Throughout the interview, Bulls tugged off and on at her T-shirt's round neck, as if she felt constrained by it. When it was evident that her recounting had ended, Toombs said, "Let's go back to where he started calling you."

"Okay," she said, nodding.

More details came out as Toombs asked questions about what Matt had said. "He told me that Kari had attempted suicide once before." That time, as well, it had been with sleeping pills, and Matt insisted that the Dulins knew about all that had transpired.

Bulls said she hadn't noticed any changes in Matt in the weeks before or the weeks after Kari's death. At the Dulins' home the day after Kari's death, Vanessa, like so many others, had noticed how calm Matt looked. "He told me he was that way when Kassidy passed away, too," she said. "So I thought that different people just act differently."

Bulls never mentioned the Christmas potluck where Matt cornered her and suggested they date. Instead, she insisted that Matt had never come on to her. Theirs, she said, had not been a sexual relationship. But there were strange things, like the day he told people at church, soon after Kari's death, that five-year-old Grace already "knows who she wants her new mommy to be."

"You didn't believe that?" Toombs asked.

"It didn't sound like something a five-year-old would say."

There were things that, in hindsight, she found odd, including the way Matt talked to his daughters: asking them a question, listening to their answers, then asking them another question. "It was like he kept asking until he got them to say what he wanted," she said. "I didn't think about it at the time, but it was manipulative."

When Toombs asked Vanessa if it was possible that Matt was upset with Kari because he wanted to be with her, Bulls covered her mouth with her hand, as if aghast. "Well, that didn't cross my mind until a couple of weeks ago," Bulls said. "I was like, that can't be . . . I've seen too many Lifetime movies."

Rather than be upset on Kari's behalf, that Matt might have killed his wife, Bulls seemed to take the suggestion more as a personal insult: "If he did that . . . if he thought that I just got divorced . . . he was . . . going to slide me into their lives . . . That's wrong."

Then Toombs asked *the* question: Did she believe Matt murdered his wife?

She grimaced, then said: "Nothing is out of possibility after I found out about the stuff he lied to me about. I think he might have done it."

"Did you and Matt have any kind of romantic relationship before Kari died?"

"No," Bulls said, shaking her head. "No!"

"Did you have any kind of relationship anyone else could perceive as romantic?"

"Obviously, other people have perceived it, which to a point offends me," Bulls said, rather indignantly. When asked, she insisted that Matt had never said anything to her she interpreted as wishing Kari was dead. All he'd said, she repeated, was that Kari was depressed and hard to live with at times.

When asked to, Vanessa, long bare legs crossed and the water bottle close at hand, recounted what Matt had told her about the night Kari died, everything from running to the store and gas station to unlocking the door and finding Kari dead, her lips blue and cold. The story matched what Matt had told Sergeant Cooper the night of Kari's death, including that he'd been gone about forty-five minutes.

Then Toombs asked something that appeared to take Bulls by surprise. "Did Matt ever mention that Kari found medication in his briefcase?"

"She found medicine in his briefcase?" Vanessa repeated. "No."

Before long, Vanessa was talking more about what she'd heard, including that the church had found records of Matt's calling the Bulls's house when her parents weren't home. At times, it would be obvious how uncomfortable Toombs was at his close involvement, knowing Vanessa and her parents. As the interview progressed, it would seem ever more apparent that many of those on the edges of the case had been talking and comparing notes. Vanessa even pointed out that Ben's mother had assured hers that Vanessa wouldn't be questioned.

When Toombs and Spear stood up and said they wanted to talk a bit, and they'd be back, she asked if she could call her mother. "She'll be worried," Vanessa said.

"Sure," Toombs told her.

Alone in the room, the camera rolling, Vanessa stared at her cell phone, then punched in a number. "Hey, I just wanted to call and let you know it's going to be a little while longer before I'm home. Ben Toombs asked me if I'd come talk to him."

Although only one side of the conversation was recorded, it was apparent that Vanessa's mother was concerned. "I just answered some questions," Vanessa said. "I'm being truthful."

Again, she repeated, "It's okay. I'm just answering questions."

The one piece of new information she quickly imparted was what she'd just heard from Toombs, that Kari found pills in Matt's briefcase. Hunched over, her elbows on her knees, Vanessa talked. "I was surprised they hadn't questioned me before since we dated a little bit afterward," she said. "It's good we're getting this over with now . . . It was scary at first. It was like whoa, why didn't you just call me and ask me to come in . . . Basically everything I told y'all . . . I stopped talking to him when I found out things were facts . . . I'm nervous, too, Mom. I hate that I ever even showed up at Crossroads and chose to let Matt into our lives once Kari passed away."

Apparently to still her mother's fears, Vanessa then said, "I didn't hide anything, so you don't have to worry. I really think I'm okay because I don't have anything to hide."

Moments later, Toombs and Spear returned, and a few minutes later, two more men entered, one a Secret Service agent who happened to be at Hewitt PD and offered help. Vanessa looked concerned but didn't miss a beat, answering the questions Toombs asked but turning her chair to look more toward the new arrivals. With that, the visiting Secret Service agent took over, and Vanessa, without protesting, answered again, giving the same description of the events as they'd unfolded.

"Do you think he had anything to do with her death?" the man asked.

"After I found out about his lying, I think anything is possible now," she answered.

"Was there anything that you found suspicious?"

That was when Vanessa went into more detail about what Matt had told her about Kassidy's death. In that conversation, he'd said that when he found Kassidy not breathing, he'd had to replace her trach tube. That it wasn't attached as it should have been seemed odd, and Vanessa later discussed it with a friend, who told her that if someone has a tracheotomy, the tube is left in, not removed. "I began to worry if he did something to his daughter," she said.

Again she repeated, this time for the two new arrivals, that the relationship with Matt had never become "inappropriate" and that it didn't begin until after Kari's death.

When she described telling Matt that the relationship was over, Vanessa cried.

Comforting her, the Secret Service agent said: "I've been interviewing the Matt Bakers of the world . . . What he did is use you. There's no doubt in my mind that he did something to his wife. There's no doubt in my mind that he may have done something to his daughter. Maybe he saw this as getting rid of his wife to have a relationship with you. The person caught in the middle is the twenty-four-year-old divorced woman."

"He had girls. I had a girl. He was a pastor . . ." Vanessa said. "I didn't think it would come back to bite me."

"It didn't, Vanessa," the agent again assured her. "It's just one of those things where it's up to us to get an insight into his life. The Matt Bakers of the world use young women like you who are vulnerable."

They talked, Vanessa insisting that they had no need to have Ranger Cawthon or anyone else call her, and that she'd talk with them again if they had any questions. "I was surprised it took you so long to question me," she said.

"We appreciate your coming in. We all know who Matt is now. He's a dirtbag."

"Why'd it take me so long to see that," Vanessa said, again crying.

In their haste to make her feel better, it would later seem there were many questions left unasked that day. The investigators gathered around her in that room never asked the pretty young blonde when she'd first gone to Matt's house. They never asked if Matt had ever told her that he planned to kill his wife. And, perhaps most importantly, they never spelled out that Vanessa needed to be careful. If she wasn't telling the truth, if she lied and they found out, she could be considered a party to a murder. In hindsight, there was much left unasked and unanswered in that dismal interview room in the run-down Hewitt police station.

Two hours after the interview began, the investigators left the room, and Vanessa again waited. Outside of her earshot, they discussed the interview. "The Secret Service agent said he was sure she was telling the truth," Toombs would say later. "He told me there was no reason to ask her to take a lie detector test."

Back in the room, Toombs and Spear prepared to take Vanessa back to Temple to pick up her car. "My mother's going to be upset," she said to Toombs.

"I'll talk to her," he said. "You are in no . . . trouble about this . . . you weren't involved."

How were they all so sure? Was Vanessa Bulls telling the truth? Did she know more than she'd told them? Perhaps the Secret Service agent should have listened to his own warnings, when he'd told her, "You just never know about people, you really don't."

Chapter 42

After Johnston filed his motions for subpoenas, Matt's attorneys filed countermotions, attempting to block Johnston from obtaining the records and depositions he'd requested, including those involving Kari's and Kassidy's deaths. In the end, the judge ruled that Kassidy's records weren't relevant to the wrongful death suit but upheld the subpoenas for information on Kari. Quickly, the records began pouring in.

Among the first to arrive were those from Hewitt PD and the EMT service. Once they had those in hand, Johnston and Bennett traveled to Edmond, Oklahoma, to meet with Tom Bevel, a crime-scene and blood-splatter expert who'd worked for twenty-seven years for the Oklahoma City Police Department. With them they carried copies of the scene photos, the autopsy, the EMTs' reports, a DVD of Matt's interview with Cooper, and a time line they'd constructed based on Matt's statement and the receipts he'd produced to police.

"They were basically looking for an independent analysis of what the scene said," says Bevel, who'd specialized in forensic science for eighteen years, testifying in high-profile cases including that of Darlie Routier, the Dallas housewife convicted of murdering her two young sons.

After they left, Bevel began by looking at the scene

photos, taking in any clues he could find based on what he saw of Kari's body and the room itself. After he'd absorbed what he could, he turned to the autopsy, statement, and time line, comparing those to what he'd already gleaned from the photos.

Later, Bevel put his findings into a formal letter for Johnston, writing: "I would not expect to be able to observe any visible signs of lividity in less than thirty minutes minimum and up to two hours maximum . . . The extent of lividity seen in the photographs of Mrs. Baker and that reported by the EMT personnel does not comport with the time line given by Mr. Baker. In my opinion much more time has elapsed from Mrs. Baker's death until it is reported, than stated by Mr. Baker."

Bevel then pointed out that death is a process that takes time. If Matt was gone for forty-five minutes, and Kari was alive when he left, Kari had to take the pills and the pills had to have time to work. Lividity wouldn't have begun until Kari's heart stopped, until she was dead. "This does not comport with the time frame as given by Mr. Baker." Bevel also questioned how Kari had so quickly become cold to the touch.

As troubling was Matt's description of dressing Kari's body before the EMTs arrived. "I have worked a number of cases in which an unconscious or deceased person has been dressed," he wrote. "Due to their 'dead body weight,' this dressing by another is very difficult and usually obvious. The position of Mrs. Baker's panties are much more consistent with her dressing herself, as they appear in a normal position."

Bevel also noted what appeared to be bruising on Kari's nose and lips in the scene and autopsy photos. When he talked with Johnston, Bevel mentioned that this type of injury suggested that Kari might have first been drugged, then smothered.

After bringing up the typewritten, unsigned suicide note, Bevel concluded: "There is enough contradictory information in this case that I would highly recommend further action on this investigation."

Johnston already had the opinion from the toxicologist, Dr. Stafford, who said unequivocally that Kari hadn't died of an overdose. Now the lawyer turned to another expert, William Lee Carter, a Waco psychologist who testified in criminal trials. This time, Johnston supplied his expert with information on Matt's past with women. "I wanted to know what a professional thought of Matt's personality type," says Johnston.

When Carter called with his conclusions, they weren't a surprise to any of those involved in the investigation. "Mr. Baker has a history of serious sexual indiscretion with females. There is an elusive, manipulative quality to his personality. A relationship with a female gave him reason to desire his wife's absence from his life, creating motive for murder."

Carter pointed out that Matt himself had made it clear to police that he was the only one with Kari on the night of her death. Also not to be discounted were Kari's words to Bristol: "Research validates that a woman's reports of perceived death intentions by a husband is one of the most telling diagnostic precursors to spousal murder."

Adding Matt's "dark personal history" to the other evidence the team had pulled together surrounding Kari's death, including Matt's apparent lack of grief, Carter said, painted a damning picture.

After Johnston filled Linda and Jim in on the reports, she called the experts, wanting to hear firsthand. Afterward, she was ever more certain that Kari had not died by her own hand. "I thought, oh, my gosh, Matt really is a sexual predator, and he murdered our daughter," she says. "Everything my sisters had wondered about, it was all true."

Off and on, Toombs and Spear went to the DA's Office as Cawthon did, talking to Melanie Walker, asking for guidance. "I told them that they didn't have enough for probable cause," says Walker. "The scene wasn't even processed like a questionable death. Without homicide on the autopsy or death certificate, the potential for reasonable doubt was huge."

Yet the evidence kept mounting. Matt had suggested that the police talk to a woman named Holly Romano, someone who'd seen Kari the evening before her death at the Y during swim practice. What Matt told Cooper was that Romano remarked about how tired Kari appeared. When Toombs talked to the woman, however, Romano said, "That's not true."

In fact, Kari mentioned that she'd interviewed for a new job and it had gone well that day, seeming to look forward to the change to middle school. "Did Kari leave to go get sick in the restroom?" Toombs asked, repeating what Baker had told Cooper.

"Not that I saw," Romano replied.

At about that time, Mike McNamara met with the director of the Y, who showed him records documenting Matt's firing from the staff. Waiting for an official subpoena, which she hadn't yet been served, the woman wouldn't let him take the records, only read them. When McNamara was done, another Y employee approached him. "I always worried about Kari," she said. "Matt has a terrible temper. I was afraid he could hurt her. When she died, I immediately thought something had to be wrong."

After McNamara left, he filled in Bennett and Johnston, then talked to Spear and Toombs, suggesting they interview the same women. The two officers followed up quickly and left with another piece in the puzzle of Matt Baker's personality.

Then, in mid-August, McNamara returned to WCY, this time with the power of a subpoena, one for everything on the facility's network generated by Matt's missing computer.

Afterward, McNamara took the CDs to Johnston's office and began looking through them on a computer. But he and Bennett couldn't open the files. Deciding it must be encrypted, they returned to WCY and asked to have the documents transferred into "something we can read."

From there, McNamara and Johnston went on to other matters while Bennett and Johnston's secretary searched the files. Before long, what Bennett saw gave him chills: Internet searches on drug sites. "We've got something," he said, calling out to McNamara and Johnston.

That evening, Bennett and Johnston worked late, combing through the disks. "We found what looked like a history of Matt shopping for drugs, and we couldn't be sure, but it looked like he'd purchased Ambien."

In July, after Linda had taken the disks out of Matt's garbage, the one with the chilling description of Kassidy's blue eyes, Johnston had hired another expert to work the case, a computer guru named Noel Kersh, a Texas Tech grad who worked with Pathway Forensics, a Houston-based consulting firm. Now, Johnston called Kersh, asking him to come to Waco. When he did, Kersh and Johnston met with Linda at the office. A short time later, Kersh left with the WCY disks and the Crossroads Dell laptop, the one Waco police had found nothing of interest on.

Back in Houston, Kersh began with the laptop. He wasn't looking long before he found a history that seemed unusual for a man of the cloth. Baker had been using the computer to access dating and pornographic Web sites, among them private.camz.com and coolanalsite.com. It wasn't shocking news. Besides Linda's description of the porn that had shown up on Matt and Kari's home computer, Bennett had looked at the laptop earlier, finding the porn sites intermingled with Matt's searches for Internet sermons. "Look at what that idiot's been up to," Bennett had told Johnston.

From the laptop, Kersh turned to the WCY disks. Over a period of days, he slowly worked through the material. One of the first things he found was a folder marked Dulin Family Crap. In it were e-mails between Kari and Matt and Linda and Matt. He copied those to a disk and kept going.

As he delved even further, Kersh saw more records illustrating that the chaplain's eye often strayed from the heavens. Matt's work-computer trail also led to a long list of dating and pornographic Internet sites. The URLs were descriptive of where the minister's interests lay, from widewomen.com, to sexlist.com, hotmatchup.com, sextracker. com, sexdatenetwork.com, bustydustystash.com, playboy. com, iwantanewgirlfriend.com, and hornymatches.com.

While that was interesting, perhaps opening the window wider into Matt's mind, it didn't answer the important question: Had Matt murdered Kari? Rather than Matt's sexual leanings, what Johnston was interested in was any computer activity that indicated that Matt Baker had shopped for drugs, most importantly Ambien, the drug found in Kari's body on autopsy. Before long, there, too, Kersh hit pay dirt.

The list of drug Web sites Matt had visited was long, including drugs.com, medicinenet.com, search.drugs.com, Rxlist.com, hydrocodone.com, drugslist.com, and 1stmeds. com. He'd even dropped in at ambien.com. As Kersh combed through the information, one site stood out, and that was the one Kersh mentioned to Johnston when he called with the results. Explaining that to complete an Internet purchase a buyer had to go to a shopping cart, Kersh pointed to one Web page in particular that popped up on Matt's history: secure.rx-cart.com. On March 23, two weeks before Kari's death, Matt's account accessed that page on the site of a Canadian-based, online pharmacy. It appeared that he'd placed an order in his shopping cart.

After talking to Johnston, Kersh followed through and contacted the company. Before long, he was put in touch with the owner, a man named Mark Henry. "Can you make sure that all of it checks out, find out what he put in the cart?" Kersh asked.

When Henry called back, he confirmed that it was the WCY computer that logged on with the user name mattdb7722. What was even more interesting was the item in mattdb7722's shopping cart: generic Ambien.

"Did he buy it?" Kersh asked.

It was there that it became more complicated. The purchase was never completed, Henry explained, but that wasn't unusual. Many potential buyers backed out at that particular juncture, after they had the drugs in their cart. Henry attributed the lost sales to the fact that it was at that very point that buyers learned of a two-week delay before the drugs could be delivered.

Yet if Kersh hadn't found conclusive proof that Matt Baker had bought the sleeping pills, the computer expert had uncovered evidence that someone on the former minister's computer was shopping for Ambien.

After documenting all he'd discovered, Kersh again returned to the WCY CDs. It didn't take long before he found something else intriguing: Matt's computer had accessed sites that sold hydrocodone painkillers and GHB, a drug similar to roofies, the date rape drug that renders victims unconscious and wipes out their memories.

Yet something else waited for Kersh on the computer. On March 9, a month before Kari's death, mattdb7722 had Googled the phrase "overdose on sleeping pills."

Considering what he'd uncovered, Kersh knew he had one more step to pull it all together. While interesting, there was one big question mark: Could Kersh determine who'd been on Matt's computer when the sites were accessed? Could he prove the mattdb7722 who shopped for Ambien was Matt Baker?

To find the answer, Kersh charted the computer's activity. What he documented was an interwoven Internet history between Matt Baker and mattdb7722. For instance at 8:30 A.M. on March 9, Matt sent an e-mail to a work associate. Thirteen minutes later, he scoured the Internet for pharmaceutical sites. After looking up Ambien, Matt then went to a page that included the safety warnings: *The most commonly observed side effects in controlled clinical trials were drowsi-*

ness, dizziness, and diarrhea . . . Don't take with alcohol, as it may increase these behaviors.

Then, after Googling "overdose on sleeping pills" at 9:27 that morning, thirty-six minutes later, Matt sent an e-mail to Kari at school. What those documents proved was that on the morning mattdb7722 was scouting for drugs, Matt Baker was sitting at the computer.

One other thing Kersh found wouldn't mean anything to those involved in the case until later, that Matt had used his computer to purchase herbal sexual stimulants, over-the-counter capsules that the Web site described as aphrodisiacs "ten times better than herbal ecstasy."

When they heard the news about the Ambien, Johnston, McNamara, and Bennett felt the sky open up. "We'd found as close as we could to a smoking gun," says Bennett.

When they told Toombs, his early doubts about the case vanished. "This is the real deal," he thought.

With the evidence piling up, Bennett and McNamara dropped in at the district attorney's office and talked to Walker. Cawthon hadn't been successful getting the prosecutors interested in the case in the past, but the two investigators wanted to keep the assistant district attorney up to date. "We couldn't prove to her what had happened, but we could show that what Matt Baker said had happened couldn't have happened," says McNamara.

Walker listened but didn't offer to take it on. "It wasn't handled as a murder investigation from the beginning. It was handled as a suicide," she's say later. "There was a lack of evidence. They had a dead girl and a family who cared about her, and Mike and John were doing their jobs, but the finding on the autopsy was still a big problem."

Although disappointed, Bennett and McNamara weren't ready to give up. Instead, they pored through the e-mails in the folder marked Dulin Family Crap. Before long, Mike McNamara thought he saw a pattern. In the fall of 2005, the e-mails from Matt to Kari were sweet, even solicitous. But from February on, during the time Matt was calling Vanessa Bulls, "You could see the change of attitude on Matt's part. It was sickening," says McNamara.

Other information kept being produced in connection with the subpoenas Johnston's office cranked out. When they issued one for Kari's Bible, Matt didn't produce it, but when the Hewitt PD records showed up, they found the copy Sadler had made of Kari's plea for God's protection. "I read it and thought about how frightened Kari was," says McNamara. "How alone she must have felt."

Like Cawthon, Bennett and McNamara both believed that Vanessa Bulls was the key to the case. On August 30, McNamara called and asked her to meet with them at Johnston's office. She agreed. When they asked questions, she answered much as she had to Toombs and Spear nearly a month earlier, maintaining there'd been no sexual relationship with Matt Baker. Neither McNamara nor Bennett believed her. "She wasn't being truthful," says Bennett. You could tell."

"She claimed everything was lily-white with Baker, no flirting, no kissing, no sexual encounters. It was unbelievable," says McNamara. "She kept saying that she had never been attracted to him but that she thought he might make a good father for her daughter."

One thing Bennett noticed was that Bulls used some of the same phrasing Matt had when describing their relationship. "I felt like he'd schooled her well," says Bennett.

Meanwhile, at Hewitt PD, the criminal case was stalled. Toombs sent the suicide note to the lab, and when it came back, the report said that it had been printed on a Hewlett Packard inkjet printer. Although Johnston had asked repeatedly, Matt hadn't turned over the home computer and printer he'd had at the time of Kari's death, so the only one available for testing was the one from WCY, which turned out to be a Hewlett Packard. Yet when the tests were run, it wasn't a match.

On October 6, 2006, Ben Toombs performed his final official act on the Baker investigation: He returned the printer to WCY. "I felt like Matt had probably killed Kari," says Toombs. "I just wasn't sure that we'd ever be able to prove it."

Chapter 43

Despite the disappointments and the lack of encouragement from law enforcement, Linda and Jim remained steadfast, hopeful that eventually they'd prevail. "We weren't going to just let this fade away," Linda says. "We were convinced that Matt Baker murdered our daughter."

With the District Attorney's Office unwilling to take on the case, the wrongful death suit continued, each side filing motions and countermotions. The first depositions took place in October, beginning with the EMTs. What came through loud and clear was that when they arrived on the scene, Kari's body was already cool. When it came to being any more precise than that, the shoddy investigation was a problem. Since it had been so quickly written off as a suicide, no one had inserted a thermometer into the liver to record Kari's core body temperature. They hadn't even noted the ambient temperature of the bedroom.

Yet common sense said that what the EMTs and paramedics saw contradicted Matt's account. As a rule, dead bodies only lose 1.5 degrees Fahrenheit per hour. With average human body temperature at 98.6, if Kari had been dead for an hour or less, her body should have been 96 degrees or warmer, not so unnaturally cool that the EMTs noted it on their reports.

Finally, at 9:03 on the morning of November 3, seven

months after their daughter's death, Linda and Jim arrived at the offices of Matt's attorney, James Rainey. The date for the depositions had arrived, including one the Dulins had anticipated for a very long time. Both Matt and Linda were scheduled to be deposed that day, but it was Matt's questioning that loomed the largest.

While Matt's deposition was officially for the wrongful death suit the Dulins had brought on behalf of their grand-daughters, everyone gathered knew that the stakes were much higher. Linda and Jim weren't pursuing money but justice. Matt had successfully sidestepped them for a long time, but on this afternoon, that finally promised to be over.

For the first time, Bill Johnston would be able to question Matt, putting him on the record about so many things, from his relationship with Vanessa Bulls to his account of the events on the night Kari died. That information could help on many levels. Locking Matt into his story on videotape during a sworn deposition could allow Johnston to show inconsistencies with his prior statements to police and with the physical evidence. As important, Johnston could ask questions relating to all Mike and John had uncovered about important topics, including Matt's tawdry past. Everything they learned could open up more leads and potentially move the investigation forward.

The conference room filled. Both of Matt's attorneys, James Rainey for the civil case and Gerald Villarrial for the criminal investigation, were there, along with Johnston and the Dulins. Matt looked different than he had in the months following Kari's death. His hair was longer, and he had bangs, but it wasn't all gelled up, as it had been when Linda judged he was attempting to look younger for Vanessa. Johnston didn't recognize a woman with thick, coarse gray hair and a placid countenance, who'd accompanied the others, but Linda did. She was perhaps a little surprised to see Barbara Baker in the room but thought little of it. For his part, Matt barely looked in Linda's direction.

As they congregated around a table in the conference

room, before beginning his questioning, Johnston inquired about evidence Matt had been ordered to bring, items he'd promised to produce. Despite the subpoenas, Matt had arrived empty-handed.

"You felt that you didn't have adequate time to search for them?" Johnston asked.

"That's correct," Matt replied.

At that point, Johnston asked about the individual items: First, Kari's photographs, journals, diaries, notes, greeting cards, and writings. "Will you agree to diligently search for same, for those and provide them?" Johnston asked.

"Yes," Matt agreed.

Category two included Matt and Kari's home computer and printer and everything associated with it, including CDs and memory devices.

"I can search for them, I can," Matt said. "But I've told my attorneys that that computer is no longer in my possession."

"Can you state what happened to the computer?" Johnston asked.

In Matt's account, the computer became slow and wasn't working property, so he used the church laptop instead. Later, he gave the home computer to his father, but the hard drive had crashed and he'd had to rebuild it. "But it does exist?" Johnston asked.

"It does exist," Matt agreed, saying that he would turn it over. When it came to that crashed hard drive, Matt said he no longer had it but had thrown it into the trash.

The printer was a similar story. Matt said that it wasn't compatible with his new computer, so he'd disposed of it. "I believe it was a Canon," he said. The brand was important, because the analysis of the suicide note indicated it had been printed on an HP inkjet. Still, the only evidence of the brand name was Matt's word. When Johnston asked about the missing computer from the Waco Center for Youth, Matt said simply, "That is unknown . . . I am not sure when they were switched."

"Do you possess or have you ever possessed an HP printer?" Johnston asked.

"Yeah," Matt said. Yet, he said he didn't know when they'd had one or what had happened to it. He said he didn't believe that he had an HP at the time of Kari's death.

The final items on Johnston's list were any Bibles or religious materials of any sort owned or possessed by Kari Baker. "Do you agree to look for those?"

"Correct," Matt said.

After a series of additional questions about circumstances surrounding the missing WCY computer, Johnston turned to the other important purpose of the deposition: "I would really like to ask you a number of questions about your life and your life with Kari Baker, of the events over the last few years, and the events of this last spring. Will you answer those questions for me today?"

Matt pursed his lips and shook his head slightly. "I will take the Fifth Amendment. I will assert my right for the Fifth Amendment."

"You previously spoke with the Hewitt Police about this matter?" Johnston prodded.

"That's correct," Matt agreed.

"I'm asking you today to do the same courtesy for me that you've done for the police, who have much more authority than I, and answer questions for me similar to those asked of you then, and others I may have in mind," Johnston said. "Will you do that?"

"Under the advice of my attorneys, I assert my right for the Fifth Amendment."

"Will that be your response if I continue asking questions that are substantive regarding this case?"

"Correct," Baker said.

With that, Matt's deposition ended thirteen minutes after it began. Although Johnston had warned the Dulins this could happen, the reality was still crushing. Jim looked at Linda, and she shook her head in disgust.

It took only moments for the room to be resettled, and for

the tables to turn from Johnston questioning Matt to James Rainey setting his sights on Linda. To begin, Rainey asked: "Why have you filed a wrongful death suit?"

"Because we believe that Matt Baker took our daughter's life and set it up as suicide."

"By 'took her life' you mean he killed her?"

Linda didn't mince words: "I mean he murdered her. Yes, sir."

"Why do you believe these things?" Rainey asked.

Twice Linda started and stopped, trying to get her words together. "I would have preferred that my daughter had taken her life and have my granddaughters safe." She sighed, then continued, "I fought these feelings for quite a while, but there were circumstances that happened beginning shortly after Kari died that would not allow us to ignore what was becoming increasingly clear."

"What do you mean by shortly?" Rainey asked.

"Right after she was buried."

At times, Rainey seemed surprised, as when he asked twice if Kari had truly been buried just two days after her death. "Yes, sir," Linda said, not adding that it was at the insistence of his client. When Rainey asked what spurred her suspicions about Matt, Linda laid out what she'd heard from her sisters.

As his client talked, Johnston wondered about the gray-haired woman seated at the table next to Matt and suddenly questioned if she belonged there. When he discovered the interloper was Matt's mother, Johnston asked Rainey incredulously, "Is she a party to this case?"

"She's not," Rainey admitted.

"I invoke the rule," Johnston said, marveling that the woman would interject herself into the morning's events. "I object to a nonparty being present."

Rainey asked Barbara to leave, and she did.

From that point on, Rainey asked questions about the process that had taken Linda from standing up for her son-in-law to believing that he'd murdered her daughter. They talked of Kari's words to Bristol, and the matters Johnston and his investigators had worked so hard to uncover, including nailing down the allegations in Matt's past. Through it all, Linda detailed everything from finding Vanessa's number on Matt's bills to the way he'd kept the Dulins' granddaughters from them.

At times, the testimony became highly emotional, Linda needing to pause and calm her tumbling emotions. She apologized, then forged ahead. She couldn't answer everything Rainey wanted to know, and she told him so, explaining that the investigation was ongoing. In particular, she wouldn't speculate on how Matt murdered Kari.

Apologetic at times, Linda acknowledged that she was a novice at pulling together the strands of an inquiry into a mysterious death. "I'm not an investigator," she said.

That day, Linda put on the record that she disagreed with much of what Matt had said, including how he portrayed the ride home from the doctor, in which he claimed Kari attempted to jump out on the freeway.

"Did it seem like Matt was overreacting to that or something?" Rainey asked.

"It sounded like Kari thought Matt was being kind of silly," Linda responded.

Perhaps, Rainey suggested, Kari blamed herself for Kassidy's death, agreeing with Matt's charge that she'd been the one responsible. But it wasn't that Kari blamed herself, Linda said: "She thought Matt blamed her . . . She loved Matt, and she was very hurt . . . She defended Matt, always defended Matt."

The conviction that Kari hadn't died as Matt described came in bits and pieces, including the hours Linda spent at the computer researching Unisom. "It was just me being Nancy Drew," she said.

"What do you take for a sleep aid?" Rainey asked.

"I have a prescription my doctor gave me for Ambien, but I don't take it often," Linda said. Then, knowing Matt's attorney could suggest Kari had gotten the drugs from her,

Linda cleared up precisely when she'd started taking the sleeping pill. "My doctor gave me that prescription *after* Kari died."

"After Kari died?" Rainey asked.

"Yes."

At times, Linda became aware of Matt watching, listening to her every word. Usually, she tried to ignore his presence, concentrating on the attorneys, but when Rainey asked how Matt had changed after Kari's death, Linda turned to the man she blamed for her daughter's death. "Excuse me, Matt, for saying it this way," she said. "But, I mean, he just started trying to be some little cool hip daddy guy, you know?"

"You think that the fact that there were pictures of Vanessa up and none of Kari that went to motive, thinking that's a reason why Matt killed Kari?" Rainey asked.

"You know," Linda said. "It was another little piece of the puzzle."

Now it seemed ironic that Kari so believed in Matt that she'd ignored everything that suggested he wasn't the good Christian she thought she married. That thought flooded Linda with sadness. "Kari loved passionately," she explained. "The people she loved, she stood up for. And she stood up for Matt."

"So what you're telling me then doesn't sound like Matt Baker was actually ever indicted or actual formal criminal charges brought against Matt Baker?" Rainey asked. When it came to the pornography on the laptop computer from Crossroads, Matt's attorney asked, "And did the church have a policy against people looking at it?"

"He's a preacher," Linda said.

"I understand," Rainey said.

"Understand, that I'm giving you information that is just little piece by piece that by itself seems fairly harmless, until you start adding up all the pieces . . . I mean, Matt is a minister . . . He preyed on women."

"Do you have a smoking gun?" Rainey asked a while later.

"Oh, if I had a smoking gun, it would be right here on this table," Linda said.

"As we sit here today, you don't have any major piece of evidence that you would call a smoking gun, do you?"

"I do not have a smoking gun," she said. " . . . I have pieces of a puzzle that show Kari did not commit suicide, but we're not at the finish line yet. By the time we get there, we will have the answers we need."

This was a civil suit, and as the afternoon ground to a close, Rainey wanted to establish what harm had been done to Linda. "Have you had any physical ailments or physical problems since your daughter has died that you might think are related to the stress or anything related to Kari's death?"

"I've lost my daughter, and that has forever changed my life," Linda replied, her voice thick with emotion. "My daughter was my heart, and my life will never be the same . . . That is a big deal."

Looking at Rainey, she asked, "Do you have a child?"

"I have two," he said.

"Then you understand."

At 2:09 that afternoon, five hours after it began, Linda's deposition ended. The Dulins had arrived that day hoping that Matt would be made to go on the record. Instead, he'd refused, and Linda had been the one who'd endured a grueling day of questions.

Chapter 44

In Waco, many were discussing the case. "People began taking sides," says Nancy. "At church, some would say, 'We know he did it. They'll get him.' Others wanted to stay neutral or thought Matt was innocent. They really wanted to believe in him."

At the girls' school in Kerrville, Matt e-mailed the counselor eight months after Kari's death. Ostensibly it was about Christmas traditions, but what he asked was to meet with her. On the table was a discussion about the Dulins and what part they should play in the girls' lives. "My attorney needs to know of any detrimental effects Kensi and Grace are forced to undergo due to the visits with their maternal grandparents. As well as the girls' understanding of the court issues and negative feelings that are manifested toward me, their father, from their maternal grandparents."

Throughout the first months of 2007, motions in the civil suit flew back and forth, involving bank records, the girls' elementary-school records, and Bill Johnston's motions to allow him to bring into evidence extramarital affairs and past inappropriate sexual behavior. Matt denied each new charge leveled against him. Through it all, Johnston's eye was on spurring a criminal action more than continuing the civil one.

Toward that end, in early August 2007, Linda Dulin sat at her computer and composed a letter to Judge Billy Martin, asking for an inquest into her daughter's death. There'd been much discussion before getting to this point, conferences and phone calls between Linda, Bennett, McNamara, and Johnston, in which they had considered how to proceed. It was the next logical step, the only way to start up the nonexistent investigation. Johnston made suggestions, and Linda incorporated them into her letter to Martin, beginning by focusing on the crux of the situation: "Unfortunately, local police quickly accepted the story provided by Kari's husband, that the death was a suicide. It was not."

Over the past year, Linda explained, Mike McNamara and John Bennett had investigated Kari's death, and experts had reviewed the evidence. To bring Martin up to date, she included a printed summary of what the investigation had uncovered about Matt, his history, his relationship with Vanessa, and the events leading up to Kari's death. She closed by writing, "My husband and I deeply appreciate the job you do, and we trust this matter to your judgment."

The response to Linda's letter arrived in mid-August in the form of subpoenas sent to those involved in the case, ordering them to gather in two weeks in Judge Martin's courtroom for the purpose of an inquest. Not long after, an Associated Press reporter caught wind of the storm brewing over the death of a young Waco mother. She penned an article entitled: "Parents request inquest in Hewitt teacher's death." Matt's attorney was quoted as saying that Matt had been subpoenaed for an upcoming inquest in the case but would not testify. Backing up his client, he said, Matt "was not involved in his wife's death."

Despite Matt's announcement that he wouldn't cooperate, Martin's action could have been interpreted as a triumph for the Dulins. Yet Linda and Jim were keenly aware that this was simply another step into uncertain territory. Although many had worked hard to investigate, the results of the inquest were far from assured. As excited as she was, Linda had a difficult time knowing what to think. Finally, she had what she wanted, the potential that Kari's death would be looked at logically, in a clinical, unemotional manner in which the evidence could be assessed, not just waved off without consideration. But would that happen?

Evaluating the situation, those involved judged that there were three probable results of Martin's impending examination. One was that he would hear the evidence and do nothing, leaving a ruling of suicide on Kari's death certificate. That was the worst possible outcome for the Dulins, for it meant that the case would be difficult if not nearly impossible to prosecute and that the district attorney's office probably wouldn't even consider taking it before a jury.

The second was a rather tepid improvement, but one that at least opened the door for an open-minded prosecutor. Martin had the option of coming to the same opinion written on Kari's autopsy, that the manner of her death was undetermined. What the Dulins hoped was that Martin would consider all the evidence, including the expert opinions. If he did, they believed he had to rule their daughter's death a homicide.

The main problem, however, continued to be the mistakes made during the initial investigation by Hewitt PD. Unfortunately, much had been neglected and lost, leaving Martin little in the way of concrete evidence to consider. First, there was the autopsy, conducted months after Kari was embalmed and buried, with its inconclusive finding. Next there were the photos taken at the scene, or perhaps the lack of photos. There were no close-ups of the lividity in Kari's back, arms, and hands. Those in attendance hadn't even made a sketch of the scene or collected the bed linens. The crime-scene unit wasn't dispatched, and even the most obvious pieces of evidence weren't collected, including the Bartles & James bottles.

Then again, even if everything had been documented, would Martin have pulled it together? Linda and Jim worried that the judge wouldn't be open to changing his ruling. Still, as she dressed to go to the courthouse, she held out hope that Martin would be flexible enough to consider all the evidence. "Everyone makes mistakes, but the honorable thing to do is to correct them," she'd say later. "I saw the inquest as an opportunity for the JP to set things right. Billy Martin had made a mistake by not initially ordering an autopsy. Now he had the opportunity to rectify his mistake."

To get their opinions into the hands of the judge, Johnston asked the experts to lay out their conclusions in writing. The crime-scene expert, Tom Bevel, the psychologist, William Lee Carter, and the retired professor of pathology at the University of Tennessee, David Stafford, all wrote letters addressed to Martin in which they detailed their findings, all pointing to Kari's death being a homicide. A fourth letter came from the computer guru, Noel Kersh, and it included a long list of the drug Web sites Matt perused in the two weeks leading up to Kari's death and that he'd put Ambien in a shopping cart. All of the experts added that they would be happy to speak to Martin personally to answer questions should he have any about their conclusions.

Linda also had a letter from Jo Ann Bristol ready for Martin, in which she laid out her final meeting with Kari just days before her death. Reading the letters, Linda couldn't understand how anyone could consider what had happened and come to the conclusion that Kari had committed suicide.

Judge Billy Martin opened the inquest the afternoon of August 29, 2007, a year and four months after Kari Baker's death, in his courtroom in the McLennan County Courthouse. Gathered in the hallway waiting to be called were Jim and Linda, along with Hewitt officers Cooper, Irving, Kasting, and Toombs, Dr. Quinton, who'd performed the autopsy, Texas Ranger Matt Cawthon, and paramedic Shelton Chapman. Linda and Toombs carried with them the experts' letters to hand to the judge.

Also in attendance was the subject of the discussion, Matt Baker.

Although he never even glanced in her direction, Linda stared at her former son-in-law, assessing him. It surprised her that she felt so unemotional as she watched Matt, dressed in a business suit, laugh with his attorneys. *How does someone like you live with yourself knowing what you've done?* she wondered.

The witnesses were called to enter Martin's small courtroom, and like a teacher calling a class to order, the judge took roll. When Linda's name was called, she responded with a firm, "Yes, sir."

"Is there anyone here exercising their Fifth Amendment right not to testify?" Martin asked.

All eyes turned to Matt when he called out, "I am."

With that, Matt and his attorney approached the judge. After a short discussion, Matt Baker and his attorney left the room. It seemed incongruous. Everyone gathered in Martin's courtroom would be talking about Kari and Matt and what had happened that night on Crested Butte, but the one person who'd been there had walked away without answering a single question. Still, that didn't mean that those congregated wouldn't report what he'd said and done.

After the witnesses were sworn in, Jim and Linda joined the others in a hallway lined with chairs, to wait until they were called back into the courtroom. Linda felt nervous, anxious. So much was at stake. Silently, she and Jim prayed, asking that this inquiry would be the first step in a path that would lead to what they so wanted, for all the questions finally to be asked and answered, and for justice to be done.

In his courtroom, meanwhile, Judge Martin queried the first witness, Dr. Reade Quinton. As the medical examiner testified, he reviewed his records, stating that Kari's body had been in relatively good condition, considering she'd been buried for months, and that he'd seen no signs of injuries. The important area was the toxicology. While such tests are most accurate when run on blood, in this case that wasn't possible, since all Kari's blood had all been drained and replaced by embalming fluid in preparation for her burial.

Instead, the toxicology screen was run was on muscle tissue, a less accurate option. The result was that the lab was able to document what drugs were in Kari's system at the time of her death: alcohol, phentermine, Unisom, and Ambien. The embalming process accounted for the alcohols, which left the phentermine, Unisom, and Ambien. Because there were so few good studies exploring drug levels in muscle tissue, however, Quinton didn't have enough information to calculate how much of each drug was present in Kari's body at the time of her death. The result was that the M.E. couldn't say if any or a mixture of all of the drugs could have been responsible for Kari's death.

After the M.E. left the courtroom, the first officer on the scene the night Kari died entered. Officer Michael Irving recounted how he had arrived shortly after the first two EMTs. "I met Mr. Baker outside," Irving recounted. "He did bring us inside, to where his wife was in the bedroom."

As the EMTs worked on Kari, Irving described how Baker detailed the situation, including that he'd found his wife unresponsive and nude, dressed her and removed her from the bed to do CPR. When he looked about the room, there were things that caught the officer's attention, including the nearly empty Unisom container and the note.

"And how many pills would the bottle have normally contained?" Martin asked.

"Thirty-two," Irving said. "When Sergeant Cooper arrived, he found the pills in the bathroom, prescribed by the Waco Weight Loss Center."

"And they were prescribed to?" Martin asked.

"Her. Kari Baker," Irving responded.

Although admittedly early in the inquest, it didn't appear to be going well for the Dulins. First, the medical examiner had said that he couldn't determine what caused Kari's death, and now the first officer on the scene talked about pills on the nightstand as well as diet pills in the bathroom, both used by Kari.

After Irving, his superior, Sergeant Kasting, testified. One of the first things the sergeant recounted was something that could have given him pause as he stood in the Bakers' bedroom the night of Kari's death; one of the first EMTs on the scene, Gates, had told Kasting that the condition of Kari's body suggested she might have been dead for quite a while. "He said he felt that she'd been unresponsive for some time," Kasting said. "They ran a strip, a test to determine if there were any signs of life at that time. It was negative."

Perhaps to remind the judge of the part he'd personally played in the decisions made that night, Kasting then pointed out that he'd contacted Martin and told him what he'd seen at the scene, including reading the suicide note to the judge, "word by word."

"Was the note typed?" Martin asked, as if he were still unsure.

"Yes, sir," Kasting said.

"Was it signed?"

"I don't remember," the officer admitted.

As to what the officer had heard from Matt, it would be what others echoed throughout the day, that Kari had been depressed since Kassidy's death and in the preceding weeks talked of suicide. And then there was that incident in the car, when Matt contended that his wife tried to jump out on the freeway.

If that were true, why hadn't Matt sounded the alarm then? Why hadn't he gotten help for his wife? As to Matt's demeanor, did it indicate a man grieving for a dead wife? Kasting saw a man he judged to be saddened and in shock. Yet, was he? On the scene, Matt wasn't crying. In fact, he wasn't even "tearing up."

Next, a paramedic testified to the condition of Kari's lifeless body. On his report, Shelton Chapman had described Kari as without a pulse, cold, and not breathing. The cardiac monitor showed no electrical activity in her heart, no signs of life, and he'd noted lividity visible in the back of her neck. "On our protocols, she was D.A.S.," Chapman said. "Dead at scene."

One by one the witnesses answered Martin's questions. When it was his turn, Sergeant Cooper, like Kasting before him, it seemed, wanted the judge to remember his part in the decisions made the night of Kari's death. When Cooper arrived, he and Kasting called the judge again, inquiring about an autopsy. After giving a quick rundown of the situation, Cooper told the judge: "An autopsy still was not ordered."

Yet the critical information that the note was typed and without a signature, had Cooper told that to Martin during that middle-of-the-night conversation? "I can't remember," the sergeant said.

Was the decision not to autopsy Kari's body simply the result of a lack of communication between an officer who didn't divulge all the information and a justice of the peace who didn't ask all the questions? At the inquest, Martin didn't add any personal explanations into the official record.

At the scene, Cooper wrote down the details Matt told him about the events leading to Kari's death. "I did find records that his debit card had been used [to buy gas] and at Hollywood Video during the time he stated," Cooper offered.

Later that same afternoon, after the inquest took a short break, Ben Toombs's name was called. That left Jim, Linda, and Matt Cawthon alone in the hallway. Where Toombs had looked nervous during the wait, fidgeting with his necktie, Cawthon, an old hand who'd been in many such circumstances, was laid-back. He talked casually with the Dulins, about family and the small enjoyments in life. Until at one point, he turned to them, and said, "I just want you to know that I'm disgusted about the way this case has been handled." Cawthon didn't give any specifics, but the Dulins understood what the Ranger meant and appreciated that he understood what they'd gone through.

Meanwhile, inside the courtroom, Toombs recounted how he entered the case with the Crossroads laptop, followed by the disinterment and autopsy. Then he brought in, for the first time, evidence that Matt had lied. That came from Holly Romano, who Matt said had seen Kari sick at the Family Y's pool that last night. Instead, Holly insisted that Kari seemed well and was excited about the prospect of a new job.

At that point, Toombs mentioned the paperwork he'd brought in with him, expert opinions he wanted to give the judge so it would be available to consider, much of it regarding the condition of Kari's body when the EMTs arrived. On that topic, Toombs mentioned one letter in particular, the one from Bevel. "In his opinion, there's no way possible that it could have happened [the condition of the body], if she'd been alive at eleven fifteen."

Martin cut him off. "That is an opinion, and I'd rather stick to the facts."

Assessing that the judge's mind wasn't to be changed, the young detective took it in stride. He didn't push but instead dropped another bombshell, opening a window into what kind of man the young pastor truly was by recounting the information from the YMCA. While Matt worked there, the focus of their inquiry had "basically solicited sex" from teenage girls. Perhaps Martin was finally getting a view of Matt Baker as something other than a devoted man of God.

Still, there was one woman who described Matt in more flattering terms: Vanessa Bulls. Recounting the previous July's interview with the music minister's daughter, Toombs said Bulls denied any romantic relationship with Matt until after Kari's death. "She felt like Matt had grieved at the loss of Kari," Toombs related from his notes. "She just didn't notice anything abnormal about it."

After going through his failed attempts to find the computer and printer the suicide note was written on, Toombs explained that he had done nothing on the case since early October of the previous year. Then Toombs voiced the opinion that the most important evidence was the conflict between the time line Matt gave and the condition of the body.

"That's the one thing that's the most suspicious to you?" Martin asked.

"Yes," Toombs confirmed.

It was Texas Ranger Matt Cawthon who next presented himself, more than eager to answer Martin's questions. While the other had been more reserved, the Ranger didn't mince words. "Matt Baker was a womanizer," Cawthon told the judge. "One who couldn't control his urges, his needs."

As Toombs had done, Cawthon painted a picture of the young pastor as a man who sexually harassed women. "There had even been one allegation to police about a sexual assault," Cawthon said, referencing the attack on Lora Wilson. And then, despite Vanessa's denials, Cawthon called it as he saw it, describing Matt's "ongoing illicit sexual affair" with the music minister's daughter.

Before long, Cawthon turned to the heart of the matter, how Kari might have really died., While not conclusive, the autopsy had revealed that she had the drug Ambien in her muscle tissue. "Ambien was not a prescription drug Kari Baker possessed," he pointed out. And what had a review of Matt's computer turned up? That he'd visited a long list of prescription Web sites where Ambien was sold. "These are circumstantial situations that at this point are just too much to ignore," Cawthon said. Kari was "cold to the touch, lividity was fixed . . . It is our opinion in law enforcement that this couldn't have happened the way Matt Baker said it happened."

There was no doubt in Cawthon's mind about Matt's having a motive. He'd interviewed a woman who clerked in a local jewelry store, one who told him that within weeks of Kari's death, Matt was shopping with Vanessa for an engagement ring. "It's the totality of these things that we believe forms a pretty substantial case against Matt Baker for the death of his wife," Cawthon concluded.

When the judge asked if Cawthon had anything to add,

the Ranger, it appeared, wanted to get what he'd told Linda Dulin earlier that morning on the record. "I'll even be candid enough to tell you that this was handled poorly . . . by the police," he said. "Had we been able to gather forensic evidence in a more timely fashion . . . this may have been different."

What had Matt to gain by murdering Kari? Cawthon again answered without hesitation: $50,000 from her teacher retirement and his freedom to be with Vanessa.

In the hallway, Linda had been both anxiously awaiting and dreading this moment, but now she took her place before the judge. Along with others from her group of experts, she held a letter from Bristol in her hands, one in which the therapist recounted her last visit with Kari.

To begin, Linda told Martin about her last phone call with Kari on that final Friday afternoon. As she had so many times before, Linda stressed how excited her daughter was about her performance at the job interview.

Mere hours later, the house phone rang sending Linda and Jim rushing through the night, only to arrive at the house after Kari was pronounced dead. Once the investigators left, Matt fell into an untroubled sleep on the couch. When Martin asked about Kari's grief over Kassidy's death, Linda said, "Kari grieved for her daughter. I grieve for my daughter." But it hadn't paralyzed Kari. The reverse was true. At the end, Kari had talked about using her experiences to reach out to other grieving parents.

"Two weeks before Kari died, it became very apparent that she and Matt were having problems," Linda recounted. "I suggested she see Jo Ann Bristol."

At that, Linda attempted to give Martin the letter from Bristol along with the others, including those from Bevel and Stafford. As he had when Toombs tried to share Bevel's opinion about the condition of the body, Martin refused to take the letters, saying they were opinions, not evidence. But where Toombs had backed down, Linda firmly disagreed.

"Jo Ann Bristol did see Kari, and this letter documents what she saw."

There were more exchanges, back and forth between a grieving mother and a justice of the peace who held the key to righting what she saw as a great wrong, but in the end, just minutes after she entered the room, Linda was dismissed by Martin, who said that all he wanted to hear from her was about Kari's mood on that final day. "That's all you want?" Linda said, incredulous. He'd refused to look at the opinion of a trained therapist yet had solicited the opinion of the victim's mother. To Linda, it was nonsensical, and she wondered about Martin's logic.

"That's it," Martin confirmed.

Reluctantly, Linda walked out the door wishing she could say so much more. She motioned Jim in and sat back on a chair. As she waited for her husband, Linda considered her brief time before the judge. She still held the experts' letters in her hands, the ones Billy Martin had no desire to read. So much work and expense. Was it all for naught?

Jim Dulin was that afternoon's final witness. Kari's dad verified what his wife had said, that although Kari mourned Kassidy, their daughter was an upbeat, gregarious woman, one who never appeared even vaguely suicidal. And he cleared up something Sergeant Cooper had floundered about earlier. "There was no handwritten signature on the note at all."

After Jim left the room, Martin said: "This will conclude the death inquest investigation into Kari Lynn Baker."

Still, the business of the day wasn't done. Before adjourning, Martin entered three documents into evidence: the EMTs' run records, the autopsy, and Kari's death certificate. At that, the afternoon's session formally ended.

As she and Jim walked from the courthouse to their car, Linda thought back to her less-than-satisfying experience in the courtroom and decided she knew what Martin would do. "This case was a monkey on Judge Martin's back, and he wanted it gone," she'd say later. "I felt certain he wasn't looking for justice, just to get rid of us. So it wasn't hard to figure out what he was thinking and what he'd decide."

The next day, the fact-finding continued, this time when Judge Martin issued an order for the Waco Center for Youth to turn over to Hewitt Police any and all computer equipment used by Matt Baker during his employment there. Not long after, Toombs and Cawthon showed up at WCY. When Greenfield met them, however, he recounted what they'd already heard from McNamara and Bennett; Matt's computer was missing.

Nerves on edge, the Dulins and their extended family waited. Finally, on September 18, Martin called a press conference to announce his decision. Although she wanted to be there, Linda had to teach, and she felt certain she'd learn quickly what the justice of the peace had to say. Media descended on the courthouse, and Nancy and Lindsey went as well.

After the press conference, Nancy and Lindsey rushed to the college and found Linda in her classroom. They bounced outside her window, waving at her. When she joined them, they gushed with excitement, announcing that Martin had changed the manner of Kari's death from suicide to undetermined. It was what Linda had suspected, and she was less than pleased.

"My sister and niece saw it as a door opening, and it was," Linda would later say. But as she envisioned it, that door had only inched opened a crack. A ruling of undetermined allowed the district attorney to investigate but only if he wanted to. It was far from a demand for action. "I'd hoped Martin would have had the courage to do the right thing and rule Kari's death a homicide."

Chapter 45

Despite their disappointment in Martin's decision, Linda and Jim held onto hope, believing that although they hadn't gotten all they wanted, the inquest had worked in their favor and that they'd moved a step closer to the day their son-in-law would be forced to answer for their daughter's death. For their part, Bennett and McNamara were focused on making sure that happened. "We thought about this case every day. Talked about it every day," says McNamara. "We knew that Matt Baker was guilty, and we couldn't abide that he'd get away with murder."

Now that the door to an arrest had been nudged slightly ajar by Martin's ruling, the two seasoned investigators were determined to put on pressure and swing it wide open. In their quest to make that happen, two days after Martin changed the manner of Kari's death to undetermined, Bennett and McNamara again met with Texas Ranger Matt Cawthon, and the topic of conversation was the Matt Baker case.

Over lunch, the three men once again reviewed the evidence they'd collected against Baker, discussing the scenario they agreed was most likely based on the experts Johnston had brought in and the physical evidence. The more Bennett and McNamara considered the abrasion on Kari's nose in the autopsy and crime-scene photos, the more they agreed with Bevel's assessment that Kari had been first drugged, then suffocated. As they talked, Cawthon agreed that theory made the most sense and that Matt Baker's version of his wife's death was inconsistent with the evidence. The Ranger also agreed that the investigators had accumulated enough to justify a warrant. Yet Bennett and McNamara found Cawthon's response frustrating. "We still need to work through Hewitt and the DA's Office."

"But they're not doing anything," McNamara pointed out, to no avail. Cawthon was determined to honor the Texas Rangers' code of not stepping on the toes of local law enforcement by moving in uninvited and taking over cases. Yet that didn't mean that the Ranger wouldn't pursue the case. When lunch ended, Cawthon made his first stop the McLennan County Courthouse, where he again met with the ADA they'd all been keeping informed about the Baker case, Melanie Walker. His goal remained to convince her to put Vanessa Bulls in front of a grand jury. At the end of the meeting, Cawthon walked down the courthouse steps frustrated. "My impression was that the case wouldn't go anywhere in the DA's Office."

It was at that juncture that Cawthon decided the best course of action, whether the prosecutors were interested or not, was to push the matter at Hewitt PD. "I didn't need the DA to arrest Baker," he says. "I could go to a justice of the peace and get an arrest warrant signed."

Yet still mindful of the Rangers' long-held traditions, he wanted to work through those primarily responsible for the case. In Hewitt's headquarters, Cawthon confronted Chief Barton, warning that if Hewitt didn't write a warrant for Baker, the Rangers would. "The chief was upset. He kept asking, 'Why are you pushing this case? Who are you working for?'" says Cawthon. As he had in the past, the Ranger said, "I'm working for that dead girl, and you should be, too."

After Cawthon again made it clear that he intended to move the case forward with or without Hewitt's cooperation, the chief instructed Ben Toombs to write a warrant. The finished product began: "I, Ben Toombs, a licensed peace officer in the State of Texas and employed by the Hewitt Police Department and hereafter referred to as the affiant, do solemnly swear that I have reason to believe and do believe that Matthew Dee Baker . . . intentionally or knowingly committed the offense of murder by causing the death of Kari Lynn Baker by using prescription and/or over-the-counter sleeping medication and alcohol to render her defenseless and then using a pillow or similar item to suffocate her."

From that point on, the warrant laid out the evidence, everything from the expert opinions on lividity to Kari's prophetic words to Bristol, and the computer evidence that Matt shopped for Ambien on the Internet. The last line of the warrant spelled out Cawthon's and Toombs's intentions: "Affiant asks for issuance of a warrant that will authorize the arrest of the suspected party."

The warrant completed, they drove to Billy Martin's office and presented it to the judge. "He was part of all this," says Cawthon, "so Martin was the best one to sign it."

The justice of the peace agreed. Cawthon then called the Texas Ranger stationed in Kerrville, and instructed, "Go pick him up."

Finally, it appeared that Matt Baker would be taken into custody. Yet by the time the Ranger arrived at Tivy High School, where Matt was working as a substitute teacher, Baker, alerted by a phone call, had disappeared. "I was told that it appeared that he had fled," says Cawthon. "He'd left the campus."

To ensure that Baker knew they'd be looking for him, the Kerrville Ranger tracked down Barbara, who worked on the campus as an aide, and confronted her. "She said she didn't know where Matt was," says Cawthon. "The Ranger told her, 'Well, you better find him pretty darn quick.'"

In Waco, Cawthon grew impatient, word not coming of the arrest. Only hours later did he hear that the former pastor had turned himself in at the Kerr County sheriff's office and been taken into custody.

When Linda and Jim heard that their son-in-law was under arrest, there was gratitude but no sense of jubilation. "We were deeply sad. We not only had a murdered daughter but now the father of our granddaughters had been taken from them and put in jail. Matt belonged there. He needed to be held accountable," says Linda. "But there was no joy."

When a reporter from the *Waco Tribune-Herald* called, Linda said she and Jim had been waiting for Matt to be arrested and held accountable for nearly eighteen months, and she thanked Cawthon, calling him a man of courage and determination. "Texas Ranger Matt Cawthon . . . makes Chuck Norris look like a wimp," Linda said. "Cawthon truly moved a couple of mountains to make this happen."

Yet Johnston cautioned both of Kari's parents that an arrest warrant didn't necessarily predict a trial. Cawthon, too, was well aware of the potential pitfalls ahead. "I'd done my job. I believed Baker was guilty and we had sufficient evidence to prove it," says the Ranger. "But Segrest wasn't the type of district attorney who'd work with law enforcement. My opinion of him was that he was too concerned about his win-loss record. The reality was that if the DA's Office chose not to pursue the case, I couldn't force it to. The ball was in the prosecutor's court."

Chapter 46

Once Matt was arrested, the Dulins filed a motion for a nonsuit, putting the wrongful death case on hold pending the outcome of the criminal charges. Since the case was now in the hands of the District Attorney's Office, Johnston, Bennett, and McNamara all stood down, determined to stay out of the way of law enforcement. Meanwhile, the former pastor was pictured wearing a charcoal-and-white-striped jailhouse uniform, his wrists and ankles in chains, in a front-page article on his arrest that ran in the *Waco Tribune-Herald*.

At the District Attorney's Office, Matt's fate landed in the hands of Crawford Long, the office's top prosecutor. A lean, finely built man with a gregarious manner, a wide smile, and a stiff gait, Long had been a fixture on the staff for nearly a quarter of a century. The son of a Baylor English professor, he had a halting manner of speech and a sardonic sense of humor. In a courtroom, he heightened the drama by pointing a long, thin, accusatory finger at defendants as he eyed them intently and called them murderers. At other times, he recited Shakespearean and biblical quotes, occasionally throwing in remarks from other luminaries to make his point. Unlike Segrest, Long had a good working relationship with Bill Johnston. Years earlier, they'd served together as special prosecutors on two hundred sting cases for Waco

PD. As a memento, Long kept a photo of their swearing in on his office wall. The Baker case, however, wouldn't be one where Johnston and Long initially agreed. While Johnston saw the evidence against Baker as substantial, Long wasn't so sure.

When Linda and Jim met with Long, he explained that he wasn't in a rush to pursue Baker. "It was obvious that the Dulins thought their daughter had been murdered, but they never put any pressure on me," Long says. "And I wasn't going to get pushed into prosecuting anyone unless I had a good case. Since there's no statute of limitations on murder, there wasn't any hurry."

In the weeks that followed, Long would later say that he took a hard look at the case and didn't particularly like what he saw. First, he sent the Unisom bottle and suicide note out for DNA testing and fingerprinting. What didn't come back was evidence proving Baker had ever held either one in his hands. While Johnston relied on his experts and their definition of lividity, Long called others and heard less certain opinions. "What I was told was that the doctors thought it was highly unlikely that lividity would show up in such a brief period of time, but they wouldn't absolutely rule out the possibility." The autopsy's toxicology was also a problem. In front of a jury, Long worried that a defense attorney could make it add up to reasonable doubt.

Weeks passed, and Long considered the case. "I wanted to keep an absolutely open mind. You had the two sides, and I told everyone involved that the case was not going to be rushed through the system."

Meanwhile, the former pastor remained in the McLennan County jail on $400,000 bail. Baker had frequent visitors, his two daughters and his mother. Behind the scenes, Barbara was raising money. In October, a month after his arrest, Baker's attorney went before the judge, and Matt's bond was dropped to $200,000. He made bail and returned to Kerrville, moving in with his daughters and his parents in their modest gray-sided home on the outskirts of the city.

Charged with a serious crime, he couldn't substitute teach, but instead did handyman work as his father had over the years.

In his hometown, many came to Matt's defense. "The community stood behind us," says Barbara. "People know us here, and we had a lot of support." In November, friends held a barbecue fund-raiser in a pavilion at Louise Hays Park, sixty-three acres of rolling green grass and trees. That afternoon, Matt wore a green bracelet that read: DEFENSE, as friends and his parents' fellow church members from Trinity Baptist gathered. One woman told the local newspaper that she felt "called to attend," and that she remembered Matt as "likeable" and "genuine." A former high-school classmate said about the murder charges: "No one wanted to believe it."

"I am still very puzzled by what is happening to this family," said another friend.

"It's unbelievable to know the support I have. Some of the people, I don't know who they are. It's amazing," Matt was quoted as saying.

When the festivities ended, $7,500 had been collected to help pay for Matt's defense. In all over the coming year, Baker would receive donations of more than $20,000.

From the time of his arrest, a Kerrville attorney named Keith Williams, a Baker family friend, had been handling Matt's case. That ended, however, when Williams made arrangements to leave private practice to become a district court judge.

At the time, many in Kerrville were talking about a relatively new lawyer in town, Guy James Gray, an aging former prosecutor who'd gone into private practice. Gray and Williams were acquainted, and what Gray heard from Williams was that Matt was a young father, a preacher who'd been charged with the murder of his wife. The Matt Baker Williams described was a good man from a churchgoing family who was being falsely accused. Based on what he heard,

Gray formed an opinion: "It appeared that there wasn't sufficient evidence, that it was a witch hunt."

Looking back on his long career, Gray would say that he came to the practice of law reluctantly. His grandfather was a lawyer, and Gray's father bribed him with a Corvette to get him to enter law school. Decades later, Gray still voiced regret about his decision. "I've never really been crazy about law," he says. "I did it for a living."

Yet, he did it well, not losing a case in twenty years as a deep East Texas piney woods district attorney. "The thing I liked about prosecuting was that I had control," he'd say. "If I didn't think a case should be pursued, I was free to drop it. At all times, I felt like I was on the right side."

Over the years, he'd handled high-profile cases, the most famous the 1998 murder of James Byrd, Jr., who was dragged to death by three white men in the small town of Jasper. The men chained Byrd, a black man, to the back of a pickup and drove, severing his head and arm when he hit a culvert. The murder made national headlines and inspired Texas's hate crime law. Looking back, Gray would say the Byrd case helped ease him out of prosecuting. "The dragging case just wore me out."

There were other reasons to want a change, however, when Gray's stepson died. "There wasn't an autopsy," the attorney says, shaking his head at the memory. "It was probably prescription medications that caused it, but we don't know exactly."

Considering the Baker case in relation to his own experience, Gray thought he understood how Kari could have committed suicide. "Like Mrs. Baker, I knew what it was like to lose a child," he'd say. "From what I'd heard, Kari Baker was depressed, a good candidate to take her own life."

Dealing with the loss of their son, Gray and his wife looked for a place to start over. They chose Kerrville in the beautiful hills of central Texas, where Gray settled into a comfortable brown brick and glass office building. Once there, he did some civil work and some criminal, about half the time donating his services to those he judged were getting a raw deal and couldn't afford an attorney. Based on what he'd heard from Williams about the former preacher, Gray believed Matt Baker was just such a man. What Gray heard about Linda Dulin was that she was an overly aggressive woman unwilling to accept her daughter's suicide. One thing in particular made him believe that had to be true, that the Dulins had initially tried to investigate Matt regarding Kassidy's death.

Precisely how Gray became Matt's attorney would later be controversial. Barbara would say that the slightly built, gray-haired man with a goatee inserted himself into the case, lobbying for the job to garner headlines. In stark contrast, Gray maintained that Williams referred Matt to him. One way or another, after Matt was released from jail, he and his mother stood in Gray's office. "Preachers are generally a little bit sissy. Baker didn't strike me as an outdoorsman or a hunter but someone who was raised in the environment of the church," says Gray, a taut frown on his well-lined face.

His career as a prosecutor had left its mark on Gray, however, and he had a hard time envisioning himself on what he considered "the wrong side" of a murder case. Before he took Baker on, he "needed to know that Matt was innocent." To appease his conscience, the lawyer interviewed Matt, who swore he hadn't murdered his wife. In fact, Matt denied all the allegations, including the affair with Bulls.

Yet, Baker's denial wasn't enough. To make sure he had the full story, Gray personally called Vanessa. If Matt was lying, Gray wanted to know. "She told me there'd been no physical contact and that she knew nothing about the way Kari died," says Gray. "I went a step further and had an investigator call her, and it was the same. Matt told me the affair wasn't true, and Vanessa said the same, that nothing ever happened." Without a romance with Bulls, Gray figured that Matt didn't have a motive, leading the attorney to believe that Baker was innocent.

His conscience appeased, Gray agreed to take Matt on as

a client, offering to do the case pro bono, without charging a fee. "I believed in Matt Baker," Gray would say later. "I truly thought these charges were unjust."

Assessing the circumstances, Gray had his dander up about the way the Baker case was being handled. He didn't like the affidavit Ben Toombs had written, one that talked of experts who'd looked at the case and voiced opinions that Kari couldn't have taken her life. "That affidavit made it look like Matt was lying," says Gray. "If you just read that, you'd come away believing that Matt was guilty.

Early into their lawyer-client relationship, Gray and Baker conferred about how to respond. With a Baptist preacher accused of murder, the case had caught the attention of not only local and state news outlets, but also national media programs. *Texas Monthly* was working on a cover story, and the reporter was asking for an interview, as were the news magazines *48 Hours* and *20/20*. The Dulins and others were talking to the reporters. Should Matt respond? When potential jurors might see the programs, could he afford to remain silent?

"Our discussion was whether to fight or just sit back and take it," says Gray. During his years as a prosecutor, especially working the Byrd case, Gray had experience with the media, and his advice to Matt Baker was to fight back. Yet Gray warned that if Baker did so, he had to give honest answers. "We had some eye-to-eye, hard conversations about how if you're going to talk to the media, you have got to be truthful, because the eye of the camera catches every little lie, and you can't remember everything you tell them. They catch inconsistencies."

Over the weeks that followed, Gray, Barbara, and Matt met with reporters in Gray's wood-paneled office, decorated with a worn leather saddle with a lasso looped around the horn, Western art, and cowhide chairs. On those days, Matt did a series of interviews, first with Tommy Witherspoon, the veteran *Waco Tribune-Herald* reporter who'd been a mainstay at the McLennan County Courthouse for decades,

Skip Hollandsworth with *Texas Monthly*, Erin Moriarty with *48 Hours,* and Jim Avila with *20/20.*

The months clicked off the calendar, and in the spring, the articles began appearing and the TV programs aired. *Texas Monthly* entitled their piece on the case "The Valley of the Shadow of Death," and in the lead photo, Matt Baker had his eyes closed and his hands folded in prayer. With Hollandsworth, the former pastor compared himself to Joseph in the Old Testament, a man falsely imprisoned and betrayed by his family and friends. "He came back and helped the family that had tried to destroy him," Matt said with tears in his eyes. "I have said a prayer asking God to forgive the Dulins. And I have prayed for God to let me forgive them. But I don't blame them. I understand they are hurting so deep inside that the only way for them to deal with this is to lash out at me."

Ever the model minister, Matt quoted a verse from Proverbs: "Trust in the Lord with all your heart. In all your ways, know him, and he will make your paths straight."

On some points, Baker remained steadfast, especially denying any sexual or romantic relationship with Vanessa Bulls. When the *Tribune-Herald*'s Witherspoon asked about the myriad of cell-phone calls Baker made to the beautiful young blonde, Matt insisted that she was merely a friend. And as for Bristol, Matt charged that the counselor had told him that she knew Kari was depressed.

What would stand out later were the inconsistencies. As Matt talked to reporter after reporter, his story strayed, and the poised pens of the reporters and the camera lenses caught glaring differences. At times, he said he never saw the suicide note until the police showed it to him, despite his having told the 911 dispatcher that Kari had left a note "basically saying I'm sorry." Even with the same reporter, Matt gave contradictory accounts of the night Kari died. With Moriarty, in front of the *48 Hours* cameras, Baker initially said that Kari was awake and talking when he left for the video store. When Moriarty interviewed him a second time, he described that crucial moment differently: "She'd rolled over and gone back to sleep. So when I left, she was asleep."

When Bennett and McNamara saw the interviews, they shook their heads. "It was like he'd read the arrest warrant and was changing his story to account for Kari's body being cold and the lividity," says McNamara. "It was transparent that he was lying."

In all, the media reports only cast more doubt on Baker's innocence. For their broadcast, *48 Hours* went so far as to ask a toxicologist, hired by the program, to look at the evidence. "What part of Matt Baker's story bothers you?" Moriarty asked.

"Being cold in an hour is nonexistent unless you're killed in the arctic or in an icebox," he answered.

As Baker's interviews aired, a deadline approached. The arrest warrant would be for naught unless Crawford Long took action. By law, the prosecutor had only 180 days before the warrant lapsed unless he took the case to a grand jury and secured an indictment. Yet from the perspective of those who'd worked the case, they saw nothing being done. "It surprised me that I didn't get a phone call from the DA's Office to talk about the case. It was like it had never been filed," says Ben Toombs.

Long didn't call Bennett or McNamara asking for any further information on the allegations in the arrest warrant either. "Anything that went on in that 180 days, I know nothing about," says McNamara.

"Nobody contacted us to talk about the case," says Bennett. "No one."

Then, on March 25, 2008, 180 days after Matt's arrest, at Gray's request, Judge Martin signed an order dropping the charges based on the lack of an indictment. The order stated: "The criminal accusation . . . is dismissed."

Why? Years later, Long would say that the decision not to proceed with the case was his. "After looking at everything we had, I thought that Matt Baker had done the crime, but I still thought there was reasonable doubt for a jury to find him not guilty. I didn't feel it was ready for a grand jury at that time," he says. "I wouldn't have felt comfortable about taking it in front of a jury with what we had. I'm probably careful to a fault. I'll let a case sit around for a while rather than rush things through."

Days later, Mike McNamara sauntered into the courthouse wearing his cowboy hat. In his hands he held the necessary paperwork required to reopen the civil case, the wrongful death. "It appeared that the system had failed us, but we didn't give up," says Linda. "We weren't going to let Matt Baker get away with murder."

"There will be a day of reckoning," Johnston assured the Dulins.

Chapter 47

Twice a month, Linda and Jim drove to Kerrville to pick up the girls for visitation. Matt met them in public places, appearing to be hiding where he lived, but Bennett and McNamara knew the address. At that point, Matt and the girls were living in an old parsonage donated by Trinity Baptist Church. One day, Kensi left her ball in the car, and Jim drove to the parsonage to deliver it. Matt, Barbara, and the girls were outside when Jim drove up.

Barbara walked up to him, and said, "Being nosy, aren't you?"

"No," Jim said, handing her the ball. "Just returning this."

"I believe my son is innocent, and I believe that you were swayed," she charged.

"No, I wasn't," he countered. "I have my own opinions."

Meanwhile in Dallas, Jill's husband had slowly worked his way around to believing as his wife did, that their good friend and former preacher Matt Baker had murdered Jill's best friend. "It was tough for Stephen," says Jill. "For a long time, it hurt our marriage. It was so obvious to me, but he just didn't want to believe it. I couldn't understand why he didn't see it as quickly as I did."

Meanwhile in Kerrville, Matt felt the support of the community around him. And in Williams Creek and Riesel, other small Texas towns around Waco where he'd pastored, many shook their heads, not knowing what to believe. "I just didn't see how Matt could have done this," says a Riesel resident. "I never saw that in him. I mean, after all, Matt Baker was a man of God."

"We knew Kari was depressed after Kassidy died," says a member of Matt's church in Williams Creek, the one with Kassidy's prayer garden out front. "The whole thing was just confusing. I mean, why wait seven years to commit suicide? But then, how could Matt murder his wife? That wasn't the man we all knew."

In Waco, after Matt's arrest, one woman had decided it was time to do more than talk. Tall and blond with a penchant for wearing jeans, Shannon Gamble wasn't a close friend of Kari's, but they'd shared something important, Gamble's son, Brody. "Kari was Brody's third-grade teacher that year at Spring Valley," says Gamble. "She was incredible with my son."

Brody was one of those students Kari brooded over in the months before her death, worrying about how he'd perform on the TAKS test. When Kari spotted Gamble in the school cafeteria, she "lit up" and literally skipped over to Gamble with the test results in her hand: Brody hadn't just passed but done well. "She had this giant smile," says Gamble. "She loved my boy, and she loved and taught him so well he rocked that freakin' TAKS test. She was beaming. I was beaming watching her beam over my son."

It was Gamble who'd seen Kari at Walmart the afternoon before her death, and in the year that followed, Gamble felt conflicted about Kari's death. "I couldn't believe she committed suicide," Gamble says. "And early on, I felt in my gut that it wasn't true. The Kari Baker I knew would not have committed suicide."

As news spread of the Dulins' suspicions and their fight to have police investigate Matt, Gamble watched the headlines in the papers, then, when Matt was arrested, she took action. "It's odd, I know, but I felt like I had Kari's hand on my shoulder leading me," she says. "It was time."

What Gamble did was take to the Internet, founding a blog called "Don't Even Get Me Started."

"What's worse than killing your wife?" Gamble's first post read on September 30, 2007, a week after Matt's arrest. "What's worse than having your girls always think their mother left them by her own hand?"

What Gamble said was worse was that Matt was a pastor. "So way to go, Matt Baker. You gave people who long for and dig for reasons NOT to believe in God and faith fuel for their fires," she wrote. "YOU'RE one of the reasons they detest 'religion,' and your one disgusting, evil selfish act sent waves of 'see, I told you so' through their worlds. You just slapped God in the face in the worst way."

In the months that followed, Gamble's blog became a rallying place for those who believed that Matt had murdered Kari. Friends and family checked regularly, leaving messages that included memories of Kari, quirky little anecdotes, and funny stories, and Gamble kept them up to date, posting articles as they appeared in newspapers and on TV news Web sites. She posted a link to the 911 call, and Matt's booking photos. "I've always been kind of a news junkie," she says. "It was a natural thing for me to read everything and post it on the blog."

When Linda first saw it, she e-mailed Gamble: "I read your blog and just bawled like a baby. I am so touched at the love you have shown my daughter. God has blessed me today through you. She comes back to me so sweetly when you share your memories."

In the end, many would rally around Gamble, and Waco, Jerusalem on the Brazos, would become consumed with the case, residents lining up on both sides.

After the arrest warrant lapsed and Martin dropped the charges, Gamble took her battle to the streets. Another friend of Linda's printed bumper stickers, and Gamble made them available on her blog, ones that read: JUSTICE FOR KARI. Seemingly overnight, the plea was seen on cars throughout the county, including some of those that parked outside the

courthouse where Judge Martin and Segrest, the district attorney, had offices, and on the streets of Hewitt, where Chief
Barton drove his car each day. Over the months and years
ahead, Gamble would have to reprint as the number of those
calling for "justice for Kari" grew.

"Others commented on the blog in support of Matt," says
Gamble. "There were two sides, those who believed he'd
committed murder and those who didn't. God bless those
who believed he was innocent, but they just weren't looking
at the evidence."

Chapter 48

In Kerrville, after the charges against Matt were dropped, Gray suffered another tragedy, the death of a second son, this time in a car accident. Gray and his wife were left reeling. "Suffice it to say that we've had a lot to deal with," he says. "I cleared my load. I needed time for my family."

His attorney unavailable for the continuing civil trial, Matt hired Richard Ellison, who'd moved to Kerrville eight years earlier. An affable man with shaggy gray hair, Ellison found himself curious about his new client. "Baker seemed kind of aloof and cold," says the lawyer. "He wasn't touchy and feely, the way one would picture a Baptist minister."

Despite the turmoil in his life, Matt hadn't let his sexual appetites wane. That fall, he went into a salon and flirted with a woman who cut his hair, telling her that he was a widower with two daughters. They talked, and he asked her out. On their first date, they ended up at her house, where they began making out. But Baker became aggressive, and he shouted at her, cursing during intercourse. After she saw Matt on television talking about the case, the woman called Linda. "He was rough," the hair stylist said. "I thought if I said no, he would have done it anyway."

Bennett and McNamara interviewed the woman, adding her statement to their files.

It would turn out that the woman's account would come

in handy, as Johnston prepared for what he saw as his big opportunity: Matt Baker was scheduled for another deposition,
and this time his lawyer was going to let him talk.

"I don't know why in the world they let him do that," says
Johnston with a smile.

Chapter 49

The day had been much anticipated. More than two years had been dedicated to delving into the case. And on the morning of October 20, 2008, in room 108 of Kerrville's Dispute Resolution Center, Matt Baker would finally answer Bill Johnston's questions. By then, Johnston had an opinion about Matt: "He was a pretty good liar, but there was a lot out there, lots was known about the case. I figured this was an opportunity to hand him some water, mix it up, and let it harden." Johnston hoped that once Matt had concocted his own cement, it would sink him.

On the other hand, Ellison, while he preferred that Matt not testify, was worried about the civil trial. "If he hadn't, and the civil case had gone to trial, the judge could have instructed the jury that they could assume that since he'd refused to testify that what he would have said would not have been in his best interest," says Ellison. "And I figured he'd already talked too often, to so many people. He'd already gone on the record."

The stone-sided building with narrow windows was just half a mile from the house where Matt's parents had once fostered children. As he entered the room, Baker looked older than he had just two and a half years earlier, before Kari's death. He wore a dark green, carefully pressed shirt, and a gray-and-green-striped tie. His goatee was carefully trimmed, yet his chin had broken out, and he fidgeted with change in his pocket. They took their stations in the conference room, Matt's attorney, Ellison, at his side. There was no doubt that the former pastor looked nervous. A vein in Baker's forehead bulged.

"Have you ever testified under oath before?" Johnston asked.

"No," Matt responded. On the wall behind him hung an oil painting, a pastoral scene, with flowers and tall grass surrounding a brown rail fence. In the camera's eye, cutting off all but a few posts and crossbars, the painting resembled a row of crosses.

In a patient tone, Johnston explained the importance of why they were gathered. "A deposition in a civil case has the same import as a criminal-case trial in front of a jury," he said. "In other words, my questions and your answers can be used in a proceeding after today, just as if you've testified in court."

The questions Johnston asked were, therefore, a way to get Matt to testify, to have him describe his version of the events, and his answers could someday, if the criminal case was ever taken into a courtroom, be shown to the jury. It wasn't a criminal trial, but the deposition and civil case were as close as the Dulins and Johnston could come without a way to light a fire under the McLennan County district attorney.

When Johnston finished, Matt nodded that he understood, then in response to questions, he described his family history, including that he'd been born in and grown up in Kerrville. His family consisted of his parents, his sister, Stacie, and all forty-nine foster children. When Johnston asked what that experience had taught him, Matt said, "I learned a lot: how to be a parent; how to take care of kids. And how to accept everybody."

With so much at stake, the mood in the room was edgy. Matt sometimes flashed a short, tight smile, but no one forgot why he was there. There were concerns far beyond the parameters of the civil suit he had hanging over his head. With no statute of limitations on murder, every word he said could someday be used against him.

At Baylor, Matt said he'd briefly considered premed, instead went into sports medicine, then made the change to church recreation.

"That's a degree plan?" Johnston asked.

"Yes, a four-year program," Matt answered.

There were so many jobs, some like the one at First Baptist in Kerrville, before Matt finished his undergrad work. "Was there any disciplinary action that caused you to leave First Baptist?" Johnston asked.

As he would often, Matt answered in an oblique way: "I was not told I could not work there . . . I was talked to but . . . I was never given a negative performance review."

When Johnston asked about the First Baptist allegations of sexual harassment, Matt balked, and his attorney stepped in, informing everyone in the room that when it came to this particular matter, Matt was pleading the Fifth Amendment. "You're invoking the Fifth on the issue of employment with First Baptist Church?" Johnston said.

"Yes," Ellison repeated.

"Are you intending to take the Fifth on anything else today?" the bushy-haired former prosecutor inquired.

"We'll take it on a question-by-question basis," Ellison explained.

It wasn't long before they did just that, when Johnston inquired about Matt's tenure at the Waco Family Y. Those events had happened twelve years earlier, and Johnston didn't mince words: "Mr. Baker, can you think of a way to bring a cause of action . . . to involve your Fifth Amendment rights?" But Ellison jumped in to object, and Matt never answered.

From the Family Y, Matt had gone on to pastor at Williams Creek in Axtell. "Why did you leave?" Johnston asked.

"Death of a child," Matt said, his voice unemotional, except for a condescending undercurrent. "We had another child, and my wife didn't want our baby sleeping in the room where our second child passed away."

The main inquiry was to pin Matt down on matters that related to Kari's death, but there were also many questions surrounding Kassidy's death. Matt had given different accounts over the years, some of which had raised eyebrows. While Johnston had him under oath, he asked Matt to recount the night Kassidy died.

"How long was Kassidy home from the hospital when she died?" Johnston asked.

"A month," Matt responded. He then laid out his version of the events of that night. In the past, he'd often said that he'd been the last one with Kassidy, when he checked her at midnight, but this time he said Kari had been there with him. When he returned nine minutes later, Kassidy wasn't breathing. "I yelled to my wife to call nine-one-one," he said, still showing no emotion. "I proceeded to do CPR until the paramedics came. I never felt a heartbeat or blood pressure."

As the afternoon unfolded, Johnston would see firsthand what so many had said about Matt, his need to stress how much he did for others, to emphasize how good he was at taking charge and handling tasks. Now he said something that seemed more than odd, that once the EMTs arrived, instead of taking over working on Kassidy, they asked Matt to continue because "I was doing such a great job."

Although he'd left Northlake Baptist under a cloud after a cut in pay, Matt contended that he'd enjoyed his time at the church and that he'd been the one to decide to move on. Why? Kari had told her mother she didn't want to move. She'd made close friends in Dallas, and she'd built a life there. She had a good job. But according to Matt, he left only because "my wife felt the need to be close to her home and her family."

"Were there any employment issues at Northlake?" Johnston prodded.

"No," Baker replied, with a slight shake of the head.

Matt quickly went from the Texas Youth Commission to the Waco Center for Youth. Then, that fall, he hired on as the part-time minister at Crossroads, the small church that lay between Hewitt and Lorena. How far back was the Bakers' marriage troubled? Johnston asked about the relationship in January 2006, three months before Kari's death.

"As a family you have issues. You have great times. You have sad times," Matt said. "We had ups and downs . . . but we were trying to become healthier."

"What was the illness in the marriage . . . the one you were trying to make healthier?"

"Part of the illness in the family was the loss of a child," Matt said. "That's a big, key issue, that kind of stays with you all the time."

What were they doing to heal the wound? Matt said they were trying to spend more time together, and one more thing: "Have a healthier sex life."

"Was that true January, February, and March as well?" Johnston asked.

"Yes," Matt said. It appeared that the questioning was making him uncomfortable.

"What is AdultFriendFinder?" Johnston asked, then said nothing.

The former pastor stumbled, as if not sure how to respond, then said, "Ah . . . I know I've had some friends who have used it, but I'm not sure."

"Have you ever from your computer at the Waco Center for Youth logged onto AdultFriendFinder?" Johnston asked. Calling itself the world's largest singles and swinger community, AdultFriendFinder boasts that it's "the best place online to find hotties looking for steamy hook-ups."

"Not to my knowledge," Matt said, shaking his head as if in earnest. "No."

"In January, February, and March, did you spend any time on any site that might contain obscenity or sexually related material?"

Baker straightened his posture in his chair. "Not to my

knowledge and not for any reason like that. We had to deal with issues kids had, not for any self-gratification."

"How would it have benefited the kids at WCY for someone to go onto an adult Web site?" Johnston queried.

"There would be students who would come, and one of our issues in the chaplain's department was to verify reading material and music," Matt said, appearing increasingly nervous. "And we would have to look up lyrics online, and it would sometimes take you to sites you didn't want to go to, and you would get back off."

"But if something popped up, you're not going to stay on that site for any period of time though?"

"Correct," Matt said. What perhaps he didn't understand was that Noel Kersh had found a long string of such sites, and many much worse, that Matt's WCY computer had visited.

"That would have been inadvertent, right?"

"Correct," Baker said.

"Because delving into material like that wouldn't be healthy for any marriage."

Matt shifted in his chair. "I guess it would depend upon the marriage and what you were trying to get out of it."

"Would it have been healthy for your marriage?" Johnston asked.

Kari was well-known to be a modest woman, one who felt uncomfortable with blatant sexuality, yet Matt answered, "My statement would be that my wife and I did look at pornography together at different times, the two of us together at home."

Yet how did that explain the history of pornographic Web sites on Matt's WCY computer? Had Kari come into the chaplain's office, where he worked, to view porn with him? She'd only been seen at the facility a half dozen times, and then to do things like attend chapel services. "But you didn't do it at work by yourself?" Johnston asked.

Shaking his head, Matt insisted, "I did not."

Although everyone else said Kari was enthusiastic about

her interview that final afternoon, believing she'd done well and excited about the possibility of teaching middle school in the fall, Matt disagreed, saying Kari seemed unsure of how the interview had gone. And why did she want the job? Kari had told so many how she bonded with middle-school kids, but Matt said it was because, "Linda was pushing it."

That whole month had been a difficult one, Matt said, as his dead wife struggled with the anniversary of their second child's death. "My wife was very withdrawn," he said. "So that's always a tough time of year every year."

"So what did you do to help her deal with that?" Johnston asked.

"Basically what I did all the time was take care of her, meet her needs," he said. As Matt described himself, he was the one who held the family together, including caring for the house and the girls. Kari, it seemed, worked, graded papers, but did little else.

In the weeks leading up to her death, Matt said Kari struggled with depression. Why was she so anxious? It had been a full seven years since Kassidy's death. There did seem to be some evidence that the terrible loss of her child still bothered her, including the e-mail where Kari commented she felt as if she was finally realizing that Kassidy would never return. But was that truly what was going on? Was it a coincidence that Kari's anxiety built as her marriage faltered, especially in light of the evidence that for the last week of her life, Kari struggled with the belief that her husband planned to kill her?

"Did you sense something a little more serious about a week before she passed away?" Johnston asked.

Matt recounted how they'd gone to the doctor. Although Kari had told her mother that she was furious with him for going in the examination room with her, he said his wife took his hand and led him in. Once there, he insisted he let Kari do all the talking. The story he then told was the same yet different than the one he'd told Sergeant Cooper. When the doctor diagnosed some depression, Kari spiraled into another anxiety attack that led her to attempt to jump from a moving car on the freeway. In the past, Matt had said they'd circled the block, slowly, until Kari regained her composure. To Johnston's questions, Baker now contended that they'd driven slowly home.

There was so much that Matt changed, it seemed, each time he recounted the events leading up to Kari's death. For instance, Kari had told Bristol about finding the pills, saying Matt said that they were from the kids at WCY. Matt had told Linda the same story. Yet when Johnston asked, Matt insisted he never believed the pills were from his work but rather that they were Kari's pills. He said they'd argued, and he'd told his wife that he'd never seen the pills before, challenging her statement that they'd come out of his briefcase. "She huffed and puffed and stormed off. That was it for a while, when she came back huffing and puffing some more and said I found them in the briefcase."

This time, he said that Kari was the one who asked if the pills could have come from WCY. And rather than Kari's being the one who said she wanted to have them tested, Matt now contended, as he had with Cooper, that he'd told her to have them tested to put her mind at ease.

In hindsight, Matt said he wondered if Kari would still be alive if she'd taken the antidepressants the doctor prescribed. And why didn't she? Matt blamed Linda, saying she told Kari not to.

Much of what Matt said simply didn't make sense. He'd suggested often that Kari could have been at Walmart that day to buy the Unisom, planning to use it to take her own life, and that was why she wouldn't tell him what she was picking up. But was that logical when he told Johnston that Kari used Unisom-type medicines nightly, and that he'd often picked it up for her in the past? Now that he'd seen the autopsy, now that he knew the toxicology found traces of sleeping pills, Matt said he'd seen Kari take Ambien.

"She didn't have a prescription for those . . . Where did she get them?" Johnston asked.

This, too, Matt suggested was Linda's fault, that Kari had gotten them out of what he described as her mother's well-stocked medicine cabinet. The problem with the theory was that at that time Linda Dulin didn't have a prescription for Ambien.

The hours wore on, Matt looking increasingly agitated. He told of that afternoon at the Y. Kari had left the middle school hours earlier on a high, yet she arrived at the Family Y angry and sad. Something had clearly happened in the few hours between the interview and swim practice, but what? He seemed unable to explain.

As the questioning continued, Johnston nailed down details. Matt said Kari threw up shortly after they arrived at the Y. Johnston wanted to know if once she sat down in the hallway, had Kari ever left the black leather couch. Matt said no. The importance was that Kari hadn't slipped away to the bathroom to ingest anything.

Then Johnston led Matt through his account of the last hours of Kari's life, from the time they left the Y until he called 911 at just after midnight: On the drive home, they decided to forgo pizza for Happy Meals for the girls. Not feeling well, this time Matt said Kari ate a single french fry. As soon as they arrived at the house, she threw up for a second time that evening. By eight that evening Kari was in the bathtub, soaking. Afterward, she lay in bed watching television, drifting in and out of sleep. By nine or nine thirty, Matt said he'd joined her in the bedroom, taken a shower in the adjoining master bath, then watched TV and talked.

"What did you talk about?" Johnston asked.

"There wasn't a lot of talking," Matt said, dismissively. "She was asleep, awake, asleep, awake. That's basically how she was. She asked me to run some errands."

Was she so tired, so out of it, that he worried she'd be unable to care for the girls?

"No," he said. " . . . They were sleeping, and I'd left them with her before."

At ten forty-five, when he said Kari asked him to fill the

gas tank in her SUV and rent a movie, pick up a soda and M&Ms, how was she then? "It was still kind of that half-awake talking, still really drowsy," Matt said.

"Were you worried she couldn't take care of herself at that point?"

"No, I just thought she was tired."

Again and again, Matt said that Kari was awake if tired when he left at what he pegged as approximately eleven fifteen. "I knew I'd only be gone an hour or so," he said. "I walked over to her in bed and told her that I was leaving."

"How did she respond?" Johnston asked.

"She said, 'Okay.'"

"You weren't concerned at that point?"

"I knew she wasn't feeling well, very lethargic, tired, drowsy, eyes are droopy."

"But she wasn't mentally unclear?" Johnston asked.

"She was slower," the former preacher contended.

"You didn't have a concern that if you left her in that condition, she was so out of it she couldn't take care of the kids?" Johnston asked yet again. This was an important point. If Kari had already taken the pills, if she was unconscious, that set the clock back, gave her body more time to develop lividity and cool, explaining the condition her corpse was in when the first EMTs arrived. But if she was alive, talking and lucid? Then how did she die, cool, and develop lividity in forty-five minutes?

"Correct," Baker said with a nod.

As for his foray to run errands, that the ex-pastor described in much the same terms as he had to Cooper: the stop at the closed convenience store near the house, the gas station that sold only diesel, the stop to fill up the tank, then the run through Hollywood Video, where he rented the video, *When a Man Loves a Woman*.

So much of what Matt had described about Kari's death resonated with those who remembered Kassidy's final night. From finding them both in fetal positions, on their sides, to the time of night, just after midnight. Now, Matt drew the parallel, saying that after he walked into the room, Kari's stillness, the paleness of her body, her lips a faint blue, reminded him of their dead daughter. "That was a familiar look," he said. "Kari was not responsive and not breathing. I'm trained in CPR. I looked for her heart rate and blood pressure, any of that. Didn't find any signs of breathing."

"What did you do next?" Johnston asked, moving on to a subject he wanted to etch into stone: Matt's depiction of his actions once he entered the bedroom.

"I reached for the phone and I called 911," he said.

"And then what happened?"

As he reached for the phone, he said he saw the note on the table but didn't take time to read it. Instead, as he cupped the cordless phone between his ear and his shoulder, he got to work. Kari was naked, and instead of immediately beginning CPR, he took the time to dress her, putting her silky panties on while she was still on the bed, then pulling her off onto the floor to start compressions, yet first dressing her in the Snoopy Santa T-shirt she'd had on earlier that evening, threading her limp arms through the sleeves and pulling it down behind her back.

"How long did it take to dress her?" Johnston asked, his voice bland, giving away none of the importance of the question.

"Seconds," Matt said. "It was a loose shirt and panties, very easy to put on."

Just dressing a dead body could be an arduous task, the experts had told Johnston, but the way Matt was describing it was that he did it at the same time he balanced a phone against his ear, talked to the 911 dispatcher, and pulled Kari from the bed. He'd accomplished all of this in less than a minute. At that point, he gave her CPR for one minute, then rushed to the door and got there just in time to open it before the EMTs rang the bell and woke the children.

In his description, it seemed that Matt was everywhere at once, doing everything perfectly, not just attempting to breathe life back into his wife but protecting her modesty.

When questioned, Matt said he saw no abrasion on Kari's nose although Bevel had noted one in the photos. But then Matt hadn't noticed the lividity either, writing off what Johnston pointed out in the photos as "shadows." And instead of cold to the touch, the way the first EMT on the scene described the body, Matt said Kari felt "clammy."

"How hard was it to move her?" Johnston asked.

"I didn't think about that at the time," Matt said, yet he agreed that he'd actually had to drag Kari's body off the bed and claimed that at one point he'd dropped her and her head had hit the floor. At Johnston's request, Matt drew a diagram of the bedroom, placing the furniture and Kari's body both in the bed and on the floor. Always appearing to be more than helpful, he asked, "Do you want me to time and date it?"

Johnston declined the offer.

"How much did you receive in death benefits?" Johnston asked. The answer from Matt was somewhere between $50,000 and $60,000. People in Kerrville had donated about $20,000 that Matt said had gone to pay his lawyers. Why had they opened their wallets? Staring down Johnston, Matt said, "Because they believe in my innocence, believe in the attack mode that's been against me."

"When did you meet Vanessa Bulls?" Johnston asked.

Here, too, Matt deviated only slightly from the description of the relationship he'd given Sergeant Cooper. As the ex-pastor had in the past, he talked as if Vanessa had initially been Kari's friend, and that they only became close after his wife's death. He admitted calling her, but said he was talking to Vanessa as a counselor might. Their relationship didn't change until midsummer 2006, and only because his children were the ones who wanted to spend time with her. "She was nice to my family," he said.

He had asked her father for permission to date Vanessa, that he admitted, but it was in the summer. They'd only kissed twice, he said. In fact, Matt insisted that he'd had no sexual relations with a woman since Kari's death. No, he said, he hadn't gone shopping for engagement rings with Vanessa just weeks after Kari's funeral. Instead, he said they'd been in Kay Jewelers looking at earrings for Grace. In Matt's version, the only time Vanessa had stayed over was the night of the slumber party. That, too, was the only time she had her car parked at his house. "I don't believe it was in the garage."

Again Johnston asked, "Did you have sexual relations with any woman in the year prior to Kari's death other than Kari?"

"No," Matt said.

"Do you have a conclusion as to what caused Kari's death?" Johnston asked.

"I believe she took too many sleeping pills in combination with the alcohol, and that she stopped breathing," Matt said.

"Where did she get Ambien?" Johnston asked.

"I don't know," Matt said. "Unless she borrowed some from her mom."

When it came to the searches on his WCY computer, scouring pharmacies and drug information, Matt insisted it was merely out of concern for Kari, his fear that she was taking too many sleeping pills. "So you raised that concern with the doctor?" Johnston asked, pointedly.

"I did not," Baker admitted.

"It was such a concern that you had felt like you should do Internet research . . . But you didn't mention it at all to the doctor?"

"No," he said again. "I did not."

"Did you ever order anything off the Internet?"

"Not a drug . . . a sexual stimulant," Matt said. "A liquid we were supposed to drink, and it was supposed to stimulate you."

As the questions continued, Matt Baker, the ordained Baptist minister who'd earlier talked of watching pornography to aid his sex life, said that he and Kari drank the liquid to elevate their level of excitement. "What was the sexual problem that you needed this for?" Johnston asked.

"To see if it would entice us more . . . Not necessarily that we weren't fulfilled. We just wanted to know if we could do more." According to Matt, the years had diminished their sex life, and he and Kari were both attempting to reignite it.

"Were you sexually frustrated in March 2006?" Johnston asked.

"If your question is, was I getting enough at home, the answer is yes," Baker said.

"Were you dissatisfied enough to order a sexual stimulant?" Johnson pushed.

"The two of us talked about that, and it was just to try something different," Baker said, noncommittally. Of course, since Kari wasn't there to object, he could say anything without fearing she'd contradict him, as he'd done earlier suggesting that they both enjoyed watching pornography.

"Do you remember on March 6 looking for Ambien on the Net?" Johnston asked.

"Not looking for Ambien, but looking at what side effects Ambien could cause," Baker protested.

"Did you go to a site from which you could order Ambien?" Johnston asked.

"All I know is that you can't order without a doctor's prescription," Matt said.

"How do you know that?" Johnston asked.

"I guess it's considered common knowledge," Baker shrugged.

About the possible side effects, Johnston asked if Matt knew that one was that someone could get lethargic to unconsciousness.

"I believe that's a side effect," Baker said.

As far as the missing WCY computer, Matt said that he didn't know where it had gone. When it came to the key to his office door, the one he'd had changed, he claimed that was a state-mandated order, and that he'd assumed Green-field and the other higher-ups at the center had a key that would open his door.

"Whom do you suspect in the switch of the computers?"

"I don't know that I formulated that," Baker said, his eyes red from the strain of what was becoming a long afternoon.

Earlier, Matt had filed a motion contending that the Dulins were making false statements about him. Johnston asked what those statements were. "That I killed my wife," he said.

So much would be telling that day. When Johnston asked for the names of Matt's friends, there were none to offer; Kari had been his constant companion. She had friends, but individually, Matt didn't have a name to give them. While he could have been saying that simply to keep the Dulins' attorney from contacting them, it fit what Kari had said so often, that without her, he was alone.

Again, Johnston returned to a question he'd asked many times that afternoon in many ways: "After Kari's death, how long did you wait to date anyone?"

"I've never officially dated anyone," Matt said again.

"So, since April of 2006, you have not had a dating rela-tionship with a woman . . . Certainly not a sexual relation-ship with any woman?"

"No," Matt answered.

When Johnston pressed, Matt again agreed that he'd turn over the home computer, the one Johnston had been attempt-ing to get for more than a year. Matt reiterated what he'd told the former prosecutor in the past, that the hard drive had crashed. Where he'd earlier said that he'd thrown it away, this time he said: "But I kept it." As for the printer, Matt said he'd not only thrown that away but also replaced it with another that he'd also discarded. Although money was tight, it seemed that Matt Baker had ample funds to replace two printers in a span of two years.

"Have you endeavored to be truthful with each and every answer to my questions?"

"Yes," Baker replied, straightening up in the chair.

"Did you go out with a girl who cut your hair?" Johnston asked with a slight smile. This was what the attorney had been waiting for.

"Did I go out with a girl who cut my hair?" Matt looked as if he'd been slapped across the face.

"Did you go out with a woman who cut your hair . . . ended up at her house?"

"Yes, we did," Matt admitted, looking markedly uncomfortable.

"You were intimate . . . kissing?"

"We did kiss, correct," Matt said.

Then Johnston cornered Baker, asking, "You had sex that night, didn't you?"

Baker had repeatedly said over the three-plus hours of the deposition that he hadn't been intimate with anyone since Kari's death, but now he must have known that Johnston knew about his one-night stand in Kerrville, about the woman who described a night the ex-pastor made her feel dirty and used. Matt, however, in his continual stance of maintaining that he was the one who helped others, answered with the seemingly bizarre statement: "No, what we did was I gratificated (sic) her."

Apparently he saw his actions in bed that night not as sex but as a service he was providing.

To drive his point home, that Matt Baker had been caught lying under oath, Johnston asked, "And every answer you've given me to one question has been just as truthful and just as important as each other question. Isn't it?"

"Yes, sir," Baker said, still defiant.

Johnston smiled.

In McLennan County that December, Ellison filed motions in the civil suit for Matt Baker in which he argued that the judge should rule on Matt's behalf because the Dulins hadn't supplied evidence of wrongdoing. Johnston responded, attaching the written opinions of the experts who'd reviewed the evidence, including Stafford, who'd written: "Kari Baker did not die as the result of an overdose."

Six days later, Ellison filed a countermotion, questioning Stafford's qualifications and asking to ban his testimony. "Baker looks to have civil case thrown out," read the headline in the *Kerrville Daily News* on December 16, 2008. In the piece, Ellison said the lawsuit was based solely on speculation. Johnston's response included the scintillating detail that Matt had attempted to order Ambien online just two weeks before Kari's death.

In the weeks that followed, Ellison continued to contest the testimony of nearly everyone on Johnston's witness list, from Heather Sigler, the jewelry-store clerk, to Ben Toombs, the young detective who'd written the arrest warrant. "We assumed the civil case would keep grinding along, and we'd get him there," says Bennett. "It wasn't what we wanted, but we were playing the cards we'd been dealt."

Then, right after the first of the year, something happened that none of them could have predicted, and it would change everything.

Chapter 50

In January 2009, the chief investigator in the McLennan County District Attorney's Office picked up the three-ring binder on the Baker case and walked into the office of one of the investigators on his staff, Abdon Rodriguez. A round-faced, jovial man with a friendly manner, Rodriguez was a former detective who had a reputation for getting suspects to confess. "I like police work. To me, it's all a game," he says, with a ready smile. "You do the bad things, and my part is to catch you."

Years earlier, Rodriguez had even managed to convince a good friend to confess after hiring someone to torch his shop. "I don't care who you are," Rodriguez says, a bit cocky and with a healthy share of enthusiasm. "I'm going to go after you if you commit a crime."

The other trait Rodriguez was well-known for was that he was something of a human lie detector. He could look at people, listen to their stories, judge their words and their body language, and he knew if they were lying.

"John Segrest wants you to reinvestigate this case," his boss said.

After opening the folder, Rodriguez said, "I remember this case."

Once he was alone, he began reading. He knew of the Baker case but only what he'd heard around the office, read in the newspapers, and seen on the news. So he started on page one, absorbing the crime-scene reports, assessing the photos, the inquest records, becoming familiar with the case and those involved. Once finished, Rodriguez watched videos of Hewitt PD's interview with Matt. What he saw in Baker was a nervous man. "There were tells, indications he wasn't telling the truth . . . One was that every time he lied, he closed his eyes. He wouldn't look at the person while he was lying."

That done, Rodriguez slipped Hewitt's interview with Vanessa Bulls into the DVD player. Sitting back in his chair, he knew within minutes that she, too, wasn't being truthful. "She was evading the questions, not answering, diverting the questioning. There were all kinds of red flags." What Rodriguez saw was that whenever Bulls didn't want to answer a question, she distracted Toombs. Sometimes she accomplished it by talking as she took a drink of water. At other times, she simply changed the subject. "When she didn't want to answer a question, she cried. Women do that a lot, and it worked," says Rodriguez. What did all this tell him? Based on what he saw, Rodriguez came to a conclusion: "I knew she was either involved, or she knew more than she was saying."

After he'd finished, he did as his boss had instructed, knocking on the office door of the prosecutor who'd had the Baker case for more than a year, Crawford Long.

Why was the DA's Office suddenly interested in the case? Later, Long would say that he'd never tabled the case, but it had stalled, and that it was turned over to Rodriguez in hopes that his talent for spurring confessions would break it open. Others would see it differently, wondering if John Segrest's political situation was behind the sudden interest in the case. Elections were coming up the following year, and there were rumblings that the longtime DA would have a serious opponent, a Waco lawyer. With the streets dotted with cars bearing bumper stickers that read JUSTICE FOR

KARI, it might have seemed only prudent to take another look at the Baker case.

No matter how he got the case, that week Rodriguez drove with Long to Dallas to talk with Dr. Reade Quinton, the pathologist who had autopsied Kari's body. What they were told was what others had heard over the years: There was no way after embalming and being in the grave for months to have an accurate toxicology finding. In a courtroom, Long still saw not having homicide on the autopsy as a major hurdle.

Yet, this time that didn't stop the investigation. Once back in Waco, Rodriguez began collecting statements from witnesses, including Bristol and Jill Hotz, who'd both talked with Kari the last week of her life. They repeated what she'd told them, that she feared that Matt was having an affair. Bristol added that Kari had told her that she feared Matt was trying to kill her.

That done, Rodriguez decided it was time to make it official. At the Dulin house, he stood on the front porch and rang the bell. Linda answered and invited him inside. "I'm here to let you know that I'm going to reinvestigate your daughter's death," he said.

Tears ran down Linda's cheeks. "Do you think you'll be able to do anything with it?"

"This case has a lot of potential," Rodriguez said. "I think I can solve it. I really do."

"I think the Lord sent you to us," Linda said. "I know you're going to do it."

The following day at the office, Rodriguez thought about what to do next. He was itching to have a discussion with Vanessa Bulls, wondering, *Why is she lying if she doesn't have anything to hide?* First, however, he needed to know more about the young woman at the center of the Baker case. Although at first reluctant to talk to him, Bulls's ex-husband finally agreed to answer questions for Rodriguez, laying out

the details of their failed marriage and the paternity test
that had proven that Lilly wasn't his. Next the investigator
tracked down a few of Vanessa's friends. "What they told
me was that she didn't always tell the truth," says Rodriguez.
"After that, I was sure I was right about her. She was lying
about how much she knew about Kari Baker's death."

The account Vanessa's friends gave Rodriguez was that
she'd told them Matt had begun hitting on her in December
and that he'd say things to her like he "could make her feel
good." One friend also said that Bulls was seriously interested in Baker, thinking that he'd be a good father for Lilly.

That Friday, Rodriguez called the cell-phone number
Bulls had given Hewitt PD. When she didn't answer, he left
a message and included his cell-phone number. The following morning, an attorney called, identifying himself as representing Bulls. "Why does she need an attorney? Does she
have something to hide?" Rodriguez asked.

The conversation went back and forth, and later that day
a meeting was scheduled for the coming Monday. At first
the attorney wanted Rodriguez to travel to his office, but the
investigator insisted Bulls had to come to his office, to meet
him on his own turf. "She's going to talk to me here, or she's
going to talk to the grand jury," he said. After consulting
his client, the attorney called back and agreed to meet at the
DA's Office.

Soon after, Rodriguez was bringing Long up-to-date in
his office when another assistant DA happened to walk in.
For fourteen years, Susan Shafer's workweek had focused
on prosecuting cases, many of them murders. "So many
victims don't really have a voice," she says. "Prosecuting
gave me an opportunity to fix that as much as possible." A
motherly woman with shoulder-length dark brown hair and
glasses, Shafer spent weekends and evenings shuttling her
children to sporting events and playing bluegrass music on
her guitar.

As Rodriguez and Long talked, Shafer waited her turn.
Listening to what Rodriguez told her boss about the Baker

case, Shafer began to show interest. A few years earlier, she and Long had prosecuted the case of William Mark Gibson, another cold case. Gibson was charged with barricading his wife and her daughter in the family home, then burning the house down. "It was a difficult case to pull together, and we had to try it twice, but we finally got a conviction," she says.

Before long, Shafer volunteered to work on the Baker case with Long, an offer he gladly accepted. "It was known in the office to be a tough case, and people weren't jumping up and down offering their services," he says.

Parallels she saw between her life and Kari's spurred Shafer's interest; they had children of similar ages who went to school in the same district, and Shafer's husband, like Kari, was a teacher. Shafer even knew people who'd known Kari.

One of the first things Shafer did on the case was to consult Bennett and McNamara. The two seasoned investigators went over all they'd done on the case, Bennett turning over an inch-thick, three-ring binder of their work that he'd pulled together for Shafer. Starting out with so much information was unusual. Shafer had never been involved in a case before where a family had done so much investigation privately. "What they'd pulled together for the civil case was a help for us if we proceeded criminally. As an ex-prosecutor, Bill Johnston knew what he needed, and he'd gone out to get it," she says. "John and Mike had compiled a lot of evidence that could be helpful if we prosecuted."

It wasn't that Shafer doubted Matt Baker's guilt. After watching him on *48 Hours,* Shafer formed the opinion that Baker was a liar, one who had probably murdered his wife. "I had strong feelings based on what I knew," says Shafer. "We had enough circumstantial evidence to prove it, we thought, but you hate to take a murder case before it's ready, and you get an acquittal and you've lost it forever. Crawford and I both thought that Matt had murdered Kari, but we weren't sure we could prove it."

That Monday, Bulls and her attorney showed up as scheduled at the DA's Office. Strategizing how he'd handle the interview, Rodriguez had already asked Shafer to divert Bulls's attorney to an observation room. Shafer agreed, and the two attorneys watched on a monitor as Rodriguez interrogated Bulls.

The questioning took nearly two hours, Rodriguez asking many of the same questions Hewitt PD, Bennett, and Mc-Namara had previously asked Bulls. Rodriguez questioned Bulls repeatedly about her relationship with Matt Baker, and she told the same story she'd told before, that Matt was counseling her. But Rodriguez didn't believe her, and he let her know, pointing at the phone calls between them. "That's a lot of counseling," Rodriguez said, sarcastically, but Vanessa wouldn't change her story.

After watching her prior interview, Rodriguez knew what questions to push with Bulls, and did so. "Every time I trapped her, she got defensive and would say she didn't know why something happened," he says. "She just couldn't answer the tough questions, and it was obvious that she was lying."

Rodriguez asked if she and Baker had been lovers before Kari's death, but Bulls denied it, saying that he'd once tried to kiss her, "But I told him that he was married."

When it was over, Rodriguez gave Bulls a warning, something Toombs and the other officers had failed to do: "I'm going to get Matt Baker indicted and convicted, and if you don't tell the truth, you're going to go down with him. I'll be following up on what you've told me, and I will be getting back with you."

"We knew she was lying," says Shafer. "We didn't believe her."

Later, Rodriguez took a drive out to the Bulls's household and talked with Vanessa's parents. During his interview with their daughter, Rodriguez had asked where she was the night Kari died. Vanessa had said that she was at home, watching television with her mother. Cheryl Bulls backed her daughter up, not only saying Vanessa was home but also describing what they watched that night, a movie on the Lifetime network.

There was also the matter of Cheryl's Ambien prescription, one that Larry Bulls had talked with Bennett and McNamara about. When Rodriguez brought it up, Cheryl confirmed that she had the prescription and that it was filled the week before Kari's death. "You're the only ones we know who had Ambien. Could Vanessa have given it to Matt Baker?" Rodriguez asked.

"No," Cheryl insisted, saying none was missing. "That's not possible."

Still, the investigator wondered.

The investigation continued on, Rodriguez talking to many of the same people Bennett and McNamara had interviewed three years earlier, during the summer after Kari's death. Then two weeks after his interview with Bulls, Rodriguez was in San Antonio at a conference when he decided to place another phone call to Vanessa. Once he got her on the line, he mentioned that he was in the river city, close to Kerrville, letting Bulls think he was there working on the Baker case. "We need to sit down and talk about this, Vanessa," he said. Then he bluffed: "I know what you did. I know what Matt Baker did. I know you two were having a sexual relationship. And I know you know what happened to Kari Baker. We're willing to offer you immunity if you tell us what you know."

Rodriguez waited. "Okay," Vanessa said. "When are you going to be back in Waco?"

"Monday," Rodriguez said, certain he now had her.

Yet Monday arrived, and Vanessa Bulls never showed up in his office as promised. Instead, her attorney called and said that she wouldn't be keeping the appointment. Rather than stopping the investigator, Rodriguez called Bulls and left messages. She didn't respond. He e-mailed, and she didn't reply. "You need to call," he typed. "This isn't going away."

"I want to subpoena Vanessa Bulls and make her talk to a grand jury," Rodriguez told Crawford Long.

Soon after, the investigator had what Matt Cawthon had asked for nearly two years earlier, a subpoena in his hand as he walked into the principal's office in the Killeen, Texas, middle school where Vanessa Bulls was teaching. He asked for her, and she was called to the office. When she saw him, her mouth gaped open with surprise.

"You're going before the grand jury," Rodriguez said, handing her the subpoena. "And you will testify truthfully to everything. I'm going to be in there with you, and I'm going to make sure that you tell the truth."

At that, Vanessa began crying. "You could have been more cordial."

"I tried that," he said. "Now you're going to talk to the grand jury, and if you don't tell the truth, you're going to be charged with perjury."

The morning of March 25, 2009, the matter of the death of Kari Baker was finally scheduled to go before a grand jury. Abdon Rodriguez got to the courthouse early, wanting Vanessa Bulls to see him. When he saw her waiting to testify, he made it a point to walk past her. "I wanted to remind her that I was there and that I was listening."

When Crawford Long and Susan Shafer arrived, Bulls's attorney informed them, "She's going to plead the Fifth," meaning that she planned to invoke her constitutional right not to give incriminating evidence against herself. "But she does have information for you. We want transactional immunity."

Long balked, not willing to give Bulls the type of immunity that ensured she couldn't be tried for any crime tied to Kari Baker's death. "I didn't know what her involvement was, and I wasn't going to give her a get-out-of-jail-free card," says Long. Instead, he offered testimonial immunity, which guaranteed only that her grand jury testimony couldn't be used against her. At that, an agreement was signed.

Inside the room, the grand jurors listened as Long asked questions of Bulls, including ones about her relationship with Baker, stressing all the phone calls. "She admitted a certain extent of relationship but not boyfriend girlfriend." Bulls appeared nervous. Her eyes were red, and at times she cried, as she had with police, usually when her little girl, Lilly, was mentioned. Gradually, Long worked up to the most important question: "Did Matt Baker ever tell you anything about his wife's death?"

"He told me that he killed her to be with me," Bulls answered.

"We were all stunned," says Long. "None of us expected her to say that."

That same afternoon, the McLennan County grand jury returned an indictment on the charge of murder against Matthew Dee Baker.

John Bennett was helping a friend remodel a house when the phone rang.

"They've done it," Linda said, crying. "They've indicted Matt."

At four the following afternoon, Thursday, March 26, 2009, nearly three years after Kari's death, Matt Baker again turned himself in at the Kerr County Courthouse. On a charge of murder, based on an indictment stating that he'd drugged then suffocated his wife, the bond was set at half-a-million dollars. Two weeks later, Ellison argued successfully and had Baker's bond reduced to $250,000. The following day, Matt posted bond and was released, to await his trial.

Immediately after Bulls's grand jury testimony ended, Rodriguez told Susan Shafer he wanted another interview with the woman at the center of the Baker case. "I want the whole story," Rodriguez said. Shafer agreed, and on March 20, the investigator and his prime witness came face-to-face again, this time in her attorney's office. As the interview progressed, Bulls fluctuated, initially denying then admitting that her relationship with Baker had been sexual, but still claiming it didn't start until after Kari's death. At Kensi's party, she said she slept on the couch while Matt slept in his bedroom. "I have information that you slept in the same bed," Rodriguez bluffed.

"Okay," she said. "We did."

"I have information that even before Kari's death, you were at his house," Rodriguez challenged, gradually pulling out more detail. To get her to talk, over and again, Rodriguez acted as if he understood Bulls, and that he sided with her, saying repeatedly that Baker had used the pretty young woman.

"Yes," she agreed.

The account that Bulls finally gave that day was that in the beginning, Matt counseled her on the telephone, until one day when he insisted they needed to continue their work at his house on Friday afternoons, while his wife and children were at school.

"If you didn't have anything to hide, why did you park in his garage and put the door down?" Rodriguez asked.

"I don't know."

In the end, Vanessa stood fast, saying she hadn't slept with the errant preacher until Kensi's birthday party.

As their time together drew to a close, Rodriguez turned off his tape recorder.

"Do you believe me now?" she asked.

"No," he said. "Because I know you all had sex prior to Kari's death. Y'all were having an affair, and you had sex at his house."

"Just one," she said. "One Friday only. One of those Fridays we did have sex."

"Well, okay."

"Do you believe me now?"

"Well, I still believe that you provided that," Rodriguez said, referring to a more frequent sexual relationship.

"No," she said. "I promise. I would never tell you I did that."

As the trial approached, Bulls hired a new attorney, this one a criminal defense lawyer, Russ Hunt, Sr. A bearded man with glasses, Hunt was a Baylor University law graduate and a former prosecutor. One of his first acts was to inform Shafer and Long that his client refused to have any further contact with Abdon Rodriguez. When he heard the news, the investigator laughed. He understood why. "That's fine," he said to Shafer. "But tell them I need to have one last interview with her. She's still not telling us everything."

Over Labor Day weekend 2009, that interview took place at the DA's Office in the book-lined law library, with Vanessa's attorney present. At first, Bulls appeared reluctant, saying, "You know, this is going to make me look bad. What about my job?"

"Vanessa, you could be charged with this, too," Rodriguez said. "You could be going to prison and leaving your daughter and family. Just think, you're going to be free. I don't know what's going to happen with your job. It's not going to look good for you, all the involvement you've had. But you will be free rather than behind bars."

At that, Rodriguez and Shafer left the room, so that Hunt could talk to his client. Afterward, Shafer would form the opinion that the woman at the center of the Baker case finally comprehended that the charade was over. "I think she realized that it was becoming ridiculous, that we didn't believe her," says Shafer. "We were all catching her in so many lies."

When they returned, Hunt said, "She'd like to talk to you."

"We just want the truth," Shafer said. "We don't want you to elaborate, we just want to know what really happened, what you really know."

For the next three hours, Bulls appeared to open up, telling Shafer and Rodriguez the details of how the affair began months before Kari's death. By late February and into March, she said Matt began planning how to kill his wife. As they continued their affair, Bulls said Matt discussed a variety of plans to dispose of his wife, so that he and Bulls could be together, including tampering with the brakes on Kari's car, staging a drive-by shooting, using chloroform or roofies, the date rape drug, to knock her out, then making it look like a suicide. The methods included hanging Kari or making it appear that she'd intentionally overdosed.

Nonchalantly relaying the conversations, Bulls showed no regret. Instead, she laughed, saying she'd brushed off his ideas as preposterous. In the end, Bulls said Baker focused on drugging Kari. "He talked about putting it in a milk shake," she said.

When Rodriguez pressed Bulls about where Matt got the Ambien, she said that Matt told her that he'd taken it from Kari's mother's medicine cabinet. That wouldn't have been possible since Linda didn't have a prescription for the drug, but that day in the DA's Office, Vanessa had center stage and she told her version of the events surrounding Kari's death. "Matt said he was going to type the suicide note," Bulls said. "I told him, 'You can't type it. Suicide notes are handwritten.'"

"Kari types everything, so I can do it that way," he said.

This time, the preacher's ex-mistress admitted that Matt Baker told her beforehand that he'd murder Kari that Friday night. "He had it all planned," she said.

The next morning, he called her and let her know it was done.

Yet Rodriguez still wondered if Bulls was telling them everything. "Vanessa showed no remorse, and when she talked about Kari's death, it was as if she didn't even acknowledge that a woman had died."

Then Bulls described how Baker said he'd killed Kari. After buying capsules for sexual enhancement on the Net, he emptied the contents and filled the shell with Ambien. Kari was trying hard to keep the marriage together, and she'd been more amenable to doing what he asked. Bulls said Matt realized that, and he planned to use it to get her to take the Ambien by pretending it was a drug to stimulate their sex life.

"Vanessa said that Matt and Kari were drinking the Fuzzy Navel wine coolers, and he gave her the pills," says Rodriguez. "He handcuffed her to the bed when they were having foreplay, then, of course, she passed out with all the alcohol and Ambien, and he took a pillow and put it over her face."

Rodriguez had wondered how Kari had pieced it together, how she'd come to suspect that Matt might be having an affair and planning to take her life. Something Vanessa told him that day gave an inkling of a possibility. One day at church while Vanessa was talking to Kari, Vanessa mentioned something Matt had said to her on the telephone. As Vanessa told the story, Kari homed in on the fact that Matt was talking to the music minister's attractive, young daughter.

"Why were you talking to Matt?" Kari asked, sounding suspicious.

Rodriguez guessed that was when Kari began to suspect the affair. Then when she found the crushed pills, "I think she put it all together."

In the end, Kari's mistake was that despite everything, she still loved and believed in Matt, and she never allowed herself to make the leap from suspicion to certainty.

One area that Rodriguez didn't delve into was Kassidy. One of the accounts Bulls gave that day left a dark cloud over the infant's death. When she heard that Kari's body was being exhumed, she called Matt. He was at the cemetery, going to the grave. "Yes, her body's gone," he told her. What was so frightening was that he then ran over to see if the authorities had dug up Kassidy's grave as well. Why would he think that the police might get his daughter autopsied? What did that mean?

"We suspected he might have murdered Kassidy, too," says the investigator. "But we had no evidence."

In the days that followed that interview, Shafer thought about the woman who'd been Matt Baker's lover. In a court-room, Bulls's testimony could be damning, but there were problems, the major one that Bulls had lied for so long and so often about what she knew. Would a jury believe that now she was telling the truth?

What Shafer needed was physical evidence corroborating Vanessa Bulls's testimony. One thing immediately came to Shafer's mind: Bulls said that Matt attempted to murder Kari weeks before her death by feeding her drugs in a milk shake. When Shafer looked through Matt's e-mails, ones retrieved off the WCY network, she found what she was looking for in an exchange between Kari and Matt dated March 21, 2006, the day before the seventh anniversary of Kassidy's death. "Do you want anything special tonight?" Matt wrote. "How about a chocolate shake with even MORE chocolate syrup? Just joking. :-) Love you!"

There it was, evidence that two weeks before Kari's death, Matt had fed his wife a milk shake, one Vanessa Bulls said he'd bragged about lacing with drugs.

One afternoon, Shafer called Bulls and asked another question: Had Matt Baker ever sent her any e-cards or songs? Kersh had explained to Shafer that he had batches of information off Matt's computers, but it was like being in a library filled with books without a card catalogue. What he needed were specific search terms, things he could use to find the right book/batch of information. When Shafer asked that question, Bulls was silent, then described something that had happened after the murder: "There was this song Matt sang to me, to intimidate me. "Dirty Little Secret" by the All-American Rejects."

When Shafer looked up the lyrics, she understood why Bulls saw the song as a threat. The words cautioned to keep silent. If secrets were divulged, the chorus warned that she could become "just another regret."

"Would you look for the song on his computer?" Shafer asked Kersh. "Or the lyrics, anything that ties into it?"

"Sure," Kersh said. Before long, he called back. "I found it. I found the MP3!"

As Shafer's dialogue with Bulls continued, other discoveries followed. After Bulls divulged Baker's passwords, including that he used her name, "Vanessa," Kersh searched again. This time he found an account with a Fiji travel site. Adding even more confirmation to Shafer's belief that Bulls was finally telling the truth was an e-mail sent by a booking agent, one that offered Baker congratulations on his upcoming marriage and discussed the details of a Fiji honeymoon.

"It was all checking out," says Shafer. "The little bits and pieces fit together."

As they talked, Bulls sounded embarrassed that she'd ever had a relationship with Baker. Says Shafer, "She sounded stunned that she'd trusted him and frustrated with her own willing blindness, that she'd known he was going to kill Kari and never did anything about it." Now that Vanessa had opened up, "She really did seem to be trying to assist as much as possible."

The immunity Bulls had been granted wasn't all-inclusive, so if Shafer and Long discovered any evidence that Vanessa had been instrumental in either planning or carrying out the murder, they had the latitude to prosecute her. "The immunity only covered the grand jury," says Shafer. "And Vanessa never asked for it again. We never found any evidence that she had done anything other than know about Matt's plans."

When they talked, Long and Shafer both believed Vanessa was being honest. First, they saw no reason for her to say what she did if it weren't true since everything she'd told them made her look bad. Secondly, Bulls didn't know about the e-mails and other evidence, yet what she said dovetailed with all they had.

At times, Shafer wrestled with the fact that Vanessa knew Matt Baker was going to kill his wife and did nothing. While the prosecutor felt strongly that Bulls should have spoken up, in Shafer's analysis, she wasn't sure it would have changed the outcome. "I don't think anyone would have believed Vanessa," says Shafer. "Maybe Kari, but that would have taken the mistress calling the wife, and Kari had already voiced suspicions and written them off. She wasn't ready to believe her husband could kill her."

If Bulls had talked and prevented Matt from carrying through, Shafer speculated that Matt would have taken action at a later date. "Kari wasn't in the life Matt wanted for himself," says Shafer. "If Vanessa wasn't the one, someone else would have been, and Kari was in the way. With or without Vanessa, Matt would have murdered his wife."

That spring in Kerrville, still reeling after the death of his second son, Guy James Gray would later say he wasn't looking to get back into the Baker case. "I don't think I was in the frame of mind," he says. "After losing my son, I understood how Kari Baker could have committed suicide. I'd had some of those same thoughts and fought through them."

The way he'd tell it, Baker and his mother convinced him otherwise, pushing him to sign back on as Matt's attorney. "They pleaded and begged, and they didn't let up," says Gray. "I finally gave in, and said I'd take the case back." Again, stressing why he felt compelled to represent Matt, Gray would say that the general opinion in Kerrville hadn't changed; those who knew Matt viewed him as a martyr, a good man persecuted by a domineering mother-in-law who couldn't accept her daughter's suicide.

Once he took the case, Gray again considered the evidence. As he saw it, little had changed with one exception: Vanessa Bulls. "She'd talked to the grand jury, and they'd indicted," he says. "So she must have told them something different than she told me."

Yet he wasn't as worried as he might have been because he had three tape-recorded interviews in which Bulls had denied knowing anything: the first with his investigator; the second with Hewitt PD; and the third, her initial talk with Rodriguez. "If she was telling a different story, she was contradicting her own words," says Gray. "She would have lied not once but three times."

There was one thing that did bother Gray, however: Matt

wasn't acting the way he'd expect when facing a possible life sentence. "It was odd. He didn't appear worried," says Gray.

The Baker case would fill 2009 for Shafer. "It was pretty much all I worked on," she'd say later. "We had many of the pieces without Vanessa's testimony, but we didn't have the picture, like the one on a puzzle box that ties it all together."

As they actively readied it for trial, Shafer sent the only physical evidence they had from the scene, the note and pill bottle, out for retesting. What they were looking for was DNA or fingerprints. Again, Matt's fingerprints and DNA weren't found, but there were interesting results. Most intriguing was that Vanessa Bulls was a possible contributor to DNA found on the Unisom bottle.

Again, Bulls was questioned. "We went at her hard about the DNA," Long says. "She was steadfast that she wasn't there, and we didn't have any evidence to the contrary."

In the end, the DNA numbers were so low that they were far from conclusive. "The findings weren't solid," says Long. "They were small numbers, meaning that they could have been from someone else. There wasn't anything there we could use."

For instance, Linda Dulin was a possible source of DNA found on the suicide note, but she'd never touched it. "All these numbers weren't reliable," he says. "But we knew Gray would make use in a courtroom of the fact that Vanessa was a possible contributor to the DNA on the bottle."

Fall 2009 arrived, and Shafer got ready for trial, interviewing witnesses and studying the intricacies of computer records, so she'd be able to explain such complicated matters to jurors as the way drugs are purchased on the Internet. As the weeks counted down to the January trial date, she culled through the interviews Matt Baker had given the press, TV, and written media, along with his testimony during the deposition for the civil trial. Shafer drew up a chart, comparing Matt's quotes, listing what he told whom and when, to illustrate his inconsistencies. "That was something you almost never have in a trial," says Long. "We had Matt Baker's own words in the press. And we had this thorough interview Bill Johnston had done with Matt Baker, in which he locked himself into his account."

As the case came together, there were aha moments, times when a bit of evidence came into focus; one was when Shafer interviewed the first responders to the scene. On the 911 call, Matt claimed to be in the bedroom, feverishly attempting to revive his wife. But the EMTs arriving on the scene had another version. "They told us Matt wasn't even in the house," says Shafer. "He was standing at the front door, still on the phone."

There was also the matter of the telephone; Matt said he used the cordless phone next to the bed to call 911. In the photos, that phone was on its base on a nightstand. Matt was still on the phone when the EMTs arrived, and the police said that he never reentered the bedroom while they were there. If Matt had used the bedroom phone, how did he put it back on the base? "We realized it was a show, all of it," Shafer says. "Nothing he claimed on the 911 tape happened."

Another day, Shafer inspected the crime-scene photos and noticed that the lividity in Kari's left arm was more pronounced than in the right arm. To get another set of expert eyes on the crime-scene photos and the autopsy, Long hired Dr. Sridhar Natarajan, the head pathologist in Lubbock, Texas. First, Shafer sent the M.E. all the photos and the autopsy. Then, shortly before Thanksgiving, Long and Shafer flew to Lubbock to meet with the pathologist in person.

The lividity pattern was one of the questions Shafer put before Natarajan. When Shafer asked about the left arm, the ME said what she'd anticipated, that the arm in question had to have been lower than the rest of the body. "I saw that as pretty important," she says. "I mean, why in the world would someone lie about something like the position of the body? Matt Baker lies about things he doesn't even have to lie about."

As Shafer saw it, Baker was someone who'd always been able to talk himself out of trouble and who believed he was more intelligent than everyone else. "He figured he'd get out of this, too," she says. "No matter who he's with, Matt's the kind of guy who figures he's the smartest one in the room."

Meanwhile, Long asked the medical examiner about a discoloration on Kari's nose, one clearly visible in the crime-scene and autopsy photos. From the beginning, Bennett and McNamara had voiced the theory that Kari had been first drugged, then smothered. Long wondered if the bruise was evidence pointing to that conclusion. The M.E. responded that the mark was an abrasion, one that could have come from Kari's having been smothered by a pillow.

As they got ready to walk into the courtroom, Long and Shafer assessed their case. Despite what they'd pulled together, there were still those nagging problems, the biggest that they didn't have a homicide finding on the autopsy. "There was no definitive ruling on manner of death," says Long. "We knew Gray would exploit that."

Add to that the unwillingness of the medical experts Long had contacted to say that the lividity visible in Kari's body was absolutely impossible during the forty-five-minute time period of Matt's alibi, and the prospects were troublesome.

When it came to the scientific evidence seen on programs like *CSI,* they had little. Instead, the case's linchpin was Bulls. But she'd lied so often, would a jury believe her?

Yet there were the strong points, too. One: So much would be allowed in the trial simply because of Matt's own actions. In most cases the statements of a dead person are hearsay and inadmissible, since the person is unable to take the stand. But Matt had talked to others about what Kari had said, and he was alive. "Matt Baker's statements were not hearsay, so we could bring all of that before the jury because he'd talked about those things with Linda Dulin and Jo Ann Bristol," explains Long. "All of it became admissible through his own words, plus what he'd said in the deposition. He screwed up. The way it worked out, he couldn't object because they were his own statements."

As the days counted down, Shafer saw the case come together. But was it solid enough? As they prepared opening arguments, Shafer and Long agreed that Matt would want to testify. "Baker has a history of talking, even when it's not in his best interest," she says.

It was then that Shafer had an idea. The plan came to her while listening to the 911 tape. The entire phone call took little more than four minutes, a brief time to do all Matt said he did, from dressing Kari and pulling her off the bed to administering CPR. "Baker would have to be Superman. There's no way," says Shafer.

She thought about ways to illustrate the incongruity between what Matt said he'd done and what was possible. In the end, what Shafer devised was a trap she'd bait with Matt Baker's own words.

Meanwhile, in Guy James Gray's office in Kerrville, a drama unfolded that threatened to postpone the trial. Over the months, Gray had pushed Matt to tell him everything, so that he'd be prepared in the courtroom, and high on the list was what Bulls might say. Steadfastly, Matt had denied that the relationship had been sexual. Then, in December, with the trial looming, Matt and Barbara again talked to his defense attorney. "At that meeting, what Matt Baker told me was that he'd been lying, and that he did have a sexual relationship with Vanessa Bulls before his wife died," says Gray.

The defense attorney was furious. The next day, Gray and his cocounsel, a Kerrville attorney Gray had brought on named Harold Danford, both filed motions in which they asked to be taken off the case, saying they had a serious breach of confidence with their client. Yet new counsel could delay a trial for months or more, and the judge ruled against them.

That didn't sit well with Gray, who'd convinced himself early on that he had an innocent client. Suddenly Gray, like the prosecutors, had Baker pegged as a liar. "I think the judge should have let me leave," he says, with a frown. "From that point on, I never talked to Baker unless I legally had to. I wanted nothing to do with him."

Chapter 51

Texas *v.* Matthew Dee Baker was called to order on the morning of Wednesday, January 13, 2010, in McLennan County's 19th District Court. Presiding from behind the bench was Judge Ralph Strother, a rosy-cheeked man with a balding pate and a stark white beard and mustache.

In the audience, Kari's family filled two rows, Jim sitting beside Linda much of the time, with his arm protectively wrapping her shoulders. Linda's father attended and, of course, the angels: Lindsey, Nancy, and Kay. Jennifer, who'd backed her sisters throughout their fight, had flown in from Florida. Others included extended family and friends, and Shannon Gamble, who founded the blog that had become a rallying point for supporters. In the months leading up to the trial, the music Gamble had on the blog was Johnny Cash's gruff voice singing: "You can run . . . but sooner or later, God'll cut you down."

The press filled the front row, and behind them on the right-hand side in a reserved row sat Barbara Baker, severely dressed, with dry eyes and a taut smile. Matt's father, Oscar, hadn't come, nor his sister. When asked, Barbara said that her husband had stayed home to care for Kensi and Grace and that Matt's sister was busy with her own family. Neither ever did attend, and throughout the trial, Barbara would either sit alone or with a small handful of supporters.

Bill Johnston wasn't in the audience, but John Bennett and Mike McNamara were, listening as Susan Shafer addressed the jury, offering a window into the testimony that lay ahead. Shafer outlined the evidence that was to come, from the accounts of those who'd seen Kari and Matt that final evening to the EMTs who found Matt not administering CPR but on the front porch.

Then Shafer introduced the central figure in her case. "You are going to hear from Vanessa Bulls. You are going to see her. And she is going to come in and tell you about the affair she had with Matt Baker both before and after Kari Baker's death. Vanessa Bulls is going to tell you how Matt brought her into the marital bed while Kari was still alive. And she's going to tell you how Matt Baker killed Kari on the night of April 7. Vanessa is going to give you all the information you need . . . and we feel confident that after you hear the evidence we'll bring to you, that you'll find Matt Baker guilty."

It was the first inkling Gray had of what Bulls would say on the stand. Still digesting that the prosecutors' star witness had made a complete about-face, he stood up to address the jurors. Gray began by painting a starkly different picture. In his account, it wasn't Matt who'd lived a double life but Kari: "As a schoolteacher, she was relatively happy, very professional, and well liked. Then she had a private life, a home life that was quite a bit different . . . She had this private pain. This child that died—the middle one—it was a very, very traumatic death . . . It was something that consumed her."

As Matt had told so many, Gray argued that Kari became depressed each year around the anniversary of Kassidy's death. He cited the medical record, in which a doctor prescribed an antidepressant for Kari just days before she died. And then Gray admitted Matt's affair: "Pretty classic, preacher and the daughter of the music minister."

So much would never be known due to Hewitt PD's shoddy crime-scene work, Gray pointed out. In his opening statement, the defense detailed the problems that Long and Shafer had discussed between themselves, especially the lack of a finding of homicide on the death certificate and a toxicology report that left so many questions unanswered.

Then, once Gray finished, the prosecutors began to present their evidence. The first witness was a Spring Valley teacher who'd seen Kari that last morning, one who said Kari was excited about the prospect of the new job and fretted over getting Grace into the class she wanted for her the coming fall. Then Basy Barrera recounted Kari's final beauty-shop visit. "To me, she never seemed better," said Barrera. "Kari had just lost fifteen pounds."

Yet with Gray, Barrera admitted that Kari hadn't always been happy, especially in the days following Kassidy's death. "How was she then?" the defense attorney asked.

"Sad, of course," said Barrera.

At the Y, Kari didn't acknowledge Kim Jackson in the stands, and Matt mouthed that his wife wasn't well. "She was not her normal self that night," Jackson said. Kari looked like she'd been crying. "They both were acting very differently."

After the testimony regarding the Family Y, Shafer put the medical personnel who'd responded to the scene on the stand. In the end, their testimony would be varied. Some didn't observe any lividity, while others not only saw it but also noted it on their reports. Yet none described Kari as warm. The terms they used ranged from cool to cold. The problem for prosecutors was that Gray cross-examined and again pointed out the shoddy work done by Hewitt PD. The ambient temperature in the room was never taken, nor was Kari's body temperature. With so much left undone, how could anyone really know when Kari died?

During cross-examinations, Gray hammered away at witnesses, questioning why they administered CPR if Kari was so clearly dead, and one other thing: None of them had seen any signs of a fight. If there'd been a murder, shouldn't there have been some kind of struggle? Gray suggested. Still there was something else that struck those on the scene that night as odd. With his wife lying dead on the floor, Matt didn't appear at all upset.

Officer Michael Irving never saw the pools of vomit and foam that Matt said had come from Kari. In fact, if it had been there, the EMTs said they wouldn't have hooked up their equipment. Yet had the Hewitt police protected the meager evidence they did take? No. They hadn't even used gloves to collect the suicide note and pill bottle.

Gradually, the prosecutors brought into evidence the handful of crime-scene photos, including the four with the body. "Do you see pens on the nightstand?" Shafer asked, pointing to ballpoints near the note. The inference was that if Kari had written the note and wanted to sign it, she could have. Why then was her name only typed?

On the witness stand, Justice of the Peace Billy Martin appeared uncomfortable. He'd been a justice of the peace in McLennan County for twelve years, he said. "Is one of your duties to determine if an autopsy should be ordered in a death?" Long inquired.

"Yes, sir," Martin answered, explaining that the existence of a note and what he'd heard from Hewitt PD convinced him that in this case one wasn't necessary. And after the inquest? "Did you change the ruling . . . to what?" Long asked.

"Undetermined," Martin answered.

Throughout, the jurors sat at attention while the scientific testimony left question marks. Over and over again it was apparent that law enforcement had failed Kari, never adequately investigating her death. In the end, it would be times such as Jo Ann Bristol in the witness box recounting her last meeting with Kari that would linger. "I think that Matt is planning to kill me," Kari had said.

Accounts of Matt's tenure at the Waco Center for Youth were offered by a handful of witnesses. They told of the procedure for distributing pills, one that didn't account for the pills in his briefcase, his strange change in appearance after Kari's death, and the mysterious disappearance of his computer. Not only did Matt not seem upset by Kari's death, but he talked of her as a "dark cloud," saying he'd no longer loved her.

Whenever the opportunity presented itself, Gray brought out Kari's journals. Yes, a variety of witnesses said, she'd written often saying she wanted to be with her dead daughter, but the dates, where there were any, were from years earlier. What Kari wrote in her Bible days before her death didn't even mention Kassidy; instead, it named Matt and asked God to protect her.

While she had Ben Toombs on the stand, Shafer played the 911 call and put before the jury the receipts from Matt's trip to the gas station and Hollywood Video. Off and on throughout the trial, she played DVDs of Matt's interviews for the jury, demonstrating his contradictory statements. In some, Matt Baker described Kari as awake when he left. In others, she was half asleep or "lethargic, eyes drooping."

On the stand, Dr. Reade Quinton talked of the problems he'd encountered during the autopsy. Yet although he couldn't say how much was in her system at the time of her death, he said unequivocally that Kari Baker had ingested the drug Ambien. During cross-examination, Quinton discussed the sedative effect of the alcohol, the Ambien, and the Unisom, but he couldn't say what level would be necessary to prove lethal. "Bottom line is that you don't know?" Gray asked.

"Yes," the physician admitted.

The days passed, and the trial continued. Todd and Jenny Monsey told of the birthday party and their surprise at finding Matt already inserting Vanessa into his family. With both, Gray asked about Kari's depression after Kassidy's death.

Bits and pieces, each so important, nearly all of it first pulled together by Charlie's Angels and the Dulins' investigators. Noel Kersh detailed Matt's Internet life on the days leading up to Kari's murder, in which he searched for information on overdoses and shopped for Ambien. Mark Henry, the CEO of one of the pharmacies, took the stand and in staggering detail laid out the route that brought mattdb7722 to put Ambien in his shopping cart. Yet Matt never completed the purchase.

For the prosecution, it felt like one step forward and one step back.

At times, a deep sadness filled the courtroom, perhaps never more so than when Linda testified, introducing herself as "the mother of Kari and Adam and the wife of Jim." Her eyes filled with tears, she asked, "Can you tell this is unsettling?" In the otherwise silent courtroom, Linda Dulin told of the daughter she'd lost, the ambitious young woman who'd worked hard to get her master's and poured her attention and love into building a family. "Kari was such an extrovert, loved life, a joy to be around," she said. "An excellent teacher, and more than anything, she loved her daughters . . . a wonderful wife."

Like Bristol, Linda talked of what Matt had told her about the WCY pills and about the hundreds of cell-phone calls to Vanessa Bulls that finally led her to believe Matt had committed the ultimate sin, murder.

When Gray asked about Kassidy's death, Linda answered calmly, not denying that her daughter grieved when Kassidy died. "Did she miss her child? Yes. She missed her child. But Kari had faith she would see her again in heaven."

"Isn't it a fact that she routinely used sleeping pills?" Gray asked.

"Yes, that is a fact," Linda answered.

So much for the jurors to absorb, but it all laid the groundwork for the prosecutors' twenty-seventh witness: Vanessa Bulls.

Chapter 52

Walking into the courtroom, Vanessa Bulls appeared almost luminescent, a small smile on her lips, her blond hair falling about the shoulders of her prim gray shirt. On day four of the trial, the testimony of the music minister's daughter would be chilling.

As Susan Shafer asked questions, Bulls, by then a twenty-seven-year-old middle-school teacher, recounted in shocking detail her version of the events that led up to Kari Baker's death. Her affair with Matt, Bulls said, started slowly, with Matt approaching her at church, making comments that included, "Whoever finds you is going to be a lucky man."

Consistently in the accounts of the young women who'd complained about Baker, the descriptions had been similar, that of a man stuck in adolescence, unable to talk to a woman as an adult. With Bulls, too, Baker's immaturity was evident, as he bantered with the young blonde, telling her not to date others, "just your pastor," then bragging that he'd had a vasectomy and didn't "have any sexually transmitted diseases."

As they talked more, Vanessa said Matt criticized Kari as a wife and mother. In church, Bulls had noticed Kari's attention to the girls. Yet Matt described himself as the main caretaker and called Kari "a fat bitch." By February, Bulls had agreed to counseling at the Baker house, and by early

March the relationship had turned sexual: "He asked if he could hold my hands to pray, and after that he kissed me." Then, she said, he took her by the hand and led her into the bedroom.

Afterward, she felt remorse, but she said Pastor Matt Baker told her: "Oh, you don't need to feel bad. God is such a forgiving God, it doesn't matter what anyone does. Just ask God to forgive you. It's okay. In reality, I don't think God believes that anyone can just be with one person the rest of their lives." And he said something else, that if they fell in love, he'd find a way to dispose of Kari.

Apparently Baker decided quickly that what he felt for Bulls was love, for within weeks of bedding her, Bulls said he began talking of killing his wife. For justification, he argued that Kari was already supposed to be dead. Once, years earlier, after Kassidy died, Matt claimed that Kari had threatened suicide and that he'd taken pills from her hand. Now that he wanted his wife out of his life, he described his action as "cheating death." Rather than murder, he said killing Kari would put things right by finishing what she'd started.

From that point on, there were breathless discussions of murder. One day Matt talked of killing Kari by putting drugs in a milk shake, saying he'd tried it, but the milk shake tasted like lead, and Kari refused to drink it. It was all so heartless: a husband talking of staging a hanging or a drive-by shooting, coolly plotting his wife's murder, while his mistress listened and took no action to stop him. In the courtroom, Jim and Linda Dulin softly cried.

On the stand, Bulls's manner alternated between angry and defiant. As time passed, it appeared that Matt grew more desperate to erase Kari from his life, telling Vanessa he attempted to buy roofies, the date rape drug, to render her helpless. That final week, Matt bragged that he was doing the "husbandly duty," having sex with Kari to make it appear he was attempting to work on the marriage. When Vanessa asked if anyone would question the faked suicide plan Matt had concocted, he said no: "Everyone knows how depressed she is."

That Saturday morning, even though Matt had told Vanessa that he planned to kill Kari the previous night, Vanessa said she was stunned when the phone rang and her mother told her that Kari was dead.

Two days later, Matt first said, "You know you're stuck with me now, right?" Then, she said, he told her about the murder, but he began by cautioning that if she told anyone, it would be to no avail "because he was a preacher."

"I'll tell you this once, but never again," he said. In the audience, Linda and Jim held each other, as Vanessa told a horrifying story, one in which Matt poured Ambien into the shells from sex-stimulant capsules and fed them to Kari with the wine coolers, then handcuffed her to the bed. When she passed out, he kissed her on the forehead, and said "either hug or kiss Kassidy for me."

Then Matt Baker put a pillow over his wife's face, to smother her. Yet Kari didn't die. Instead, after he removed the pillow, she gasped. Matt told Bulls he said, "Oh, shit," then climbed on top of Kari, this time cupping his hand over her mouth and nose, squeezing them shut. Afterward, he typed the suicide note on the home computer and printed it out on the printer, then ran the palm of Kari's hand over it. The scene was set with the pills and the empty wine-cooler bottles on the nightstand, and he locked the door and left. He'd chosen *When a Man Loves a Woman* because it was about a mother who treated her children badly. "He said it reminded him of Kari."

Had Kari looked up at him? Did she see her husband on top of her as she died? Did she look into his eyes, perhaps the way Kassidy might once have done?

From that moment on, Matt expunged his dead wife's possessions from the house and attempted to do the same to her memory. Only Kari's family, Linda and the angels, had kept that from happening.

How could Vanessa Bulls have ever trusted Matt Baker?

Many in the courtroom stared in disbelief when the pretty blonde said that she'd never loved Matt but initially felt safe with him "because he was a preacher." Felt safe with a man she knew had murdered his wife?

"I know that sounds ironic," she said, "But I was like, as long as someone's good to me, I don't, I don't care about being in love. I don't care about being attracted to someone." At the jewelry store, he'd inquired about trading in Kari's rings to buy new ones for Vanessa.

Shafer asked if Vanessa entertained the possibility that since Matt had killed one wife, he could kill another. "He promised me that he would be so happy, he would never hurt me," she said.

Over the summer, Bulls first grew ashamed and worried about knowing so much, then she grew to fear him. "Who would have believed me?" she asked, ignoring the police and all those who'd asked for her help over the three years of the investigation.

By July, Vanessa testified that she feared that the police would come after her. On the day Kari's body was exhumed, she called Matt from a Starbucks and told him it was over. "He couldn't do anything to me because he could never admit guilt," she said. On that day, she told him that they "didn't worship the same God."

"I killed my wife for you, and now you're leaving me?" he responded. When he asked if he could see her one last time, she simply hung up the phone. Days later, he called again, and she said she urged him to confess to the police. "God has forgiven me," he responded. When she threatened to turn him in, he replied, "You'd better not do that."

During the first break in the trial, at 10:24 that morning, while Gray looked over Vanessa's grand jury testimony, Bill Johnston was in the courthouse and heard what Vanessa had said on the stand. In the hallway, he looked for Linda and found her, hugging her. "I'm so sorry," he said.

"I know," she said, tears running down her cheeks. "I know."

When court began again, Vanessa was still on the stand, and this time Gray asked the questions. One after another he brought up the prior, inconsistent statements she'd given, those in which she denied everything she'd just testified to. She bristled, saying that whatever she said at the time was right, if perhaps she hadn't said everything. Gray continued to pick away at Bulls, and she contradicted herself time and again, confused, it would seem, by her own long trail of lies. Unable to keep straight what she'd said to which investigator when, she became flustered and angry.

"I was worried that he would come after me," she said. "Put a bullet in my head, to be blunt . . . I know he's killed one person. I think he's killed two people." What Bulls was referring to were her suspicions that Matt might have also murdered Kassidy, based on what he'd told her about the trach not being in that night and his panic when he thought that the child's body had been exhumed along with his wife's. "What's another notch?" Bulls asked. "I was afraid for my life and for my child's life."

On the stand, Bulls claimed that the entire time Matt was free after his first arrest, she slept with a nail file next to her bed. Since the murder, she'd had nightmares, including one just three nights before testifying, in which he hunted her down to kill her. Why would I lie? she asked. "This is making me look bad."

"You voluntarily went to his bed?" Gray asked.

"I did," she said. " . . . He's a master manipulator. I think you know that, too."

But was Bulls really afraid? Gray listed all the places she'd gone with Matt, from a motel to shopping, without appearing frightened. She'd been in the limo the day of Kensi's party and with him at the house. And then there was the immunity prosecutors had given her. Was Bulls lying to save herself? She testified that she'd been threatened if she didn't tell what she knew. Yet she insisted that no one had asked her to lie. "Just tell the truth."

"He used me," she said, pointing at her former lover.

" . . . He wore the mask of God, like he's doing now . . . He did it. The only thing I'm guilty of is not telling anyone sooner."

Yet Bulls seemed disconnected from reality, in denial about her part in Kari Baker's death. She'd bedded a married man, then listened as he planned his wife's murder. When Gray asked if Vanessa worried that she could be charged with a crime, Bulls looked proud. Despite admitting she'd acted as Matt's confidante as he planned a cold-blooded murder, to the astonishment of many in the courtroom, the pretty middle-school teacher said: "Absolutely not, because I didn't do anything wrong."

Again and again, Gray returned to Bulls's prior statements, all the lies she'd told over the years. Even with what she had testified to on the stand, she'd made conflicting statements about when the events had occurred. Did Matt tell her how he murdered Kari two days after the killing as she said now? Gray asked. Or was it the way she'd told Rodriguez earlier, that Matt had told her over the phone weeks later. "I told bits and pieces," she said. "I didn't tell the whole truth."

When Gray pushed harder, Bulls became incensed. "What do I have to gain from this right now? I could possibly lose my job as a teacher. Everyone is looking at me really bad right now. I'm setting things right. I made a mistake here because a manipulative liar wearing the mask of God came into my life."

On redirect, Bulls talked of "not doing the right thing" and "a mother was lost." But did she truly understand that she could have saved Kari Baker's life?

There seemed little doubt that Bulls was an unsympathetic witness. Perhaps to rehabilitate her, Shafer asked about the song lyrics Matt had e-mailed her, the words to the All-American Rejects song "Dirty Little Secret." Those lyrics became state's exhibit number fifty-seven, and Shafer had Bulls read them into the record, including the chorus: "I'll keep you my dirty little secret. Don't tell anyone, or you'll be just another regret."

Adding more detail, Bulls said that Matt had told her that they shared a "dirty little secret," and that what he was referring to wasn't their sexual liaisons but her prior knowledge of "the murder plan."

The last thing Vanessa Bulls testified to from the witness stand was Matt Baker's attitude toward murder: "He said he felt like it was a mercy killing in a way because he felt like he had already cheated death once when he claimed that she had tried to overdose previously and he'd taken the pills from her hand. So, he said that he felt like it was just time now. No, not upsetting. No long face. He was happy afterward."

The crowd gathered in the hallway watched Vanessa Bulls exit the courtroom. She looked almost regal, that same small smile she'd had when she'd walked in, her head high, her eyes glistening. She could have been walking up the aisle at her wedding or in front of a swarming crowd of paparazzi eager for news of her latest movie. The cameraman for the *Waco Tribune-Herald* caught her expression, and the headline that ran next to the photo the next morning told the story: MISTRESS: HE KILLED HER.

Chapter 53

After Vanessa Bulls's testimony, Susan Shafer put up only one more witness, the second medical examiner. On the stand, Dr. Natarajan described the abrasion on Kari's nose, one that could have been made by a pillow.

Then the state rested.

The following morning, Matt Baker entered the courtroom in a sport coat as he had the other days, but there was something that made many recall Vanessa Bulls's words from the day before, when she'd charged that the ex-pastor wore "the mask of God." Carefully knotted around his neck was a tie, one that had words written across it. Most prominent, front and center: FAITH.

From the beginning, Guy James Gray had said that his client would testify, and the mood in the courtroom was expectant. Yet as the defense began, Gray called a forensic scientist, Brent Watson, to talk about DNA found on the suicide note and the bottle. Watson confirmed what the other experts had said, that Matt Baker's DNA wasn't found on either piece of evidence. The DNA on both was a mixture, and on the Unisom bottle there was a 1 in 1,029 chance that Vanessa had touched it. Yet that was so low, what could jurors take from that?

"All you can say is that some of these people might have

touched the bottle. You can't say they are a match?" asked Crawford Long.

"That's right," Watson answered.

At that, the defense rested after a single witness.

Why didn't Matt testify? Later, he'd say he wanted to but that Gray told him not to. The reason had to do with a trap Shafer had set for Baker in the fourth-floor grand jury room, a mock-up of the bedroom on Crested Butte, with a 197-pound CPR dummy on the bed, near Kari's weight on the day of her death. "If Matt had testified, we were going to make him show us with a cordless phone to his ear, how he dressed Kari and did all the things he claimed to have done in those brief minutes," says Shafer. "We were going to make him do it in front of the jury."

"I knew he couldn't do it," says Gray. "But it was a hard decision. Not putting Matt on the stand cost us dearly since he was going to be the one to talk about Kari's depression. But he never would have been able to pull it off. Once I found out about the dummy and the bedroom, we had to advise him not to get on the stand. It would have been suicide."

Testimony ended at 10 A.M. on the fifth day, and the jurors were escorted to their room to wait, while the judge and attorneys wrote the charge. When the gallery filled and all those involved reclaimed their seats about 1:00 P.M., Susan Shafer had a diagram scrawled on the courtroom's whiteboard, a spiderweb labeled MATT BAKER'S WEB OF LIES.

Referring to it throughout her closing, Shafer had written details around the edges, everything from "It's a staged scene," to the condition of Kari's body. "If she'd been flat on her back the way Baker had said, Kari wouldn't have more lividity in her left arm," Shafer said. "He can't even remember if she was asleep or awake."

Why did Shafer theorize that Matt committed the murder: "Kari was in the way of the life he envisioned for himself."

With that, Shafer told the jurors that they didn't have to like Vanessa Bulls. They didn't have to agree with what she'd done. Yes, she'd lied in the past, Shafer said. But there was corroborating evidence that backed up the key parts of her testimony, including the e-mail that proved Matt had made Kari a milk shake. Throughout, Matt stared at his hands as Shafer detailed his attempts to buy Ambien on the Net and retraced his day at his work computer, where he fluctuated between looking up stories to illustrate sermons, e-mailing his wife and saying he loved her, and scouring online pharmacies to buy drugs to kill her.

"Kari left all the flags she could. She struggled for her life. She tried to get some air. And what she got for that was an abrasion on her nose. . . . The last face she saw was his," Shafer said, pointing at Matt. "In spite of that, he told everyone, including their two daughters, that she committed suicide. Everything is about him."

Then Shafer instructed the jurors: "Look at Matt Baker and tell him that you understand what he did, and you're not going to let him get away with it. Look at him and tell him that you're not going to let him carry on his dirty little lie. Convict him."

"It's your job to determine who you're going to believe and what you're going to believe." Gray's cocounsel, Harold Danford, told jurors. After recounting bits and pieces of the evidence, Danford attacked where the prosecutors knew the case was the most vulnerable, first at the medical examiners' testimony. "If you look at that autopsy report, there are three other doctors who sign off on it," Danford said. "Three of them sign it, and they can't find a cause of death. The most important thing is that he didn't say this was a homicide."

Secondly, Danford, a large, bulkily built man, set his sights on the second weak link. "The whole thing comes down to Vanessa-full-of-Bulls."

With that Gray took over and agreed, at times blustering, his emotions running high. "You are required to find proof that Kari was administered drugs and smothered by a pillow. In essence, this means you have to believe Vanessa Bulls," he told the jurors. "In all of the extra work the prosecutors did, in hiring expert witnesses, it really comes down to, what is the scientific proof?"

As if confiding in the men and women in the jury box, Gray said he had doubts about the state's case. First: They had no proof that Kari's death was a homicide. Second, he referred to a palm print on the suicide note, one that hadn't been traced back to any of the witnesses or Matt. Was it Kari's? If so, wasn't that evidence that she'd typed it. But was it? Vanessa had said Matt rubbed Kari's hand over the note.

"I'm not particularly proud of Matt Baker. I told you in the beginning, he had an affair, and he lied about it. And he lied about it many times. That's why he's in this spot, because he kept lying. . . . But I think Vanessa Bulls is at least as bad," Gray then said. "She may be pathological. . . . Lying and then coming along and saying 'I'm gonna turn clean, but it's gonna be in stages' and then lying to the grand jury and then changing it again . . . and then coming into the courtroom and lying."

For Danford and Gray both, the bottom line was: "The only way you can get to the facts is by believing Vanessa Bulls." The question hung in the air: Was Bulls believable?

The last one up was Crawford Long who knew he had to rehabilitate Vanessa Bulls if the jurors were to accept her testimony. "First of all, I don't think there's any human being who has never told a lie. . . . Are all of us never to be believed . . . ? Of course not." When it came to Vanessa, the lead prosecutor said, "The lies she told were because she was trying to totally distance herself from the death of Kari . . . Does anything she said make her look good? . . . Do you think she came in here to commit job suicide? Do you think she'll get anything out of that? Everything she told you makes her look worse, and that's how you know it's true." With a slight shrug, he then admitted: "Everyone is repulsed by what Vanessa Bulls told us."

With that, Long focused on the man on trial, asking why Matt hadn't given police the home computer he'd repeatedly promised? That computer could have cleared him if Kari had written the note while he was gone. Why hadn't he produced it? Because Matt was the one who'd typed the suicide note, not Kari.

His emotion building, Long said: "You know, ladies and gentlemen, people kill their spouses. It's hard for us to accept, but they do. This defendant has held himself out as a minister. This defendant perverted what's good and holy."

Turning to Kari's Bible, Long then read her plea to God to protect her from harm. "She's speaking to you from the grave," he said, his voice softer. "She's telling you what she knew, and was afraid of, what her husband was going to do to her. Folks, we can't protect Kari Baker from harm. The only thing we can do now is give her justice."

At that, Long turned and pointed at Matt Baker: "I ask you to convict this murdering minister and find him guilty for one reason only. Because he is guilty."

At 2:20 that afternoon, the jurors left to begin deliberating. From that point on, the room slowly emptied, as many milled through the courthouse, talking, wondering what was going on behind the closed doors of the jury room. Barbara appeared calm sitting in the courtroom, and Matt looked as unflustered, saying hello to reporters and those gathered, as if he were greeting them as they entered one of his churches. To one he said, "I know I'm going home to my girls tonight."

Meanwhile, Linda and her family congregated in the courthouse break room, away from prying eyes, praying for the justice Long had referred to. They'd had their days in court, the trial Linda, Jim, Lindsey, Nancy, and Kay, Bennett, McNamara, Cawthon, Rodriguez, and Johnston had worked so hard to ensure, but would the jurors believe Vanessa Bulls? Would they trust her enough to find Matt Baker guilty?

While so many waited, a rumor flitted through the courthouse, one that turned out to be true, that after her testimony, Vanessa Bulls had been put on administrative leave from her job as a teacher.

Four hours and twenty minutes after they began deliberating, the jurors sent out a note that asked whether they could exclude "suffocating her with a pillow" or if they had to find both that Baker drugged Kari and suffocated her. The judge's response referred them to the jury charge, and deliberations continued, but Shafer and Long worried. "We were afraid they'd get hung up on it, and jurors wouldn't be able to agree to both," says Shafer.

At 9:11 that evening, the courtroom filled, but it would turn out that it wasn't to hear the verdict. Instead, Gray presented a motion, one asking for a mistrial based on conflicts in Vanessa Bulls's testimony. The jurors had asked for portions of it to be given them in writing. "Vanessa Bulls's testimony is obviously giving the jurors problems," he said. Judge Strothers denied the request.

Then twenty-eight minutes later, word was sent out that the jury had reached a verdict. Although it was late, the courtroom quickly filled. Matt stood with his attorneys at the defense table, and in the gallery, Jim again put his arm protectively around Linda.

"We find the defendant guilty."

The room was somber. The judge had warned against any outbursts, and the jury was cleared. At the defense table, Matt didn't cry, instead looking as if, despite his earlier bravado, he'd expected the outcome. He glanced at his mother, who wore that same taut smile, as if she'd expected it as well. Moments later, two guards walked Matt from the courtroom to be taken to jail, while in the audience, Linda and Jim Dulin and many in their family cried.

The punishment phase began early the next morning, with a range from probation to life. Death wasn't an option since Texas law limits the ultimate penalty to cases involving either a second felony, like burglary, rape, or multiple murders, or a crime that includes special circumstances, such as the killing of an on-duty police officer or firefighter, or a child under the age of six.

Again, witnesses took the stand, at first those called by

the prosecutors. Many of them were the women Matt Baker had made improper sexual advances to over the years, including Lindsey's friend at the hospital, a young woman Matt accosted at the Y, and Dina Ahrens, Matt's high-school girlfriend, who'd had to fight him off one evening.

Afterward, Noel Kersh again took the stand, this time to detail Matt's Web history on both his church and work computer linked to pornographic and dating Web sites like bustydustystash.com, collegewildparties.com, www.americansingles.com, sexlist.com, and iwantanewgirlfriend.com.

To counter the testimony, the defense put up Sharon Rollins, a licensed counselor who'd grown up with Matt. With an air of certainty, Rollins dismissed the idea that Matt Baker could have done what he was convicted of and referred to him as "a fine pastor . . . A man of God." On the stand, Dr. Theron Hawkins, who knew the Bakers from Trinity Baptist, said Matt came from an "outstanding family that makes service to others their main mission."

"Let me ask you, does a good father kill their children's mother?" Crawford Long asked Kerri Spartman, who'd known Matt growing up. She'd called him "one of the good guys" and described Matt's relationship with Kensi and Grace in glowing terms. "I think it's possible," Spartman answered. "I think you could do that. I think you can be a good father and do other things, too."

The defense rested, and the prosecutors introduced a final witness, Lora Wilson Mueller. A meteorologist with the National Weather Service, she'd flown in from New York to finally accuse Matt Baker from the witness stand, to hold him accountable for his actions nineteen years earlier in Baylor's football stadium. Describing that harrowing day, Wilson cried softly at times. "I came here to face him, and do right by Kari," she said. When asked if the attack had affected her life, she said, "Absolutely."

The testimony completed, the attorneys again argued before the jurors. Crawford Long called for them to put Baker behind bars. "Women aren't really worth much to

him. This is a person who thought about killing his wife
. . . He robbed her of her life when she was a young woman.
Why did he do it? . . . Ministers don't get divorced. I think
the word for it is a religious word. Out of his religion. It's
evil." Long again pointed at Matt Baker, this time saying directly to him: "I can look you in the eye and say, because of
your heartless, soulless conduct, you deserve the maximum
sentence."

Guy James Gray didn't take the floor. Instead, Harold
Danford did, talking about "the good Matt Baker," the one
who did community service and helped others, from a good
Baptist family. The state searched high and low to bring you
all the bad stuff they could about Mr. Baker's life. . . . He
did some things he's not proud of," Danford acknowledged.

Bringing the arguments to an end, Susan Shafer took the
floor for the last time. She labeled Baker a narcissist and a
sociopath, one who'd victimized women, one who plotted
and carried out the murder of a wife who loved him. "We
want to send a message to any men out there who are like
Matt—and I don't think there are many. You can't just erase
a life and be out with a slap on the wrist."

The jury had been out more than seven hours to determine that Matt Baker was guilty, but they showed little hesitation about his sentence. Just two and a half hours later,
they returned. Their verdict: sixty-five years.

When Judge Strother asked if there was any legal reason
the sentence shouldn't be imposed, Matt Baker said a very
curious thing. He didn't say, "I'm innocent. I didn't kill my
wife." Instead, Baker looked at the judge, and said, "I truly
believe in my innocence. I believe the jury made a mistake."

Vanessa had testified that Matt told her God was all forgiving and that He condoned adultery and had absolved
him for murdering Kari. Could Matt have believed that the
judge was supposed to forgive him as well? He didn't, and
Matt Baker was summarily sentenced to sixty-five years in
a Texas prison.

Minutes later, Linda walked up to the witness stand. She

began by asking Matt to look at her, but he appeared unable to. His head sank down, as if ashamed. "You took her from us, Matt. You discarded her like she was yesterday's trash. You murdered the mother of your children. . . . You took Kensi and Grace's mother, then fed them lies. . . . Thank goodness this journey doesn't end here. . . . You see, Matt, you were never going to win this one. You spent your life preying on innocent people. . . . But love trumps evil. Do you hear me, Matt? Love trumps evil."

For a moment, Linda was quiet. Then she said, "When I see Kari again, she's going to run toward me and knock me over and smother me with kisses. . . . God told us He would never forsake us, and He hasn't. We have felt His arms around us through this entire process. . . . We are blessed. So, what do we do now? Well, first we thank God for bringing us here to this place. . . . But next, Jim and I commit our lives to Kensi and Grace. . . . We can't give them back their mother, but we want, more than anything in this world, for them to be whole and healthy. You poisoned them. You taught them to hate. But it won't last.

"You have to spend many years in prison," she continued. "What you did was horrific. It was horrific, Matt. And I believe you're capable of much more evil." As Linda spoke, Matt shook his head, but she didn't pause. " . . . We forgive because that's the only way, Matt." And then, once again, she said, "Love trumps evil."

Chapter 54

What forces shape a murderer, a man willing to kill the mother of his children? Before long, another trial loomed, one that would perhaps shed light into the darkness that was Matt Baker, one that suggested possible answers to that very question and exposed even more dirty little secrets.

Before he was led off to prison, Matt had already put into place Grace's and Kensi's futures. Just before his trial, he'd signed over temporary guardianship to his parents, Oscar and Barbara. The girls, it would seem, were destined to grow up in the same house and in the same atmosphere that had spawned Matt. Linda and Jim had been expecting this, yet they were concerned.

It was on the Dulins' first weekend visitation after the trial, in February 2010, that they sat down with Kensi and Grace and had what they'd later refer to as "the talk." That day, both girls were upset, blaming Jim and Linda for their father's plight. Calmly, Jim explained that they weren't the ones who'd ruled that Matt had murdered their mother, and they also weren't the ones who'd sentenced him to jail. "A jury of twelve did that," Jim said. "They looked at the evidence and weighed the facts, not us."

Understandable for a child who'd been through so much, Kensi appeared preoccupied with her personal situation, worried about even more change in her young life. "All I want to say is I do not want to move to Waco. If you really want us to be happy, leave us in Kerrville," the then-nearly-fourteen-year-old insisted.

It would, of course, have been easiest and less expensive simply to agree. The Dulins were not wealthy people and had spent hundreds of thousands of dollars on the investigation and wrongful death suit. Their financial resources had dwindled. Yet Linda feared that the consequences of leaving the girls in the Baker household could be devastating. She felt certain that the girls were being told that their father was innocent, and from talking to them, she knew that they were being fed hope in the form of assurance that the appeal Matt had filed would be granted, and he'd soon return home. That wasn't all. There was that ever-widening emotional gulf between Jim and Linda and the girls. When they picked up the girls from Kerrville for their once-a-month visits, especially Kensi seemed resentful and angry. It was only as they drove away from Oscar and Barbara's influences that their granddaughters relaxed. "We believed that the Bakers were teaching Kensi and Grace to hate us," says Linda. "Rather than trying to protect them, the Bakers were putting the girls in the middle."

It wasn't that the Dulins weren't willing to find a way to collaborate with the Bakers. In fact, Linda e-mailed Barbara and asked to meet to discuss ways they could work together for the good of the girls. The Dulins wanted to see Kensi and Grace in counseling, with the help they needed to come to terms with all that had happened. "We're all adults," Linda stressed in one e-mail to Barbara. "A custody battle won't be good for the girls. Can't we cooperate?"

Barbara responded by not responding, ignoring the suggestion that for the sake of the girls they put aside their differences, at least to try to mend their granddaughters' ruptured lives.

The result was that a little more than a month after the end of the murder trial, the Dulins formally filed for custody. The court system, however, moves slowly. Months passed, then a year, as the girls continued to live with the Bakers, growing up in Kerrville, making friends, going to school, and earning good grades. On the surface, they did well, but were they really? As part of the custody action, a house study was done, lawyers for both sides filed motions, and a therapist was appointed to assess the two sets of grandparents, Kensi and Grace, and the children's best interests. An attorney ad litem, Beverly Crowden, a woman with cropped reddish hair and an intense manner, was appointed by the court to represent the girls.

One of the first actions of Darren Obenoskey, the tall, sandy-haired Waco civil attorney the Dulins hired, was to file a subpoena for recordings of all Matt's prison phone calls and copies of his e-mails and letters. Meanwhile, John Bennett helped find Obenoskey a Kerrville private investigator to assist him. Nicknamed Batgirl for her resolve when working a case, Gina Frenzel was a middle-aged mom with long, dark hair and a brash manner. Once she'd hired on, Frenzel recommended a Kerrville attorney named Pat Maguire, a dark-haired former prosecutor. Maguire and Frenzel had both grown up in Kerrville and gone to Tivy High School with Matt, but they remembered little about him.

Her investigation began, and on Gina's desk, a file on the Dulins' custody case grew as she interviewed those in Kerrville who knew Oscar and Barbara. The hardest part, but they all agreed the most important, was determining what the Bakers were truly like. While Matt continued to insist his parents were the God-fearing, upright churchgoers they were known as in Kerrville, Gina suspected there was more to discover. How could they find out? Everyone involved believed the answer was to look into the seven years Matt's parents ran the Buckner Baptist Benevolences home.

The first thing Frenzel did was search for records from the foster home covering the time period the Bakers ran it. But the facility had closed more than a decade earlier, and after subpoenaing records from the state of Texas and the

Baptist Benevolences, they came away empty-handed. Both entities responded to the requests by saying all the records had been destroyed. That left only one possibility: Frenzel set out to find the former foster children, those who'd lived inside the home. That wasn't easy. The residents had spread far and wide over the past thirty years. Since she'd grown up in the Kerrville area, however, Frenzel had a network of contacts. At first, nothing happened, but she kept searching. Eventually she'd track down nearly thirty of the by-then-middle-aged former foster children. About twenty of those agreed to talk to her, and the accounts Frenzel heard were consistent, describing Barbara Baker as demanding and often demeaning with her young charges. What about Oscar, the mystery man who'd never made an appearance at his son's murder trial? In early 2011, Frenzel found a group of women who had horrifying stories to tell.

Aware of what the private investigator had discovered, on July 6, 2011, the day the custody trial finally began, Linda and Jim were even more anxious about its outcome. A year and a half after Matt had disappeared behind prison bars, he was again seated in a wood-paneled courtroom, this one in downtown Kerrville. In khakis, a pressed brown sport coat and shirt, his hands were cuffed and his ankles shackled.

In the 198th District Court presided over by Judge Robert Barton, a soft-spoken, grandfatherly man, Linda and Jim sat behind their attorneys, Obenoskey and Maguire, with Frenzel on their right. Left front in the courtroom Barbara, Oscar, and Matt conferred with a small battalion of their own lawyers: a short woman with a stark black French twist named Pamela King, representing Matt; a tall man named Fred Henneke, his thick mop of curly hair graying, representing Barbara and Oscar; and Crowden, the girls' attorney ad litem. By then, Crowden had made it clear to the Dulins that Kensi and Grace didn't want to live with them and that she intended to do all she could to help them remain with the Bakers.

Beginning opening statements, Pat Maguire stood at the lectern facing the jury, laying out in skeleton form what he and Obenoskey expected to show, first filling the jurors in on why they were all there: because Matt Baker had murdered his wife. "He was a Baptist minister," Maguire said. "He's a wolf in sheep's clothing . . . he used a façade to manipulate."

Maguire then described the abyss between the girls and the Dulins. No longer did they call them Grammy and Pawpaw, but Linda and Jim. Why? Maguire called it a "severe form of emotional abuse" fostered by the Bakers, one that multiplied the damage done to the girls by cutting them off from grandparents who loved them. As he spoke, Maguire described the Bakers as manipulative and said that they'd worked to alienate the girls from the Dulins. When it came to the court-ordered home study and social worker, Maguire explained that both experts had filed reports contending that the girls should live not with Matt's parents but with Kari's.

In their arsenal, Maguire and Obenoskey had among the subpoenaed material devastating ammunition, including letters in which Matt urged Kensi to write to and talk on the phone with one of his fellow inmates, a convicted murderer. And there was more. The Dulins' attorneys were prepared to expose the Bakers as very unlike the way they presented themselves to the world. For on the witness list were six of their former foster children, who Maguire said would testify about sexual and emotional abuse suffered at the hands of Oscar and Barbara. "You will hear evidence of dark secrets in the Baker family," he said. "Is that how Matt Baker became the way he is today?"

The three attorneys on the opposite side of the courtroom then countered those claims. The Bakers' attorney, Henneke, maintained that his clients were fine people and wonderful role models for their grandchildren. King, Matt's attorney, admitted that her client had made errors in judgment, especially when it came to the murderer he'd set up as Kensi's pen pal, yet that wasn't the problem. Instead, she blamed the rift between the families on the Dulins' wrongful death suit. Why were the girls angry with the Dulins? Because Kensi and Grace shared Oscar and Barbara's belief that Matt was innocent. "The hope factor," King said, was all the girls had, their conviction that their father would one day be cleared and set free.

The staunchest advocate was Crowden, the girls' attorney, who argued passionately that it would be a grave injustice to remove the girls from Kerrville and the Baker home. Why? Kensi and Grace didn't want to live with the Dulins. The girls had family, friends, and a support system in Kerrville. The girls had people who accepted them. All three of the Bakers' attorneys, King, Henneke, and Crowden, pleaded with the jurors not to uproot the girls, who by then were fifteen and nearly eleven. "Kensi and Grace have already lost a sister, a mother, and a father. Don't take this from them, too," Crowden said. "To stay in Kerrville is their deepest desire."

At that point, the testimony began. Much of that first day would be taken up with Maguire's examination of Matt, during which the ex-minister sat at the witness table with his attorney beside him, as often as not taking the Fifth Amendment and refusing to answer even basic questions. His parents, he insisted, were wonderful, loving people, the perfect ones to raise his daughters. He refused to answer any questions involving Vanessa Bulls or the events surrounding the murder, but he did admit after Maguire pushed the topic that arranging for Kensi to be a pen pal with another convicted murderer could be viewed as a mistake.

On the stand, Matt denied working to eradicate his wife's memory or separate his girls from his former in-laws, saying that he believed the girls still loved Jim and Linda. "Do you think erasing the girls' memories of their mother would be harmful to the girls?" Maguire asked.

"If that happened, yes," Matt agreed.

What became quickly apparent was that even from prison, Matt remained a big part of his daughters' lives. He called three times a week, talking for fifteen minutes each time, and wrote often. In his long letters, he assured them that he'd be home soon.

"Do you believe false hope is good . . . do you believe it's healthy to lie to your daughters?" Maguire asked.

Yet, Matt insisted that he wasn't lying, that he believed his appeals would set him free.

"This all revolves around you," Maguire charged.

"I believe it is good for my daughters, too," he said.

"Someone who kills their wife would not be a fit parent, would they?" Maguire said. Again, Matt took the Fifth. He did the same when asked about the fitness of a parent who had sexually abused children.

For Matt's cause, the most devastating exhibits would be the letters he'd written to Kensi, Grace, and his parents, who he called Gma and Gpa. While he maintained he wanted the girls to have a relationship with Kari's parents, his letters belied that. Instead, he warned the girls to stick together and protect themselves when they were at the Dulins, as if their maternal grandparents presented a threat. And he cautioned his daughters to confide in his mother, who was trying to "help me out and protect you" from Linda and Jim.

When asked why the girls had to be protected from their maternal grandparents, Matt claimed that his daughters feared the Dulins, citing as a reason the Mother's Day after Kari's death, when Linda had talked with Kensi in the bedroom. In his current version, Linda grabbed her oldest granddaughter's arm hard enough to bruise her, then shook her and locked her in a bedroom, despite the fact that those who'd been there had said that never happened. And he accused the Dulins of an "onslaught," with their fight to bring him into a courtroom to answer for Kari's murder.

Yet that wasn't all of it; in some of the letters, he detailed for his daughters what they "had" to say to the judge and everyone involved if they wanted to stay in Kerrville, which "I BELIEVE YOU BOTH DO!" he typed, all in caps.

"It reads like you might be coaching," Maguire said. But Matt said it was all predicated on the girls' desire to remain with his parents.

Letter after letter, Matt warned the girls to be careful and to tell Barbara what transpired on the visits to Waco. Over and over, he said that he knew the girls didn't want to go and predicted that their time with their maternal grandparents would be "horrible." Maguire asked if Matt wasn't keeping the girls from enjoying their visits by making it disloyal for them to do so. But Matt said he was only repeating how he knew the girls felt.

"When Kensi and Grace grow up, do you want them to marry someone like you?" Maguire asked.

Matt didn't hesitate: "Yes."

When King, Matt's attorney, took over, she concentrated on tracing back when the estrangement with the Dulins began and blaming their actions, not Matt's, for spawning the chasm. Perhaps Matt hadn't told her that he'd pushed the girls to pull away from their maternal grandparents within weeks of the murder, even before the Dulins began questioning their daughter's death. Again, Matt drove home what he pegged as the girls' feelings. Kensi, he said, was fearful to be alone with Linda, and the prospect of having to go to Waco left her in tears. "It's a tough situation, when your children are hurting, and it's family hurting them," Matt said.

There were solid arguments for leaving the girls where they were, King argued. Kensi and Grace were thriving, getting good grades, and playing sports. They had friends, the kind of relationships they could count on. His parents, Matt said, were exceptional people, full of love and acceptance. Their reputation in their community was "very respected."

When it came to the allegations that they all knew lay ahead, Matt insisted that his parents had never abused him and that he'd never seen anything inappropriate with any of the foster children.

"You don't take responsibility for the death of your wife,

do you?" Maguire asked on redirect. Again, Matt took the Fifth Amendment.

"We'll take that as a no," Maguire said.

Like her son, Barbara Baker insisted that she wasn't trying to keep the girls from their other grandparents, but like her son's, her own words came back to haunt her. E-mails she'd sent to Matt at the prison included indications of what was going on inside the house, suggesting that Kensi and Grace were being told about the battle first between the Dulins and Matt, then with the Bakers.

"Has Kensi ever told you that she hates the Dulins?" Obenoskey asked.

At first, Barbara appeared uneasy about answering, but then said, "Yes . . . she said she didn't like the way Grammy does a lot of things like Mommy."

"Do you blame the Dulins for your son's incarceration?"

"Partially, yes," Barbara admitted. She went on to contend that the Dulins had influenced the justice system, insinuating they set Matt up. But when Obenoskey asked what she meant, Barbara couldn't give an example of any influence they'd exerted.

"You had no basis for saying that, did you?" Obenoskey said.

"Correct," Barbara admitted.

In her e-mails to her son in prison, Barbara boasted of refusing to communicate with the Dulins when they wanted to find a compromise and avoid a custody battle. Her influence on Kensi seemed apparent when she divulged a plan the teenager had to sway the impressions of the social worker. When with the Bakers, Kensi would sit close, but with the Dulins, both girls would sit on the opposite side of the table. And although Barbara said she wasn't trying to keep the girls from the Dulins, in an e-mail she admitted that she wanted the girls' time with Linda and Jim reduced.

When Obenoskey asked Barbara why she didn't at least attempt to work out their differences by talking to Linda and

Jim, Barbara claimed it was "like trading with the devil . . . You end up giving her five for one."

Yet when he challenged that characterization, Barbara shrugged and admitted that, too, wasn't true. "So you just made it up?" he said.

"Yes," she said. Moments later, Barbara Baker read out loud a passage out of an e-mail where she listed all of those she wanted to "take a fall," from the attorneys in the murder trial through the Dulins to Obenoskey and Maguire. The woman on the witness stand appeared angry and vindictive, not loving and accepting as Matt described her.

When Fred Henneke, her own attorney, took over, he attempted to rehabilitate Barbara's image in front of the jury, pointing out that the e-mails were written late at night. "Were you tired?" he asked.

"Yes," Barbara answered, saying that the only one she thought would ever be reading the e-mails was her son. The letters were a lifeline, she said, one that kept him feeling as if he were tied to his children.

"Is it important that you keep Matt updated on the attacks on the Dulins . . . ? You are carrying on his vendetta," Obenoskey said on redirect.

"I don't feel I have a vendetta," objected Barbara, who'd written in one of her e-mails to her son: "I don't know if anyone knows how much you're a soul mate of mine."

The following morning, the mystery man in the case, Oscar Baker, was seated at the small witness table. In his eighties, Matt's father was balding, with a thin white comb-over, his face well lined behind wire-rimmed glasses, and his voice hoarse, as his bulky body slumped in the chair.

Beginning questioning, Pat Maguire went directly to the heart of the matter, asking about the seven years, from 1974 through 1981, when Oscar and Barbara were houseparents at the Buckner Baptist home. In response to questions, the retired farm worker and handyman estimated that they'd cared for approximately forty-nine foster kids, from elementary-school age through teenagers. Then Maguire asked about specific foster children, those he planned to call to the stand. One was a mentally challenged girl named Sherry Perkins. "Would you consider her to be a vulnerable girl?" Maguire asked.

"Very," Oscar agreed.

"Would you agree with me that someone who is a sexual predator has no business raising children?"

"I agree," the old man said.

"The girls have been told that their mother committed suicide . . . And they still hold that belief?"

"Strongly," he growled.

Much of what Oscar said that day would echo what had come through loud and clear in the e-mails his wife had written to their son in prison. Yes, they believed their son was innocent, and they reinforced that with their granddaughters. There was so much animosity between the Bakers and the Dulins that Oscar said unequivocally that he and Barbara could never coparent with them. "There's too much difference in where we're at," he said. "They have their way of parenting, and we have our way."

On cross-examination, Henneke pointed out that Kari's death had originally been ruled a suicide, and that there was a reason for Oscar and Barbara to have told the girls that. Yet on redirect, Maguire pointed out that suicide was no longer the finding and that their son was convicted of his wife's murder. "Do you and your wife still reinforce [the suicide theory] with the girls?"

"Yes, sir!" Oscar answered.

The afternoon wore on, and other witnesses took the stand, two of them Terri Corbin and Jill Hotz. They described how Matt had disparaged his parents, saying he rarely saw them and thought ill of growing up as their son. Afterward, a good friend of Linda Dulin's talked of what she'd seen with the girls since they'd been living in the Baker house, including the way Kensi picked at her skin, causing sores, often a sign of stress. When it was her turn, Kari's cousin Lindsey described hearing Matt disparage the Dulins in front of the girls.

In response, the opposing attorneys pointed out that the Dulins' witnesses knew little or nothing of the girls' lives in Kerrville. Crowden asked about the Justice for Kari bumper stickers, wondering if it hadn't been a mistake to have them on their cars, saying the girls saw the slogan as "injustice for Matt."

"The mistake is their father," Lindsey snapped back.

Emotions ran high, and at times it was easy to see that many had an undercurrent of anger close to the surface. Kensi had apparently made claims against her aunt Nancy, saying she'd once grabbed her breasts. On the stand, Nancy denied that it had ever happened, and when Crowden asked why Nancy said the girls were being taught to lie, Kari's aunt responded, "Look at what Kensi is saying about me!"

Finally, at 2:20 on the second afternoon of the trial, Linda Dulin took the stand. At times she teared up, as when describing how Matt had told her that she and Jim wouldn't be allowed to see the girls. Crowden had queried the other witnesses on why they hadn't driven to Kerrville to go to the girls' games and events. "We would never put them through that stress," Linda said. "We wouldn't want to have them pulled between their allegiance to either set of grandparents."

On their visits, Linda described the girls as guarded when they picked them up in Kerrville. "They wouldn't talk to us until we drove several miles outside Kerrville, then that would change . . . Since Kari's death, there's been a targeted campaign to erase Kari and alienate the maternal family. You don't do that. You don't take away their family."

Their plans, if the jury decided in their favor, Linda said, was to find a parental alienation program for the girls, one that would teach them that it was "safe to love their mother again, and that it was also good to love their father." If they came to live with the Dulins, Linda said the girls would be loved and nurtured. And when it came to their belief in their father, they'd be allowed, when they were ready, to do their own investigation, review what was available, and come to their own decisions.

"The girls want to stay in Kerrville. Why do you persist?" Obenoskey asked his client.

"Because we love them with everything we are, and we want them to grow into whole, healthy women," she said. "They can't do that if they are alienated from half their family and are living this lie. It's a lie that their mother took her life and she didn't love them."

Some in the courtroom were surprised when the opposing attorneys opted to postpone their cross-examination of Linda Dulin. She'd been articulate on the stand, and it seemed logical that they'd want to bury her testimony early in the trial rather than have her address the jury later. But that was the decision, and Jim followed his wife to the stand. He appeared nervous and uncomfortable, but determined. "Nothing has changed as far as our love for Kensi and Grace," he said. " . . . I don't want to have to pull them out of here, but it has to be done."

Matt's lawyer, King, began Jim's cross-examination, asking if the differences in belief between the Dulins and their granddaughters wasn't too wide to cross. In response, Jim talked of his faith in God and how he believed that the people they needed to help them through the transition would come through for them. Yet he admitted that it wouldn't be easy: "I can't hand them a lollipop when they need turnip greens."

"You've said the girls need to be extracted from Kerrville," Crowden charged, asking if he and Linda couldn't respect the girls' decision, leaving them with their paternal grandparents, where they said they wanted to be.

"If they stay here, their goose is cooked," Jim maintained, sounding like the military man he was. "We have to fight to get them out of here. Failure is not an option." When it came to why his granddaughters wanted to stay in Kerrville, Jim said, "I believe it is the result of brainwashing, day in and day out."

At the day's end, word spread through the courtroom that the following day's witnesses would be the Bakers' former foster children, and that what they would say would cast shadows on both the Bakers' reputations.

Chapter 55

The woman on the stand just after nine the following morning, the third day of the custody trial, was slender, with layered dark hair. When she'd walked in, she glanced at Barbara and Oscar, who looked dour in their seats behind Matt and their attorneys. After she was sworn in, she talked of her time living with the Bakers, from 1974 through 1976, when she was a troubled teen. "Mr. Baker was mostly in the background," Lori Hardin said. "Mrs. Baker was very aggressive. She ran a tight ship. She was the type of person who always had to have the last word. She always had to be right."

Hardin had lived at the home when Matt was very young, and she had little to say about him, but she remembered Barbara as being "very harsh with her words. Very degrading. She used to belittle people to make them feel inadequate and wrong." Among Barbara's favorite victims, Lori described two foster children who were mentally challenged, a boy with cerebral palsy named Jamey and a mentally handicapped girl named Sherry.

"Do you remember Mr. Baker doing anything inappropriate?" Obenoskey asked.

Hardin said she did. The first time was when Oscar initiated a conversation about sex with her, advising her that sex could be "a beautiful thing when it is shared with someone you love." That seemed a rather innocuous comment made to a sixteen-year-old, perhaps even fatherly advice. But then there'd been the day at the lake, when the houseful of kids had gone swimming. Sitting beside her while she lay on her blanket in her swimsuit, Oscar was talking, when Hardin said he reached over and ran his fingers up her legs and across the lower part of her buttocks. "I didn't react," she said. After saying that the young residents believed the Bakers listened in on their meetings with the caseworker, she said, "I didn't tell anyone."

"If you were the mother of a child and someone did that, what would you do?" Obenoskey asked.

"I'd call the police."

The Bakers' attorney, Henneke, asked if good things hadn't come from her years living with his clients. Hardin said she had turned herself around, but she also said that she credited not the former houseparents, but a sponsoring family who'd taken an interest in her.

"Maybe your memory isn't clear, you were drinking," Crowden asked, after Hardin said that at the time she'd had a problem with alcohol.

"My memory is very clear," the former foster child replied.

It was in the girls' bedroom, adjacent to and sharing a bathroom with the master bedroom, that Connie Mirfakhraie said Oscar kissed her, putting his tongue in her mouth. She was twelve at the time, and through the decades, she'd never forgotten how he tasted and smelled. "I'd never been French-kissed before," she said. "I was very scared. It was very alien and disgusting."

Why hadn't she told anyone? "I was a twelve-year-old foster kid, and you don't have the same rights as other people have."

Under cross-examination, Mirfakhraie said that while it never happened again, she had a hazy memory of Baker kissing one of the other girls, the mentally handicapped girl Hardin had referred to, Sherry.

At first, when Frenzel, the private investigator, contacted her, Mirfakhraie, a Florida businesswoman, said she'd denied anything untoward had happened in the Bakers' care. "Then I talked to my husband about it," she said. "And I realized how inappropriate it would be if my husband French-kissed one of my daughters' young girlfriends. So I called Gina back."

"When you knew there were young girls living with the Bakers, did you report this to anyone?" Crowden asked, pointedly.

"Why would I? There was already a trial scheduled."

"How long did it take for Mr. Baker to kiss you and stick his tongue into your mouth," Obenoskey asked. For those who'd been at the murder trial, it brought to mind Matt's sordid history with women, the times he'd cornered them, lunging out, and kissing them, fondling them, or awkwardly attempting to initiate sex.

"It was very quick," Mirfakhraie said.

Her long, graying hair in a ponytail and wearing thick glasses, Sherry Perkins rocked anxiously in the witness chair. Diagnosed with the mental capabilities of a seven-year-old, she appeared terrified. Raised in foster care from infancy to the age of eighteen, she'd lived with the Bakers from fifth grade on, and for many years she'd called the Bakers Mom and Dad. "Did anything inappropriate happen?" Maguire asked.

"He touched me in the wrong places," she said, referring to Oscar Baker.

"Did he insert his fingers into your vagina?"

"Yes," she said. "When I was vacuuming the living room."

After Perkins said that this happened often during the years she'd lived with the Bakers, Maguire asked how the alleged assaults made her feel.

"Scared," she said.

"What about Barbara Baker?"

"She used to laugh at me. She called me Porky Pig, fatso, stupid, and retarded."

"Did that make you cry?"

"Yes," the woman said, rocking ever harder.

Unlike the first two former foster children who'd testified, Sherry had told her caseworker. In response, Sherry said she was placed for a week in a San Antonio psychiatric hospital. "What happened when you were released?" Maguire asked.

"I was sent back to the foster home with the Bakers," she answered. "I was glad to go home." From that point on, afraid of returning to what she described as the "crazy hospital," she never complained to her caseworker again.

"Did anyone ever take you to a doctor for an examination," Crowden asked.

"No," Perkins answered.

Perhaps one of the saddest moments was when Crowden asked Perkins why she'd later visited the Bakers, after she'd moved out of the home and had her own apartment. "Because I thought of them as my parents," she said.

"Are you sure that your memories of what happened are real?" Crowden asked.

"Yes," Perkins said.

The charges against Oscar Baker built as the day wore on. After Sherry left the stand, a middle-aged woman named Tracy Owens replaced her. Thin, with long dark hair, Owens lived outside San Antonio. Unlike the other former foster children, her gaze never strayed from the jurors to look at the attorneys asking questions. Instead, she stared straight ahead, her voice hushed in the horrified courtroom, as she described being in foster care for two years, from the age of seven, while her mother was hospitalized. Oscar, she said, began by touching her while bathing her, then progressed to touching her in bed, through sheets and pajamas. Before long, the woman charged that the petting had progressed to Oscar instructing her to perform oral sex on him, then full sexual intercourse.

Beginning when she was just eight, Owens testified that

it occurred often during the two years she lived with the Bakers, and even that he passed her around to other men within the community who'd also sexually abused her, including a popular Kerrville Baptist minister. When asked why she didn't report it, she responded that the Bakers threatened her. "I was told God was watching me. I was told not to tell anyone. I was told that if I did, I wouldn't get to go home to my mom. She wouldn't want me and my brother."

Tracy, too, described Barbara as emotionally abusive, saying she was controlling and demeaning with the foster children. "I got very few things from my mom while I was there. Barbara took them away . . . I remember being teased by her."

When asked if the Bakers should be allowed to parent any children, the woman uttered: "No, sir."

Minutes later, the court took the daily lunch break, and Owens left the courtroom. In the hallway, she saw the earlier witnesses, the other former foster children who were now middle-aged wives and mothers, Perkins, Hardin, and Mirfakhraie. As soon as their eyes met, they all began to cry.

That afternoon, the opposing attorneys came at Owens hard, asking pointed questions about her past. They had listened to her recorded interview with Frenzel, and there were other allegations on the tape, including that during her years in foster care, Tracy had been abused by a relative, a boy a few years older than she was. Beverly Crowden asked if doctors had once suspected Owens had Munchausen syndrome, a psychiatric condition wherein parents hurt their children to get attention. In response, Owens described the event as a misunderstanding cleared up after the doctors secured the children's medical records.

Over and over again, the attorneys challenged Tracy's testimony, asking why she hadn't told anyone during her years at the foster home about the abuse. "I had opportunities," she said. "I was just scared."

There was the overdose attempt at suicide when Owens was thirteen that took her to a San Antonio psychiatric hospital for months. "Did you tell the psychiatrist there . . . Did he make a formal report?" Crowden asked.

"Yes," she said, she had told the physician, then added, "He said he wasn't sure I was telling the truth."

"The allegations were not widely accepted?" Henneke queried.

"My mom accepted it, she just didn't know what to do," Tracy replied.

"Why didn't you report it to the caseworker," the Bakers' attorney asked.

"I was scared to."

"Scared of what?"

"The Bakers . . . I was terrified."

When asked if she had any proof, Tracy said she remembered one thing about Oscar Baker: "He wasn't circumcised."

When Crowden asked why Owens didn't remember having to be taken to hospitals for infections from all the sexual abuse she claimed, she said she didn't remember needing treatment, "but I remember that it hurt."

If Oscar Baker was circumcised, the opposing attorneys never put on anyone to testify to that to dispute Tracy Owens's account. And later, with another witness, Obenoskey brought in information that appeared to corroborate at least part of the former foster child's account, that the minister in question, the friend of the Bakers who Owens named as one of her abusers, was questioned in the midseventies regarding an attempt to lure a small child into a car by promising candy. The information had come from the former Kerrville detective who'd investigated the case, Pat Wertheim. Within a week after the minister was questioned, he'd packed up and moved out of Kerrville. "The minister had a big youth outreach program in Kerrville, and if it was true, I never believed that child was the only one," says Wertheim.

On redirect, Maguire put into evidence a medical record from his witness's 2004 hospitalization. Owens's physician noted on her chart: "Patient admits she has gone through sexual abuse from her foster father."

* * *

The following Monday proved a long, complicated day in the courtroom. The first witness Obenoskey called was the court-appointed social worker, who had prepared a report recommending that sole custody be given to the Dulins. There was a glitch, however, as Crowden and Henneke objected, charging that the woman hadn't followed procedures by not notifying all the attorneys of communications and evidence she'd had on the case. There was a lot at stake, and the arguments went on for more than an hour before Judge Barton ruled that the woman would not be allowed to testify before the jury.

Instead, the expert in the witness chair that morning was Joann Murphey, an attractive, middle-aged redhead, stylishly dressed in a crisp white summer skirt and a blue, green, and white sweater set. A psychologist, Murphey had been appointed by the court to interview all those involved: Jim, Linda, Barbara, Oscar, and Kensi and Grace. Once done, she'd supplied all of the attorneys with a 116-page written report. Her recommendation: "That Jim and Linda Dulin be given sole managing conservatorship of Kensi and Grace Baker."

"Did you find that the current environment they're in is unhealthy?" Maguire queried.

"Yes, I did," Murphey said. "Every child needs a peaceful and loving family . . . I felt that Jim and Linda Dulin were the people best suited to do that."

Pulling together her decision, Murphey said she hadn't spent a lot of time considering either the sex-abuse charges leveled against Oscar or the murder. While she'd interviewed the others, she hadn't talked with Matt, saying it wasn't necessary since he wasn't one of those being considered as the girls' custodian. On some matters, she found the Bakers and Dulins both able to handle the responsibility, including stability and being able to provide a home and support.

What differed, Murphey said, was the emotional health of the two households. After interviewing both sets of grandparents, the psychologist had come to the conclusion that the Bakers were, as the Dulins charged, disparaging Kari's memory and waging a campaign to drive a wedge between Kensi and Grace and their dead mother's family. "The girls hold their maternal grandparents solely responsible for their father's situation," Murphey testified. "They have unrealistic views of the court system and the power of their grandparents."

The Bakers, including Matt, Murphey said, fostered that opinion by maintaining that the Dulins had forced the murder case through to conviction. "Rather than that a jury of their father's peers made a decision." That, the psychologist testified, forced the girls to live in an unrealistic world, one in which a successful appeal would quickly bring their father home.

"You heard the girls' desire, that they want to stay with the Bakers?" Maguire asked.

"I heard that," Murphey said. "And I felt empathy for the girls. Who would wish this on anyone? It is horrific . . . I do hear their voices."

"Should that be the determining factor?" he asked.

"No," she replied. "I don't know any adolescents who know what's best for them."

Maguire then asked about the girls' school, their friends and church. They appeared to be doing well in Kerrville. Shouldn't that be a factor? Murphey said that with professional help, the girls would adjust to living with the Dulins and that it was their best opportunity to live happy lives. Although it appeared the girls were doing well on the surface, the therapist said that didn't always reveal what was truly going on.

"Did you have concerns that the girls are being manipulated?" Maguire asked.

"Yes," Murphey said. "By their paternal grandparents." There were also indications that the girls were being talked to about the case as if they were adults, given information they didn't need that increased their stress and made them feel more torn. "The most disastrous and horrific effects from high conflict are where children become pawns . . . asked to take a side."

"Are the girls being used as pawns in this case?" Maguire asked.

"Absolutely . . . by the paternal grandparents," Murphey testified.

One of the indications, she said, was the way the girls saw everything the Dulins did as wrong and everything the Bakers did as above reproach, a common symptom in what Murphey called Parental Alienation Syndrome. "It is absolutely a form of child abuse," she said, and on a scale of one to ten, with ten the most severe, she judged the alienation of the Baker girls as between "eight and ten."

On cross-examination, the Baker family attorneys worked hard to turn Murphey's testimony to their advantage. King voiced her argument that Jim and Linda's wrongful death suit and their efforts to have Kari's death investigated were to blame for the estrangement, not anything the Bakers had done. And she argued that there was nothing wrong with the girls believing their father was wrongly convicted and that he'd be exonerated. Murphey disagreed: "To think something is a reality before it's a reality, my granny used to say, 'don't count your chickens before they hatch.' "

When Henneke challenged the contention that the Bakers were denigrating their dead daughter-in-law's memory, Murphey said that she had personally heard them attacking Kari in front of the girls. "The tones, the words were not positive."

At one point, Henneke suggested that the Dulins' best option was to just walk away since that was what the girls said they wanted. Rather than an irrational dislike of the Dulins, he argued that it was logical for the girls to be angry with their grandparents since they blamed them for their father's incarceration. "Couldn't the girls stay in Kerrville and have counseling?" Henneke asked.

"It's possible, but . . ." Murphey began before Henneke

cut her off. Maguire asked her to finish that thought. "It's possible, but in my opinion, it's not in the best interest of the girls."

After Murphey, the Dulins' attorneys called another psychologist, William Lee Carter to testify more in depth about Parental Alienation Syndrome. Like Murphey, Carter, a thin man with mostly white hair, described Parental Alienation Syndrome as a campaign to discredit a parent or grandparent in the eyes of a child. Reinforcing what the jurors had already heard, he talked of how such emotional and psychological pressure on a child could make a child turn away from family, even alter memories so that they fell more into line with the alienating parent. Children in such situations were sometimes treated as confidants and encouraged to think and feel negatively about the other parent. "They're told things like the other parent never loved them?" Obenoskey asked.

"That's a good example," Carter answered. Like Murphey, he then reviewed Matt's letters and pointed at examples of just that type of thing, including Matt's saying that he knew the girls' visits with the Dulins would be horrible.

What was the harm? "The child ends up living in a world based on a false reality. It dredges up negative feelings that create tension . . . and it emotionally harms the children." Although the problems often weren't evident until adulthood, Carter said they ranged from feelings of betrayal to an inability to trust and problems with emotional intimacy.

When it came to the girls' friends, the ones they'd leave behind in Kerrville, Carter said that while that might hurt, there was something more important: "You're only born into one family. Friends come and go."

There were those instances where the Bakers' attorneys found Carter agreed with them, as when King described a situation where events built, adding one to another, until they resulted in alienation. She included the day the girls were with their father when he was served with the wrongful death suit. "Yes, that makes sense," Carter said. When

Beverly Crowden asked if taking a fifteen-year-old away from home, school, and friends could foster anger and resentment, even acting out, there, too, Carter agreed.

In the end, however, Carter indicated that for severe cases of parental alienation, common therapies rarely worked. Like Murphey, he described the syndrome as a form of abuse.

Once the experts had finished, Obenoskey put Matt back on the stand, and for the next hour snippets of phone conversations were played in the courtroom. Some were between Matt and Barbara, many of which were focused on the Dulins and how to win the custody case. Many sounded manipulative, as when Barbara said that Kensi was old enough to "play the game," but Grace wasn't.

"She'll learn," Matt replied. What game were they talking about? It appeared the game of keeping the Dulins at bay.

The conversations between Matt and Kensi were particularly disturbing, when he discussed testimony at hearings with his daughter, in one saying that Linda Dulin had lied on the stand. He referred to the Dulins as "idiotic and weird," and Waco as "that place from hell," and Kensi responded, one day saying, "Good news. I don't have to go to Waco."

At other times, Kensi seemed the only one with common sense, as when she sounded reluctant to write the convicted murderer her father was urging her to form a relationship with. "Write back to him . . . He's diabetic. You can ask him how he's doing," Matt urged.

"That's awkward," Kensi responded, sounding disgusted. "I'm not going to do that."

One of the most disturbing phone calls was one in which Matt and his mother discussed the upcoming custody trial. During it, Matt said sarcastically that Linda Dulin could use drama to sway the jury. Mocking her, he whined, "Boohoo. I lost my daughter."

As the trial wore on, it became increasingly evident that the children, especially Kensi, were being manipulated and used, so much so that at one point Matt asked Kensi to take pictures inside the Dulins' house. One was of the inside of their medicine cabinet. Was he looking for Ambien, to prove Linda had some? Did he think this could be useful in his appeal? Is that why he had his teenage daughter spying?

The Bakers' attorneys took over the trial, and off and on, Matt and Barbara were again on the stand, denying that he'd taken pictures of Kari out of the house within a week of her death or that he'd put one of Vanessa Bulls in their place. The phone calls, e-mails, and letters the Dulins' attorneys submitted, they suggested, were culled from thousands of minutes on the phone and hundreds of letters, a small sampling. Yet on redirect, Obenoskey brought a bigger stack, putting them into evidence, and had Matt read from them. "They're representative, aren't they?" he asked. After some prodding, Matt agreed that they were.

In other e-mails, Kensi chastised Jim and Linda for attacking Matt. Linda denied it, but Kensi said Linda had "talked bad on Mother's Day with me . . . and Paw-paw said something bad about daddy the day I was sick." In another e-mail, she said, "When will you stop calling my daddy bad names. I will always protect my dad and my sister. This is from my heart."

"If it were up to me, I don't want to see you at all," Kensi e-mailed in 2008, two years after her mother's death. Were her memories true or were they distorted by what she was hearing from her father and his parents? Once after the girls visited, Linda found a note left behind: "I hate Jim and Linda." It was signed, Kensi Baker.

"Have you grieved for your daughter?" Fred Henneke asked Linda.

"Yes," she said, her eyes filling with tears. "I know that I am going to see my child again for eternity. I think that's a good promise."

The one thing Pam King agreed with Linda about was that the wrongful death lawsuit hadn't started the alienation. Instead, it had begun months earlier, on the night in April 2006 when Kari Baker died.

"Do you think it's in their best interest to put them through this pain?" Henneke challenged.

"Because I want them to grow into healthy adults . . . Sometimes, short-term pain is necessary for long-term happiness," Linda answered.

The attorneys asked if the Dulins could live with the girls' belief that their mother had died of suicide, and Linda said she could, but the debate continued, witness after witness. Many were respected members of Kerrville's community, who testified that Oscar and Barbara Baker were good people, solid members of the church who reached out to help others, and that they were good to Kensi and Grace. Some talked about how well the girls performed in school, while others maintained that they'd visited the foster home when the Bakers ran it and that they'd never seen any indication of abuse.

Early on, there'd been speculation that the Bakers would present their own former foster children to refute the charges made by the four women who claimed that Oscar abused them, but in the end only one of the nearly fifty the Bakers estimated they'd cared for came to defend them, Jamey Hodges. Explaining that he worked at Walmart and that he still called the Bakers Mom and Dad, he said, "They're my parents. They helped me grow up." When it came to the allegations of the others that testified, Hodges insisted that not only didn't he see anything inappropriate at the foster home but that it simply didn't happen. As he framed it, the women who'd testified were all lying; there was never any physical, emotional, or sexual abuse.

On cross-examination, Obenoskey asked, "How can you be so sure?" He questioned if Jamey was always present, if he ever went to school or church, perhaps out with friends, if he could have been out of the house or even in a different room when the things the women testified to happened. "You can't say it never happened, can you?"

Defiant, Jamey insisted, "It never happened."

"You were always right there with them?"

"Correct," he said.

Of the remaining witnesses, two would later stand out. The first was Matt's sister, Stacie Segars, a heavyset woman with long dark blond hair, who lived in Denton, Texas, north of Dallas. At the murder trial, many had wondered where Segars was, why she hadn't come with her mother to defend her brother. When she testified, she began by backing up her parents' contention that the abuse never happened. "If Tracy says she was sexually abused by your father, did that happen?" Henneke asked.

"No, sir," Segars answered.

Henneke repeated the other sexual allegations, and Segars refuted each one.

"Would you have any reservations about leaving children in the care of your parents?"

"No," she answered.

When Pat Maguire began asking questions, Segars said that she and her brother didn't communicate, either by telephone or in letters. "Do you have any understanding why these women would come into court and say that your father was sexually inappropriate with them? Any motives?"

"None whatsoever," she answered.

"It's possible that things happened, and you didn't know about them?"

At that, she paused just a moment, then said, "It's possible."

From the beginning, the witness the Dulins' attorneys worried the most about was Kensi Baker. "That was really their star witness," says Maguire. "It's pretty convincing putting a teenage girl on the stand who says please don't make me move to Waco."

After Matt's sister, the older Baker daughter walked into the courtroom and took the stand. Kensi's long dark blond hair was braided in the front and pulled back, and she wore a navy blue top with ruffles. Before the questioning began, Crowden asked her witness to take a deep breath. Then they discussed the lives of the fifteen-year-old and her sister, Grace, who was set to turn eleven on the coming Monday.

At Tivy High School, Kensi was following in her father's footsteps, working as a trainer under his old mentor in the sports department.

In many ways, Kensi's testimony was heartbreaking. At times, it appeared that the teenager was determined to discredit her maternal grandparents, sometimes in ways that conflicted with prior testimony, as when she complained that the Dulins made her and Grace sleep on pallets on the floor in their bedroom during visitation. The problem was that the psychologist, Murphey, had testified earlier that Kensi and Grace had told her that they'd insisted on the arrangement in order to reinforce for the Dulins that they were guests, and that they weren't moving into the two empty bedrooms in the house.

Then Crowden played an audiotape Kensi made on their first visitation after their father's conviction. Unbeknownst to the Dulins, when they sat down to talk with their granddaughters, Kensi set her cell phone to record. At first many in the courtroom assumed that there had to be something awful in the recording, something the Dulins said that explained why a granddaughter would go so far as to secretly tape record her grandparents. But there wasn't. "We can't pretend like nothing has happened," Linda could be heard saying on the tape. "We've prayed and prayed that God could put wisdom, the right words to say."

No one, Linda said, should have to go through what the girls had suffered. "I would do anything if things were different . . . You are our children. You are our hearts."

As the tape played, Kensi cried, and Linda rested her head on Jim's shoulder, while Oscar and Barbara stared at their granddaughter's profile. "We want to be part of your lives," Linda pleaded. Over and again, she said that what they wanted was for the girls to heal and for them to have good lives. "To make you whole . . . Your mom loved you. She would never leave you."

Confused, some wondered what point Crowden hoped to make with a tape that illustrated both the Dulins' love for their grandchildren and the alienation they claimed at the root of their suit. When it was finished, the girls' attorney asked Kensi how she interpreted what her grandmother had said, that she wanted the girls to heal and become whole. "She believes that we haven't grieved properly, and we're broken and unhealthy," the teenager said.

"How does that make you feel?"

"Angry."

When it came to her father, Kensi said, "I believe that he's innocent."

What about those unrealistic beliefs the psychologist said the girls had? Earlier, Crowden had told jurors that they'd hear Kensi say that she understood and accepted that her father could be in prison for many decades to come. Yet when Crowden asked the teenager that question, Kensi replied as the psychologist said she would, stating that she believed her father would not only be freed but that it would be soon.

Yet there was no mistake about what the teenager said she wanted. Not only did she want to remain in Kerrville with her sister and paternal grandparents, but Kensi wanted even less time with the Dulins than the one weekend a month. Moving to Waco? "It would be terrifying."

Darren Obenoskey's voice was soft, not confrontational, when he took over questioning the teenager on the witness stand. Kensi said she did remember a happier time, before her mother died, when the Dulins were a big part of her life. As evidence, the attorney gave her a note to read, one she'd written the year before her mother died, in which Kensi referred to the Dulins' home as her favorite place. Then he asked her to read the note found just months later: "I hate Linda and Jim."

"What happened?" Obenoskey asked?

"They took my dad away from me."

"Who did?" When she answered Jim and Linda, the attorney said, "Why do you believe that?"

"They didn't have to take it to court," she said.

Obenoskey pointed out that the state of Texas prosecuted the case, but Kensi had seen Internet news articles, including the ones that said Linda had testified against Matt at his trial. "I don't feel they love me anymore. They don't show it like they used to," she said.

That day, so much of what the psychologist had testified to was evident in Kensi's testimony. She talked of having gotten over her mother's death quickly and putting the grieving behind her, so much so that she saw little reason to talk about Kari, who'd been such a big part of her life. And her certainty that her maternal grandparents were to be blamed for her father's conviction didn't waver. "I don't love them . . . they've caused me so much pain. I don't want to be around them," she said.

"Did they kill your mother?" he asked.

"No," and she conceded that they hadn't convicted their father. Yet she insisted that the Dulins had gone after Matt without evidence. "Because he didn't do it."

"If something happened to Grace, wouldn't you want to know what happened to her?" Obenoskey asked.

"Yes," Kensi said.

"Do you blame a parent for wanting to get to the truth about what happened to their child?"

"No, sir," Kensi said, tears spilling from her eyes.

There would be more testimony with Linda and Barbara, but in truth the trial felt over as Kensi walked from the stand sobbing. The following day, a Thursday, the attorneys made their closing arguments, reiterating all they'd said throughout the nearly two weeks of the custody trial. They each pointed at exhibits and testimony to back their arguments. After a one-day deliberation, the jurors entered the courtroom one last time.

In the audience, Kensi sat with her friends in the gallery, while Grace waited between Barbara and Oscar. Both began crying when they heard the jury's decision: As the psychologist recommended, both girls would be moving to Waco and living with the Dulins.

In their seats, the Dulins cried, too, but softly, tears of relief and sadness at all they and the girls had been through. There were tears for their daughter, who'd been stolen from them, for the girls, who'd lost their mother, then their father. Linda and Jim Dulin had won, but had they really? There would be a long road ahead, a painful journey, one they hoped would finally take them to a peaceful and brighter future.

Author's Note

It was earlier, before that final chapter unfolded at the custody trial, when I went to the Dulins' house outside Waco. Seated in the kitchen, I interviewed Jim, Linda, and the angels, Lindsey, Nancy, and Kay. It was a spirited conversation, one in which they talked of the dark suspicions that had led them to take the actions that eventually brought Matt Baker to justice. But more than that, they wanted to talk about Kari. "Kari was an extraordinary woman and mother, and we loved her. We still love her," said Nancy. "She should be here with her children. She should be here with her mom and dad."

Many of the women said they'd been inspired by her memory. Lindsey had gone back to college, determined to become a teacher. "I knew Kari would have whomped me if I dropped out," Lindsey said with a laugh. She thought about Kari, the strong woman they all knew. "The hardest thing at the trial was hearing how Matt had left Kari defenseless. But if he hadn't, she would have kicked his ass."

Vanessa's name came up often, and everyone at the table agreed that they still wondered if Matt's ex-mistress had told everything on the stand. Could she have been involved in the actual planning? No one knew, but like so many others, they had little sympathy for her. "I don't see Vanessa as a victim," said Lindsey. "It blew my mind that she didn't think she'd done anything wrong."

What had all of them learned from what they'd been through? "We made a pact," Nancy explained, reflecting on all the years they'd kept Matt's secrets by not telling Linda what they'd seen and heard. "No matter how mad someone will get, how upset, we tell each other the truth."

My interview with Matt Baker took place the fall before the custody trial, ten months after his murder trial ended. On that November day, I left my Houston home and drove north to Livingston, Texas. The Texas Department of Criminal Justice's Allan B. Polunsky Unit is off a quiet rural road, and I drove past hole-in-the-wall restaurants, ramshackle wooden houses on stilts, and a trailer park to get there. I also passed a sprinkling of small, clapboard churches, some with spires reaching toward the heavens. At least two were Baptist, and they reminded me of Pecan Grove, the historic church where Baker began his ministerial career.

At the prison gates, I identified myself and was waved through. The prison houses approximately three thousand inmates, including TDCJ's death row in a two-story, boxy-looking building, detached from the main facility. Like most prisons, Polunsky is a concrete building with slits for windows, watched over by armed guards in high towers, enclosed by a razor-wire-topped fence.

In the parking lot, I left my purse with my cell phone and wallet in my trunk. All I took in was a folder with a pad of paper, my typed questions, two pens, two tape recorders, extra batteries and tapes, and my driver's license, which I turned in to be held until I left. In its place, I was given a red plastic visitor's pass to wear around my neck.

No matter how many times I've entered a jail or prison, the echoing clank of the metal doors slamming behind me always sends a cold shiver through me. Intellectually, I know I can leave at any time, but there's a finality about hearing the doors lock. At that moment, I've entered another world.

In the visitors' room, I sat in booth 31 and waited, my tape recorder plugged into the phone line. A thick sheet of Plexiglas separated me from the enclosure in which Matt would sit. Our appointment was for one o'clock, but the minutes passed. He was late. "Does he know I'm here?" I asked a guard.

"Yes," I was told. She then mentioned that Matt had signed a form with the date and time of our meeting. "They're saying that he went to his cell to get cleaned up."

That was fine. I didn't mind. So I reviewed my questions and waited. About forty minutes later, metal gates swung open and shut, and there was Matt, looking dapper in his prison whites, his hair carefully combed. The guard locked the door and left us. One reason I was there, of course, was to get a feel for Matt Baker, to judge for myself, yet it took me aback when the first thing he said to me was a lie. Scoffing, he shook his head. "I'm sorry you had to wait. They never let me know when you were coming."

Rather than confront him, I began asking questions. My first was the one I always ask in this type of situation. People are, after all, unjustly convicted. We know that. In fact, just weeks before my visit, a Texas man named Anthony Graves, who'd served nineteen years for a murder he didn't commit, was finally released and reunited with his family. So I needed information from Matt. I needed to know whom I could talk with who could shed light on his innocence. I needed to know the name of anyone with any evidence that pointed to any other conclusion than that he'd murdered his wife.

When I asked, Matt shook his head, his blue eyes wide and his mouth curled into a slight smirk. At thirty-nine, his face was still round and boyish, but he had a light stubble covering his chin and cheeks. "That's hard because no one else was in the room that night," he said. "Just me and Kari."

I persisted. "Tell me the names of people I can talk to who will back up your side of any of the events surrounding Kari's death. Anyone who can substantiate what you've said, for instance, about Kari being depressed."

"Her depression is huge," he said, describing its importance in the trial. "Have the people who knew about it been manipulated to not testify correctly? I think so."

"This is important, Matt," I said. "Tell me whom I can talk to who would have information that would help your case."

He pursed his lips, as if thinking for a moment, then said, "I can't think of anyone."

"Would you consider that, write me a letter, and let me know whom to talk to?" I asked. "I want to make sure I cover all sides of the case."

He nodded, but no such letter would ever arrive.

At first, he said, his marriage to Kari was good. "We had fun together, enjoyed doing things together . . . After Kassidy's death, things really changed. Kari changed. I don't know what would have happened if Kari hadn't died," he said. "I don't know where we would have ended up. We were struggling, yes. But we loved each other. If we hadn't loved each other, we would have walked away from each other a whole lot earlier."

I'd talked to so many who described Kari as a wonderful mother, dedicated to her girls. Matt hadn't described her that way. I asked what the truth was. "My wife was very good in front of others putting on a show toward the end. Part of that show was because she was using Xanax."

Yet that, too, was a lie. Kari didn't have a prescription for Xanax. She'd asked for one the week she died, but the doctor hadn't given it to her. It was confirmed by the physician's own notes, which I'd seen in evidence. None was found in her system in the autopsy.

So much of what Matt would tell me contradicted all that had been testified to at the trial and the documents put in evidence. Under oath, Jo Ann Bristol testified that at the visitation, he'd asked her: "Did Kari tell you that I was planning to kill her?"

"I don't know if Kari ever said that," Matt now insisted when I asked why his wife would believe that. "I don't trust Jo Ann Bristol as far as I can throw her."

Yet wasn't Bristol's statement backed up by what Kari wrote in her Bible, her plea for God to protect her?

As we talked, Matt claimed that many others had lied. His list included Kari, her family, Bristol, the police, everyone who'd testified against him. Throughout, Matt portrayed himself as the innocent victim mistreated by all around him.

We talked about all the women who'd accused him of inappropriate sexual remarks and conduct, even Lora Wilson, who described an attempted sexual assault. Were they all lying? "Yes," he said. "But then, some people get different impressions from things that are said. They misinterpret."

"But there are so many women making these allegations, Matt," I said. Even in the county jail shortly after his trial, two women inmates complained that Matt made an obscene gesture toward them. "Doesn't that strain your credibility that this keeps happening?"

"I can't control the credibility of what other people say," he said, his words measured. I thought that perhaps this was how he'd talked to Kari, sounding so reasonable yet taking a truly irrational stand. "You can't control what other people think. All I know is some people take things the wrong way and out of context. And some people will say things to get a response and then say you've said things wrong. That happens so often."

We continued to talk, and the conversation turned to Vanessa Bulls. He didn't dispute the time line she'd presented in court, saying that they'd become intimate months before Kari's death. But he did disagree with how it had all come about. "She approached me," he insisted, as if that were a matter of pride.

"What did she say?"

"Her comment to me was along the lines of, 'Hey, I think you're cute. Have you ever had an affair? Would you like to have one?'" he said. "I thought, well, I've never been approached like this, but it was tempting."

"So she initiated it?" I asked.

"Yes," he said, with a self-satisfied smile. "I was struggling with my marriage . . . The eternal battle takes over, and the good did not win in that."

When I asked what I should know about Vanessa, he described her as "manipulative" and "calculating." Yet about her testimony, so damaging at his trial, Matt appeared to not completely hold his ex-lover accountable, instead blaming the prosecutors, who, he claimed, had threatened Vanessa into testifying against him. "Vanessa decided she'd rather make up stories and converse with the DA rather than tell the truth."

He talked of being a preacher and feeling the calling as a young man and of his children on the morning he told them that their mother was dead. "It was tortuous. Just heartbreaking," he said. "We told them, 'Your mom isn't here anymore. She's in heaven.' It wasn't the proper time, age, all those things to give details. Just, she's not here anymore. We'll see her when we get to heaven."

How did the girls first hear that Kari committed suicide? Matt claimed that Linda told them during that Mother's Day of 2006, a month after her death. The way he described it, Linda pulled at the girls, screaming: "We know your dad's lying. We know your dad killed your mom. We know your mom did not commit suicide." Matt said the girls returned home crying, Kensi asking, "What do you mean suicide?"

"So the subject was not broached until Kensi was grabbed physically, and yelled and screamed at by the Dulin family," Matt insisted.

The problem with this account was one of his own e-mails, one he sent Linda at 1:07 the morning following that Mother's Day. It said nothing of this. Instead, he'd written that he was upset about Linda asking Kensi questions. In her response to him, Linda answered with the same account she'd later tell me, that Kensi had arrived upset, and the questioning had been a grandmother trying to determine what was wrong with her granddaughter. Linda wrote:

"What I saw was a little girl going through so much pain and crying so hard. I saw her feeling pulled in two and it broke my heart for her."

Weeks after that Mother's Day, Matt had also told Cooper that Jim and Linda had never accused him of Kari's murder.

It was the Dulins, however, especially Linda, whom Matt appeared to despise the most.

"Why do you believe most people believe you're guilty of murdering Kari?" I asked.

"Because of the Dulins," he said. "Because they've spread misinformation about me."

"Why would they do that?" I asked.

"Because if I'm innocent, Kari's not perfect," he said. "If I'm not guilty, they can't think of her as a victim. Kari has become a martyr."

That afternoon in the prison, Matt Baker charged many with lying and manipulation, from the Dulins and Vanessa Bulls, to the prosecutor, the judge, the investigators, all the women who'd said he'd engaged in improper behavior. He was innocent. He was blameless. Someone else used his computer to view pornography. Not Matt. In his version of his life, especially the years since Kari's death, Baker described himself as not unlike Job in the Bible, a righteous man subjected to trial after trial.

As in so many instances in the past, he changed much of his story as he talked. In the version he told me, he didn't balance the telephone between his shoulder and his ear as he'd said in the deposition. Instead, he now said he put the telephone down on the nightstand. Yet he maintained that he hadn't put it on speaker, so how he was talking to the 911 dispatcher seemed unclear. And when it came to Kari's position in the bed, he had an explanation for the increased lividity in her left arm; the mattress, he said, was a four-year-old pillow top, with a gully in the center. When he found her, she was lying turned slightly to her left, her arm in the mattress's indentation.

Our talk continued, and Matt at times grew, if not angry,

resentful. It appeared that he was a man who was used to giving his version of the world without being questioned. When I again pressed him for the names of those who might be willing to talk to me on his behalf, his shoulders straightened, and his chin climbed, throwing his forehead back. "I respect the privacy of others," he said, piously. "I won't give out names unless people give me permission to."

"Will you ask them?"

"Yes," he told me. "I will."

Along with blaming Linda Dulin, Matt Baker blamed Guy James Gray.

"Why were you convicted?" I asked.

"Because my in-laws told lies . . . purchased the legal system," he said. "And because I had an attorney who didn't care. He honestly didn't care. In fact, he wanted me gone."

Why hadn't Matt testified? "I wanted to," he said. "I told them, put me up there." When I mentioned the stage waiting for him on an upper floor, the room with a bed, nightstand, and a 197-pound dummy, Matt scoffed. "I could have shown them how I did it. I could have dressed her, pulled her onto the floor, and done CPR. It was easy."

Since it is the only method available to me, I judge whether someone is telling the truth based on what I can verify with other sources. There was much that Matt said during our interview that I had no way of checking, but there were those things that came up that I noted on my legal pad with a star. When I returned to Houston, I worked my way down the list. First, I e-mailed an assistant medical examiner I know. During my talk with Matt, he'd described in detail pulling Kari's body off the bed: "When I moved her, bits of french fries and everything else came out of her mouth, and the smell of alcohol."

"I thought you'd said she only had one french fry that night?" I questioned, doubtful that after so many hours he'd see even a trace of the food.

"She ate like two or three French fries," he said, suddenly looking a bit uncomfortable.

My e-mail to the pathologist read: "If a healthy 31-year-old woman eats three French fries at 7:30 in the evening and throws up around midnight, will there be any visible evidence of the potatoes?"

As I suspected, she answered: "The French fries will be long gone." Making it even more doubtful, Matt had said repeatedly that Kari threw up not long after arriving home that last evening.

The other thing I could check on was Matt's home computer, the one so many from Bill Johnston to the prosecutors said that Matt had repeatedly failed to produce. Why not? After all, if he was telling the truth, there was the possibility that the note was written on the home computer during the time he was gone from the house. If that was so, it was powerful evidence. "Why didn't you give it to the police?" I asked.

"I did produce the computer," he insisted. "I took it to my attorney's office in Kerrville and gave it to him."

"Which attorney?" I asked.

"Richard Ellison," he said. "He told me he kept it in his safe. I don't know why he didn't give it to the police. I never tried to hide anything."

The next day, I called Matt's former attorney. When I asked him if he'd *ever* had possession of Matt Baker's home computer, Ellison said, "No. I never had it. I never saw it. He talked about bringing it in, but he never did."

At that point, I found it difficult to believe anything Matt had told me, but there was one time, when he looked reflective, and I thought maybe, just maybe we got close to the truth. Near the end of our time together, I asked what had happened between three and six on April 7, 2006, the afternoon before his wife died.

"What do you mean?" he said.

"Kari saw Todd Monsey sometime around three," I said. "She was happy. She high-fived him. She talked to her mother, and she was in a good mood. The next thing we know, she's at Kensi's swim-team practice, and she's visibly upset. Something happened, Matt. What happened?"

Matt Baker frowned and shook his head. "Well, we did have a disagreement because she didn't want to go into the Y," he said. "I said, fine. She didn't want to go, and she said, 'Well, maybe I'll just move out and move in with my mom.' I said, 'If you have to do that, fine. I'm not going to help you move out. I don't want you to move out.'"

"Why was she upset?" I asked.

For just a moment, I thought he was going to answer me. Then he shook his head again. "I don't know what the core of the issue was. She just loses it every once in a while, like a switch turned off and on."

"Had she learned about the affair with Vanessa Bulls?"

"At that point, she had never confronted me on it," he said. "She never accused me of it, not to my face. If she'd felt that way, she would have confronted me, told her mom or Jill, and she never did."

But that wasn't true. Kari had told Jill earlier that week. In the conversation in the car, she'd said, "I think Matt is having an affair."

It seemed so odd. Kari was excited that afternoon, enthused by the prospect of a new job. She was on a high. Something brought her down quickly. It was a Friday, Matt's day off, his day with Vanessa. There were so many possibilities, including that Kari left Walmart that afternoon and somewhere saw Matt and Vanessa together. Or she returned home and found something Vanessa left behind, the type of thing that would tip her off that another woman had been in the house.

Kari was upset enough that when one of the moms at swim team asked her not to divulge a secret, she'd sarcastically replied, "Everyone knows you can trust the Bakers."

Clearly, something had happened that brought home to Kari that she couldn't, perhaps especially when the Baker in question was her husband.

As the interview continued, I asked about all those lives he'd touched as a pastor, those who'd once looked at him as an emissary from God who now struggled with their faith.

In Dallas, one couple he'd married had conducted an entire second wedding. "I didn't want my memories of my wedding to include Matt Baker," the bride told me.

There were others I'd talked to, those who hadn't attended a church service since the day they'd come to the conclusion that Matt had murdered Kari. "I can't," said one woman. "I think about it sometimes, but I can't walk through the door. I can't look in the eyes of another minister or pastor and believe him."

Matt appeared untroubled by the damage he'd caused. "I can probably tell you who those people are," he said with a sardonic frown, as if the people I referred to were somehow unworthy and therefore not to be considered.

In the end, the damage Matt Baker had done radiated out from that bedroom on Crested Butte where Kari's body was found, like long, thin, icy fingers, invading the lives of so many. Yet no one had been so injured as two young girls, his own daughters.

As I write these last paragraphs, in Waco, Linda and Jim Dulin are bringing their dead daughter's children into their home, hoping to do for Grace and Kensi what they can no longer do for Kari: save them from the darkness that is Matt Baker. Will the girls ever come to terms with the truth, that their father murdered their mother? Maybe not, but at least with the Dulins, away from all the manipulation, one day they'll be able to look at all the evidence and come to their own conclusions. Finally, they're free to grieve for their mother and all they have lost, to put aside the hate and sadness and reclaim their place in the world, as two girls, dearly loved, free to be young, not ensnared in a web of lies.

Amazingly, through all they've suffered, the Dulins aren't among those who have lost their faith. When I last interviewed Linda, as she got ready to welcome her granddaughters into her home, I asked her to reflect on all that had happened. She said, "This has been the most difficult journey of our lives. Parents aren't supposed to survive their children. A wife isn't supposed to be murdered by her husband. And precious granddaughters aren't supposed to have their childhoods ripped from them. But I have witnessed God's love and grace in the most incredible way during these five years. You see, love really does trump evil."